Greetings from
PRICKLY
CITY

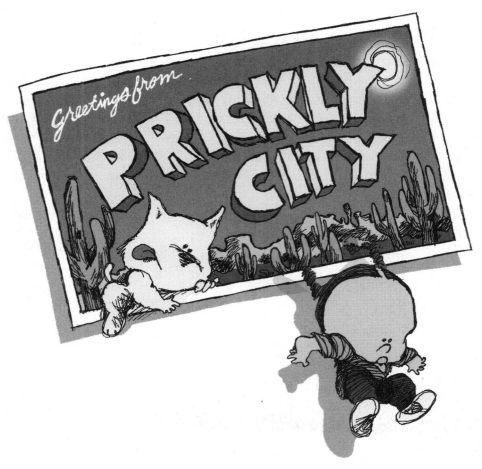

by Scott Stantis

Andrews McMeel
Publishing
Kansas City

Prickly City is syndicated by Universal Press Syndicate.

Prickly City copyright © 2005 by Scott Stantis. All rights reserved. Printed in the United States of America. No part of this book may be used or reproduced in any manner whatsoever without written permission except in the case of reprints in the context of reviews. For information, write Andrews McMeel Publishing, an Andrews McMeel Universal company, 4520 Main Street, Kansas City, Missouri 64111.

05 06 07 08 09 BBG 10 9 8 7 6 5 4 3 2 1

ISBN-13: 978-0-7407-5451-7
ISBN-10: 0-7407-5451-3

Library of Congress Control Number: 2005925665

www.andrewsmcmeel.com

For Jack Prakl, who convinced me to do *Prickly City*.
For John Matthews, who convinced me I could do *Prickly City*.
And for 'Nien, always.

Find Your Super-Secret Password to Access Special Bonus Features from *Prickly City* and Creator Scott Stantis!

Go to www.PricklyCity.com. When you get there look for the *Prickly City* book portal. Enter your SUPER-SECRET PASSWORD (which can be found somewhere hidden within the pages of this book). Then enter a new realm of *Prickly City*, one that goes far beyond the comics pages. There you'll find a bunch of bonus material available only to the smart people who buy this book—things like an extended podcast describing the background of Carmen and Winslow, behind-the-scenes stories of some of your favorite strips, never-before-seen images of the very first drawings of Carmen and Winslow, strips that didn't make the cut for the book, a guide that shows how a *Prickly City* strip goes from start to print by creator Scott Stantis, and much, much more!

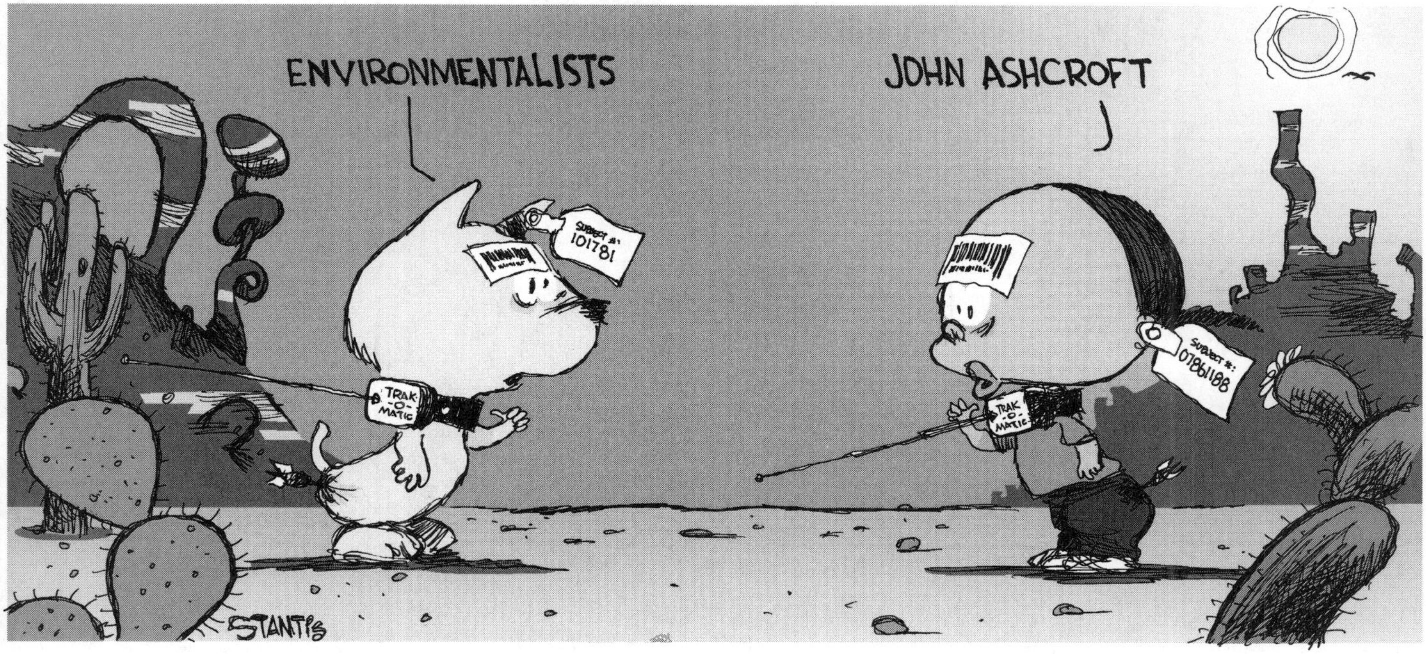
ENVIRONMENTALISTS
JOHN ASHCROFT
SUBJECT #: 101781
TRAK-O-MATIC
SUBJECT #: 07861188
TRAK-O-MATIC
STANTIS

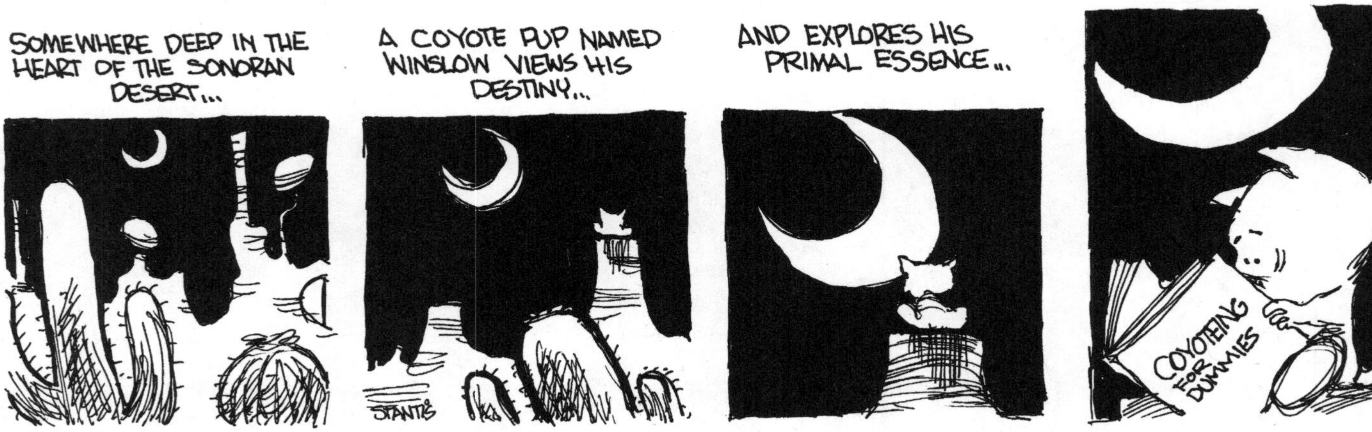
SOMEWHERE DEEP IN THE HEART OF THE SONORAN DESERT...
A COYOTE PUP NAMED WINSLOW VIEWS HIS DESTINY...
AND EXPLORES HIS PRIMAL ESSENCE...
COYOTEING FOR DUMMIES

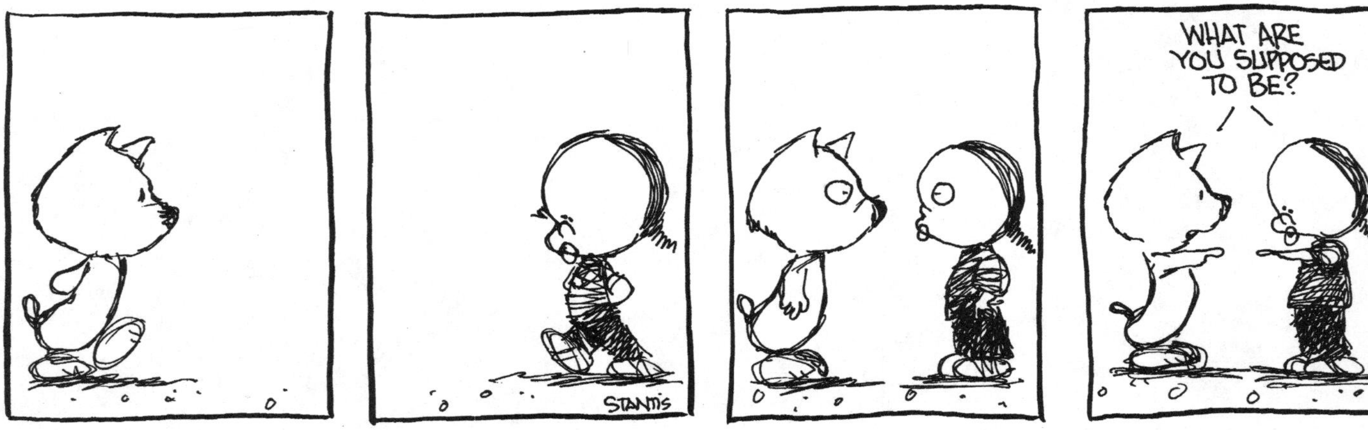
WHAT ARE YOU SUPPOSED TO BE?

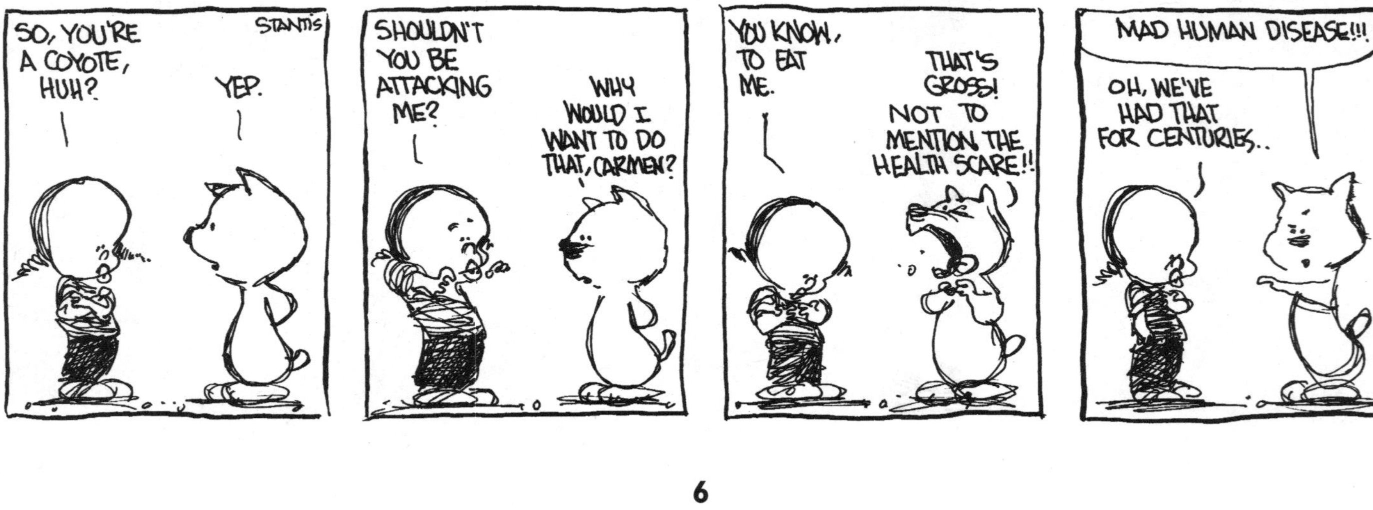
SO, YOU'RE A COYOTE, HUH?
YEP.
SHOULDN'T YOU BE ATTACKING ME?
WHY WOULD I WANT TO DO THAT, CARMEN?
YOU KNOW, TO EAT ME.
THAT'S GROSS! NOT TO MENTION THE HEALTH SCARE!!
MAD HUMAN DISEASE!!!
OH, WE'VE HAD THAT FOR CENTURIES..

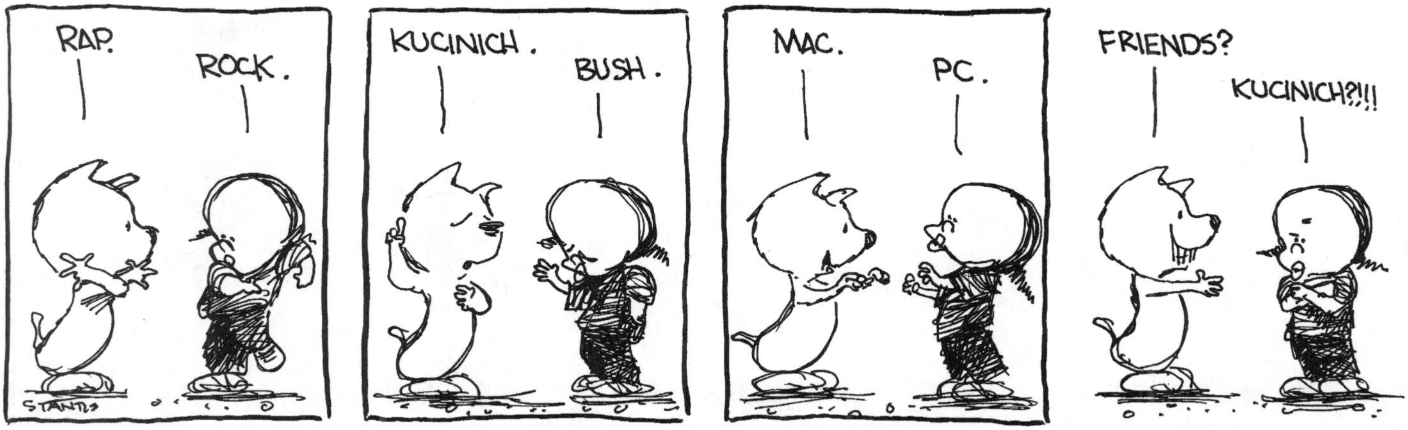
RAP.
ROCK.
STANTIS
KUCINICH.
BUSH.
MAC.
PC.
FRIENDS?
KUCINICH?!!!

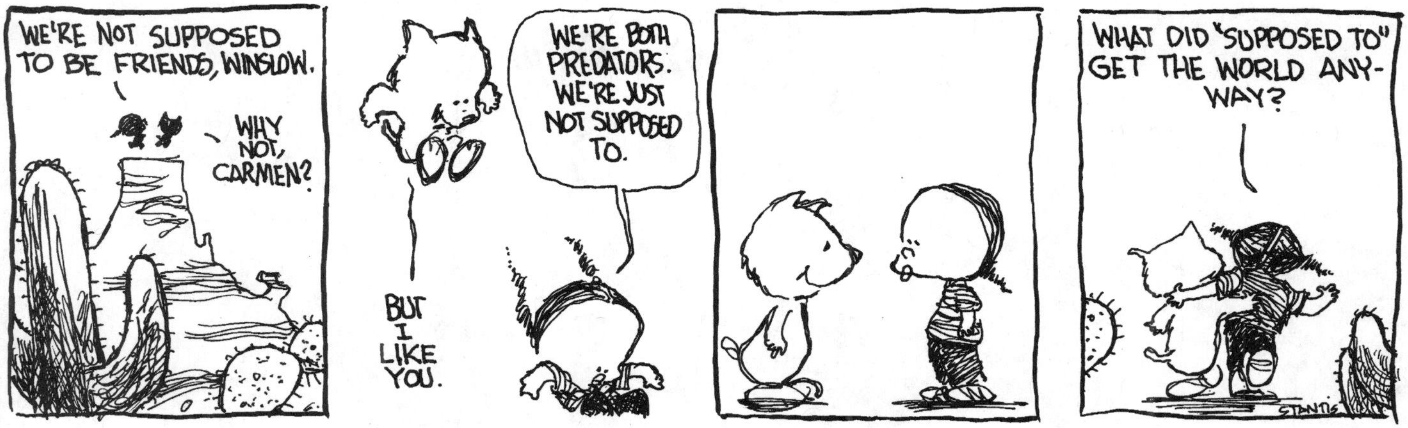
WE'RE NOT SUPPOSED TO BE FRIENDS, WINSLOW.
WHY NOT, CARMEN?
BUT I LIKE YOU.
WE'RE BOTH PREDATORS. WE'RE JUST NOT SUPPOSED TO.
WHAT DID "SUPPOSED TO" GET THE WORLD ANYWAY?
STANTIS

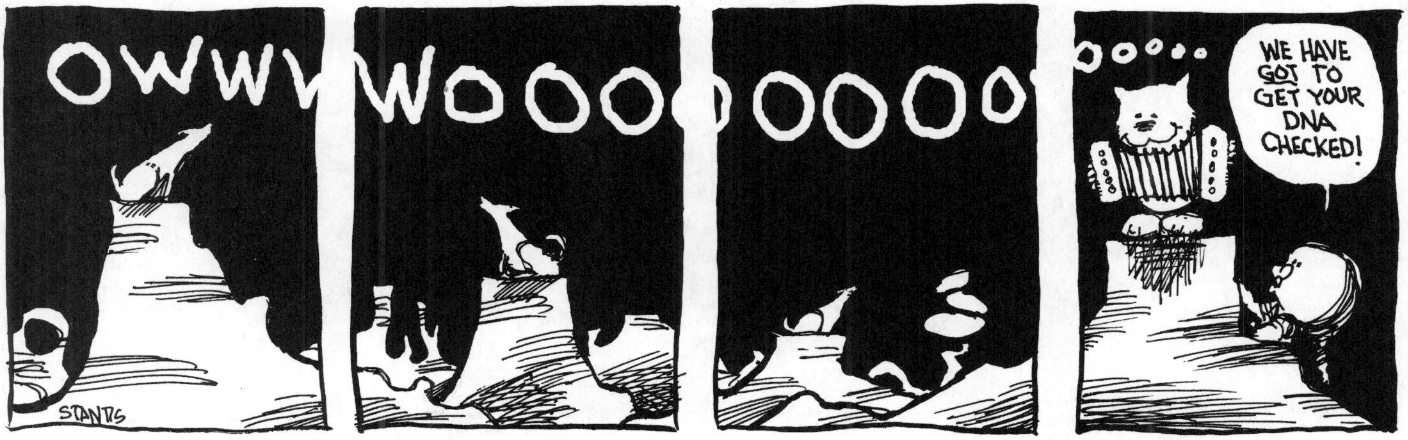
OWWWWOOOOOOOOO'oooo..
STANTIS
WE HAVE GOT TO GET YOUR DNA CHECKED!

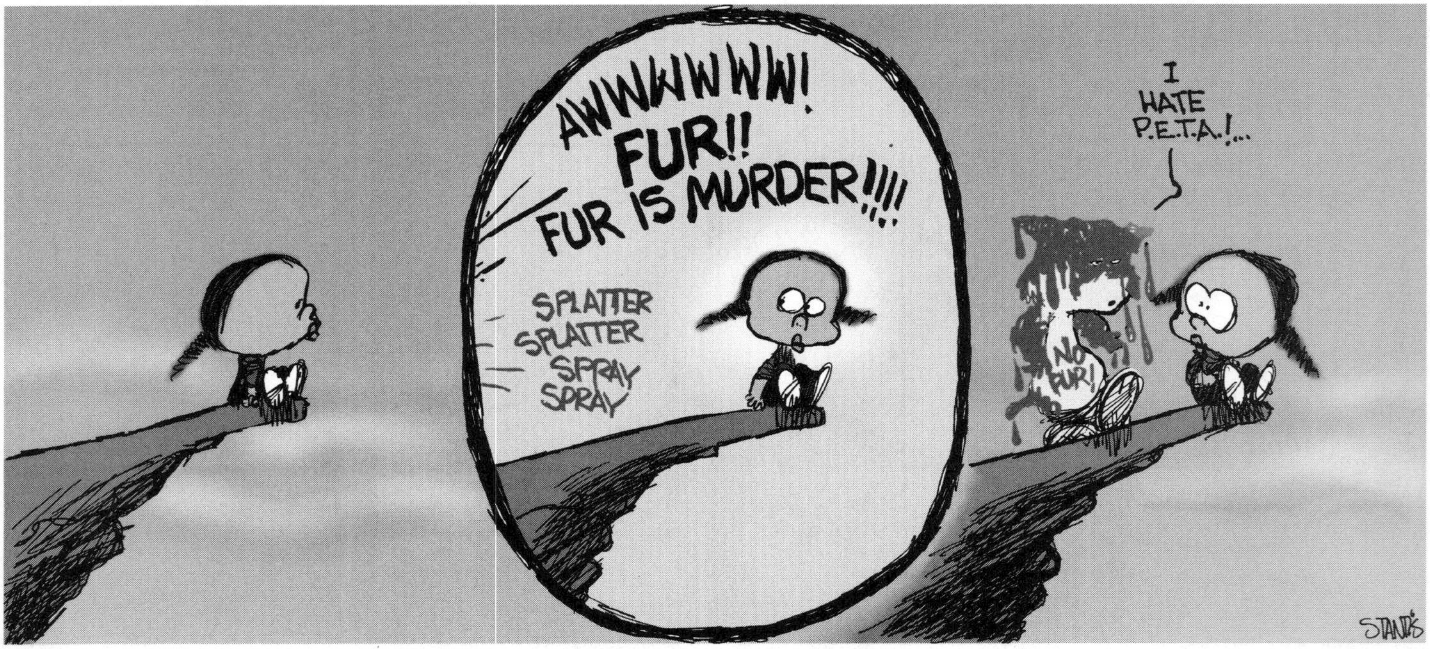
AWWWWWW!
FUR!!
FUR IS MURDER!!!!
SPLATTER
SPLATTER
SPRAY
SPRAY
NO FUR!
I HATE P.E.T.A.!...
STANIS

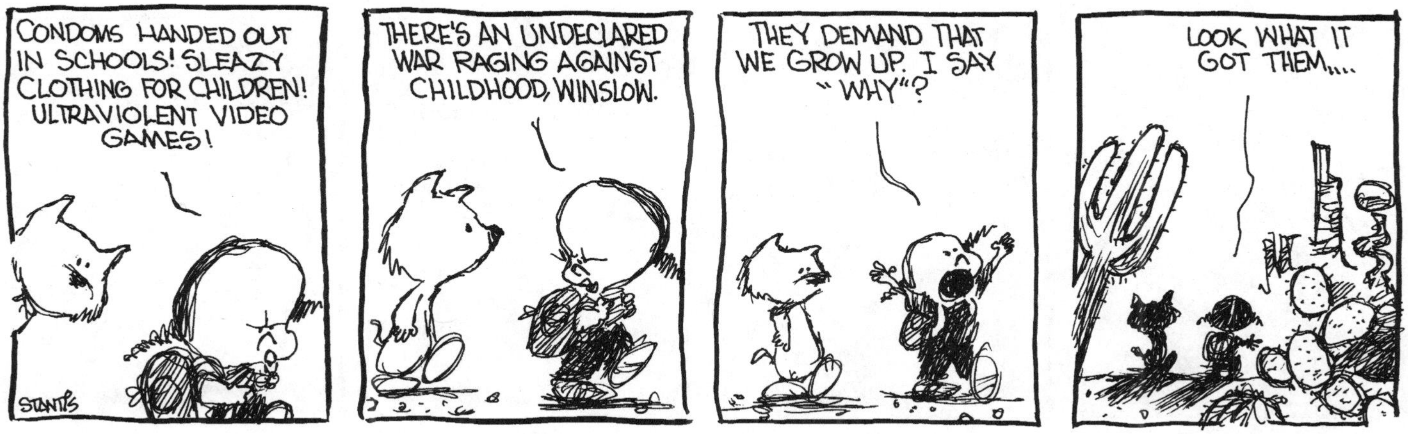
CONDOMS HANDED OUT IN SCHOOLS! SLEAZY CLOTHING FOR CHILDREN! ULTRAVIOLENT VIDEO GAMES!
THERE'S AN UNDECLARED WAR RAGING AGAINST CHILDHOOD, WINSLOW.
THEY DEMAND THAT WE GROW UP. I SAY "WHY"?
LOOK WHAT IT GOT THEM....
STANTIS

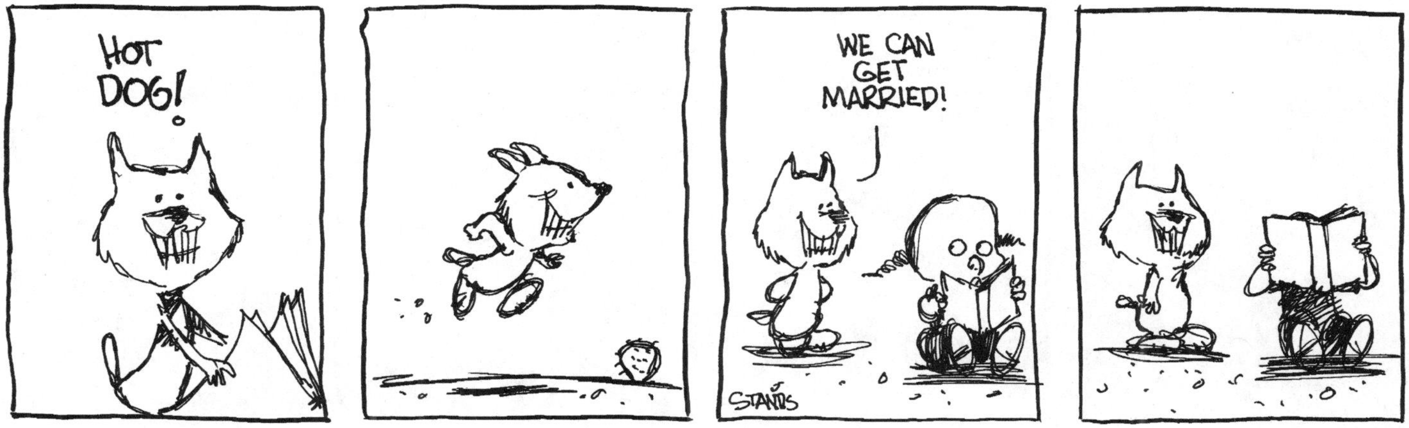
HOT DOG!
WE CAN GET MARRIED!
STANTIS

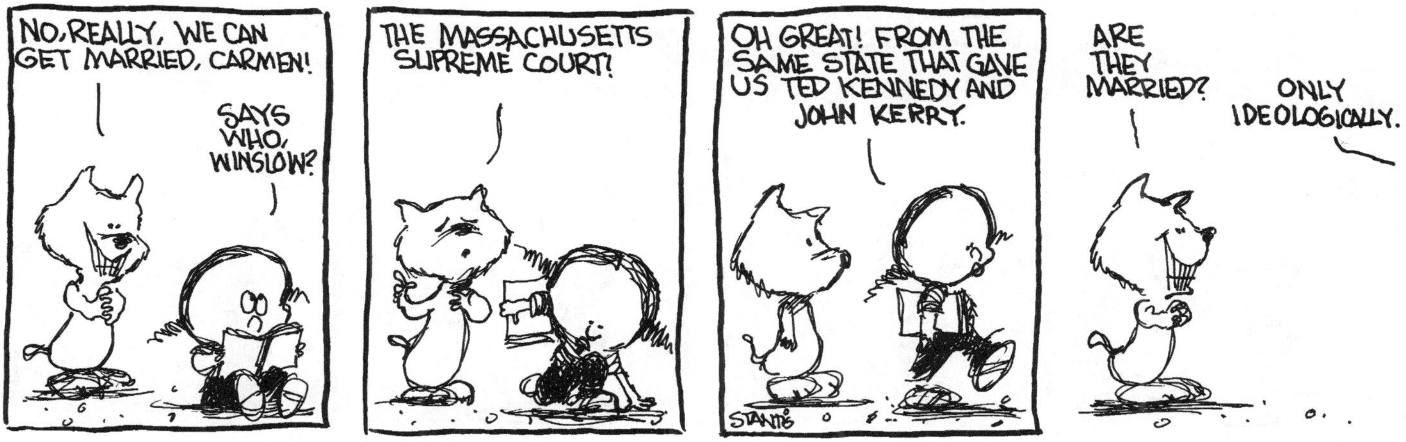
NO, REALLY, WE CAN GET MARRIED, CARMEN!
SAYS WHO, WINSLOW?
THE MASSACHUSETTS SUPREME COURT!
OH GREAT! FROM THE SAME STATE THAT GAVE US TED KENNEDY AND JOHN KERRY.
ARE THEY MARRIED?
ONLY IDEOLOGICALLY.
STANTIS

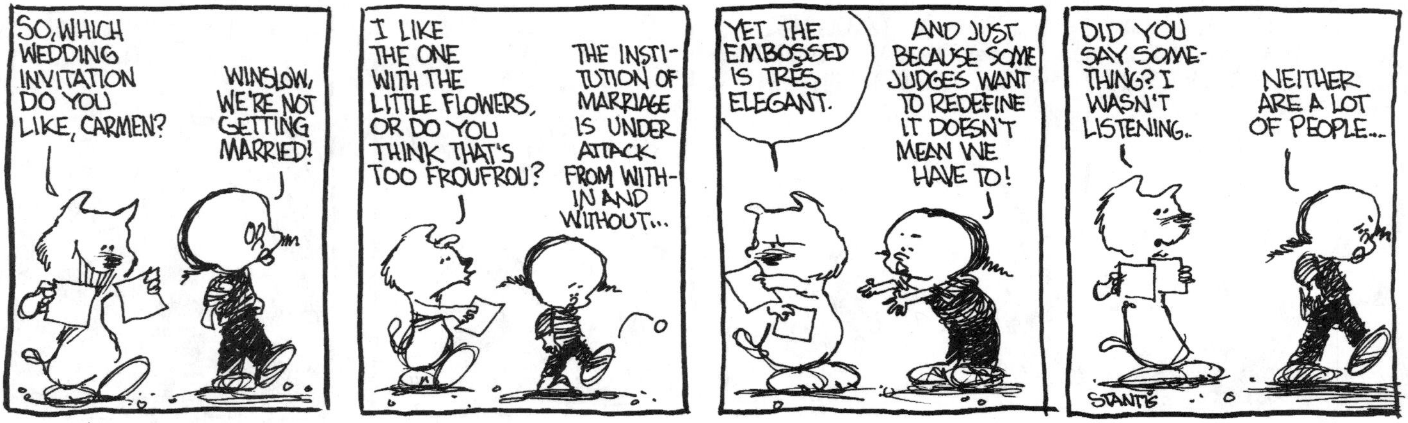
SO, WHICH WEDDING INVITATION DO YOU LIKE, CARMEN?
WINSLOW, WE'RE NOT GETTING MARRIED!
I LIKE THE ONE WITH THE LITTLE FLOWERS, OR DO YOU THINK THAT'S TOO FROUFROU?
THE INSTI-TUTION OF MARRIAGE IS UNDER ATTACK FROM WITH-IN AND WITHOUT...
YET THE EMBOSSED IS TRÉS ELEGANT.
AND JUST BECAUSE SOME JUDGES WANT TO REDEFINE IT DOESN'T MEAN WE HAVE TO!
DID YOU SAY SOME-THING? I WASN'T LISTENING..
NEITHER ARE A LOT OF PEOPLE...
STANTIS

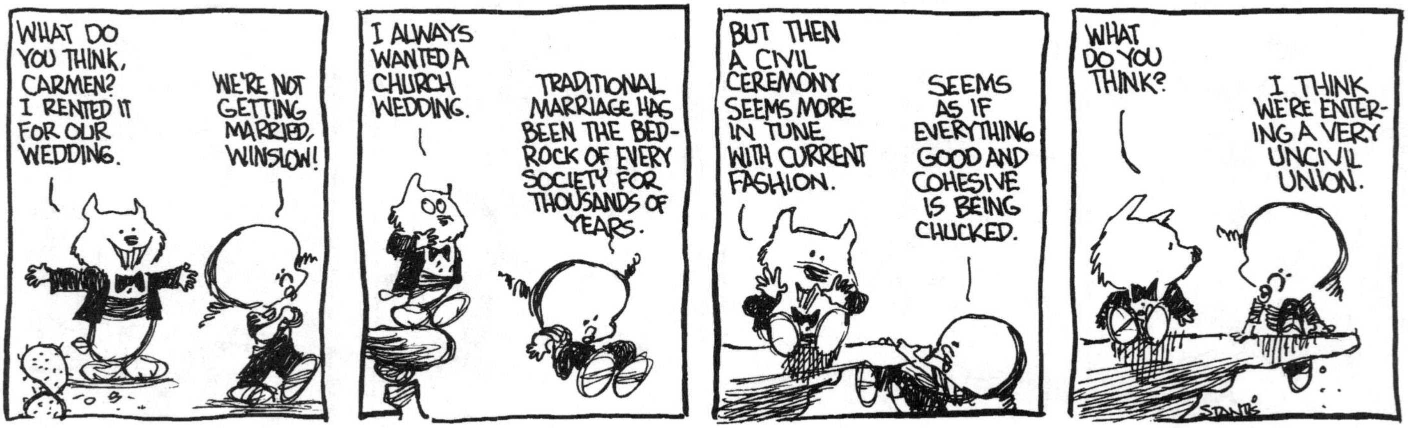
WHAT DO YOU THINK, CARMEN? I RENTED IT FOR OUR WEDDING.
WE'RE NOT GETTING MARRIED, WINSLOW!
I ALWAYS WANTED A CHURCH WEDDING.
TRADITIONAL MARRIAGE HAS BEEN THE BED-ROCK OF EVERY SOCIETY FOR THOUSANDS OF YEARS.
BUT THEN A CIVIL CEREMONY SEEMS MORE IN TUNE WITH CURRENT FASHION.
SEEMS AS IF EVERYTHING GOOD AND COHESIVE IS BEING CHUCKED.
WHAT DO YOU THINK?
I THINK WE'RE ENTER-ING A VERY UNCIVIL UNION.
STANTIS

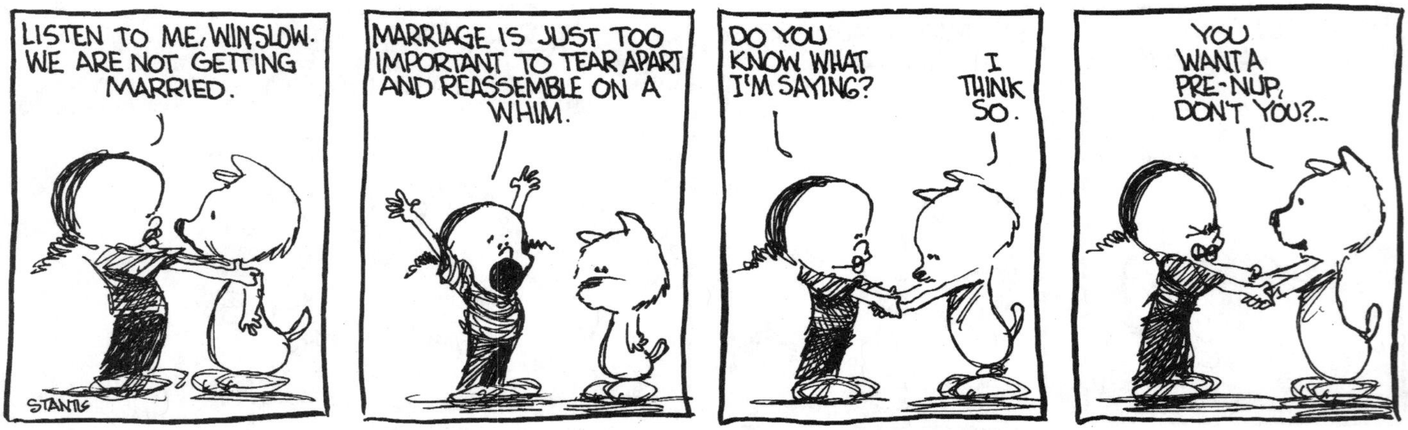
LISTEN TO ME, WINSLOW. WE ARE NOT GETTING MARRIED.
STANTIS
MARRIAGE IS JUST TOO IMPORTANT TO TEAR APART AND REASSEMBLE ON A WHIM.
DO YOU KNOW WHAT I'M SAYING?
I THINK SO.
YOU WANT A PRE-NUP, DON'T YOU?..

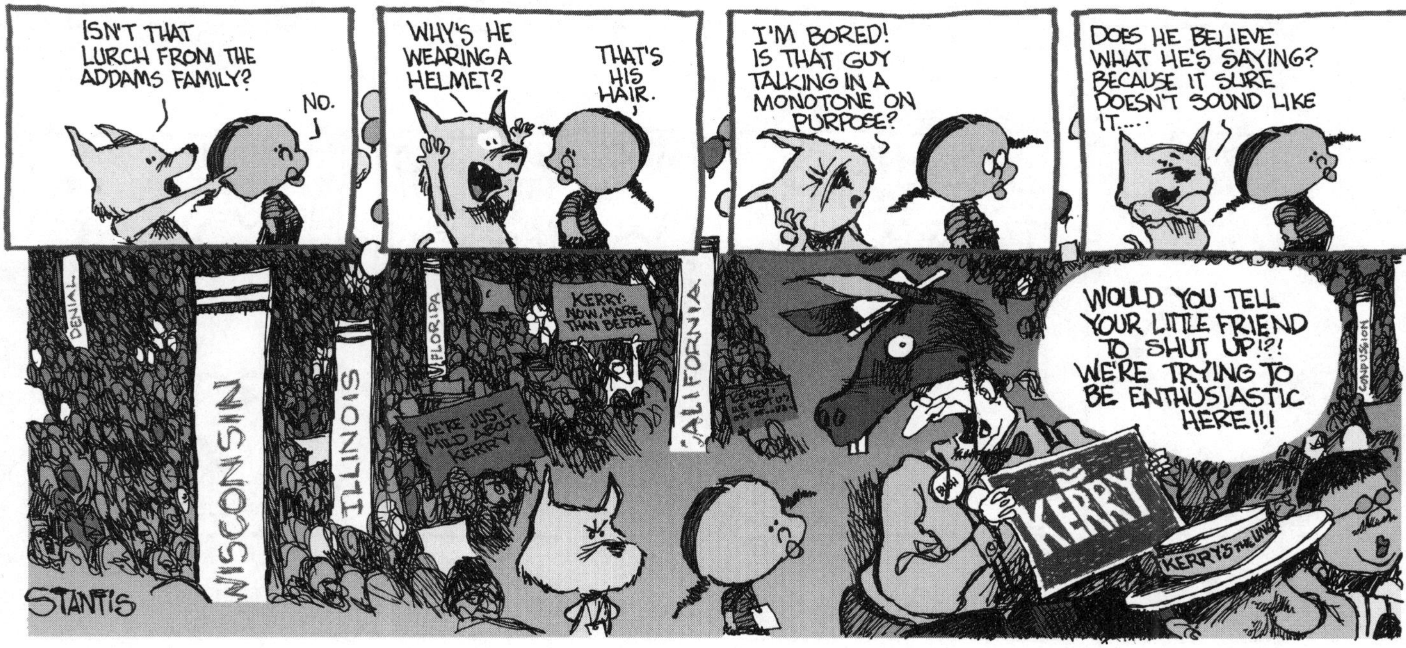
ISN'T THAT LURCH FROM THE ADDAMS FAMILY?
NO.
WHY'S HE WEARING A HELMET?
THAT'S HIS HAIR.
I'M BORED! IS THAT GUY TALKING IN A MONOTONE ON PURPOSE?
DOES HE BELIEVE WHAT HE'S SAYING? BECAUSE IT SURE DOESN'T SOUND LIKE IT....
DENIAL
WISCONSIN
ILLINOIS
FLORIDA
KERRY: NOW, MORE THAN BEFORE
WE'RE JUST MILD ABOUT KERRY
CALIFORNIA
WOULD YOU TELL YOUR LITTLE FRIEND TO SHUT UP!?! WE'RE TRYING TO BE ENTHUSIASTIC HERE!!!
CONFUSSION
KERRY
STANTIS

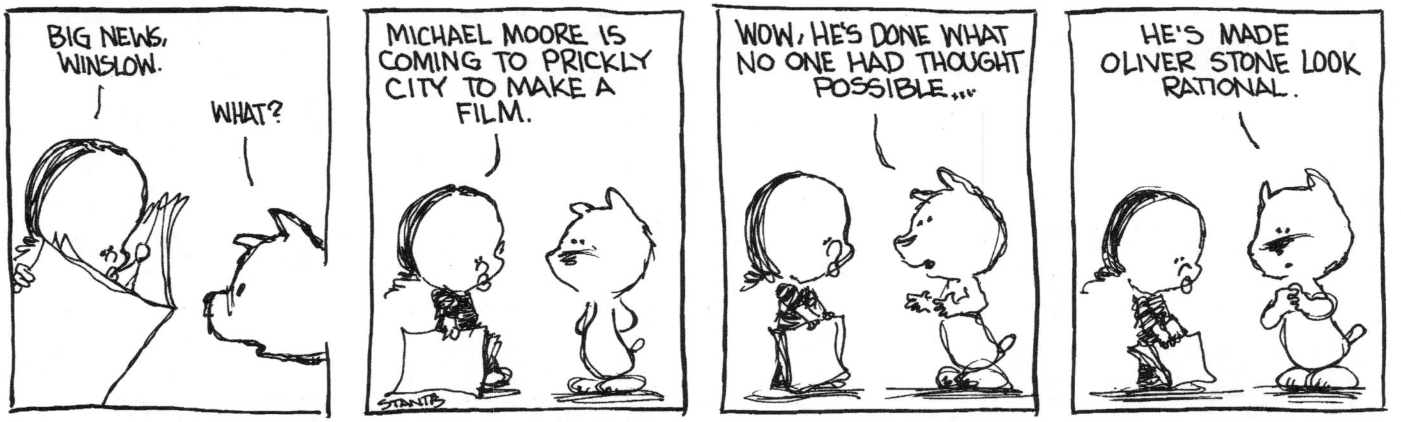
BIG NEWS, WINSLOW.
WHAT?
MICHAEL MOORE IS COMING TO PRICKLY CITY TO MAKE A FILM.
STANTIS
WOW, HE'S DONE WHAT NO ONE HAD THOUGHT POSSIBLE...
HE'S MADE OLIVER STONE LOOK RATIONAL.

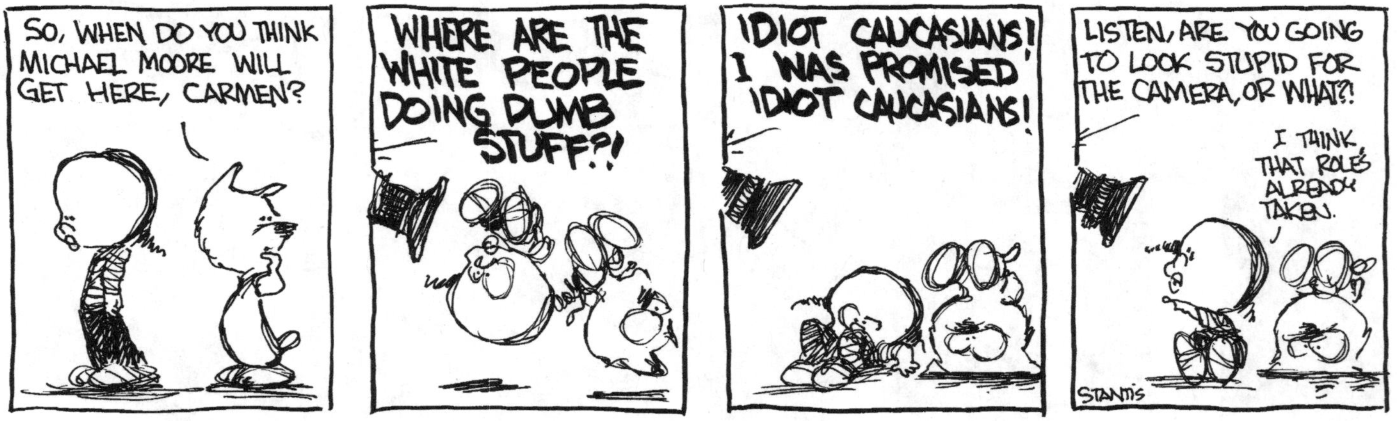
SO, WHEN DO YOU THINK MICHAEL MOORE WILL GET HERE, CARMEN?
WHERE ARE THE WHITE PEOPLE DOING DUMB STUFF?!
¡IDIOT CAUCASIANS! I WAS PROMISED ¡IDIOT CAUCASIANS!
LISTEN, ARE YOU GOING TO LOOK STUPID FOR THE CAMERA, OR WHAT?!
I THINK THAT ROLE'S ALREADY TAKEN.
STANTIS

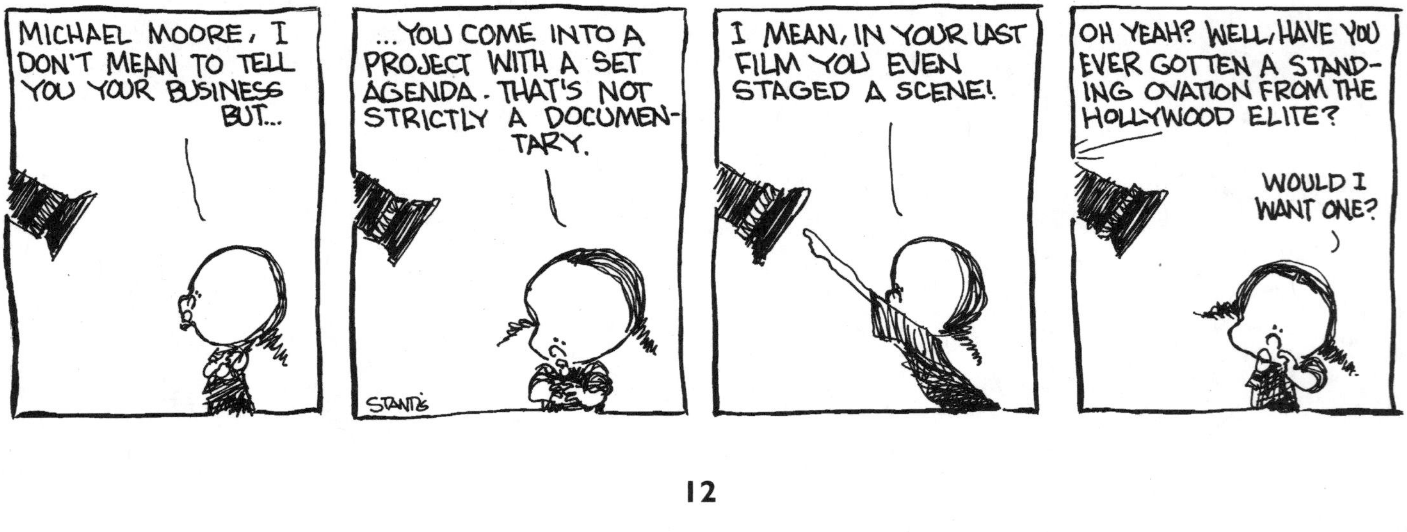
MICHAEL MOORE, I DON'T MEAN TO TELL YOU YOUR BUSINESS BUT...
...YOU COME INTO A PROJECT WITH A SET AGENDA. THAT'S NOT STRICTLY A DOCUMENTARY.
STANTIS
I MEAN, IN YOUR LAST FILM YOU EVEN STAGED A SCENE!
OH YEAH? WELL, HAVE YOU EVER GOTTEN A STANDING OVATION FROM THE HOLLYWOOD ELITE?
WOULD I WANT ONE?

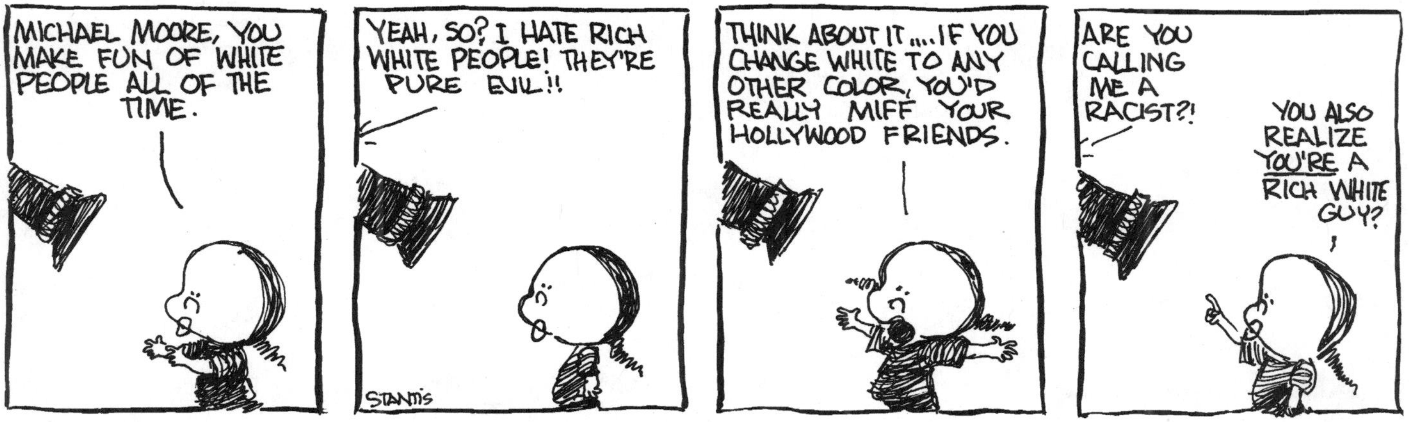
MICHAEL MOORE, YOU MAKE FUN OF WHITE PEOPLE ALL OF THE TIME.
YEAH, SO? I HATE RICH WHITE PEOPLE! THEY'RE PURE EVIL!!
STANTIS
THINK ABOUT IT....IF YOU CHANGE WHITE TO ANY OTHER COLOR, YOU'D REALLY MIFF YOUR HOLLYWOOD FRIENDS.
ARE YOU CALLING ME A RACIST?!
YOU ALSO REALIZE YOU'RE A RICH WHITE GUY?

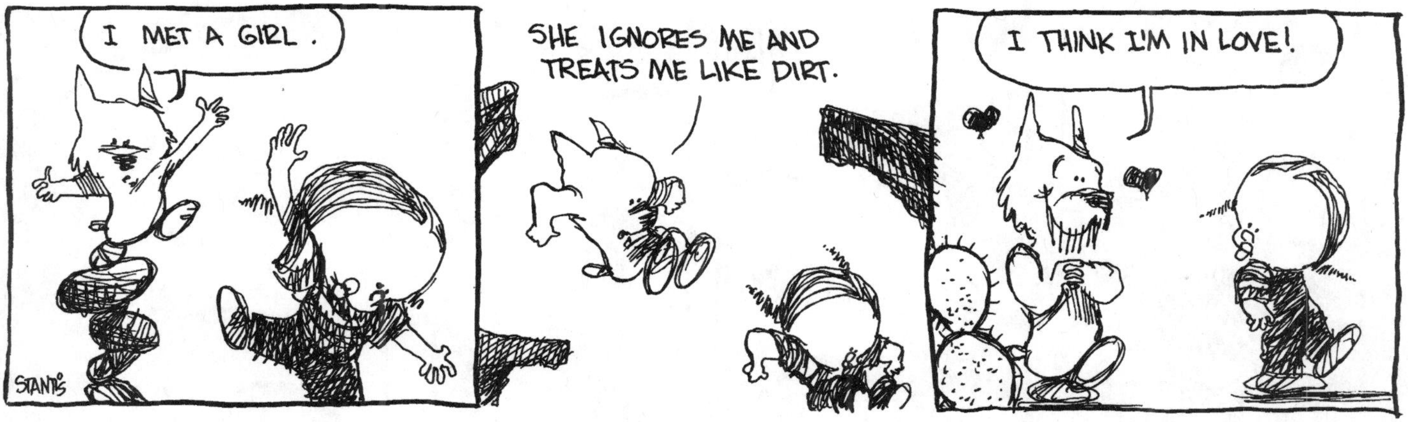
I MET A GIRL.
STANTIS
SHE IGNORES ME AND TREATS ME LIKE DIRT.
I THINK I'M IN LOVE!

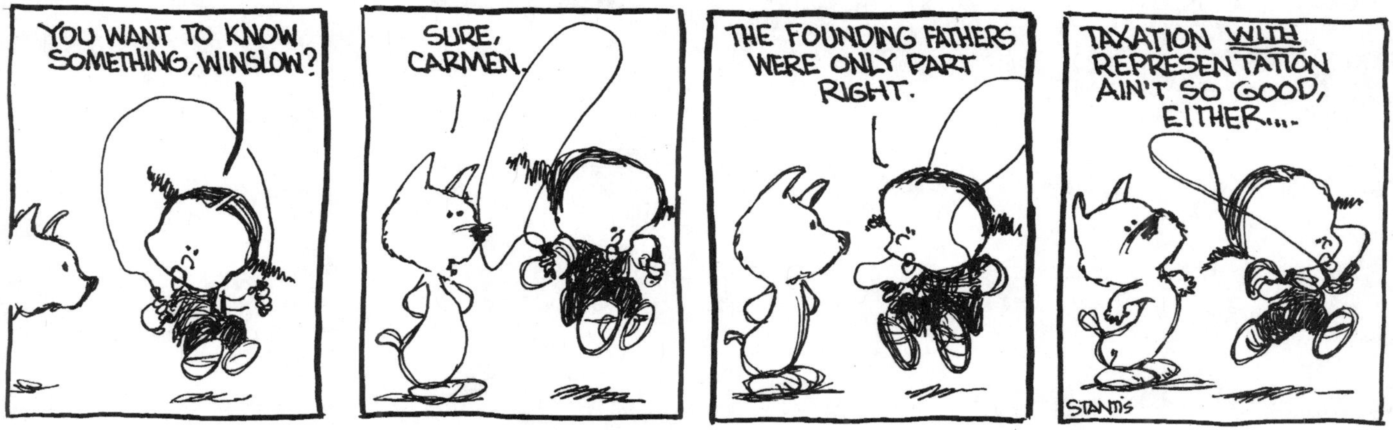
YOU WANT TO KNOW SOMETHING, WINSLOW?
SURE, CARMEN.
THE FOUNDING FATHERS WERE ONLY PART RIGHT.
TAXATION WITH REPRESENTATION AIN'T SO GOOD, EITHER....
STANTIS

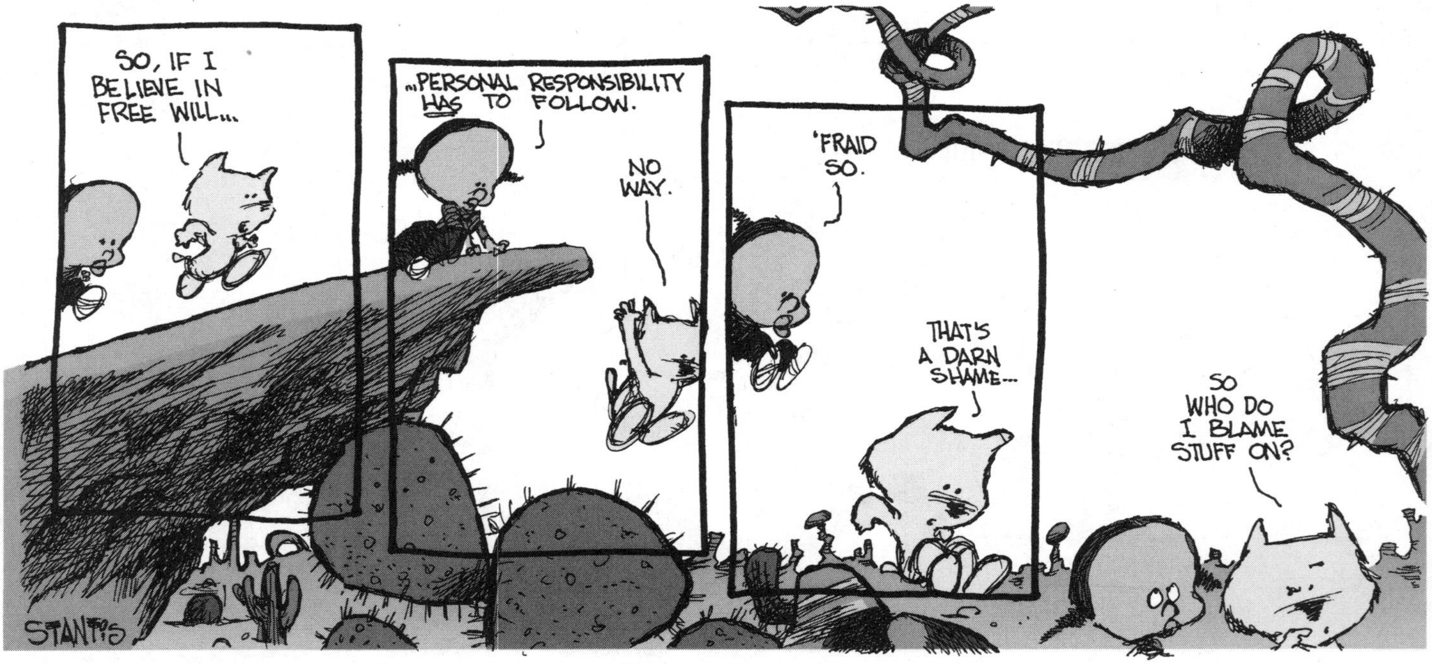

SO, IF I BELIEVE IN FREE WILL...
...PERSONAL RESPONSIBILITY HAS TO FOLLOW.
NO WAY.
'FRAID SO.
THAT'S A DARN SHAME...
SO WHO DO I BLAME STUFF ON?
STANTIS

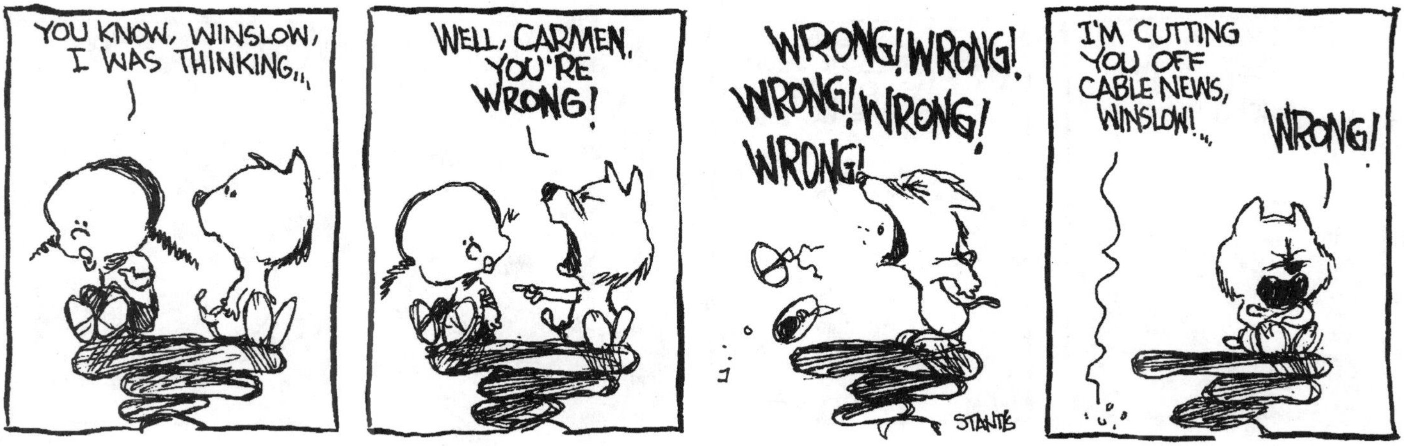
YOU KNOW, WINSLOW, I WAS THINKING...
WELL, CARMEN, YOU'RE WRONG!
WRONG! WRONG! WRONG! WRONG! WRONG!
STANTIS
I'M CUTTING YOU OFF CABLE NEWS, WINSLOW!...
WRONG!

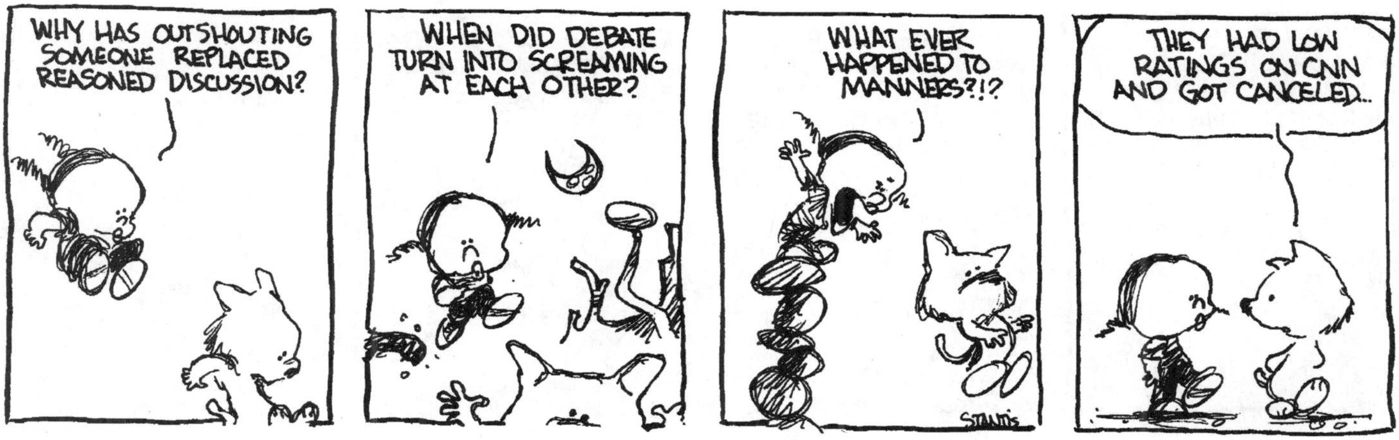
WHY HAS OUTSHOUTING SOMEONE REPLACED REASONED DISCUSSION?
WHEN DID DEBATE TURN INTO SCREAMING AT EACH OTHER?
WHAT EVER HAPPENED TO MANNERS?!?
STANTIS
THEY HAD LOW RATINGS ON CNN AND GOT CANCELED...

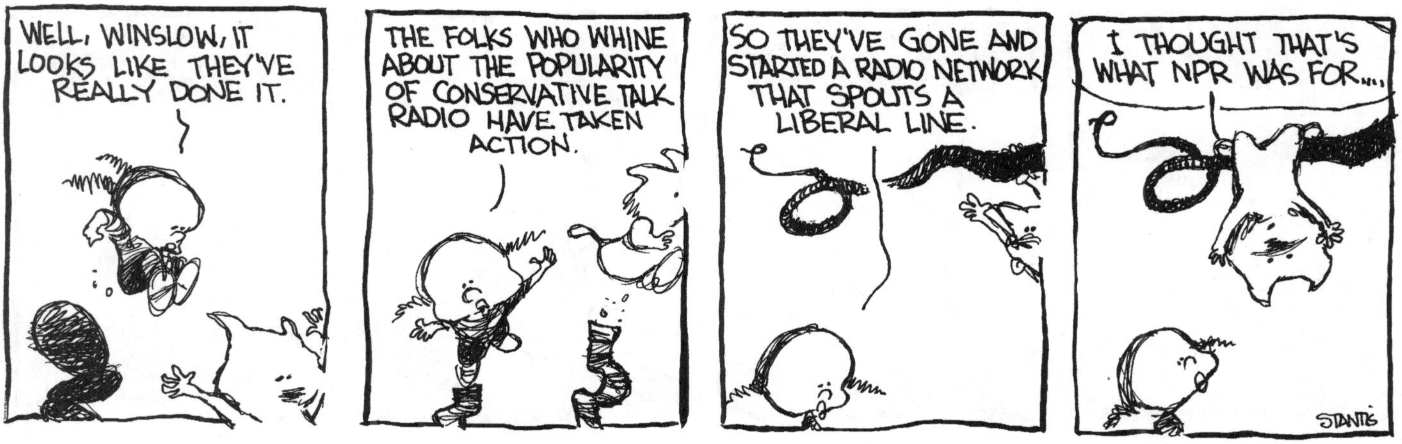
WELL, WINSLOW, IT LOOKS LIKE THEY'VE REALLY DONE IT.
THE FOLKS WHO WHINE ABOUT THE POPULARITY OF CONSERVATIVE TALK RADIO HAVE TAKEN ACTION.
SO THEY'VE GONE AND STARTED A RADIO NETWORK THAT SPOUTS A LIBERAL LINE.
I THOUGHT THAT'S WHAT NPR WAS FOR...
STANTIS

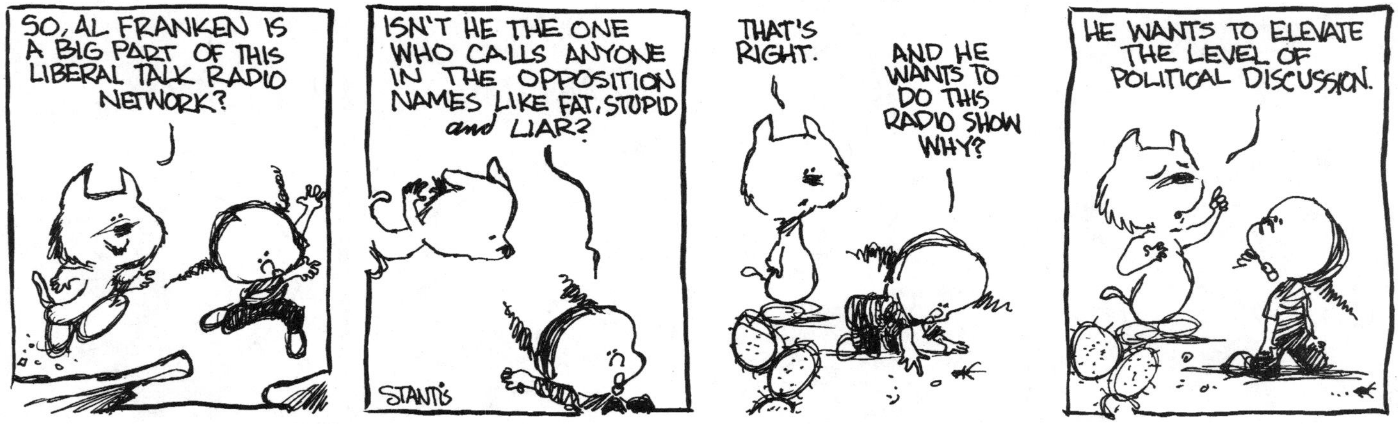
SO, AL FRANKEN IS A BIG PART OF THIS LIBERAL TALK RADIO NETWORK?
ISN'T HE THE ONE WHO CALLS ANYONE IN THE OPPOSITION NAMES LIKE FAT, STUPID and LIAR?
STANTIS
THAT'S RIGHT.
AND HE WANTS TO DO THIS RADIO SHOW WHY?
HE WANTS TO ELEVATE THE LEVEL OF POLITICAL DISCUSSION.

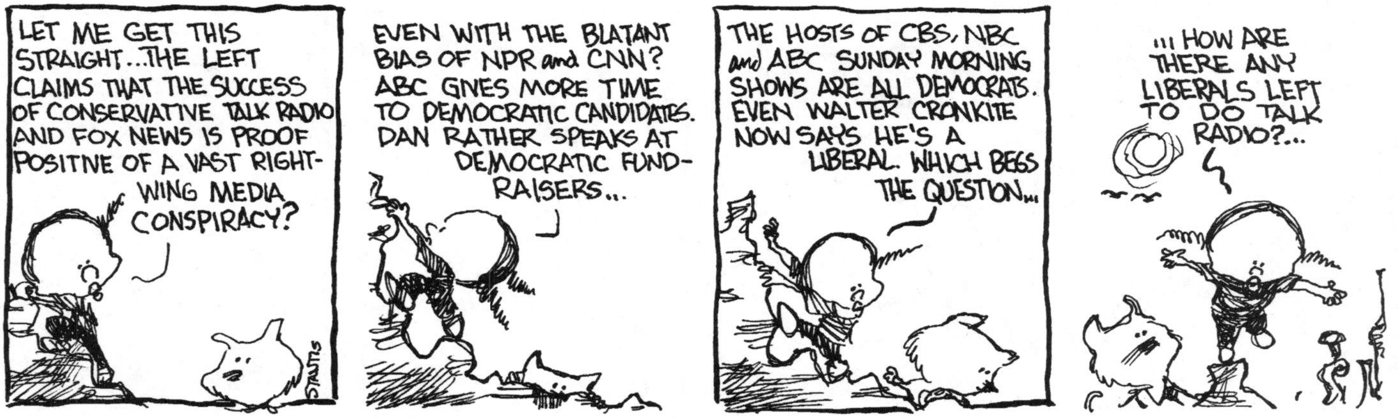
LET ME GET THIS STRAIGHT... THE LEFT CLAIMS THAT THE SUCCESS OF CONSERVATIVE TALK RADIO AND FOX NEWS IS PROOF POSITIVE OF A VAST RIGHT-WING MEDIA CONSPIRACY?
STANTIS
EVEN WITH THE BLATANT BIAS OF NPR and CNN? ABC GIVES MORE TIME TO DEMOCRATIC CANDIDATES. DAN RATHER SPEAKS AT DEMOCRATIC FUND-RAISERS...
THE HOSTS OF CBS, NBC and ABC SUNDAY MORNING SHOWS ARE ALL DEMOCRATS. EVEN WALTER CRONKITE NOW SAYS HE'S A LIBERAL. WHICH BEGS THE QUESTION...
...HOW ARE THERE ANY LIBERALS LEFT TO DO TALK RADIO?...

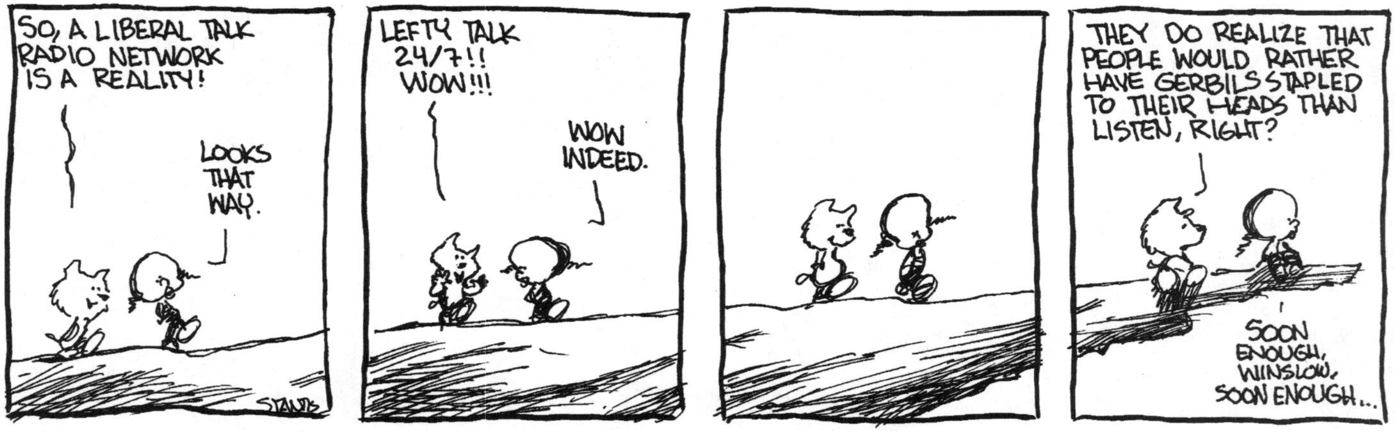
SO, A LIBERAL TALK RADIO NETWORK IS A REALITY!
LOOKS THAT WAY.
STANTIS
LEFTY TALK 24/7!! WOW!!!
WOW INDEED.
THEY DO REALIZE THAT PEOPLE WOULD RATHER HAVE GERBILS STAPLED TO THEIR HEADS THAN LISTEN, RIGHT?
SOON ENOUGH, WINSLOW, SOON ENOUGH...

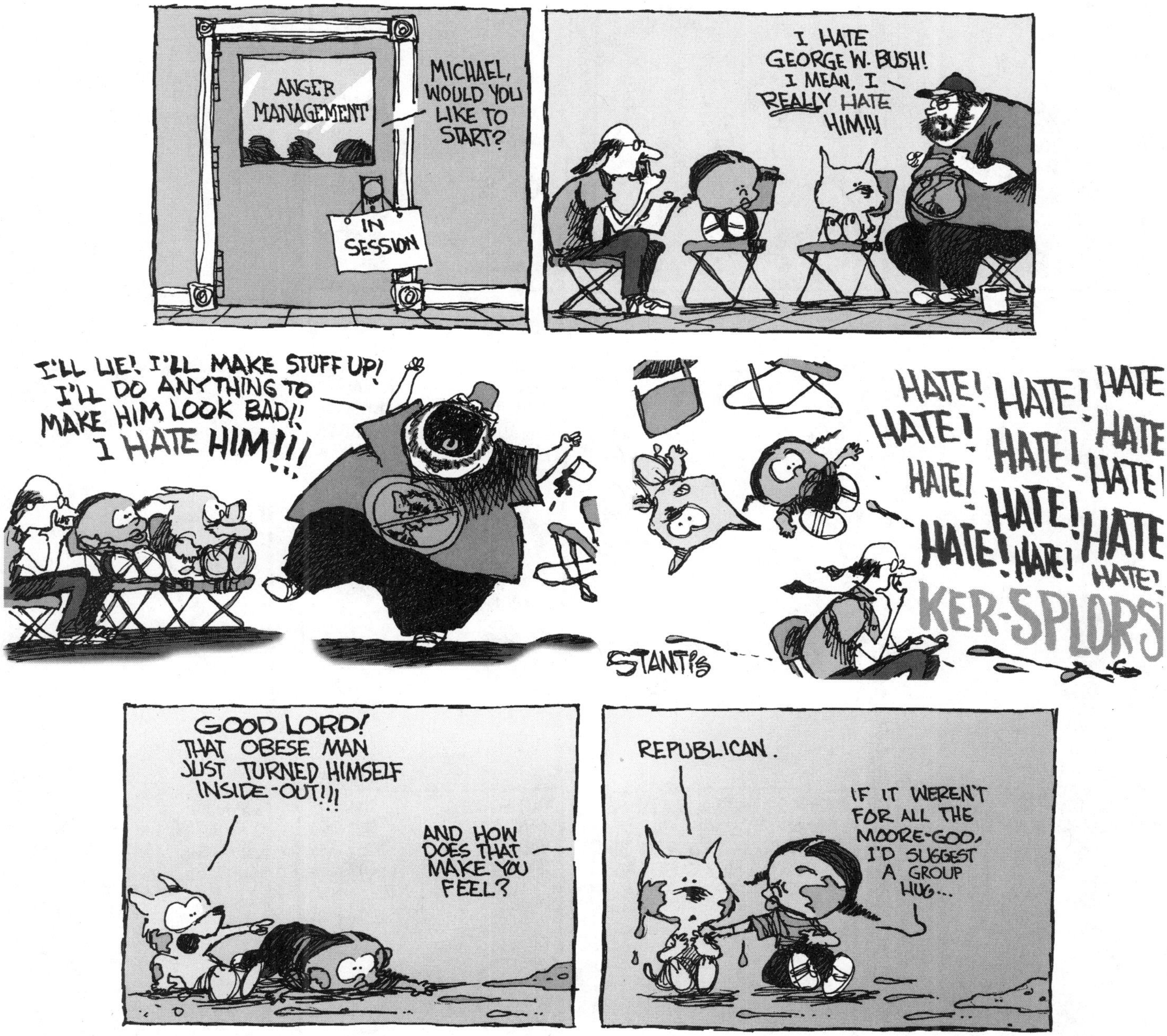
ANGER MANAGEMENT
MICHAEL, WOULD YOU LIKE TO START?
IN SESSION
I HATE GEORGE W. BUSH! I MEAN, I REALLY HATE HIM!!!
I'LL LIE! I'LL MAKE STUFF UP! I'LL DO ANYTHING TO MAKE HIM LOOK BAD!! I HATE HIM!!!
HATE! HATE! HATE HATE! HATE! HATE HATE! HATE! HATE! HATE! HATE! HATE! HATE! HATE HATE!
KER-SPLORSH
STANTIS
GOOD LORD! THAT OBESE MAN JUST TURNED HIMSELF INSIDE-OUT!!!
AND HOW DOES THAT MAKE YOU FEEL?
REPUBLICAN.
IF IT WEREN'T FOR ALL THE MOORE-GOO, I'D SUGGEST A GROUP HUG...

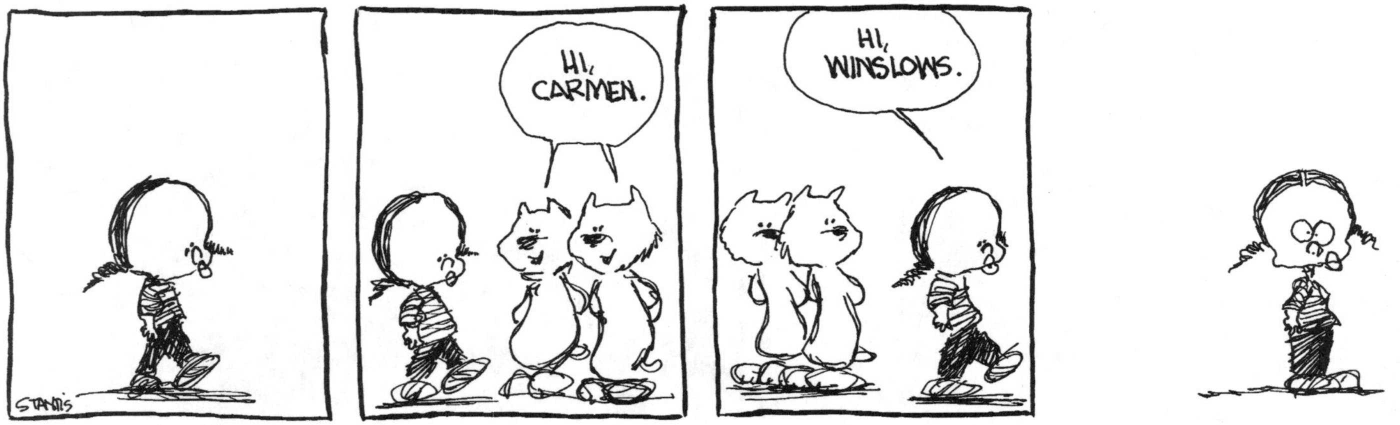
STANTIS
HI, CARMEN.
HI, WINSLOWS.

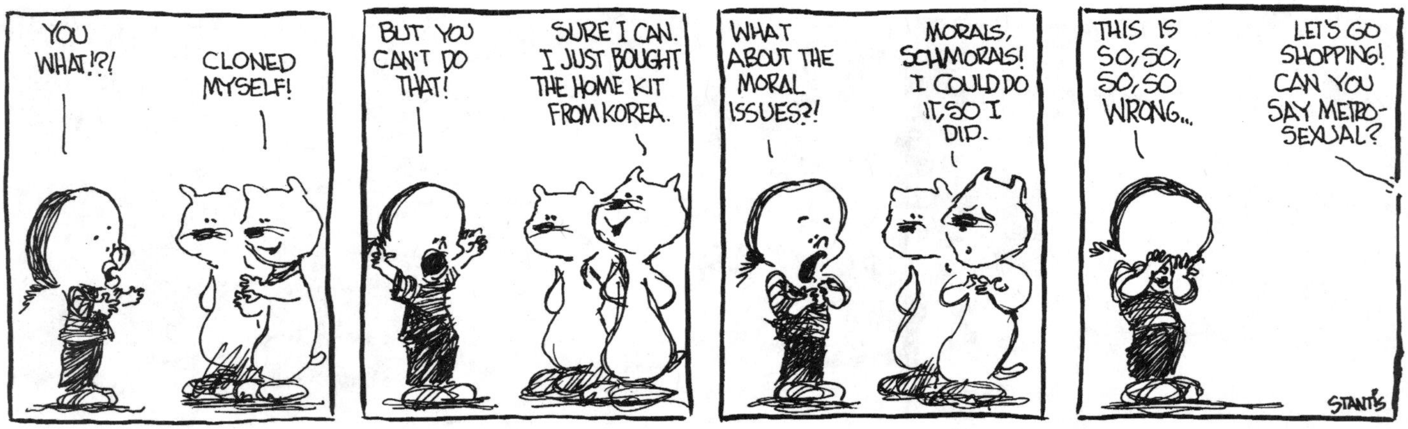
YOU WHAT!?!
CLONED MYSELF!
BUT YOU CAN'T DO THAT!
SURE I CAN. I JUST BOUGHT THE HOME KIT FROM KOREA.
WHAT ABOUT THE MORAL ISSUES?!
MORALS, SCHMORALS! I COULD DO IT, SO I DID.
THIS IS SO, SO, SO, SO WRONG...
LET'S GO SHOPPING! CAN YOU SAY METRO-SEXUAL?
STANTIS

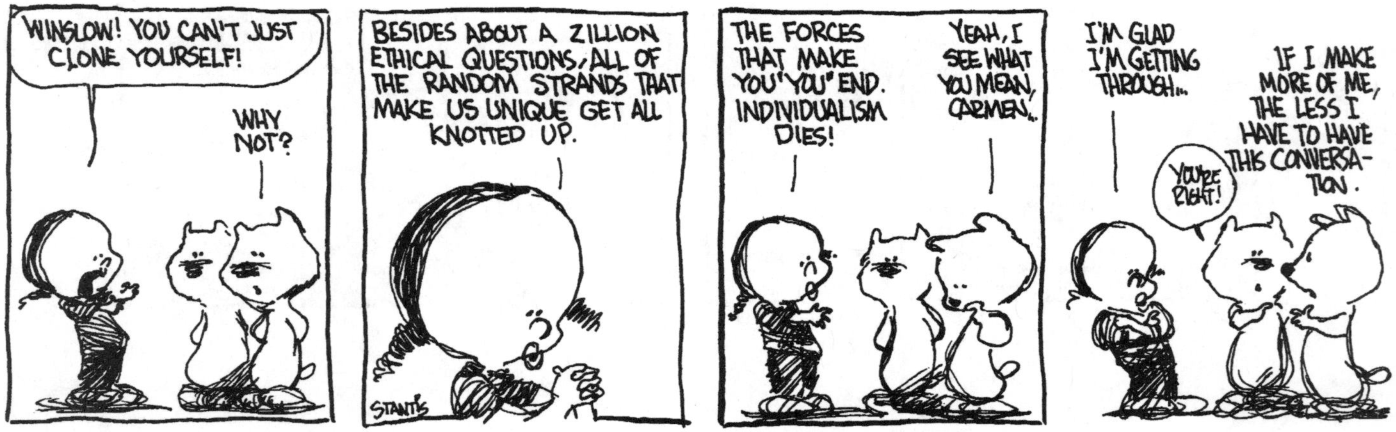
WINSLOW! YOU CAN'T JUST CLONE YOURSELF!
WHY NOT?
BESIDES ABOUT A ZILLION ETHICAL QUESTIONS, ALL OF THE RANDOM STRANDS THAT MAKE US UNIQUE GET ALL KNOTTED UP.
STANTIS
THE FORCES THAT MAKE YOU "YOU" END. INDIVIDUALISM DIES!
YEAH, I SEE WHAT YOU MEAN, CARMEN...
I'M GLAD I'M GETTING THROUGH...
IF I MAKE MORE OF ME, THE LESS I HAVE TO HAVE THIS CONVERSA-TION.
YOU'RE RIGHT!

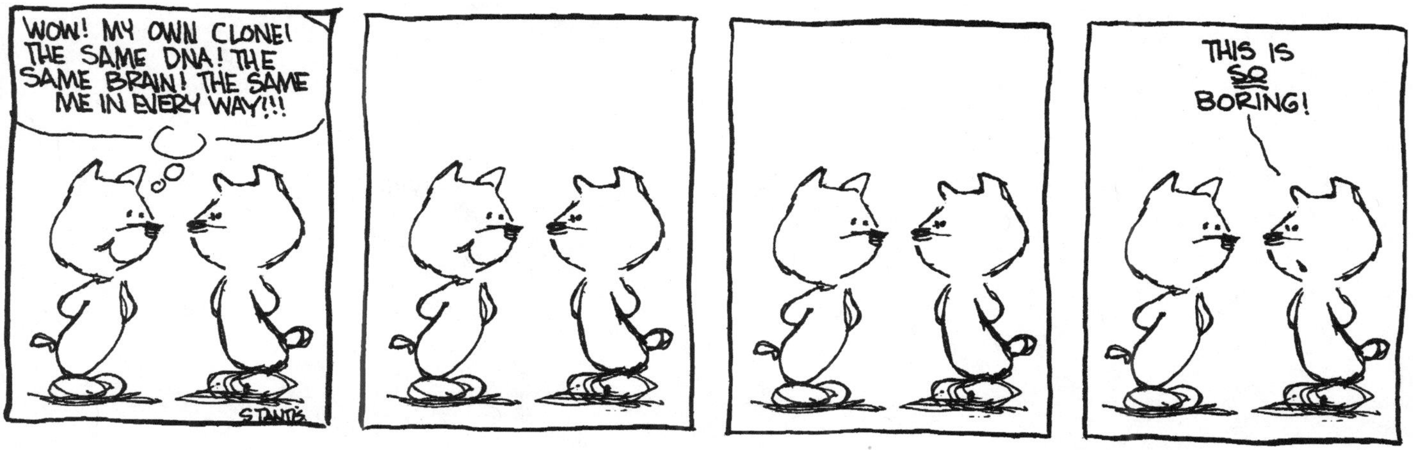
WOW! MY OWN CLONE! THE SAME DNA! THE SAME BRAIN! THE SAME ME IN EVERY WAY!!!
STANTIS
THIS IS SO BORING!

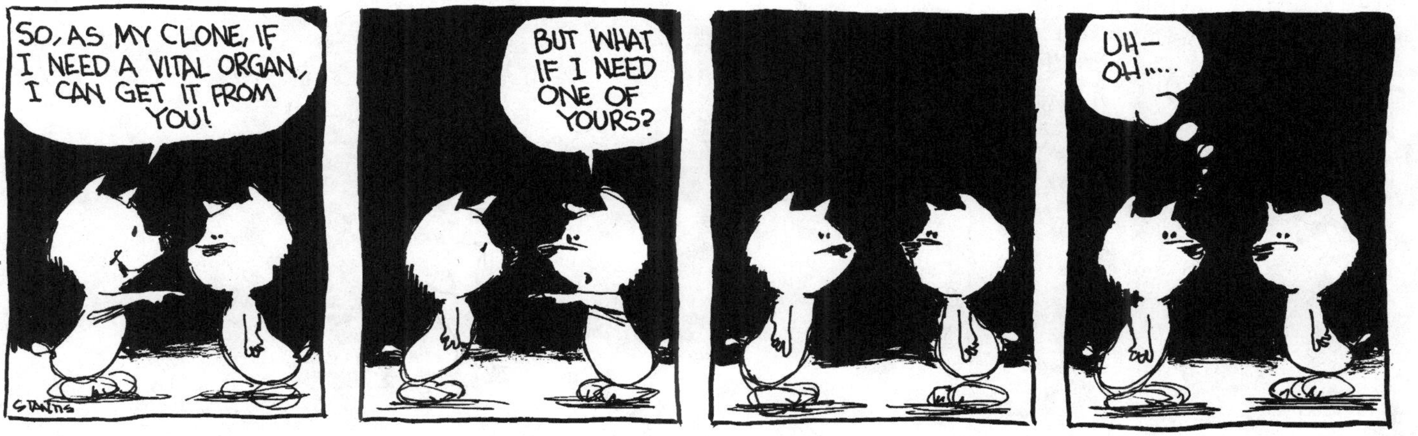
SO, AS MY CLONE, IF I NEED A VITAL ORGAN, I CAN GET IT FROM YOU!
STANTIS
BUT WHAT IF I NEED ONE OF YOURS?
UH-OH.....

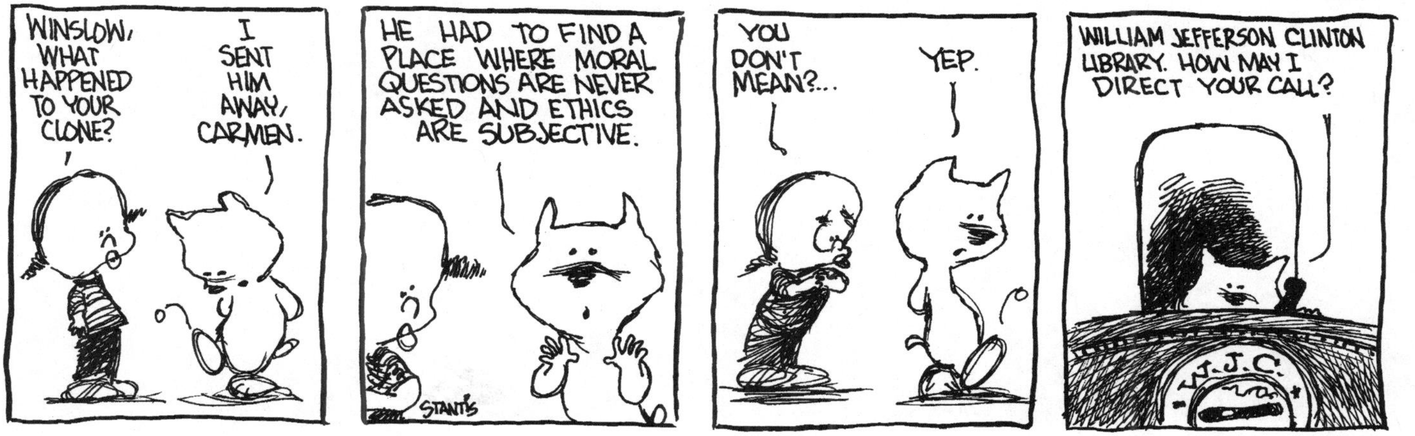
WINSLOW, WHAT HAPPENED TO YOUR CLONE?
I SENT HIM AWAY, CARMEN.
HE HAD TO FIND A PLACE WHERE MORAL QUESTIONS ARE NEVER ASKED AND ETHICS ARE SUBJECTIVE.
STANTIS
YOU DON'T MEAN?...
YEP.
WILLIAM JEFFERSON CLINTON LIBRARY. HOW MAY I DIRECT YOUR CALL?
W.J.C.

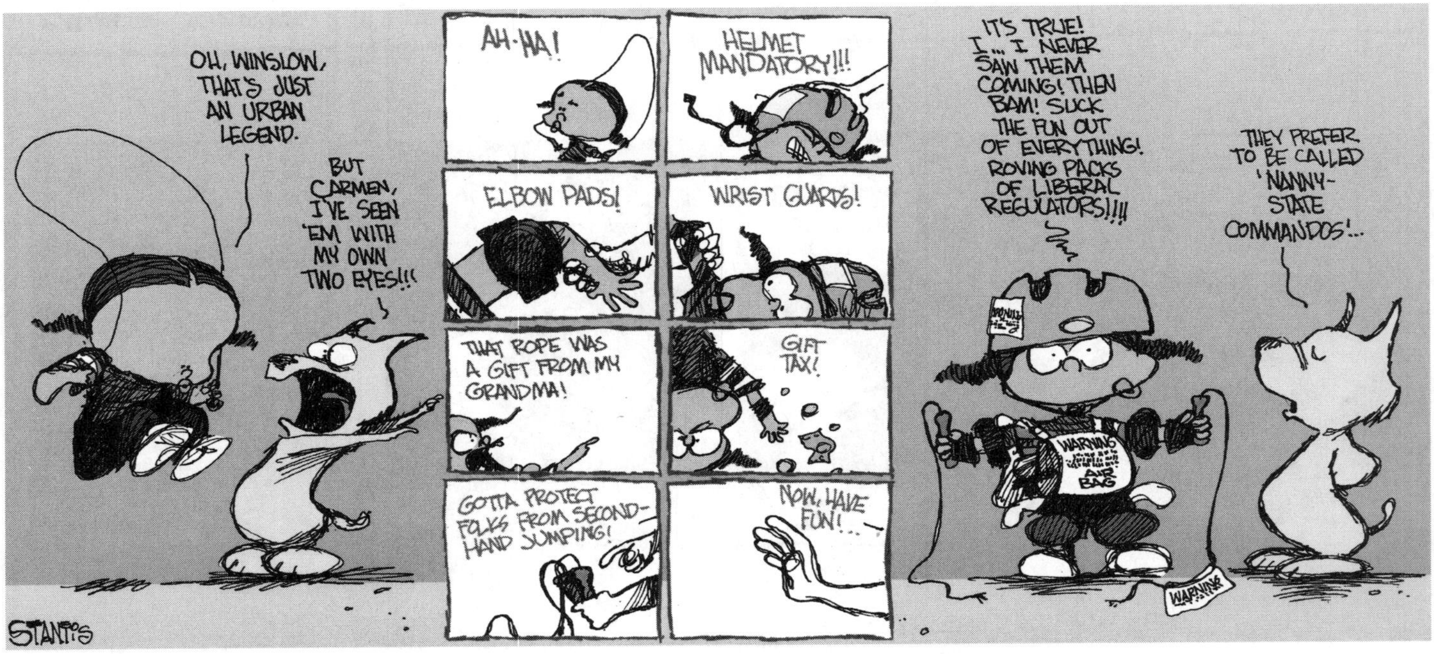

OH, WINSLOW, THAT'S JUST AN URBAN LEGEND.
BUT CARMEN, I'VE SEEN 'EM WITH MY OWN TWO EYES!!!
AH-HA!
HELMET MANDATORY!!!
ELBOW PADS!
WRIST GUARDS!
THAT ROPE WAS A GIFT FROM MY GRANDMA!
GIFT TAX!
GOTTA PROTECT FOLKS FROM SECOND-HAND JUMPING!
NOW, HAVE FUN!...
IT'S TRUE! I... I NEVER SAW THEM COMING! THEN BAM! SUCK THE FUN OUT OF EVERYTHING! ROVING PACKS OF LIBERAL REGULATORS!!!!
THEY PREFER TO BE CALLED 'NANNY-STATE COMMANDOS'...
WARNING
AIR BAG
WARNING
STANTIS

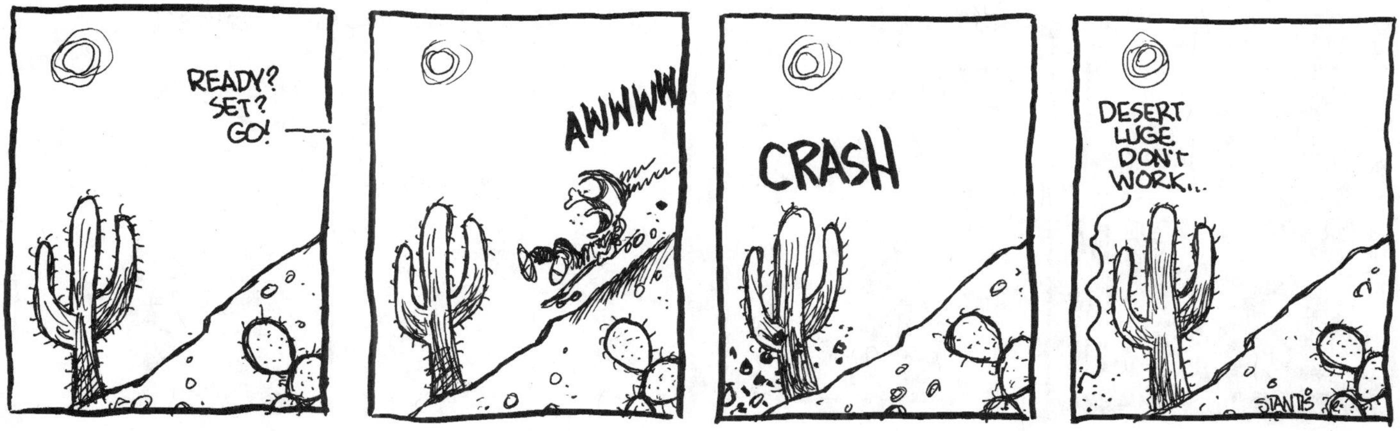
READY? SET? GO!
AWWWW
CRASH
DESERT LUGE DON'T WORK...
STANTIS

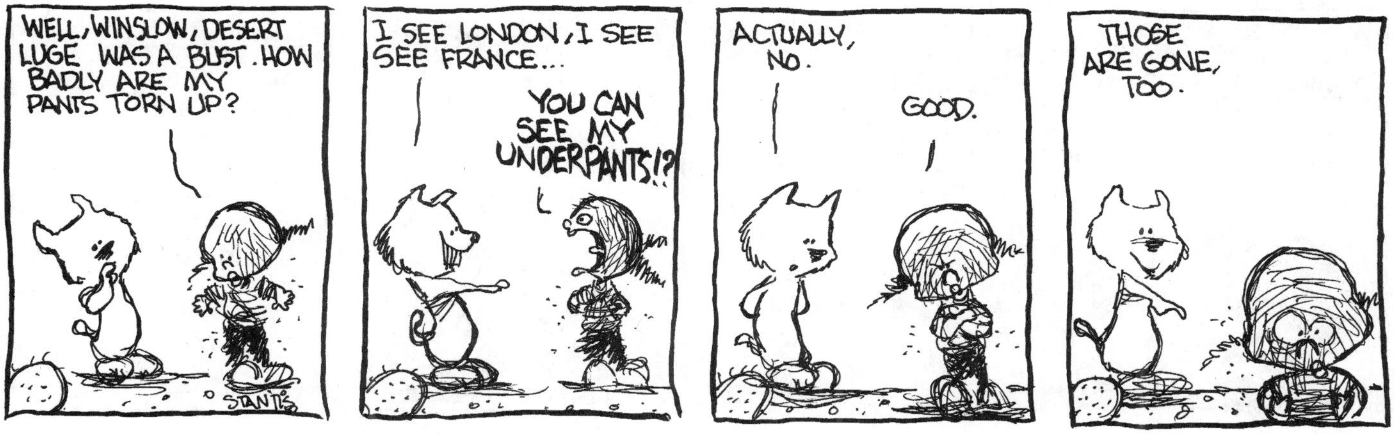
WELL, WINSLOW, DESERT LUGE WAS A BUST. HOW BADLY ARE MY PANTS TORN UP?
STANTIS
I SEE LONDON, I SEE SEE FRANCE...
YOU CAN SEE MY UNDERPANTS!?
ACTUALLY, NO.
GOOD.
THOSE ARE GONE, TOO.

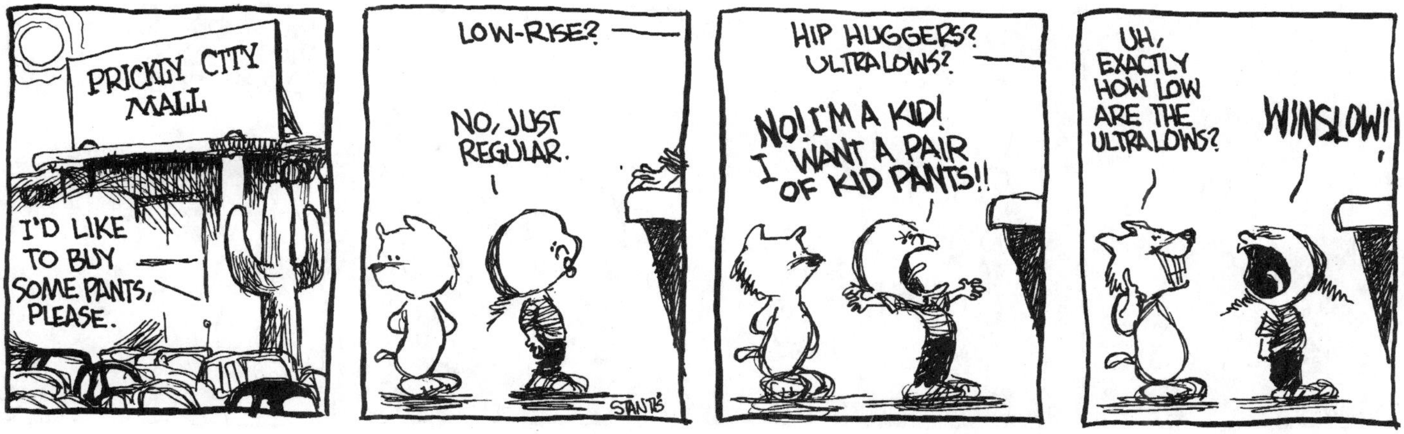
PRICKLY CITY MALL
I'D LIKE TO BUY SOME PANTS, PLEASE.
LOW-RISE?
NO, JUST REGULAR.
STANTIS
HIP HUGGERS? ULTRALOWS?
NO! I'M A KID! I WANT A PAIR OF KID PANTS!!
UH, EXACTLY HOW LOW ARE THE ULTRALOWS?
WINSLOW!

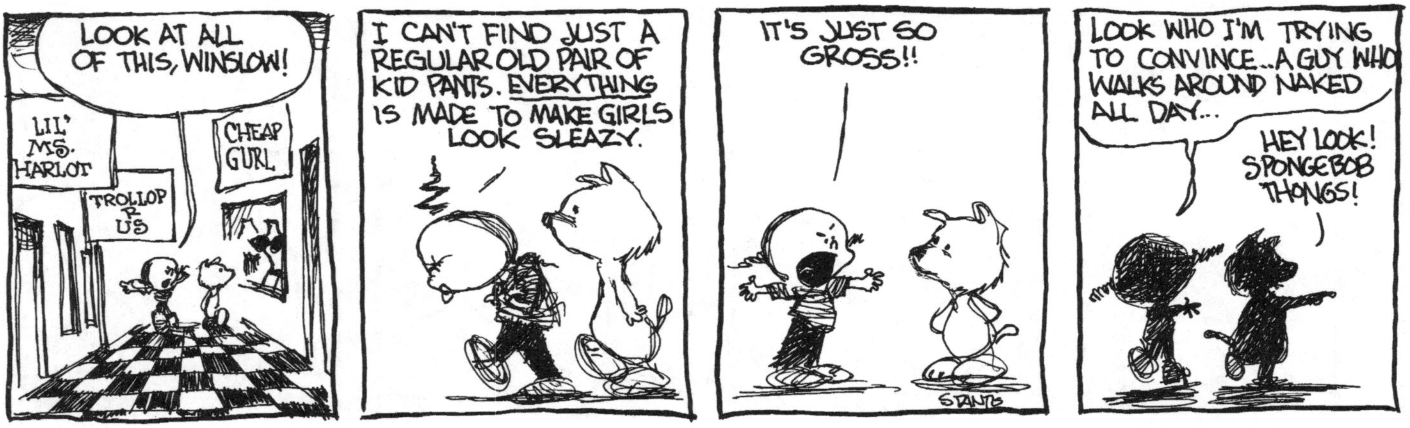
LOOK AT ALL OF THIS, WINSLOW!
LIL' MS. HARLOT
TROLLOP R US
CHEAP GURL
I CAN'T FIND JUST A REGULAR OLD PAIR OF KID PANTS. EVERYTHING IS MADE TO MAKE GIRLS LOOK SLEAZY.
IT'S JUST SO GROSS!!
STANTIS
LOOK WHO I'M TRYING TO CONVINCE...A GUY WHO WALKS AROUND NAKED ALL DAY...
HEY LOOK! SPONGEBOB THONGS!

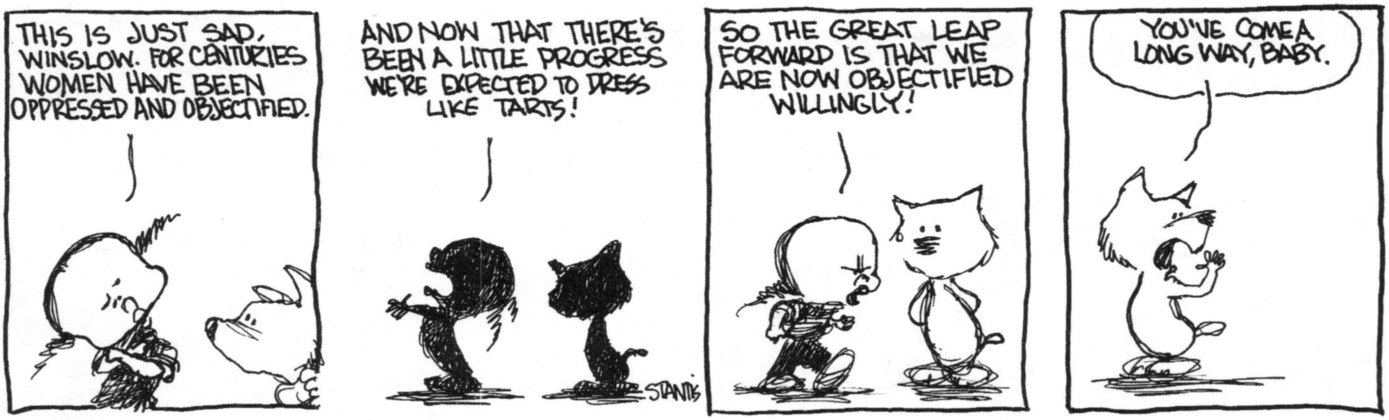
THIS IS JUST SAD, WINSLOW. FOR CENTURIES WOMEN HAVE BEEN OPPRESSED AND OBJECTIFIED.
AND NOW THAT THERE'S BEEN A LITTLE PROGRESS WE'RE EXPECTED TO DRESS LIKE TARTS!
STANTIS
SO THE GREAT LEAP FORWARD IS THAT WE ARE NOW OBJECTIFIED WILLINGLY!
YOU'VE COME A LONG WAY, BABY.

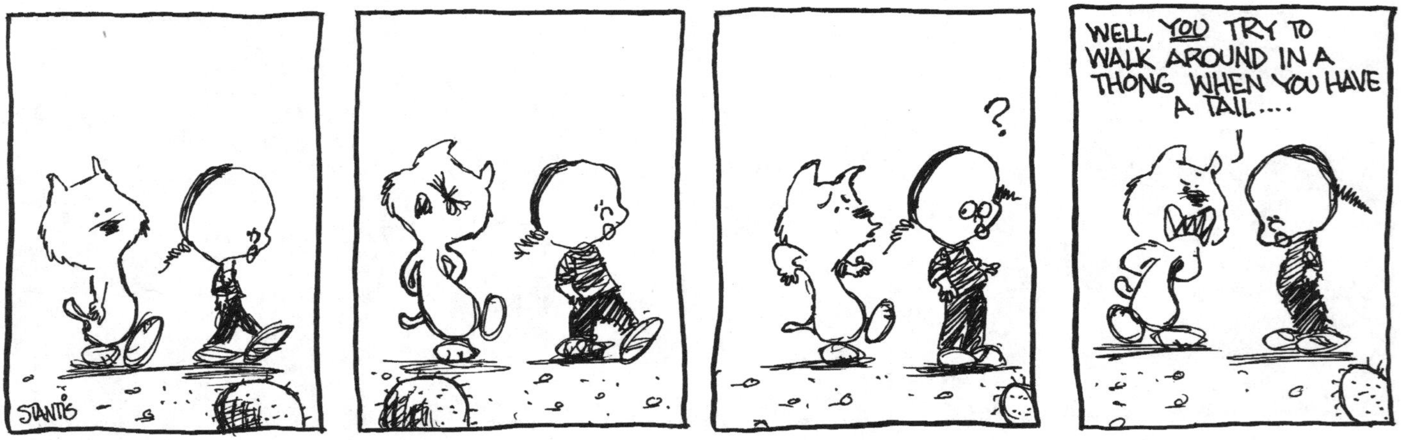
STANTIS
?
WELL, YOU TRY TO WALK AROUND IN A THONG WHEN YOU HAVE A TAIL....

I THINK. THEREFORE, I AM.
YEAH, BUT, WHAT IF YOU THINK YOU'RE NOT?
STANTIS

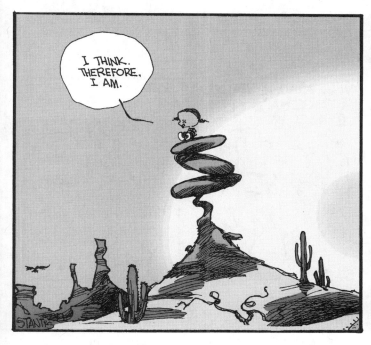

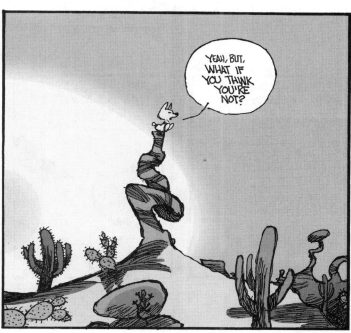

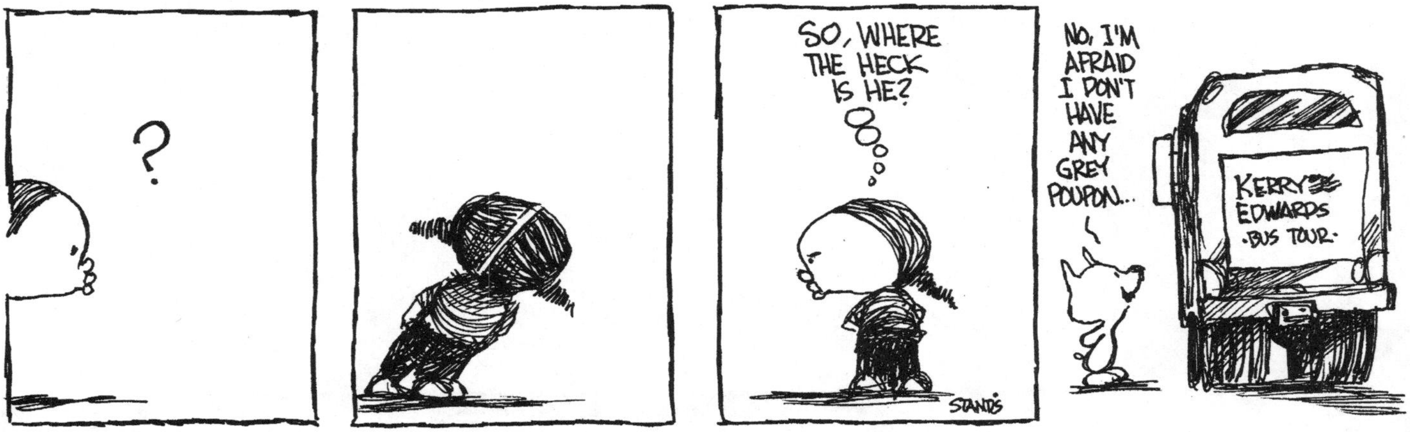
?
SO, WHERE THE HECK IS HE?
STANTIS
NO, I'M AFRAID I DON'T HAVE ANY GREY POUPON...
KERRY EDWARDS ·BUS TOUR·

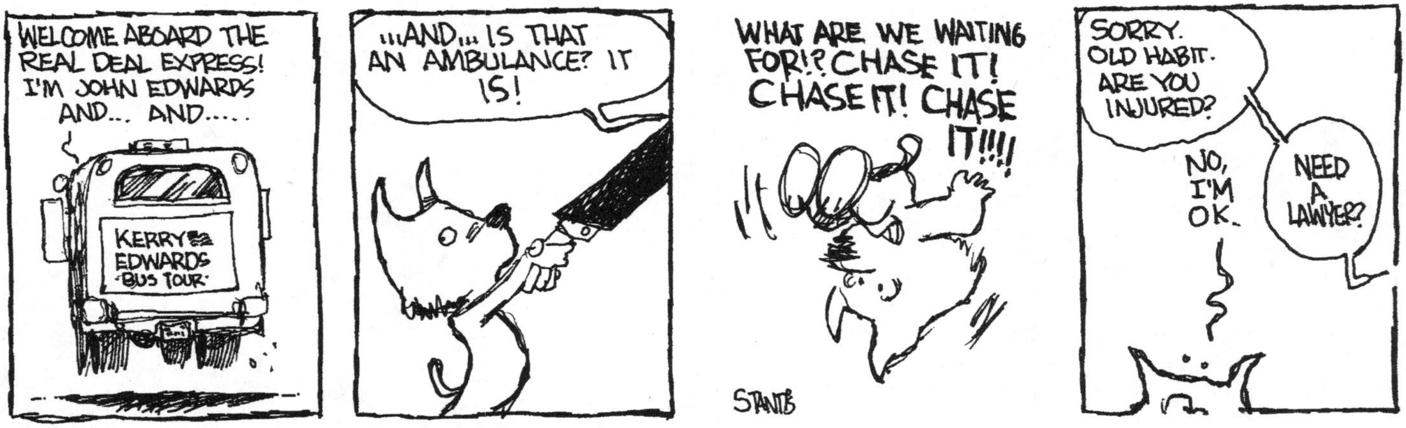
WELCOME ABOARD THE REAL DEAL EXPRESS! I'M JOHN EDWARDS AND... AND.....
KERRY EDWARDS ·BUS TOUR·
...AND... IS THAT AN AMBULANCE? IT IS!
WHAT ARE WE WAITING FOR!? CHASE IT! CHASE IT! CHASE IT!!!!
STANTIS
SORRY. OLD HABIT. ARE YOU INJURED?
NEED A LAWYER?
NO, I'M OK.

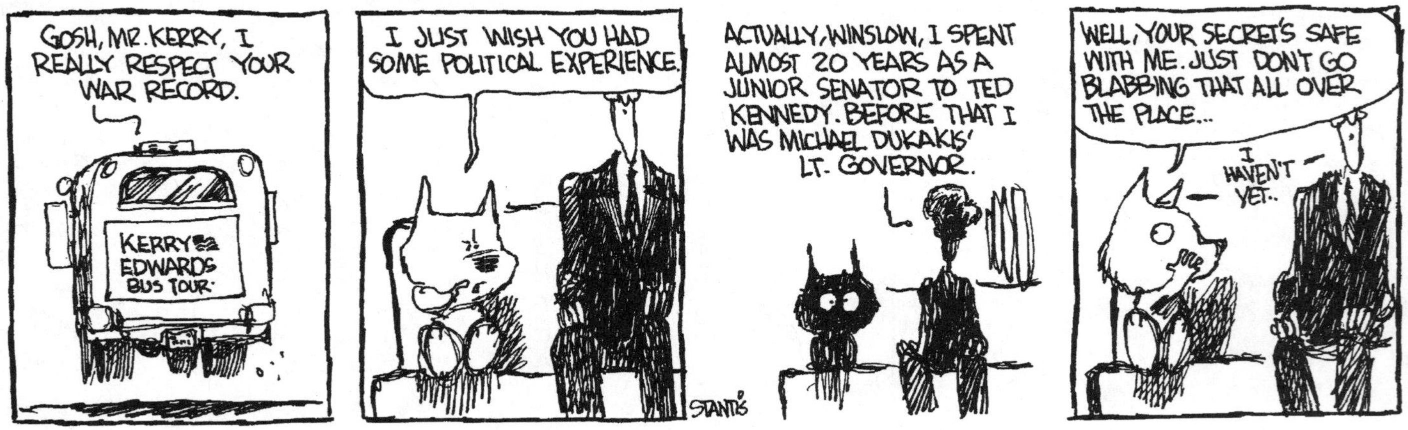
GOSH, MR. KERRY, I REALLY RESPECT YOUR WAR RECORD.
KERRY EDWARDS BUS TOUR
I JUST WISH YOU HAD SOME POLITICAL EXPERIENCE.
STANTIS
ACTUALLY, WINSLOW, I SPENT ALMOST 20 YEARS AS A JUNIOR SENATOR TO TED KENNEDY. BEFORE THAT I WAS MICHAEL DUKAKIS' LT. GOVERNOR.
WELL, YOUR SECRET'S SAFE WITH ME. JUST DON'T GO BLABBING THAT ALL OVER THE PLACE...
I HAVEN'T YET.

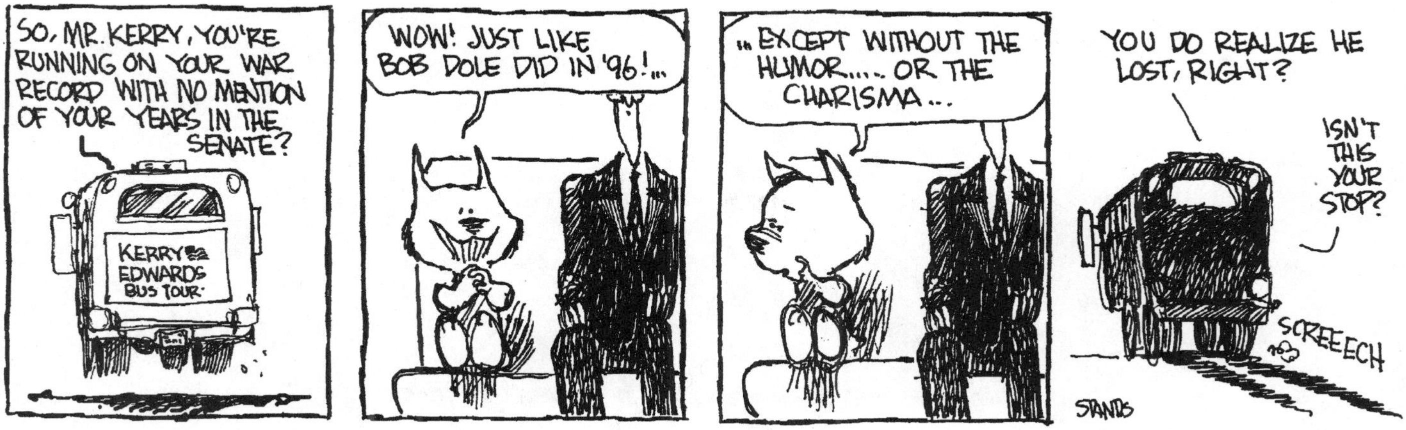
SO, MR. KERRY, YOU'RE RUNNING ON YOUR WAR RECORD WITH NO MENTION OF YOUR YEARS IN THE SENATE?
KERRY EDWARDS BUS TOUR
WOW! JUST LIKE BOB DOLE DID IN '96!...
...EXCEPT WITHOUT THE HUMOR..... OR THE CHARISMA...
YOU DO REALIZE HE LOST, RIGHT?
ISN'T THIS YOUR STOP?
SCREEECH
STANTIS

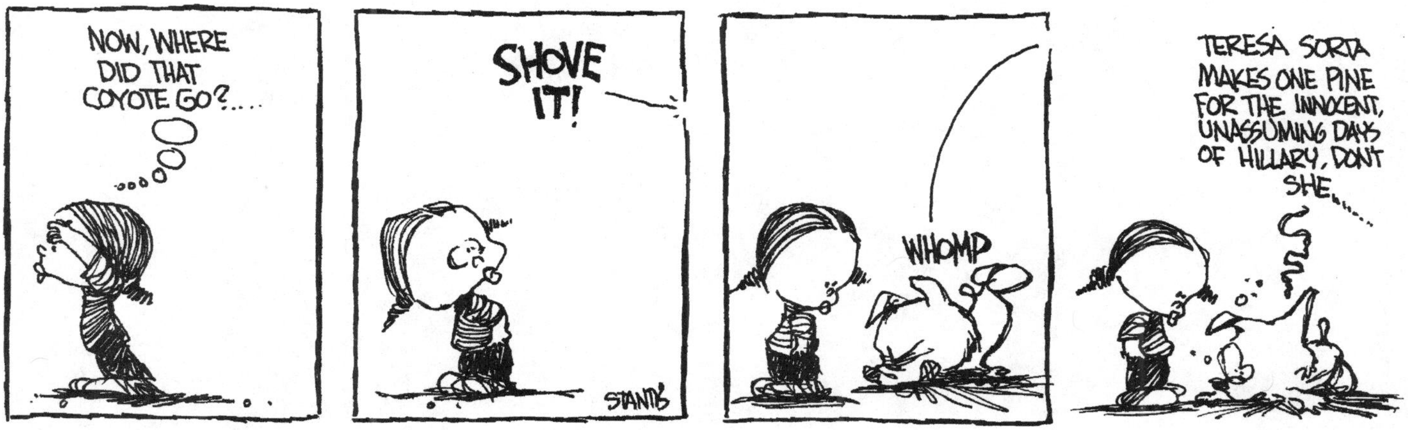
NOW, WHERE DID THAT COYOTE GO?....
SHOVE IT!
STANTIS
WHOMP
TERESA SORTA MAKES ONE PINE FOR THE INNOCENT, UNASSUMING DAYS OF HILLARY, DON'T SHE......

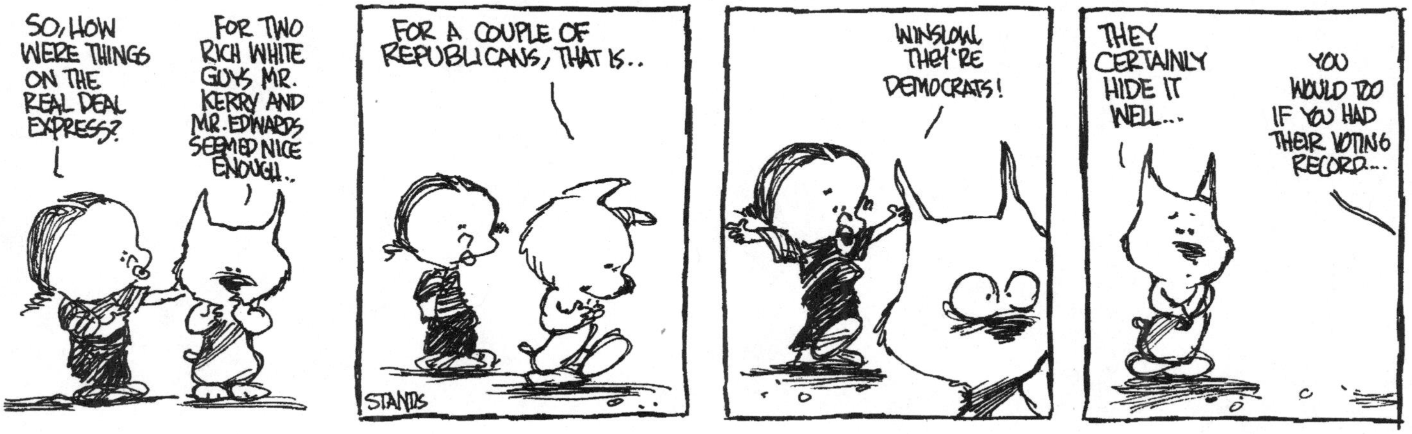
SO, HOW WERE THINGS ON THE REAL DEAL EXPRESS?
FOR TWO RICH WHITE GUYS MR. KERRY AND MR. EDWARDS SEEMED NICE ENOUGH..
FOR A COUPLE OF REPUBLICANS, THAT IS..
STANTIS
WINSLOW, THEY'RE DEMOCRATS!
THEY CERTAINLY HIDE IT WELL...
YOU WOULD TOO IF YOU HAD THEIR VOTING RECORD...

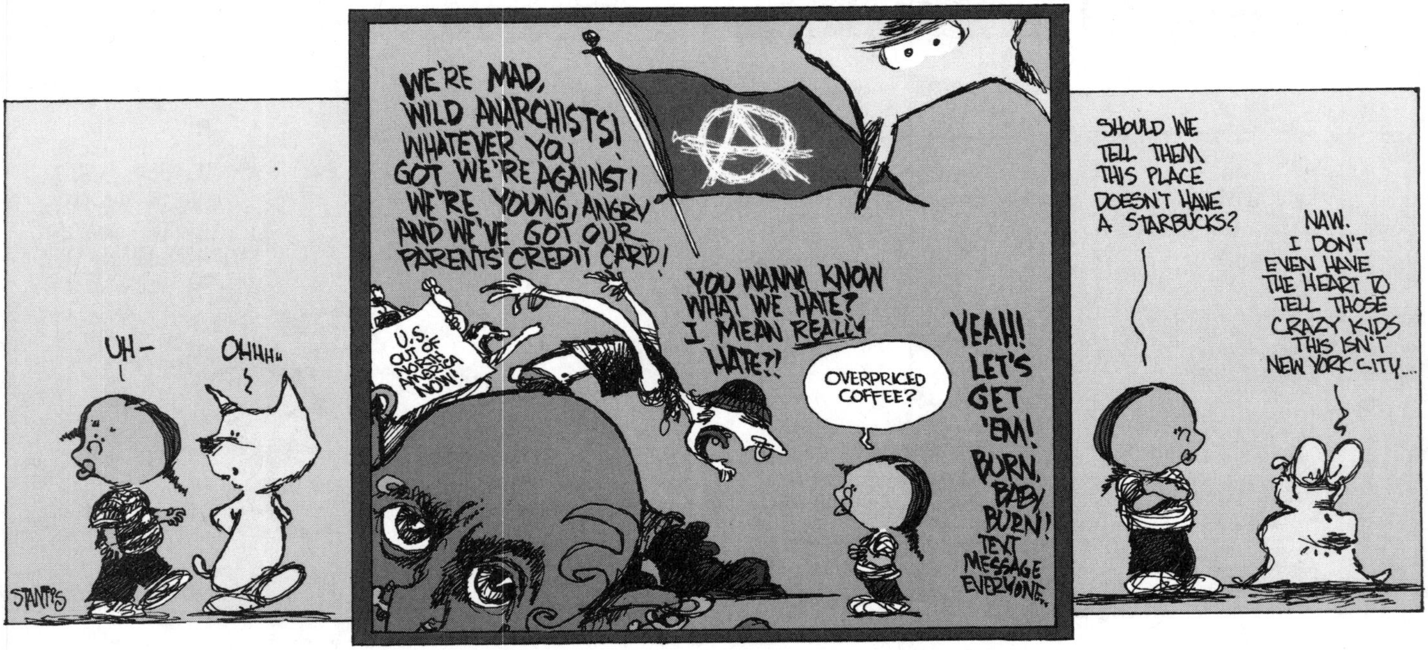

UH-
OHHH..
WE'RE MAD, WILD ANARCHISTS! WHATEVER YOU GOT WE'RE AGAINST! WE'RE YOUNG, ANGRY AND WE'VE GOT OUR PARENTS' CREDIT CARD!
U.S. OUT OF NORTH AMERICA NOW!
YOU WANNA KNOW WHAT WE HATE? I MEAN REALLY HATE?!
OVERPRICED COFFEE?
YEAH! LET'S GET 'EM! BURN, BABY, BURN! TEXT MESSAGE EVERYONE..
SHOULD WE TELL THEM THIS PLACE DOESN'T HAVE A STARBUCKS?
NAW. I DON'T EVEN HAVE THE HEART TO TELL THOSE CRAZY KIDS THIS ISN'T NEW YORK CITY...
STANTIS

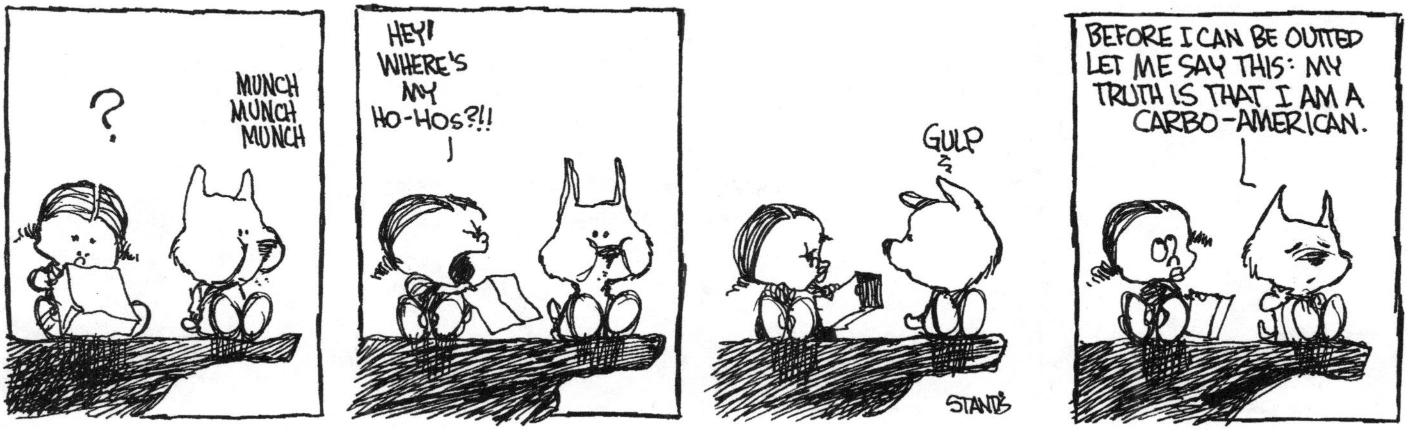
?
MUNCH MUNCH MUNCH
HEY! WHERE'S MY HO-HOS?!!
GULP
BEFORE I CAN BE OUTTED LET ME SAY THIS: MY TRUTH IS THAT I AM A CARBO-AMERICAN.
STANTIS

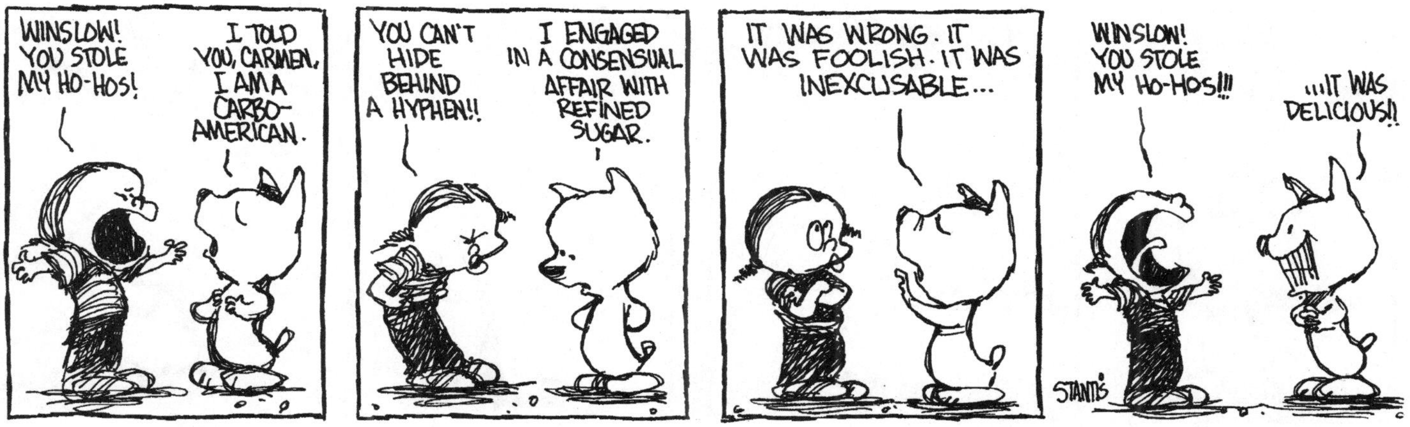
WINSLOW! YOU STOLE MY HO-HOS!
I TOLD YOU, CARMEN, I AM A CARBO-AMERICAN.
YOU CAN'T HIDE BEHIND A HYPHEN!!
I ENGAGED IN A CONSENSUAL AFFAIR WITH REFINED SUGAR.
IT WAS WRONG. IT WAS FOOLISH. IT WAS INEXCUSABLE...
WINSLOW! YOU STOLE MY HO-HOS!!!
...IT WAS DELICIOUS!!
STANTIS

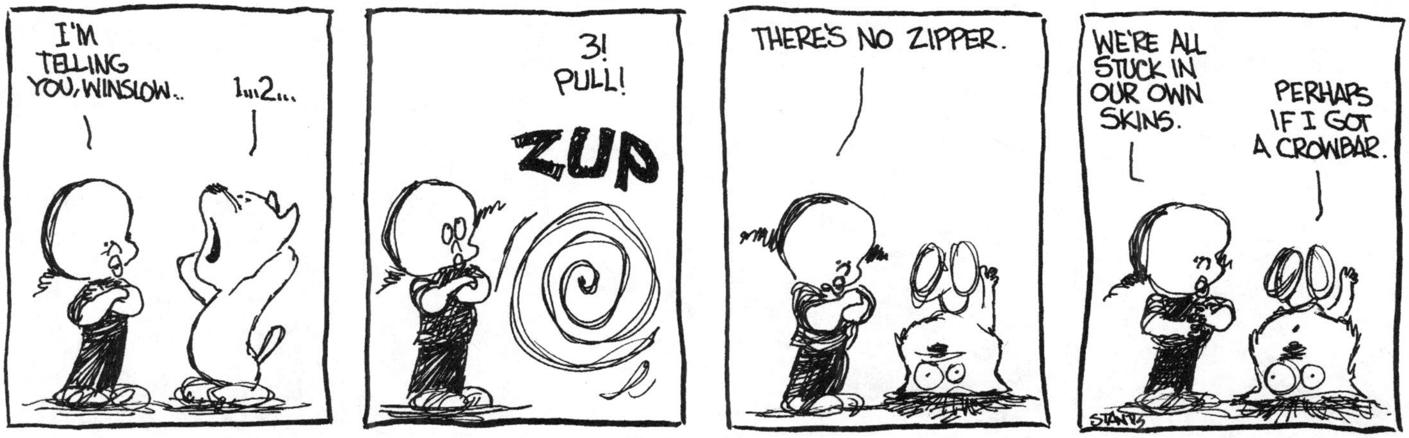
I'M TELLING YOU, WINSLOW..
1...2...
3! PULL!
ZUP
THERE'S NO ZIPPER.
WE'RE ALL STUCK IN OUR OWN SKINS.
PERHAPS IF I GOT A CROWBAR.
STANTIS

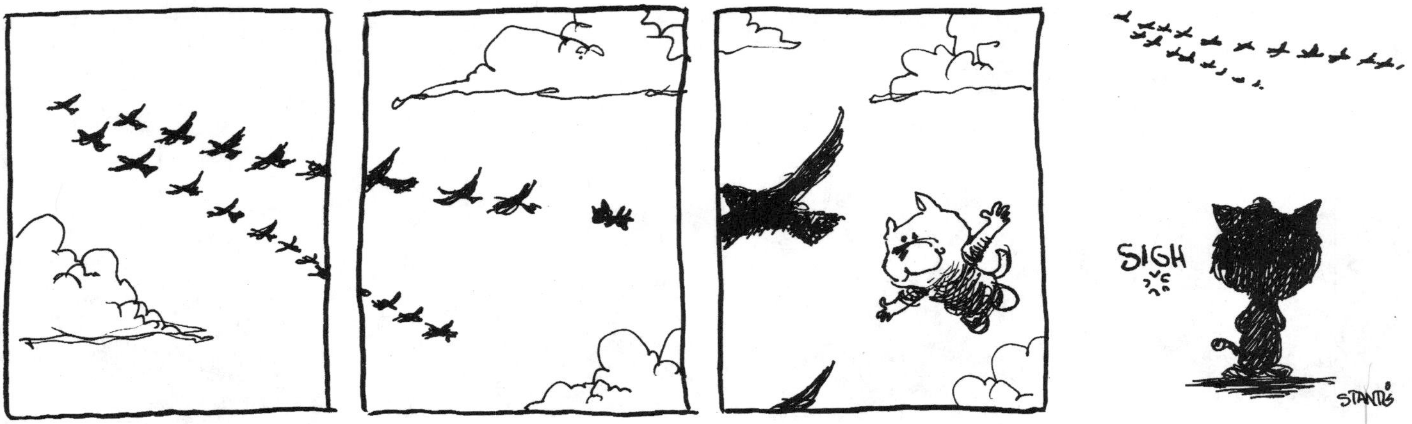
SIGH
STANTIS

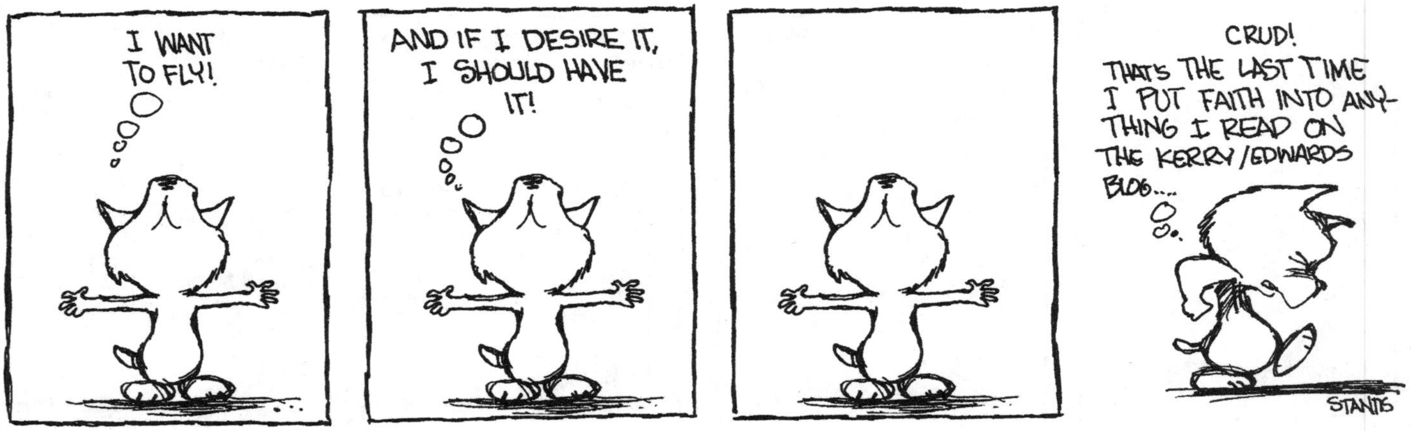
I WANT TO FLY!
AND IF I DESIRE IT, I SHOULD HAVE IT!
CRUD! THAT'S THE LAST TIME I PUT FAITH INTO ANY-THING I READ ON THE KERRY/EDWARDS BLOG....
STANTIS

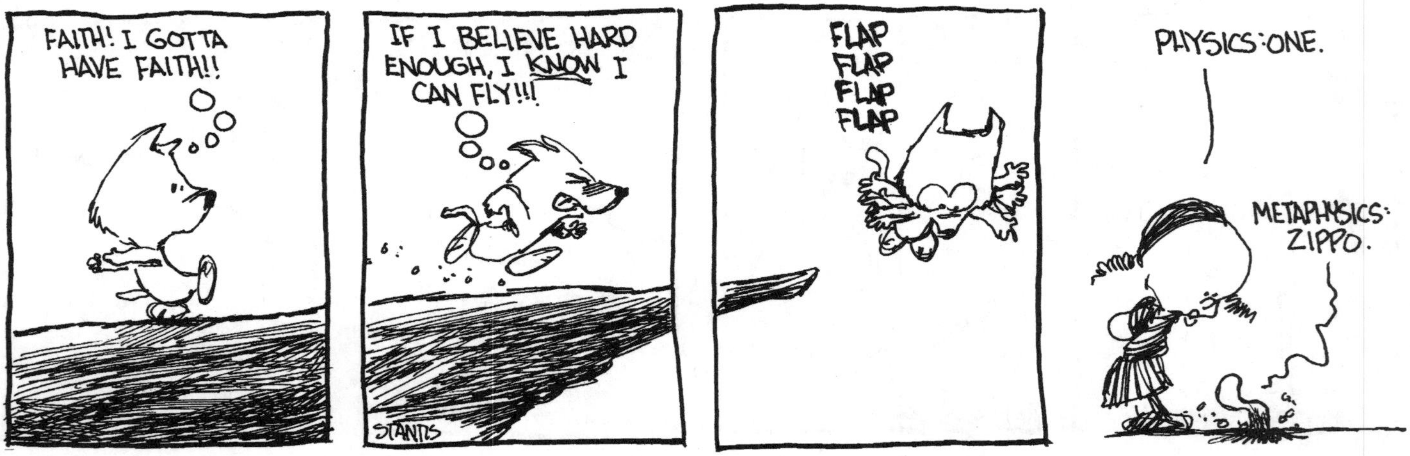
FAITH! I GOTTA HAVE FAITH!!
IF I BELIEVE HARD ENOUGH, I KNOW I CAN FLY!!!
STANTIS
FLAP
FLAP
FLAP
FLAP
PHYSICS: ONE.
METAPHYSICS: ZIPPO.

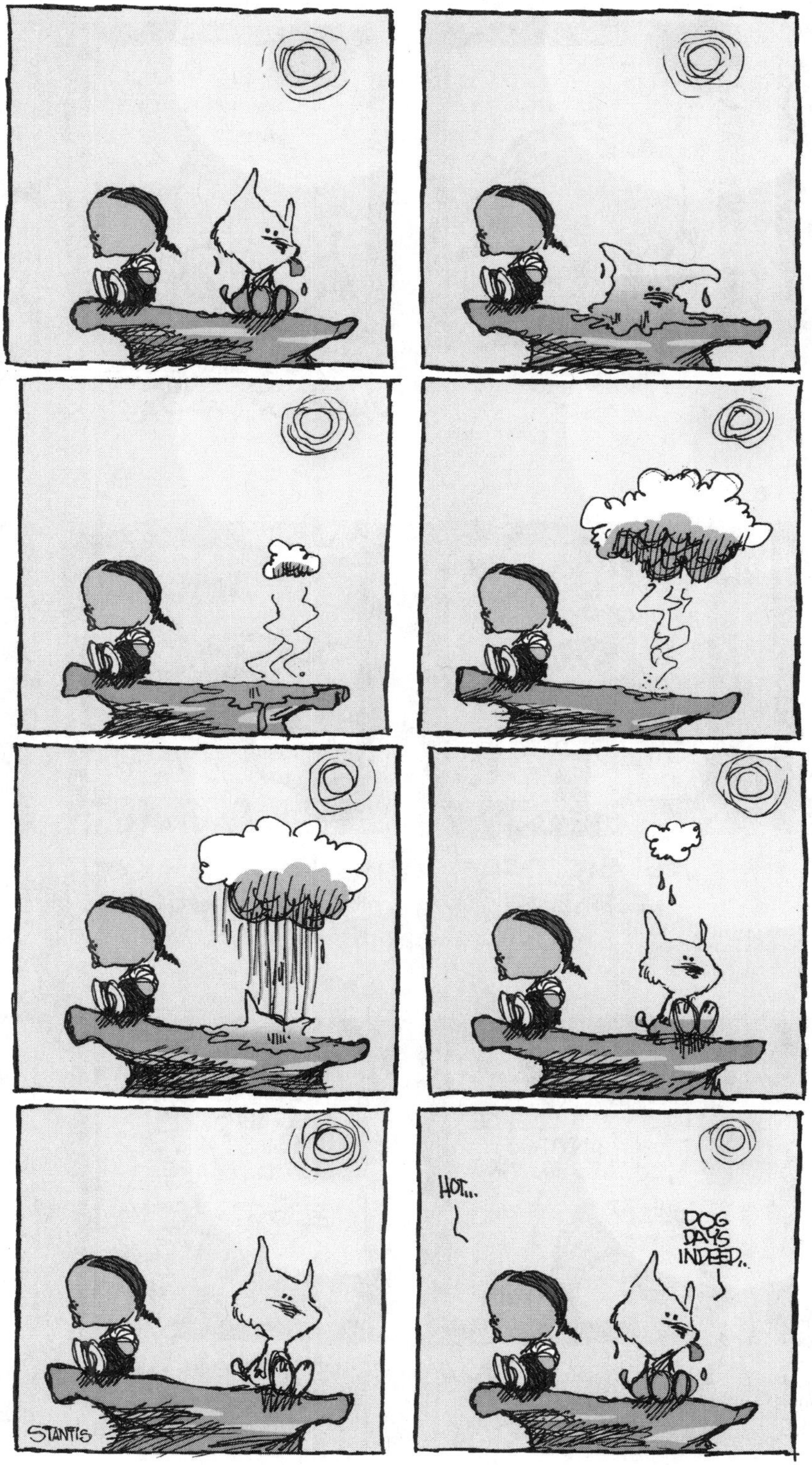
STANTIS
HOT...
DOG DAYS INDEED...

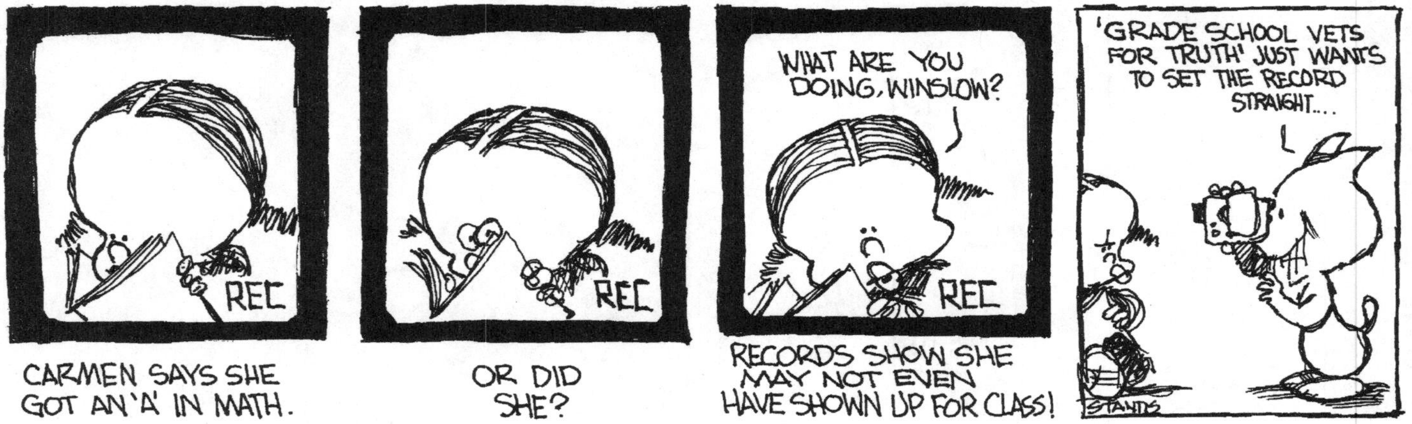
REC
CARMEN SAYS SHE GOT AN 'A' IN MATH.
REC
OR DID SHE?
WHAT ARE YOU DOING, WINSLOW?
REC
RECORDS SHOW SHE MAY NOT EVEN HAVE SHOWN UP FOR CLASS!
'GRADE SCHOOL VETS FOR TRUTH' JUST WANTS TO SET THE RECORD STRAIGHT...
STANTIS

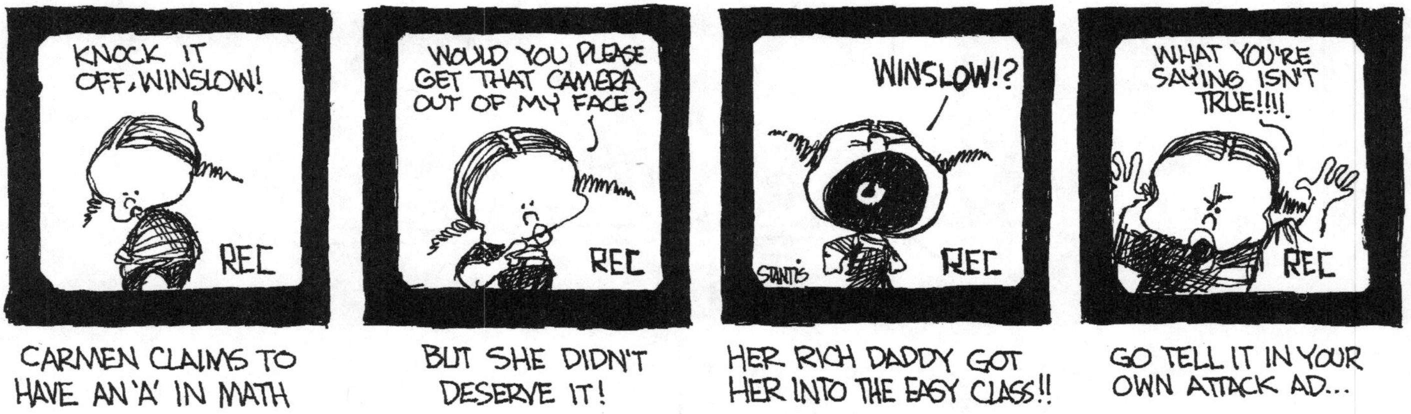
KNOCK IT OFF, WINSLOW!
REC
CARMEN CLAIMS TO HAVE AN 'A' IN MATH
WOULD YOU PLEASE GET THAT CAMERA OUT OF MY FACE?
REC
BUT SHE DIDN'T DESERVE IT!
WINSLOW!?
STANTIS
REC
HER RICH DADDY GOT HER INTO THE EASY CLASS!!
WHAT YOU'RE SAYING ISN'T TRUE!!!!
REC
GO TELL IT IN YOUR OWN ATTACK AD...

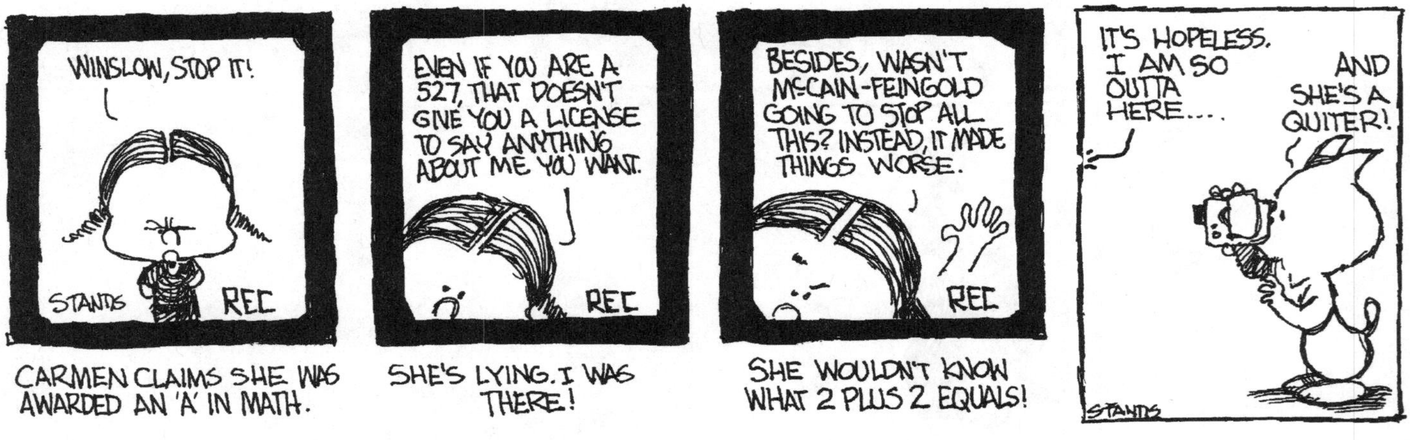
WINSLOW, STOP IT!
STANTIS
REC
CARMEN CLAIMS SHE WAS AWARDED AN 'A' IN MATH.
EVEN IF YOU ARE A 527, THAT DOESN'T GIVE YOU A LICENSE TO SAY ANYTHING ABOUT ME YOU WANT.
REC
SHE'S LYING. I WAS THERE!
BESIDES, WASN'T McCAIN-FEINGOLD GOING TO STOP ALL THIS? INSTEAD, IT MADE THINGS WORSE.
REC
SHE WOULDN'T KNOW WHAT 2 PLUS 2 EQUALS!
IT'S HOPELESS. I AM SO OUTTA HERE....
AND SHE'S A QUITER!
STANTIS

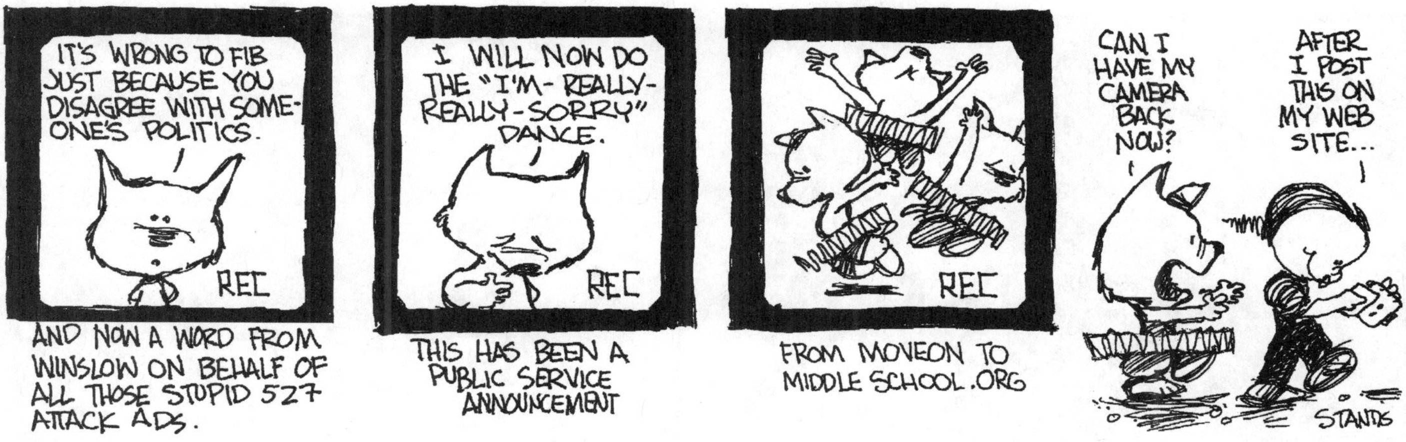
IT'S WRONG TO FIB JUST BECAUSE YOU DISAGREE WITH SOME-ONE'S POLITICS.
REC
AND NOW A WORD FROM WINSLOW ON BEHALF OF ALL THOSE STUPID 527 ATTACK ADS.
I WILL NOW DO THE "I'M-REALLY-REALLY-SORRY" DANCE.
REC
THIS HAS BEEN A PUBLIC SERVICE ANNOUNCEMENT
REC
FROM MOVEON TO MIDDLE SCHOOL.ORG
CAN I HAVE MY CAMERA BACK NOW?
AFTER I POST THIS ON MY WEB SITE...
STANTIS

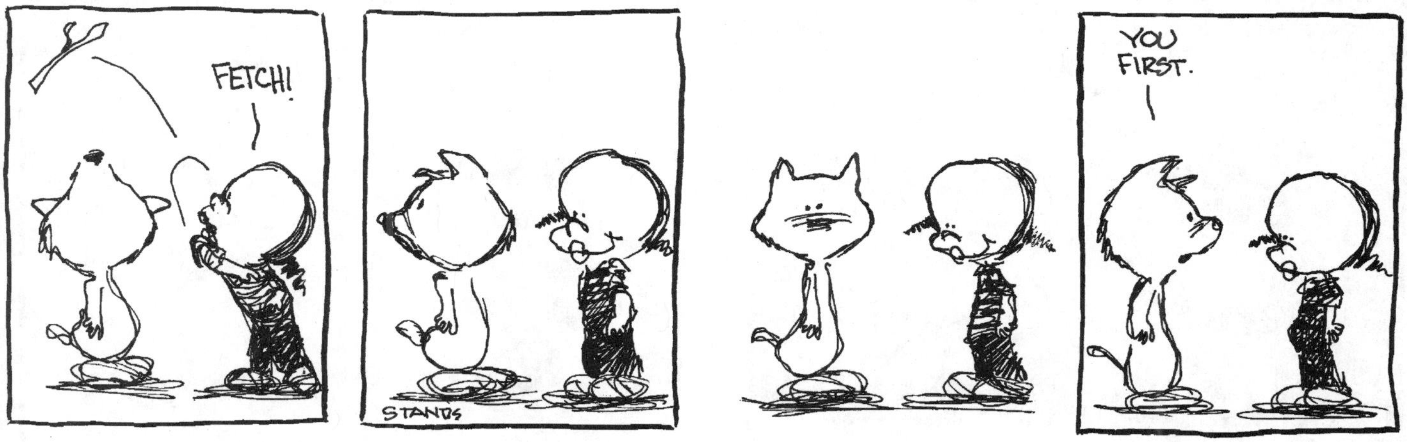
FETCH!
STANTIS
YOU FIRST.

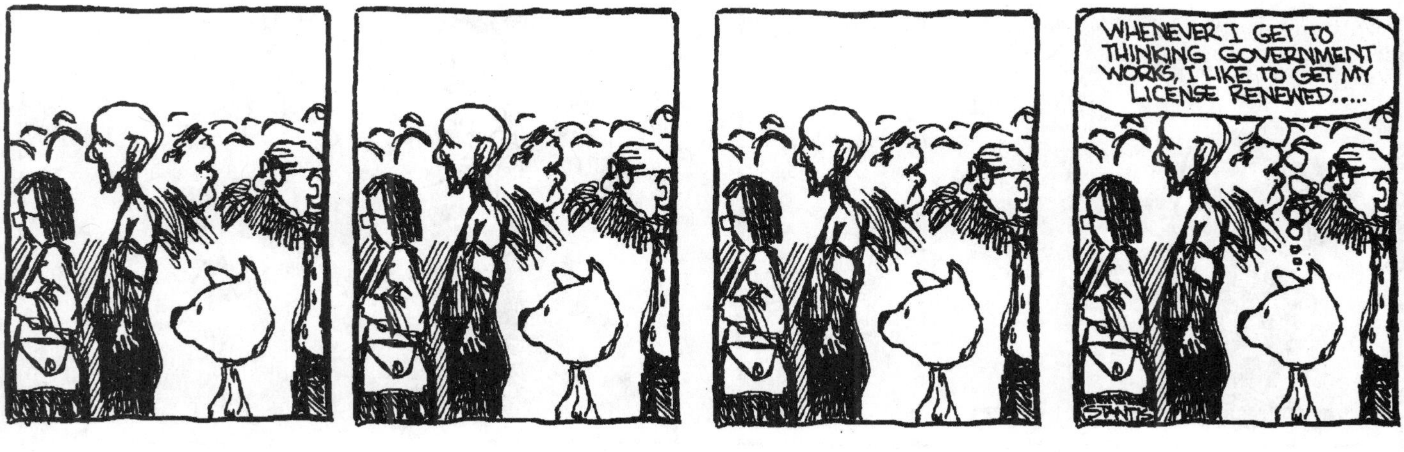
WHENEVER I GET TO THINKING GOVERNMENT WORKS, I LIKE TO GET MY LICENSE RENEWED.....
STANTIS

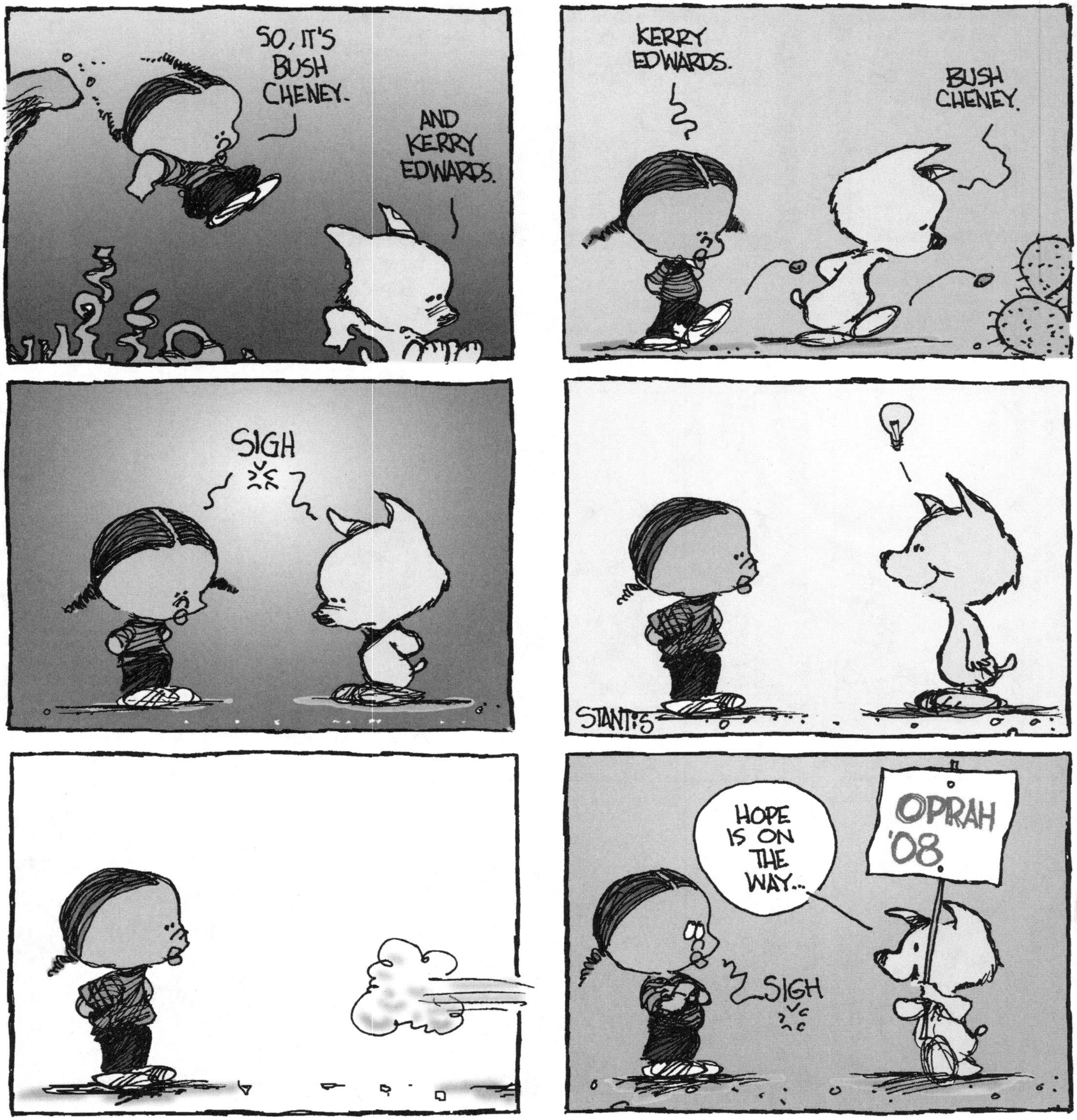

SO, IT'S BUSH CHENEY.
AND KERRY EDWARDS.
KERRY EDWARDS.
BUSH CHENEY.
SIGH
STANTIS
HOPE IS ON THE WAY...
OPRAH '08
SIGH

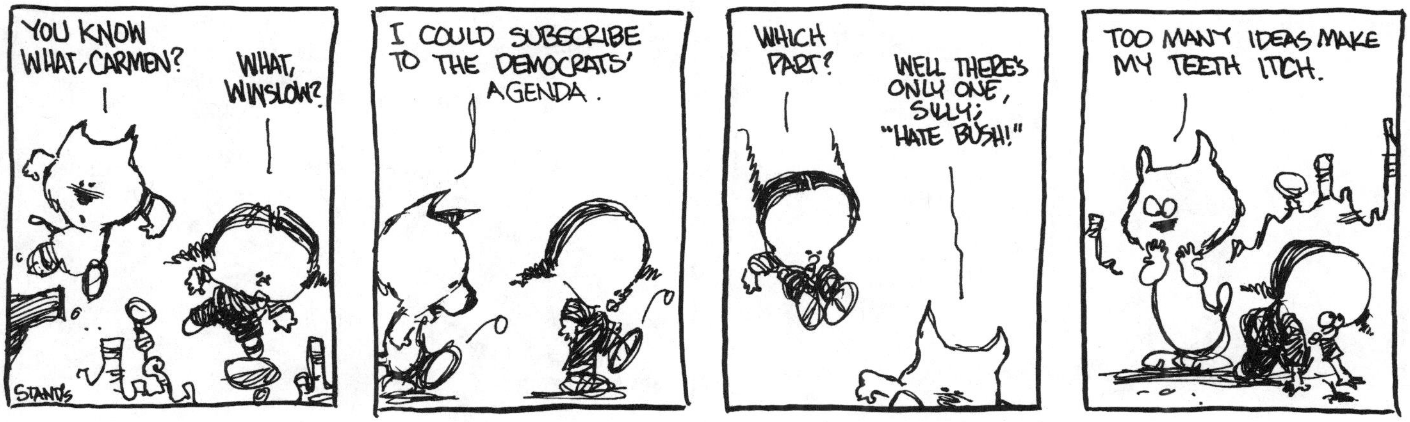
YOU KNOW WHAT, CARMEN?
WHAT, WINSLOW?
STANTIS
I COULD SUBSCRIBE TO THE DEMOCRATS' AGENDA.
WHICH PART?
WELL THERE'S ONLY ONE, SILLY; "HATE BUSH!"
TOO MANY IDEAS MAKE MY TEETH ITCH.

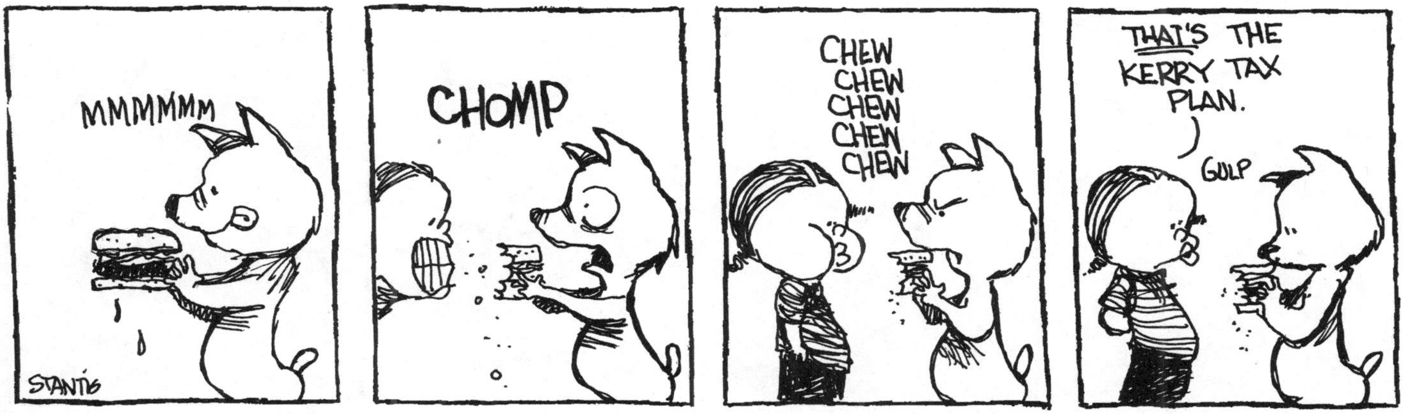
MMMMMM
STANTIS
CHOMP
CHEW CHEW CHEW CHEW CHEW
THAT'S THE KERRY TAX PLAN.
GULP

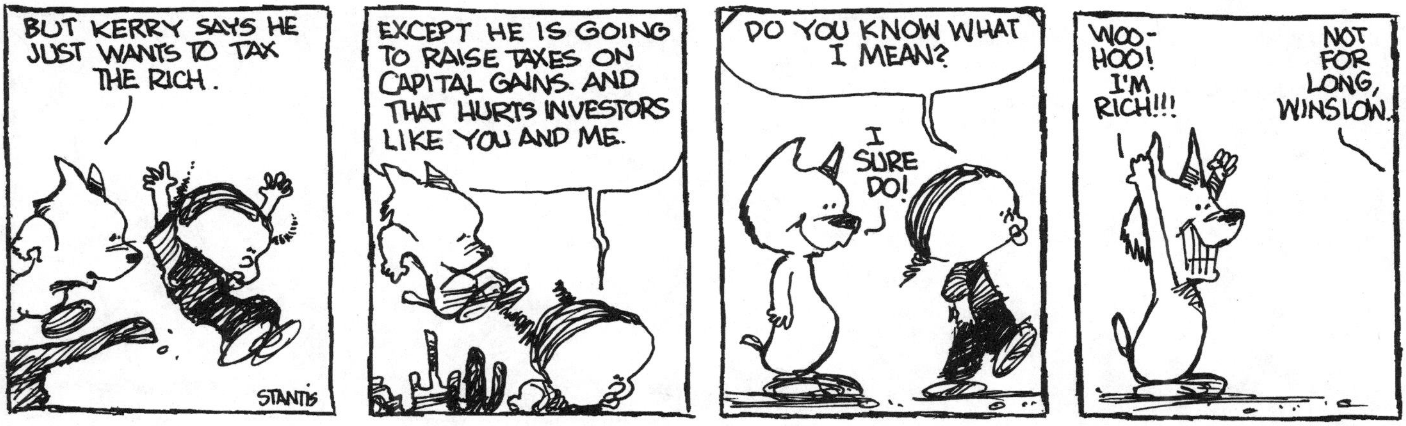
BUT KERRY SAYS HE JUST WANTS TO TAX THE RICH.
STANTIS
EXCEPT HE IS GOING TO RAISE TAXES ON CAPITAL GAINS. AND THAT HURTS INVESTORS LIKE YOU AND ME.
DO YOU KNOW WHAT I MEAN?
I SURE DO!
WOO-HOO! I'M RICH!!!
NOT FOR LONG, WINSLOW.

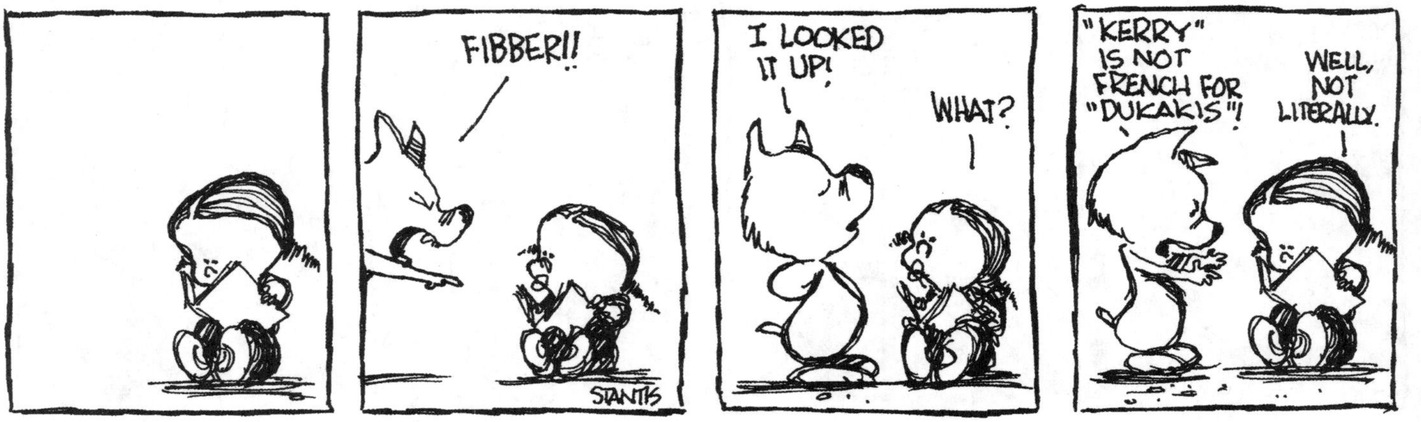
FIBBER!!
STANTIS
I LOOKED IT UP!
WHAT?
"KERRY" IS NOT FRENCH FOR "DUKAKIS"!
WELL, NOT LITERALLY.

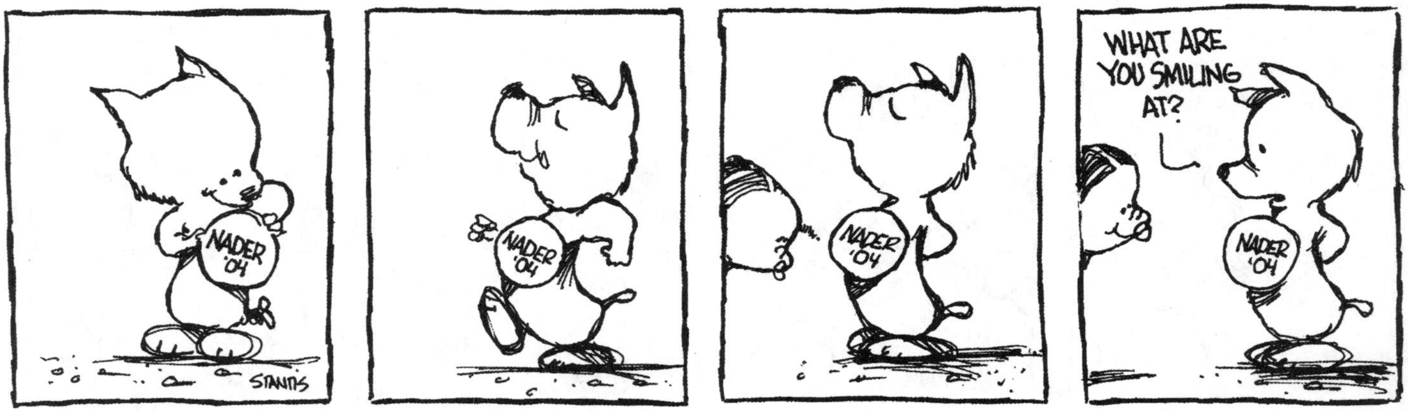
NADER '04
STANTIS
NADER '04
NADER '04
WHAT ARE YOU SMILING AT?
NADER '04

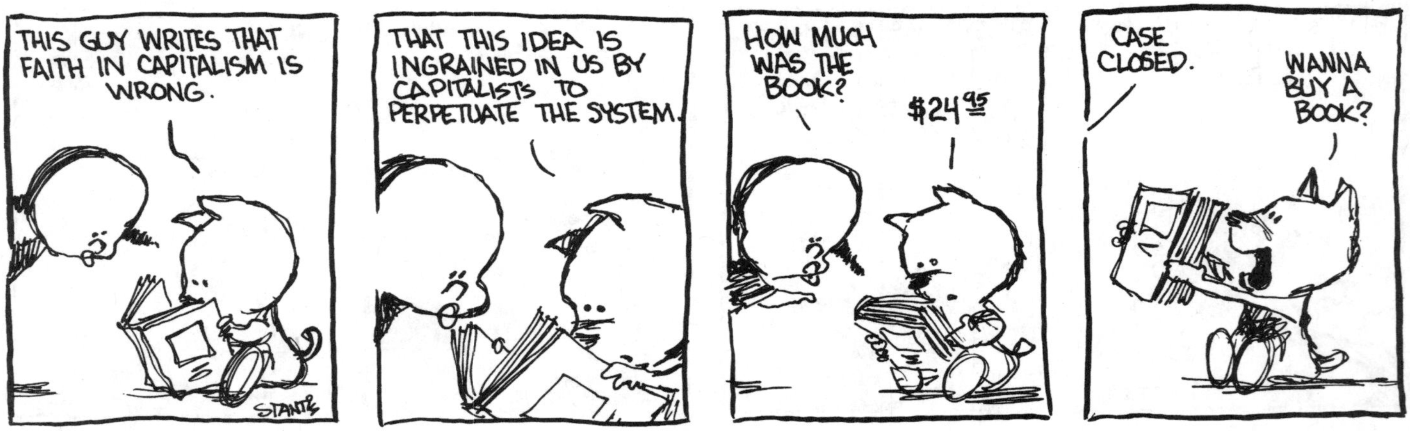
THIS GUY WRITES THAT FAITH IN CAPITALISM IS WRONG.
STANTIS
THAT THIS IDEA IS INGRAINED IN US BY CAPITALISTS TO PERPETUATE THE SYSTEM.
HOW MUCH WAS THE BOOK?
$24.95
CASE CLOSED.
WANNA BUY A BOOK?

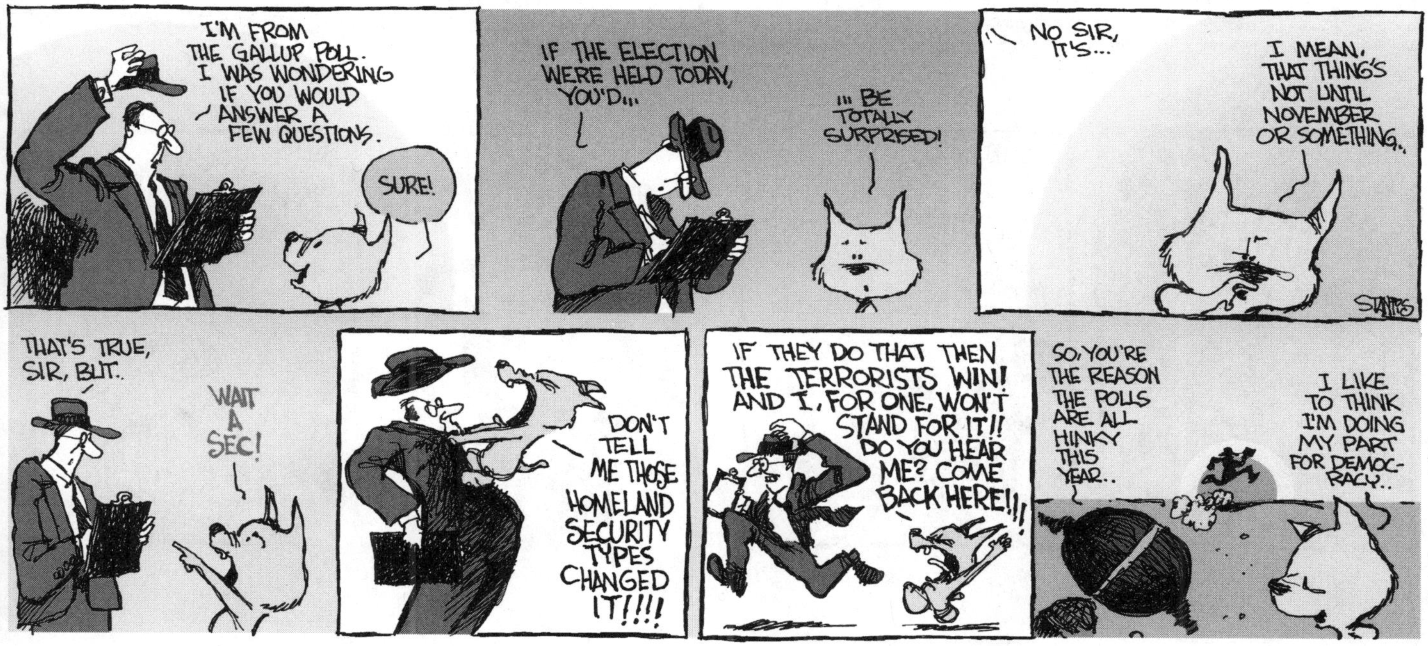
I'M FROM THE GALLUP POLL. I WAS WONDERING IF YOU WOULD ANSWER A FEW QUESTIONS.
SURE!
IF THE ELECTION WERE HELD TODAY, YOU'D...
... BE TOTALLY SURPRISED!
NO SIR, IT'S...
I MEAN, THAT THING'S NOT UNTIL NOVEMBER OR SOMETHING..
STANTIS
THAT'S TRUE, SIR, BUT..
WAIT A SEC!
DON'T TELL ME THOSE HOMELAND SECURITY TYPES CHANGED IT!!!!
IF THEY DO THAT THEN THE TERRORISTS WIN! AND I, FOR ONE, WON'T STAND FOR IT!! DO YOU HEAR ME? COME BACK HERE!!!
SO, YOU'RE THE REASON THE POLLS ARE ALL HINKY THIS YEAR..
I LIKE TO THINK I'M DOING MY PART FOR DEMOC-RACY..

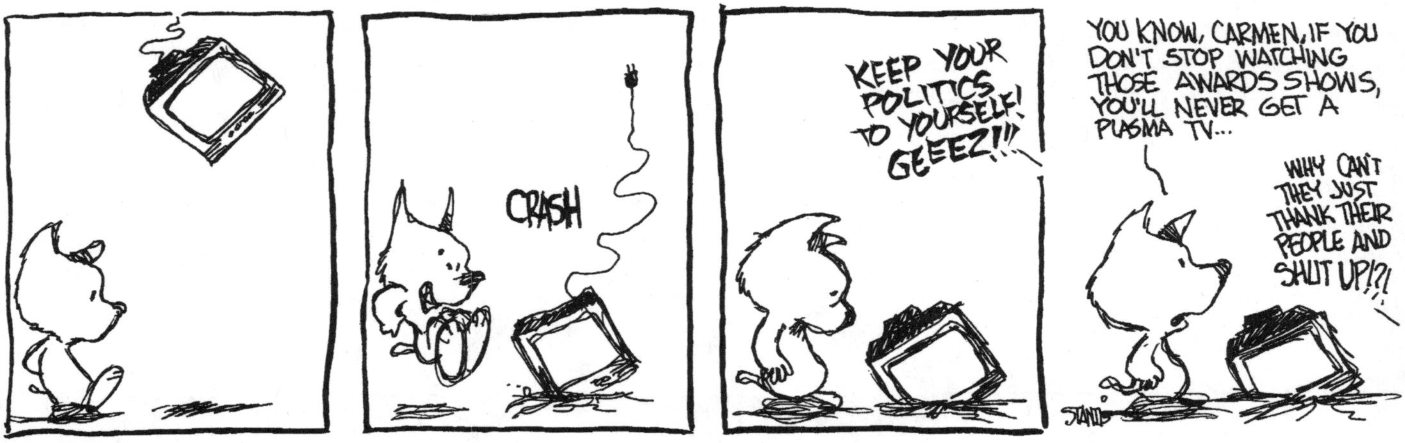
CRASH
KEEP YOUR POLITICS TO YOURSELF! GEEEZ!!!
YOU KNOW, CARMEN, IF YOU DON'T STOP WATCHING THOSE AWARDS SHOWS, YOU'LL NEVER GET A PLASMA TV...
WHY CAN'T THEY JUST THANK THEIR PEOPLE AND SHUT UP!?!
STANTIS

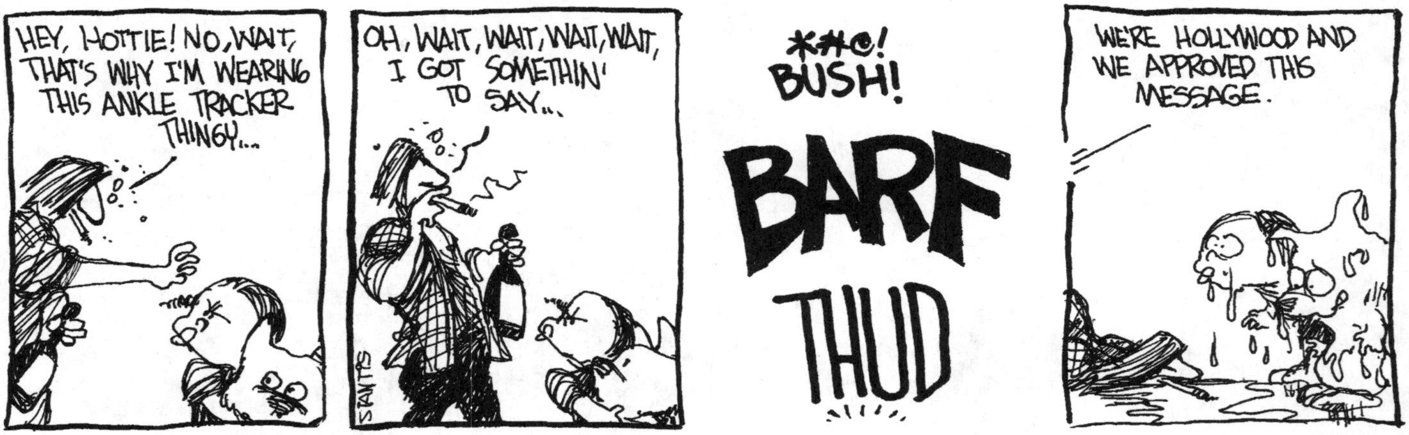
HEY, HOTTIE! NO, WAIT, THAT'S WHY I'M WEARING THIS ANKLE TRACKER THINGY...
OH, WAIT, WAIT, WAIT, WAIT, I GOT SOMETHIN' TO SAY...
STANTIS
*#@! BUSH!
BARF
THUD
WE'RE HOLLYWOOD AND WE APPROVED THIS MESSAGE.

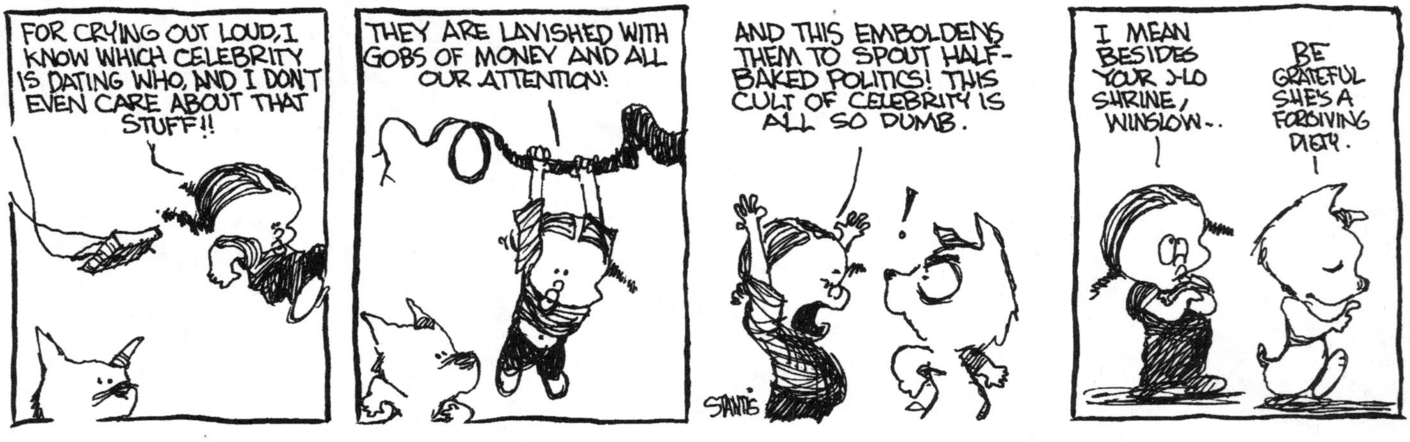
FOR CRYING OUT LOUD, I KNOW WHICH CELEBRITY IS DATING WHO, AND I DON'T EVEN CARE ABOUT THAT STUFF!!
THEY ARE LAVISHED WITH GOBS OF MONEY AND ALL OUR ATTENTION!
AND THIS EMBOLDENS THEM TO SPOUT HALF-BAKED POLITICS! THIS CULT OF CELEBRITY IS ALL SO DUMB.
!
STANTIS
I MEAN BESIDES YOUR J-LO SHRINE, WINSLOW...
BE GRATEFUL SHE'S A FORGIVING DIETY.

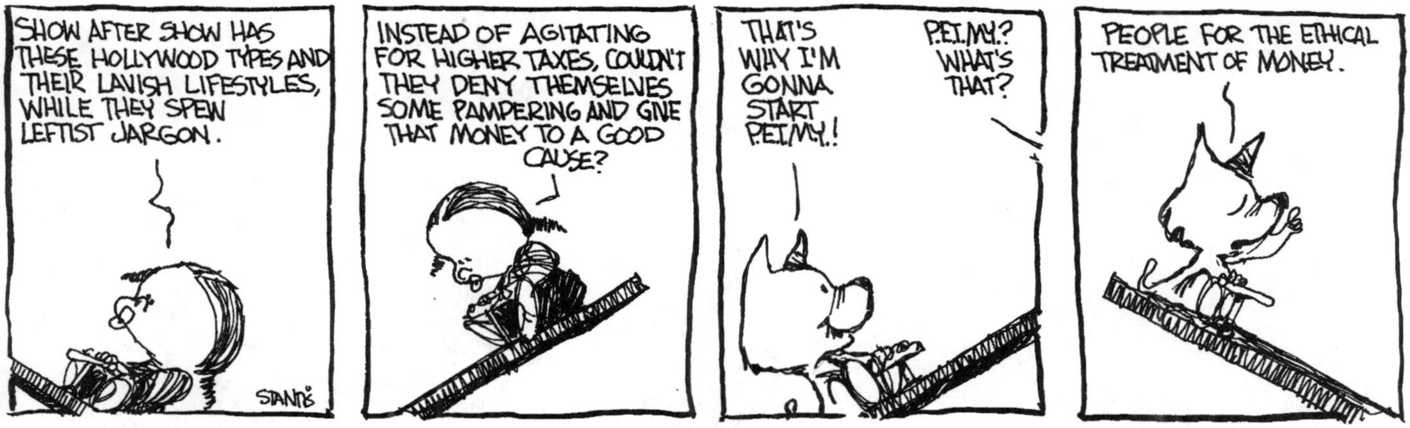
SHOW AFTER SHOW HAS THESE HOLLYWOOD TYPES AND THEIR LAVISH LIFESTYLES, WHILE THEY SPEW LEFTIST JARGON.
INSTEAD OF AGITATING FOR HIGHER TAXES, COULDN'T THEY DENY THEMSELVES SOME PAMPERING AND GIVE THAT MONEY TO A GOOD CAUSE?
THAT'S WHY I'M GONNA START P.E.T.M.Y.!
P.E.T.M.Y.? WHAT'S THAT?
PEOPLE FOR THE ETHICAL TREATMENT OF MONEY.
STANTIS

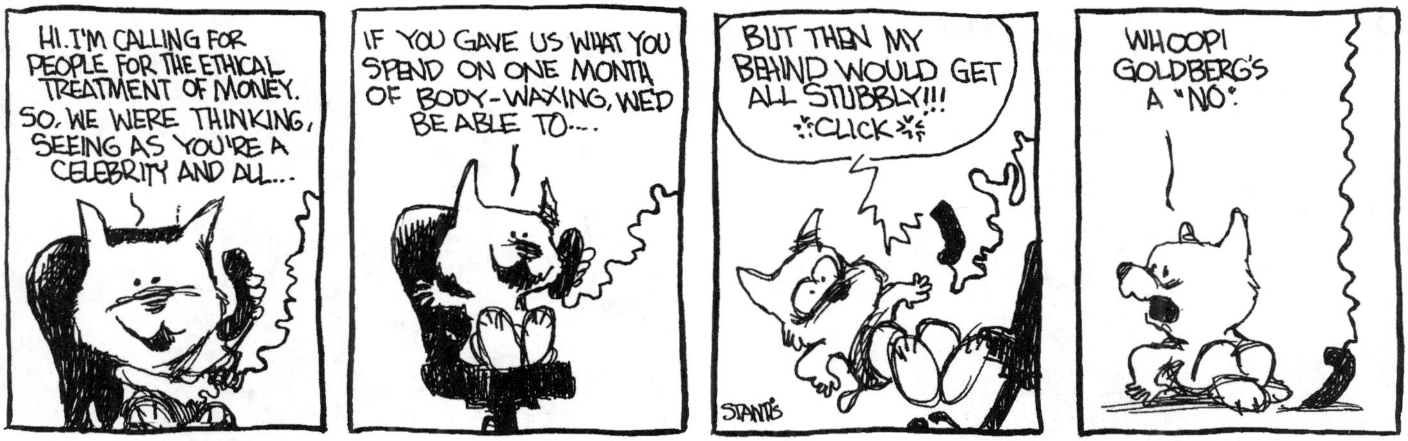
HI. I'M CALLING FOR PEOPLE FOR THE ETHICAL TREATMENT OF MONEY. SO, WE WERE THINKING, SEEING AS YOU'RE A CELEBRITY AND ALL...
IF YOU GAVE US WHAT YOU SPEND ON ONE MONTH OF BODY-WAXING, WE'D BE ABLE TO...
BUT THEN MY BEHIND WOULD GET ALL STUBBLY!!!
CLICK
WHOOPI GOLDBERG'S A "NO."
STANTIS

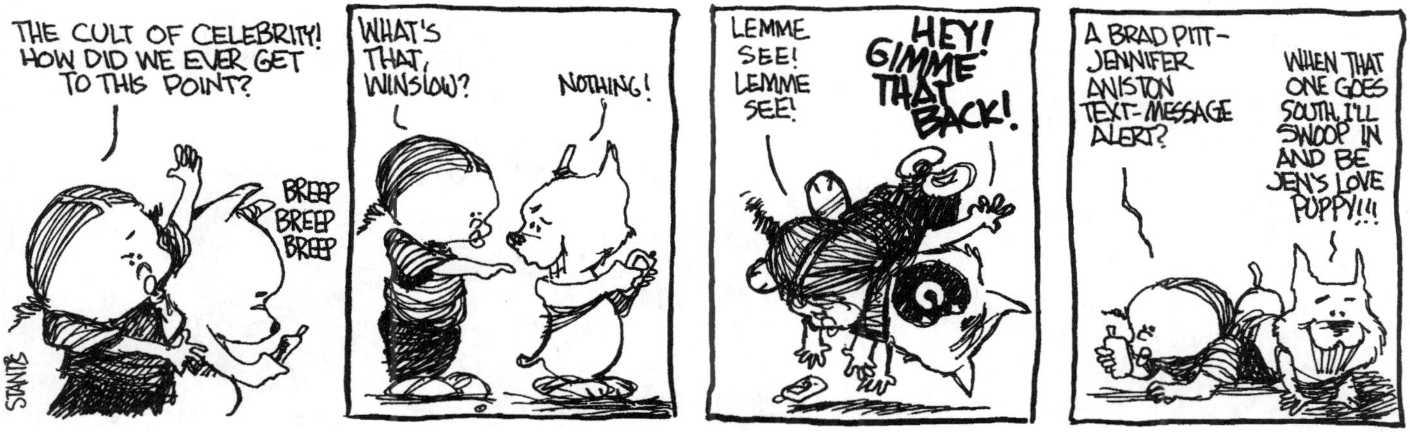
THE CULT OF CELEBRITY! HOW DID WE EVER GET TO THIS POINT?
BREEP BREEP BREEP
WHAT'S THAT, WINSLOW?
NOTHING!
LEMME SEE! LEMME SEE!
HEY! GIMME THAT BACK!
A BRAD PITT-JENNIFER ANISTON TEXT-MESSAGE ALERT?
WHEN THAT ONE GOES SOUTH, I'LL SWOOP IN AND BE JEN'S LOVE PUPPY!!!
STANTIS

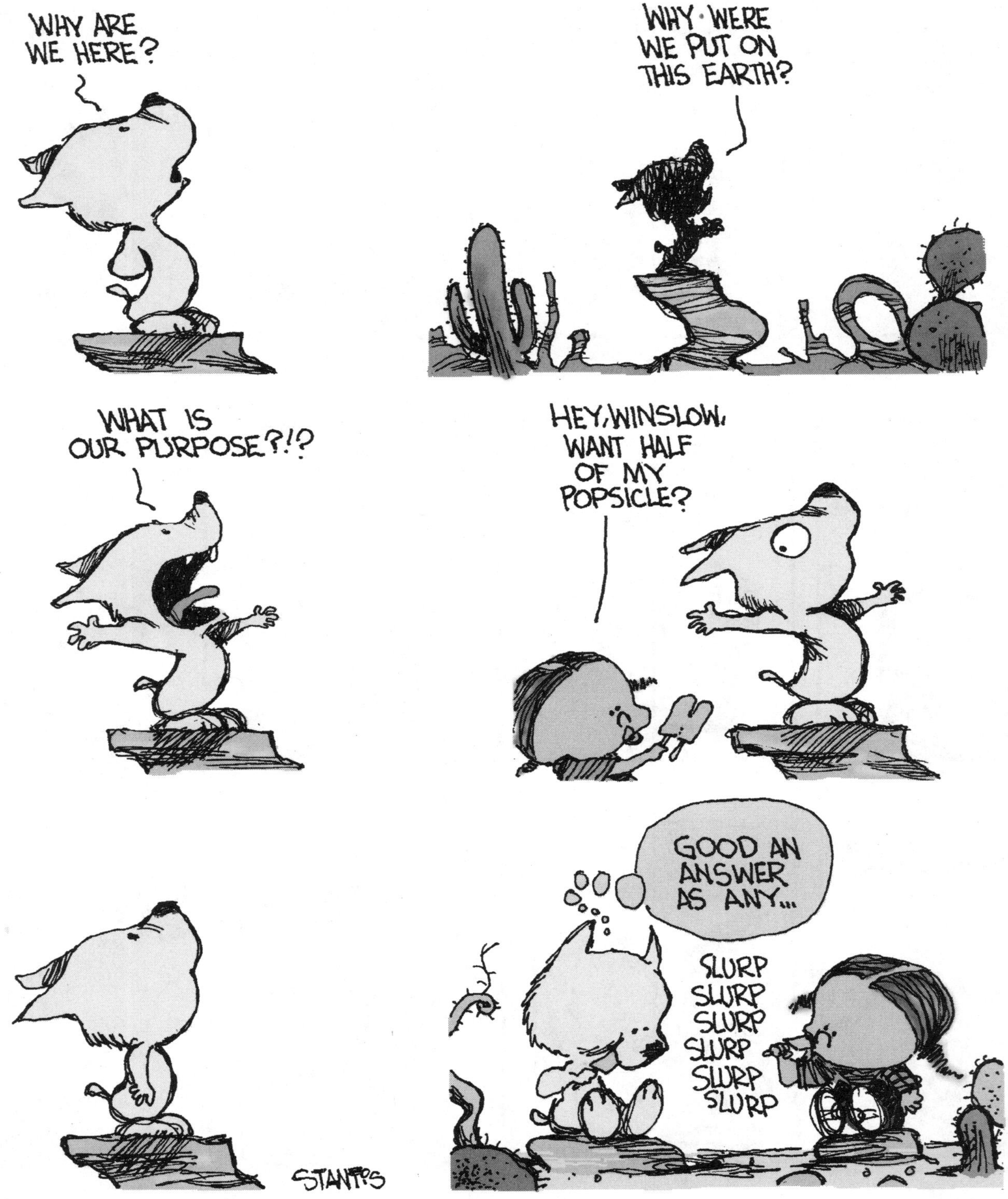
WHY ARE WE HERE?
WHY WERE WE PUT ON THIS EARTH?
WHAT IS OUR PURPOSE?!?
HEY, WINSLOW, WANT HALF OF MY POPSICLE?
GOOD AN ANSWER AS ANY...
SLURP SLURP SLURP SLURP SLURP SLURP
STANTIS

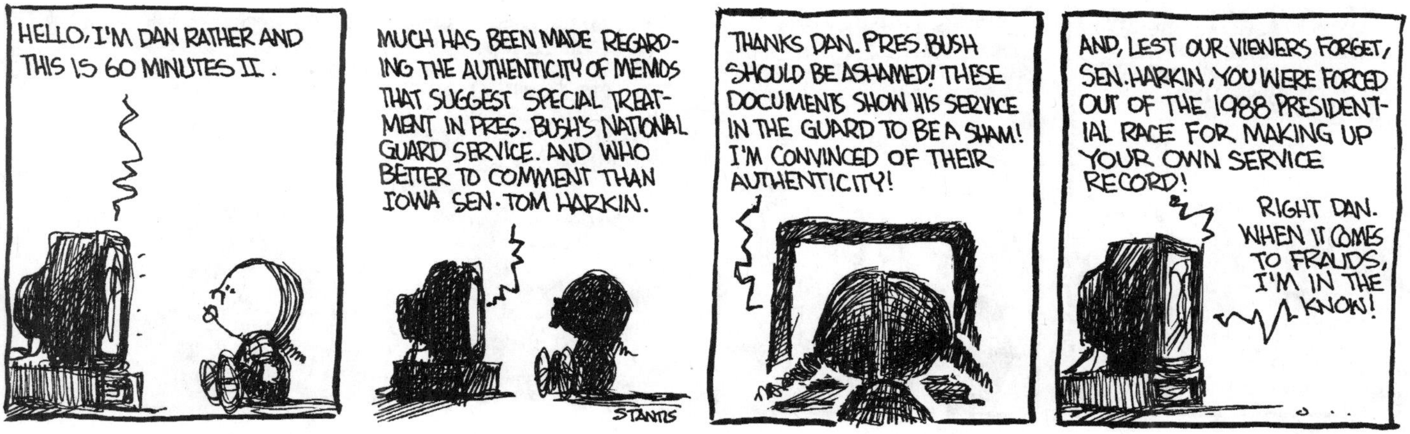
HELLO, I'M DAN RATHER AND THIS IS 60 MINUTES II.
MUCH HAS BEEN MADE REGARDING THE AUTHENTICITY OF MEMOS THAT SUGGEST SPECIAL TREATMENT IN PRES. BUSH'S NATIONAL GUARD SERVICE. AND WHO BETTER TO COMMENT THAN IOWA SEN. TOM HARKIN.
STANTIS
THANKS DAN. PRES. BUSH SHOULD BE ASHAMED! THESE DOCUMENTS SHOW HIS SERVICE IN THE GUARD TO BE A SHAM! I'M CONVINCED OF THEIR AUTHENTICITY!
AND, LEST OUR VIEWERS FORGET, SEN. HARKIN, YOU WERE FORCED OUT OF THE 1988 PRESIDENTIAL RACE FOR MAKING UP YOUR OWN SERVICE RECORD!
RIGHT DAN. WHEN IT COMES TO FRAUDS, I'M IN THE KNOW!

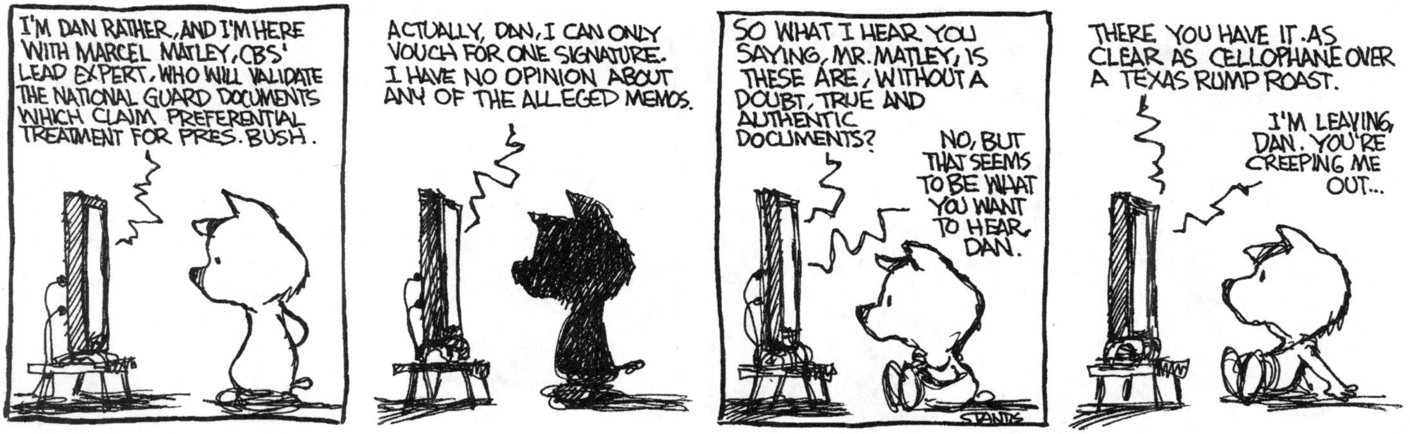
I'M DAN RATHER, AND I'M HERE WITH MARCEL MATLEY, CBS' LEAD EXPERT, WHO WILL VALIDATE THE NATIONAL GUARD DOCUMENTS WHICH CLAIM PREFERENTIAL TREATMENT FOR PRES. BUSH.
ACTUALLY, DAN, I CAN ONLY VOUCH FOR ONE SIGNATURE. I HAVE NO OPINION ABOUT ANY OF THE ALLEGED MEMOS.
SO WHAT I HEAR YOU SAYING, MR. MATLEY, IS THESE ARE, WITHOUT A DOUBT, TRUE AND AUTHENTIC DOCUMENTS?
NO, BUT THAT SEEMS TO BE WHAT YOU WANT TO HEAR, DAN.
STANTIS
THERE YOU HAVE IT. AS CLEAR AS CELLOPHANE OVER A TEXAS RUMP ROAST.
I'M LEAVING, DAN. YOU'RE CREEPING ME OUT...

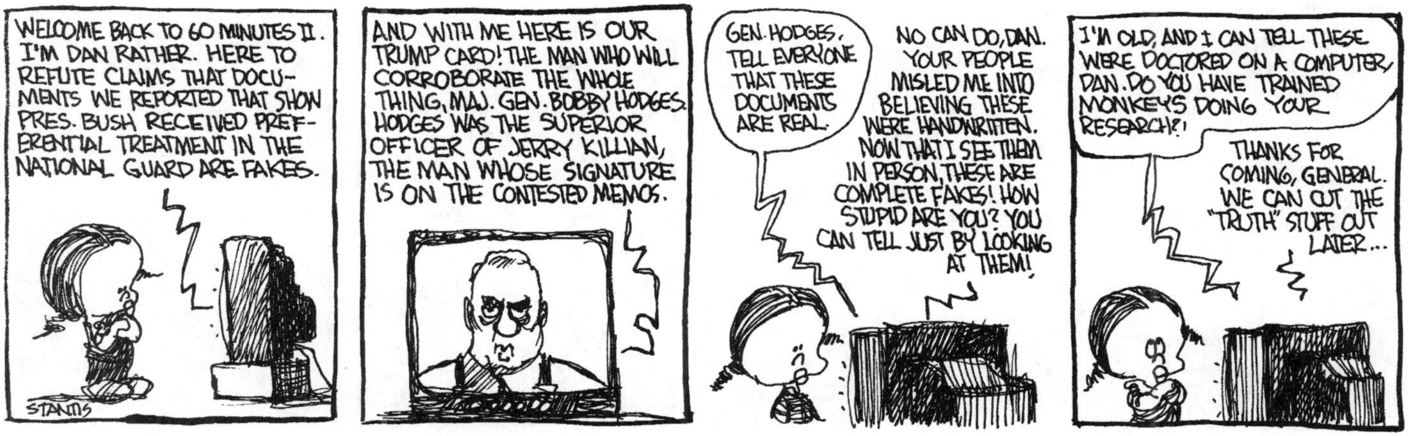
WELCOME BACK TO 60 MINUTES II. I'M DAN RATHER. HERE TO REFUTE CLAIMS THAT DOCUMENTS WE REPORTED THAT SHOW PRES. BUSH RECEIVED PREFERENTIAL TREATMENT IN THE NATIONAL GUARD ARE FAKES.
STANTIS
AND WITH ME HERE IS OUR TRUMP CARD! THE MAN WHO WILL CORROBORATE THE WHOLE THING, MAJ. GEN. BOBBY HODGES. HODGES WAS THE SUPERIOR OFFICER OF JERRY KILLIAN, THE MAN WHOSE SIGNATURE IS ON THE CONTESTED MEMOS.
GEN. HODGES, TELL EVERYONE THAT THESE DOCUMENTS ARE REAL.
NO CAN DO, DAN. YOUR PEOPLE MISLED ME INTO BELIEVING THESE WERE HANDWRITTEN. NOW THAT I SEE THEM IN PERSON, THESE ARE COMPLETE FAKES! HOW STUPID ARE YOU? YOU CAN TELL JUST BY LOOKING AT THEM!
I'M OLD, AND I CAN TELL THESE WERE DOCTORED ON A COMPUTER, DAN. DO YOU HAVE TRAINED MONKEYS DOING YOUR RESEARCH?!
THANKS FOR COMING, GENERAL. WE CAN CUT THE "TRUTH" STUFF OUT LATER...

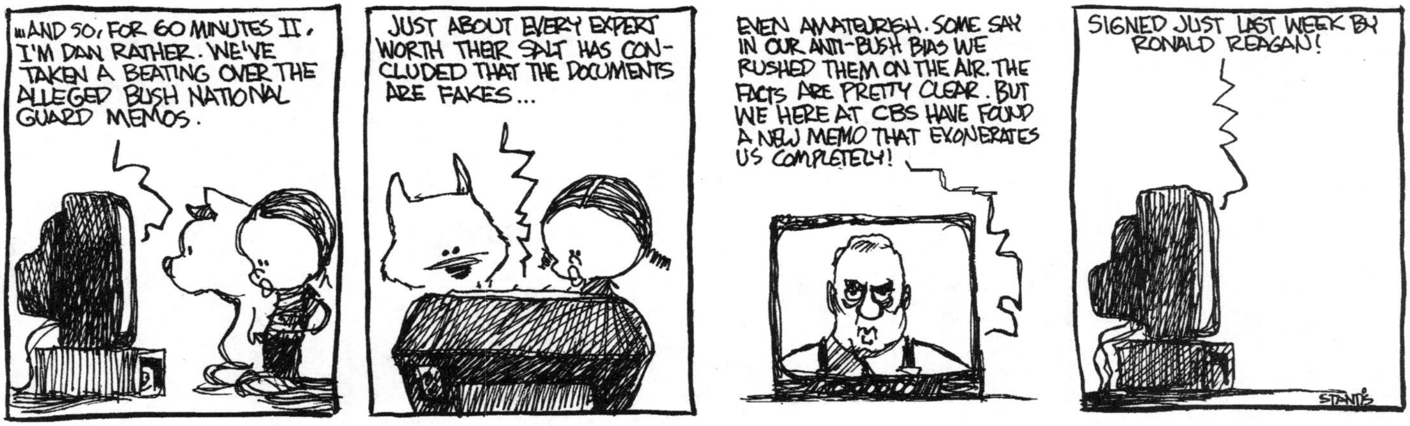
...AND SO, FOR 60 MINUTES II, I'M DAN RATHER. WE'VE TAKEN A BEATING OVER THE ALLEGED BUSH NATIONAL GUARD MEMOS.
JUST ABOUT EVERY EXPERT WORTH THEIR SALT HAS CONCLUDED THAT THE DOCUMENTS ARE FAKES...
EVEN AMATEURISH. SOME SAY IN OUR ANTI-BUSH BIAS WE RUSHED THEM ON THE AIR. THE FACTS ARE PRETTY CLEAR. BUT WE HERE AT CBS HAVE FOUND A NEW MEMO THAT EXONERATES US COMPLETELY!
SIGNED JUST LAST WEEK BY RONALD REAGAN!
STANTIS

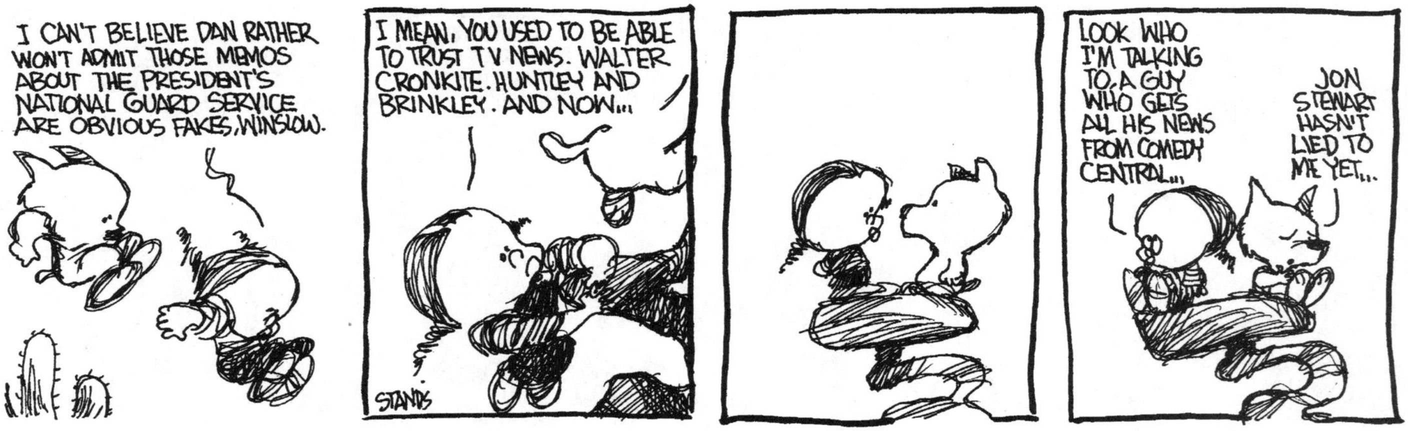
I CAN'T BELIEVE DAN RATHER WON'T ADMIT THOSE MEMOS ABOUT THE PRESIDENT'S NATIONAL GUARD SERVICE ARE OBVIOUS FAKES, WINSLOW.
I MEAN, YOU USED TO BE ABLE TO TRUST TV NEWS. WALTER CRONKITE. HUNTLEY AND BRINKLEY. AND NOW...
STANTIS
LOOK WHO I'M TALKING TO, A GUY WHO GETS ALL HIS NEWS FROM COMEDY CENTRAL...
JON STEWART HASN'T LIED TO ME YET...

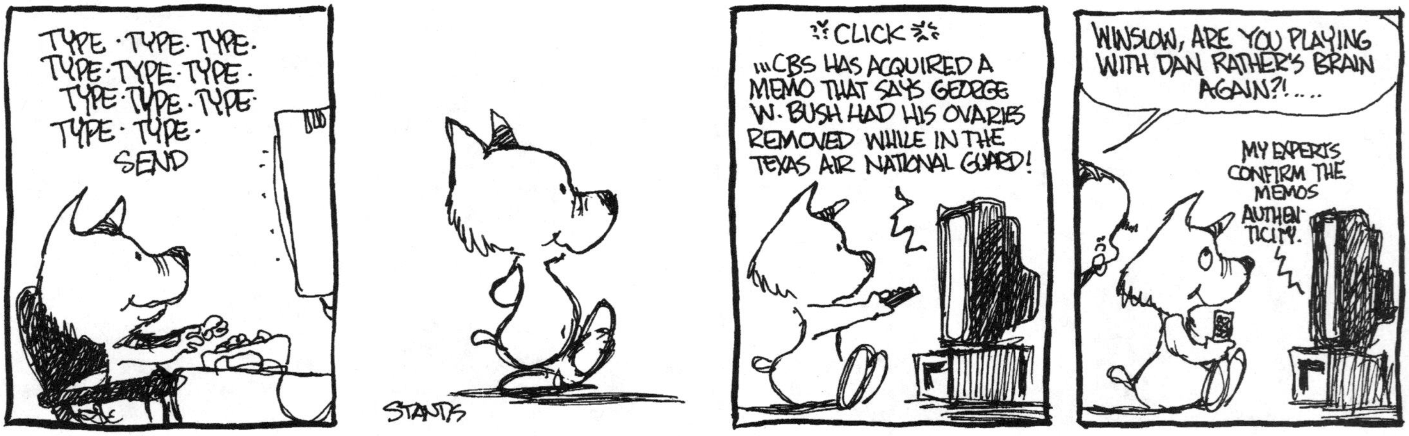
TYPE · TYPE · TYPE · TYPE · TYPE · TYPE · TYPE · TYPE · TYPE · TYPE · TYPE ·
SEND
STANTIS
CLICK
...CBS HAS ACQUIRED A MEMO THAT SAYS GEORGE W. BUSH HAD HIS OVARIES REMOVED WHILE IN THE TEXAS AIR NATIONAL GUARD!
WINSLOW, ARE YOU PLAYING WITH DAN RATHER'S BRAIN AGAIN?!....
MY EXPERTS CONFIRM THE MEMOS AUTHENTICITY.

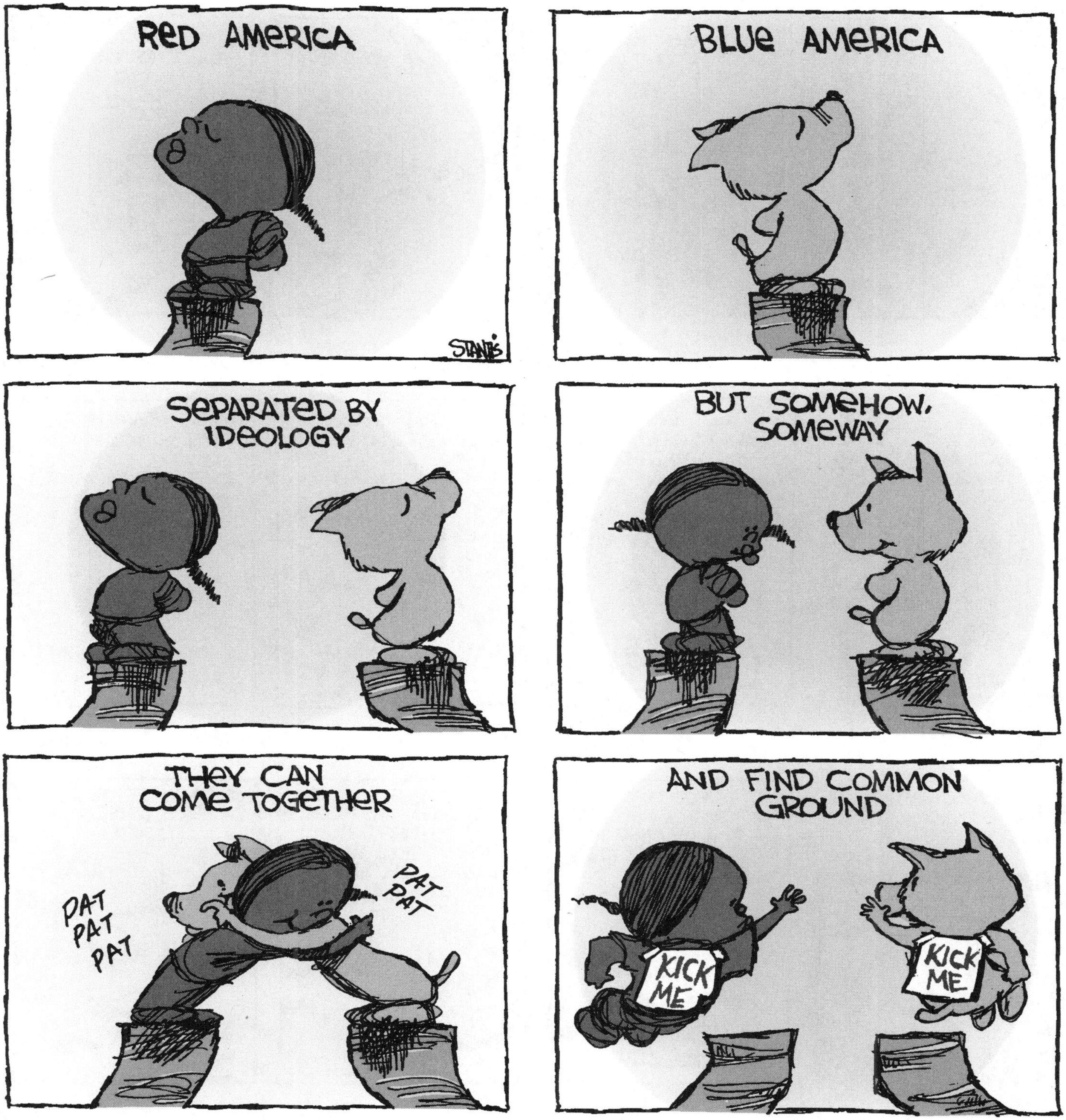

RED AMERICA
BLUE AMERICA
SEPARATED BY IDEOLOGY
BUT SOMEHOW, SOMEWAY
THEY CAN COME TOGETHER
PAT PAT PAT
PAT PAT
AND FIND COMMON GROUND
KICK ME
KICK ME

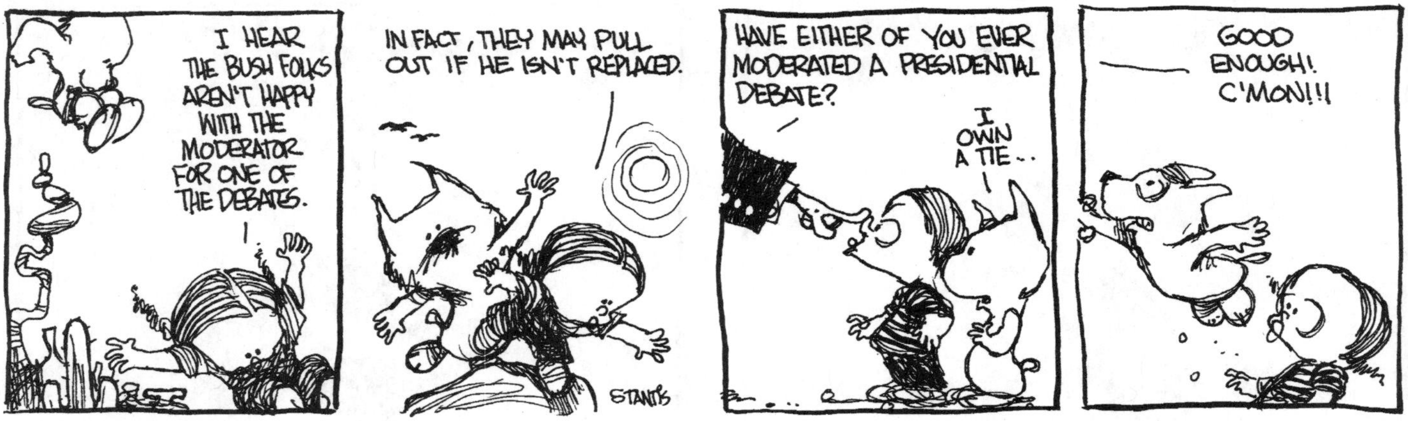
I HEAR THE BUSH FOLKS AREN'T HAPPY WITH THE MODERATOR FOR ONE OF THE DEBATES.
IN FACT, THEY MAY PULL OUT IF HE ISN'T REPLACED.
STANTIS
HAVE EITHER OF YOU EVER MODERATED A PRESIDENTIAL DEBATE?
I OWN A TIE...
GOOD ENOUGH! C'MON!!!

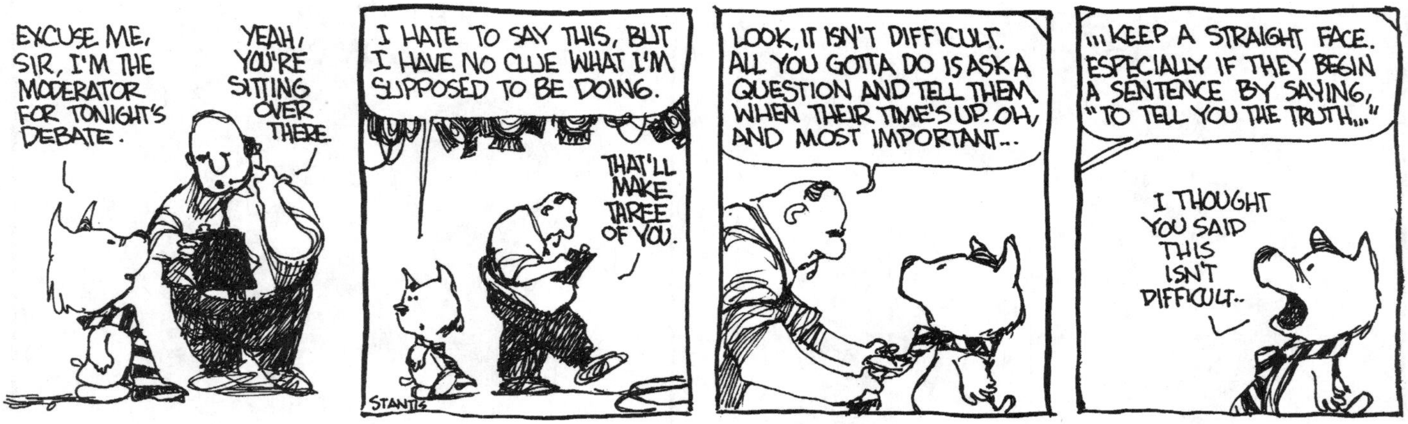
EXCUSE ME, SIR, I'M THE MODERATOR FOR TONIGHT'S DEBATE.
YEAH, YOU'RE SITTING OVER THERE.
I HATE TO SAY THIS, BUT I HAVE NO CLUE WHAT I'M SUPPOSED TO BE DOING.
THAT'LL MAKE THREE OF YOU.
STANTIS
LOOK, IT ISN'T DIFFICULT. ALL YOU GOTTA DO IS ASK A QUESTION AND TELL THEM WHEN THEIR TIME'S UP. OH, AND MOST IMPORTANT...
...KEEP A STRAIGHT FACE. ESPECIALLY IF THEY BEGIN A SENTENCE BY SAYING, "TO TELL YOU THE TRUTH..."
I THOUGHT YOU SAID THIS ISN'T DIFFICULT..

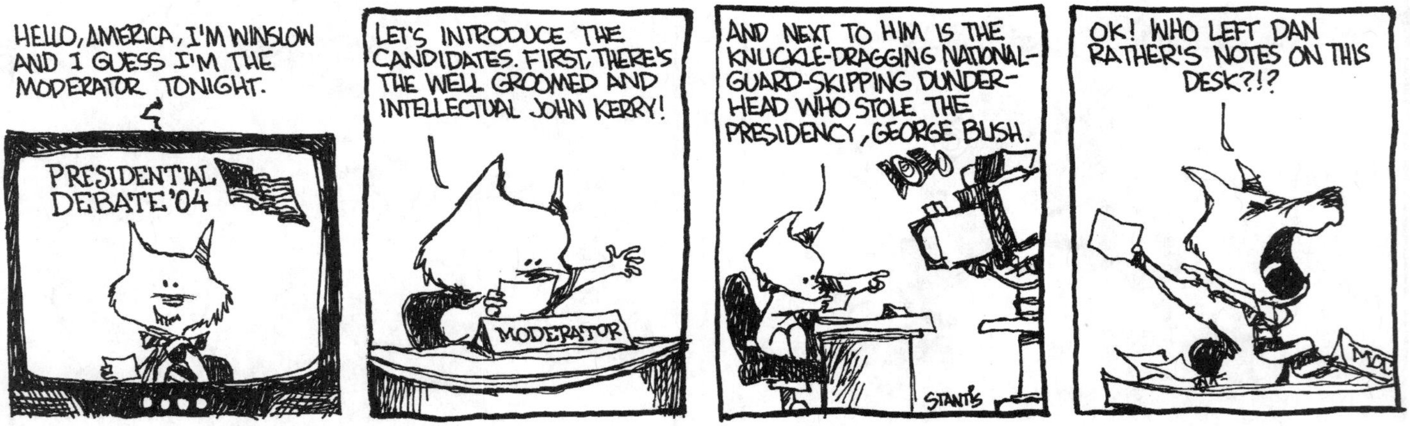
HELLO, AMERICA, I'M WINSLOW AND I GUESS I'M THE MODERATOR TONIGHT.
PRESIDENTIAL DEBATE '04
LET'S INTRODUCE THE CANDIDATES. FIRST, THERE'S THE WELL GROOMED AND INTELLECTUAL JOHN KERRY!
MODERATOR
AND NEXT TO HIM IS THE KNUCKLE-DRAGGING NATIONAL-GUARD-SKIPPING DUNDER-HEAD WHO STOLE THE PRESIDENCY, GEORGE BUSH.
STANTIS
OK! WHO LEFT DAN RATHER'S NOTES ON THIS DESK?!?

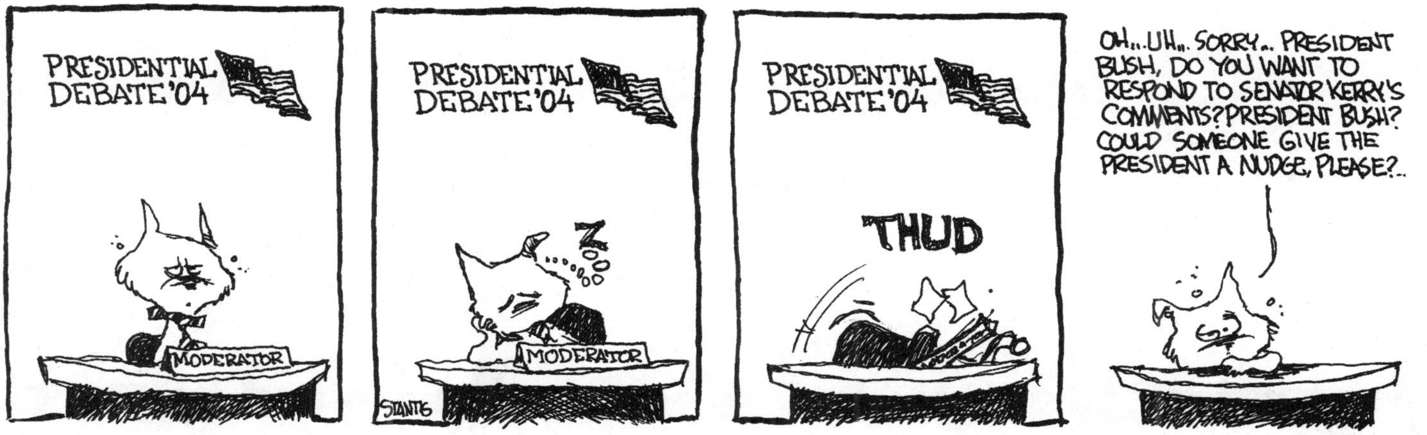
PRESIDENTIAL DEBATE '04
MODERATOR
STANTIS
Z
THUD
OH...UH... SORRY... PRESIDENT BUSH, DO YOU WANT TO RESPOND TO SENATOR KERRY'S COMMENTS? PRESIDENT BUSH? COULD SOMEONE GIVE THE PRESIDENT A NUDGE, PLEASE?...

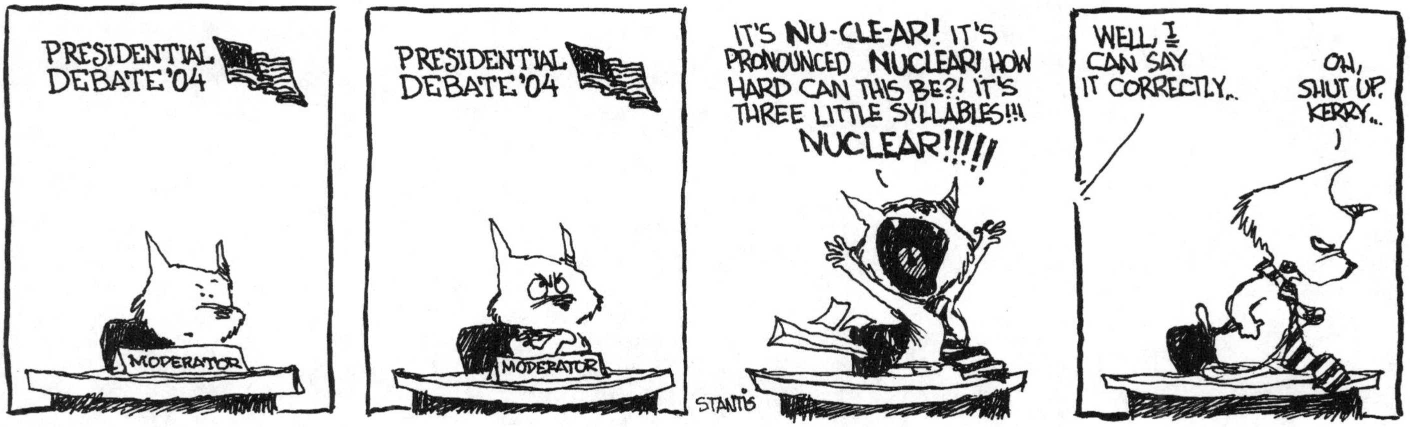
PRESIDENTIAL DEBATE '04
MODERATOR
IT'S NU-CLE-AR! IT'S PRONOUNCED NUCLEAR! HOW HARD CAN THIS BE?! IT'S THREE LITTLE SYLLABLES!!! NUCLEAR!!!!!
STANTIS
WELL, I CAN SAY IT CORRECTLY...
OH, SHUT UP, KERRY...

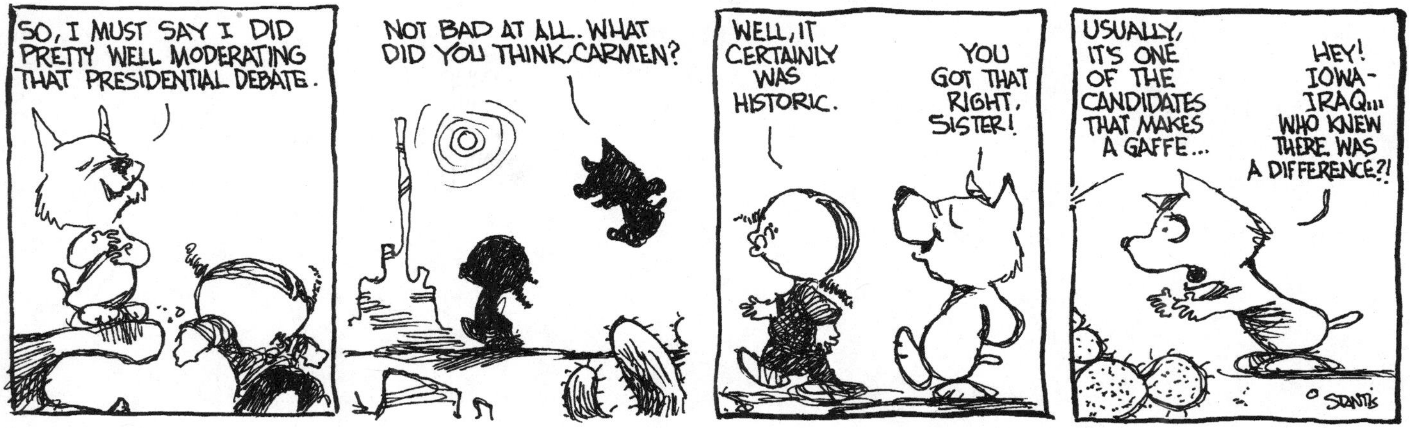
SO, I MUST SAY I DID PRETTY WELL MODERATING THAT PRESIDENTIAL DEBATE.
NOT BAD AT ALL. WHAT DID YOU THINK, CARMEN?
WELL, IT CERTAINLY WAS HISTORIC.
YOU GOT THAT RIGHT, SISTER!
USUALLY, IT'S ONE OF THE CANDIDATES THAT MAKES A GAFFE...
HEY! IOWA-IRAQ... WHO KNEW THERE WAS A DIFFERENCE?!
© STANTIS

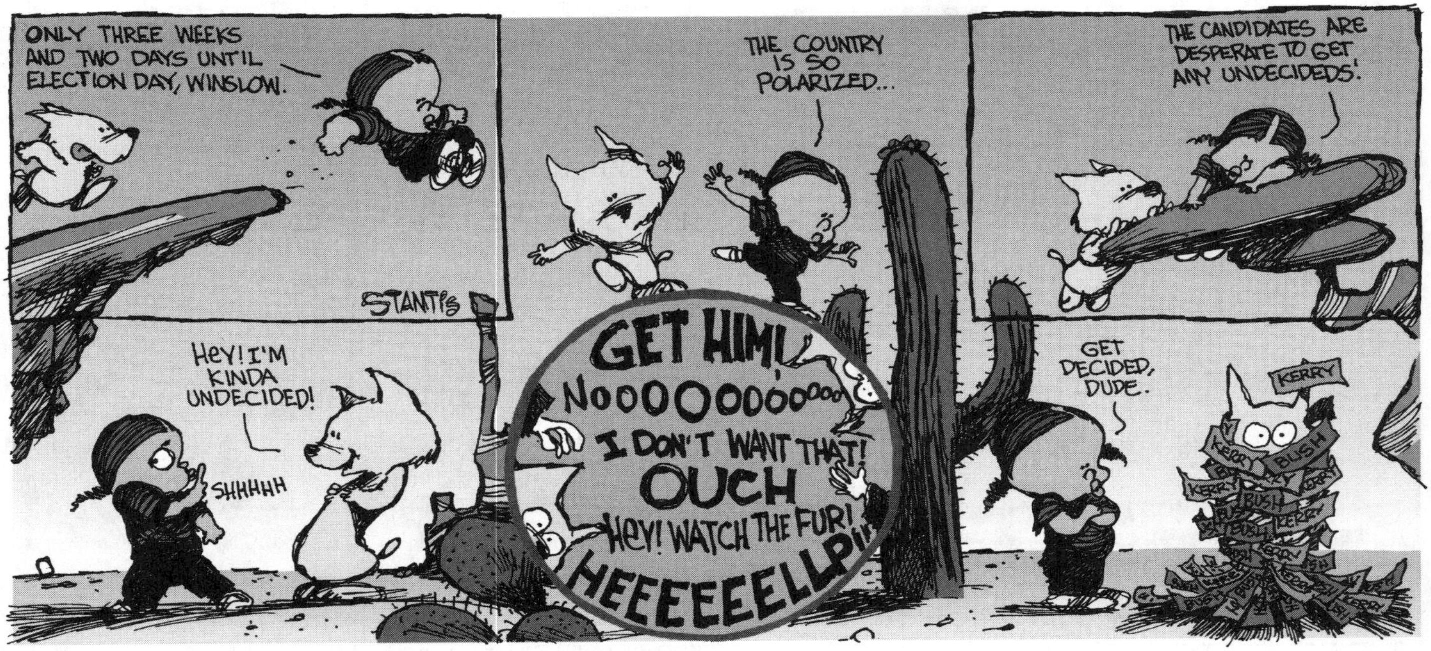
ONLY THREE WEEKS AND TWO DAYS UNTIL ELECTION DAY, WINSLOW.
STANTIS
THE COUNTRY IS SO POLARIZED...
THE CANDIDATES ARE DESPERATE TO GET ANY UNDECIDEDS!
Hey! I'M KINDA UNDECIDED!
SHHHHH
GET HIM!
NOOOOOOOOOOOO
I DON'T WANT THAT!
OUCH
Hey! WATCH THE FUR!
HEEEEEELLP!!
GET DECIDED, DUDE.
KERRY
BUSH

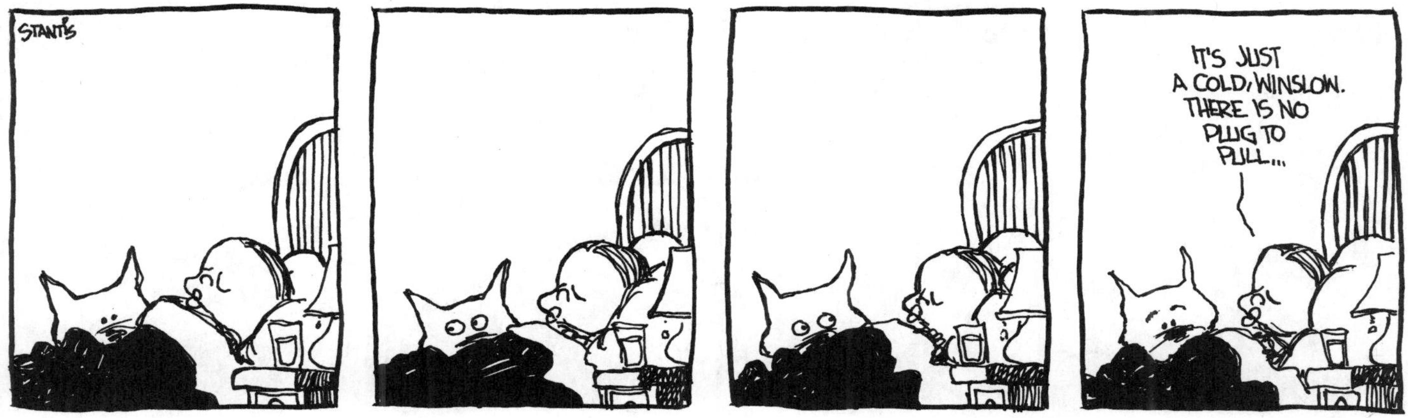
STANTIS
IT'S JUST A COLD, WINSLOW. THERE IS NO PLUG TO PULL...

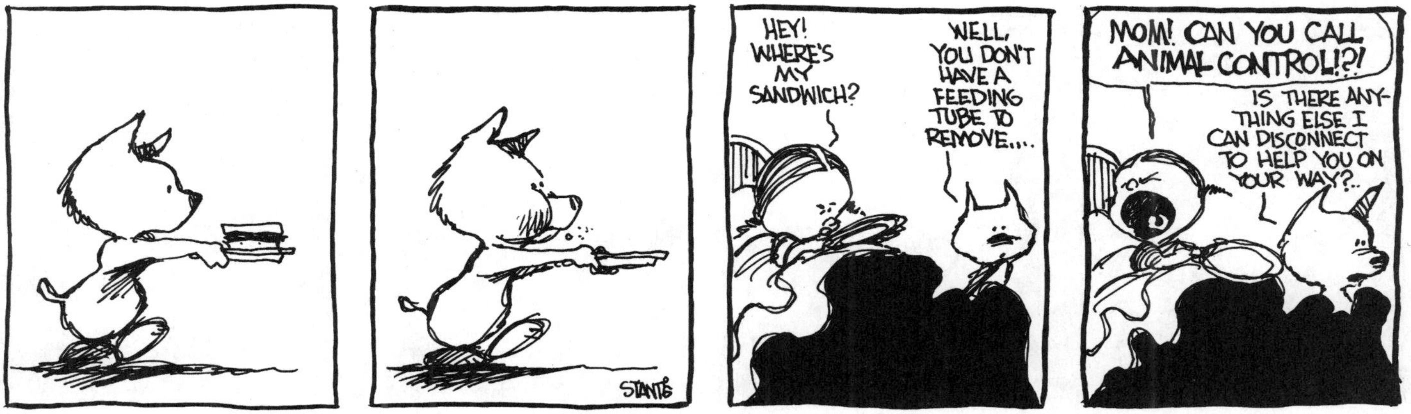
STANTIS
HEY! WHERE'S MY SANDWICH?
WELL, YOU DON'T HAVE A FEEDING TUBE TO REMOVE....
MOM! CAN YOU CALL ANIMAL CONTROL!?!
IS THERE ANY-THING ELSE I CAN DISCONNECT TO HELP YOU ON YOUR WAY?..

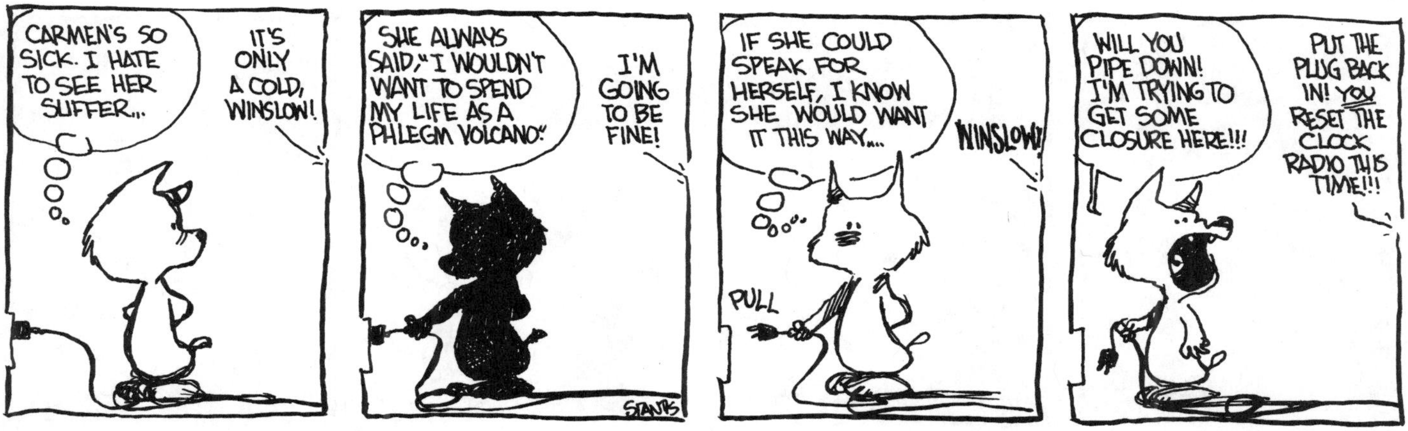
CARMEN'S SO SICK. I HATE TO SEE HER SUFFER...
IT'S ONLY A COLD, WINSLOW!
SHE ALWAYS SAID, "I WOULDN'T WANT TO SPEND MY LIFE AS A PHLEGM VOLCANO."
I'M GOING TO BE FINE!
STANTIS
IF SHE COULD SPEAK FOR HERSELF, I KNOW SHE WOULD WANT IT THIS WAY...
WINSLOW!
PULL
WILL YOU PIPE DOWN! I'M TRYING TO GET SOME CLOSURE HERE!!!
PUT THE PLUG BACK IN! YOU RESET THE CLOCK RADIO THIS TIME!!!

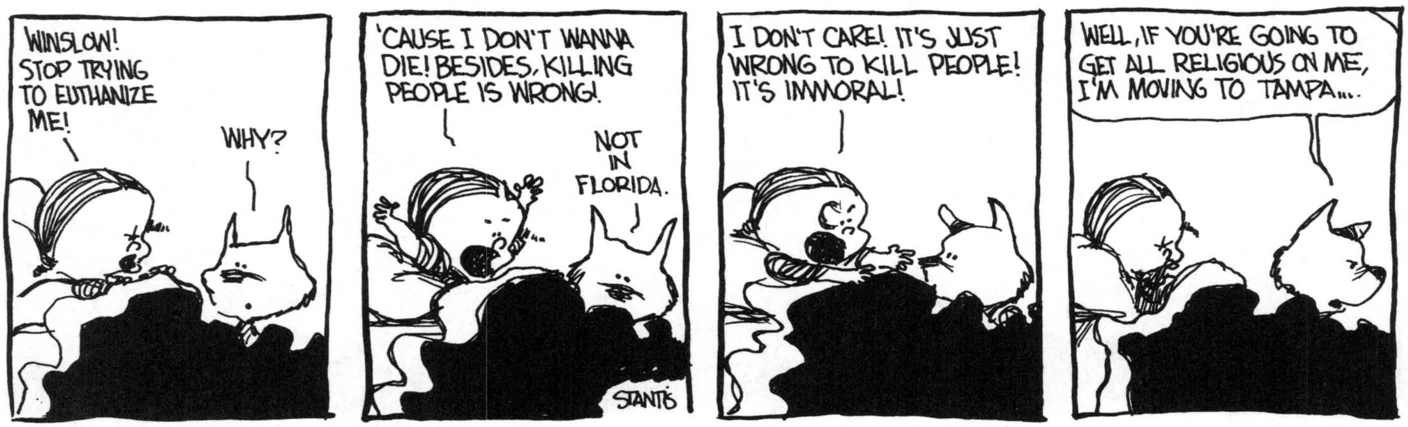
WINSLOW! STOP TRYING TO EUTHANIZE ME!
WHY?
'CAUSE I DON'T WANNA DIE! BESIDES, KILLING PEOPLE IS WRONG!
NOT IN FLORIDA.
STANTIS
I DON'T CARE! IT'S JUST WRONG TO KILL PEOPLE! IT'S IMMORAL!
WELL, IF YOU'RE GOING TO GET ALL RELIGIOUS ON ME, I'M MOVING TO TAMPA....

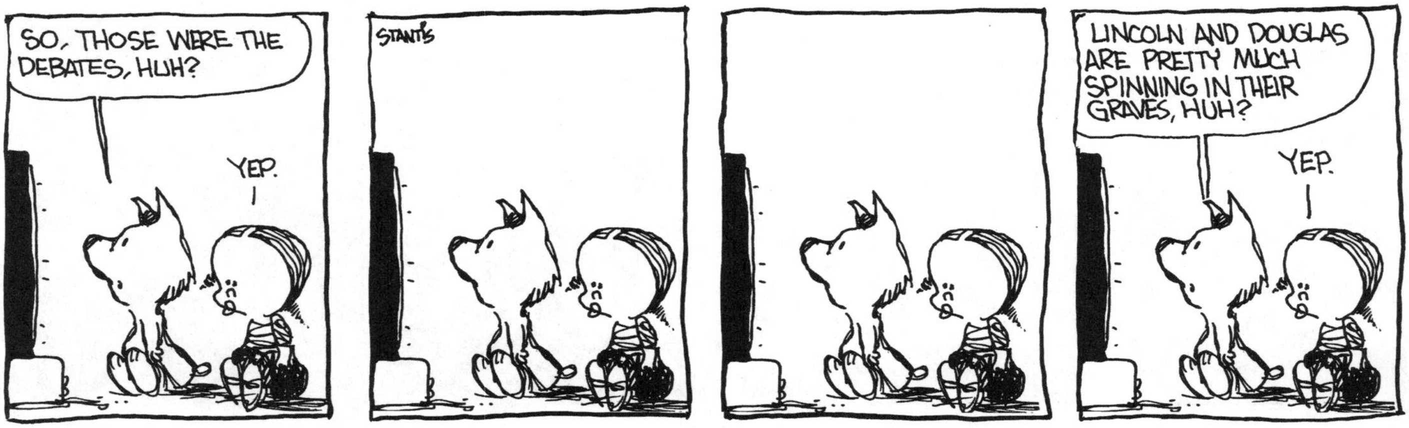
SO, THOSE WERE THE DEBATES, HUH?
YEP.
STANTIS
LINCOLN AND DOUGLAS ARE PRETTY MUCH SPINNING IN THEIR GRAVES, HUH?
YEP.

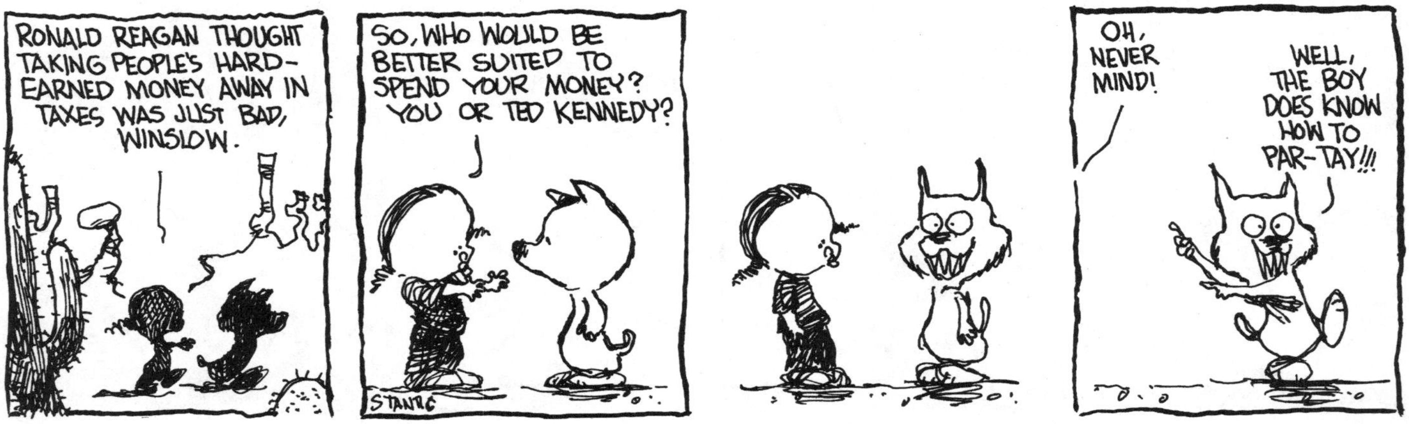
RONALD REAGAN THOUGHT TAKING PEOPLE'S HARD-EARNED MONEY AWAY IN TAXES WAS JUST BAD, WINSLOW.
SO, WHO WOULD BE BETTER SUITED TO SPEND YOUR MONEY? YOU OR TED KENNEDY?
STANTIS
OH, NEVER MIND!
WELL, THE BOY DOES KNOW HOW TO PAR-TAY!!!

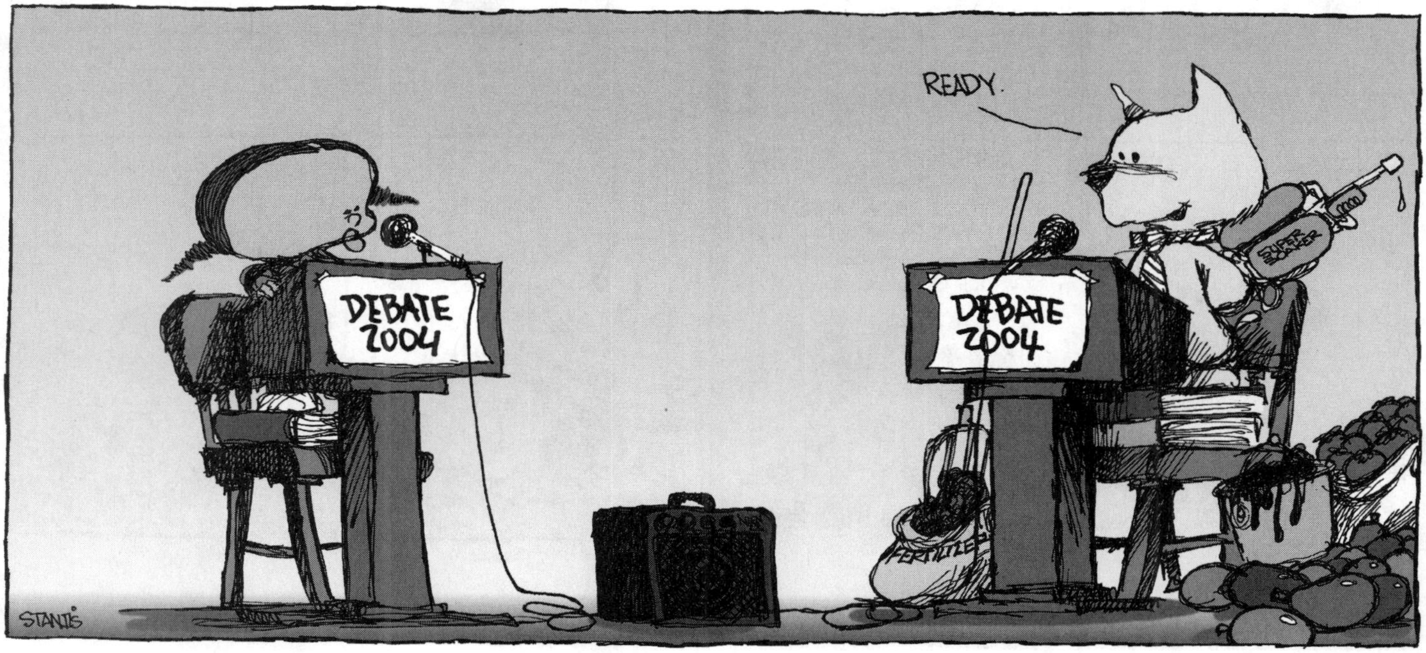
READY.
DEBATE 2004
DEBATE 2004
STANTIS

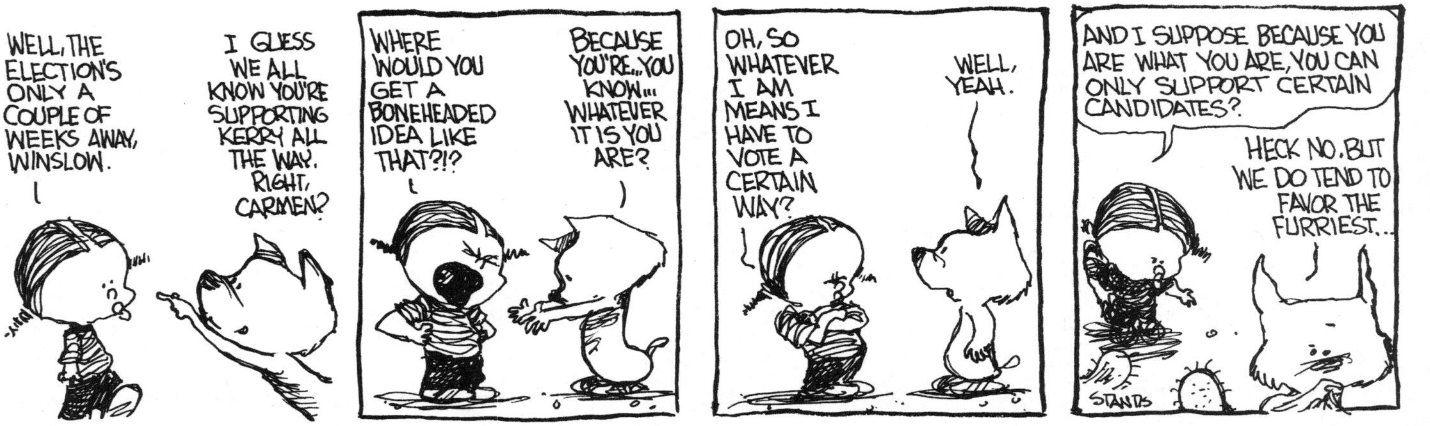
WELL, THE ELECTION'S ONLY A COUPLE OF WEEKS AWAY, WINSLOW.
I GUESS WE ALL KNOW YOU'RE SUPPORTING KERRY ALL THE WAY. RIGHT, CARMEN?
WHERE WOULD YOU GET A BONEHEADED IDEA LIKE THAT?!?
BECAUSE YOU'RE... YOU KNOW... WHATEVER IT IS YOU ARE?
OH, SO WHATEVER I AM MEANS I HAVE TO VOTE A CERTAIN WAY?
WELL, YEAH.
AND I SUPPOSE BECAUSE YOU ARE WHAT YOU ARE, YOU CAN ONLY SUPPORT CERTAIN CANDIDATES?
HECK NO. BUT WE DO TEND TO FAVOR THE FURRIEST...
STANTIS

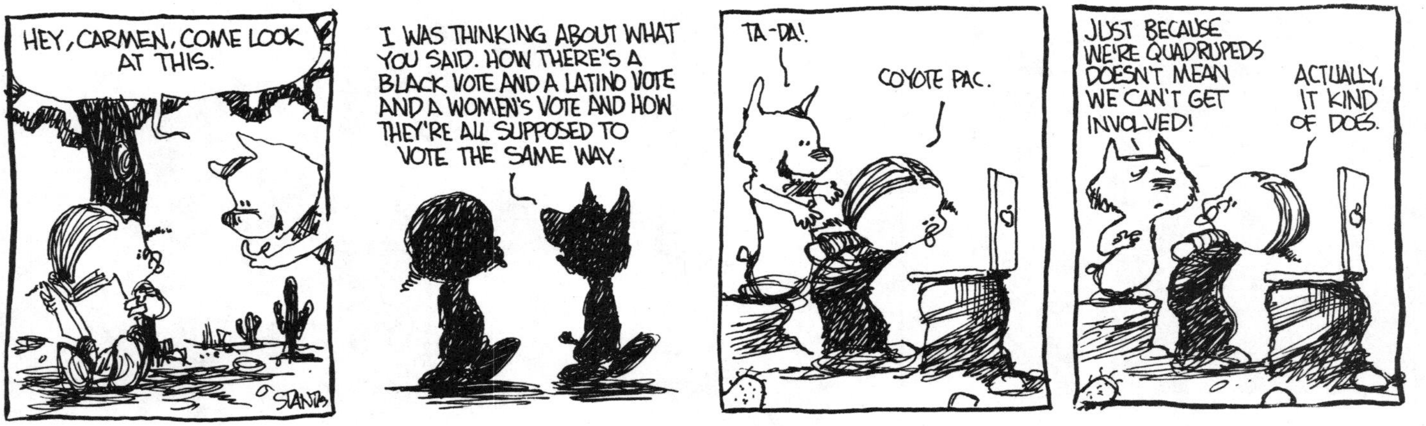
HEY, CARMEN, COME LOOK AT THIS.
STANTIS
I WAS THINKING ABOUT WHAT YOU SAID. HOW THERE'S A BLACK VOTE AND A LATINO VOTE AND A WOMEN'S VOTE AND HOW THEY'RE ALL SUPPOSED TO VOTE THE SAME WAY.
TA-DA!
COYOTE PAC.
JUST BECAUSE WE'RE QUADRUPEDS DOESN'T MEAN WE CAN'T GET INVOLVED!
ACTUALLY, IT KIND OF DOES.

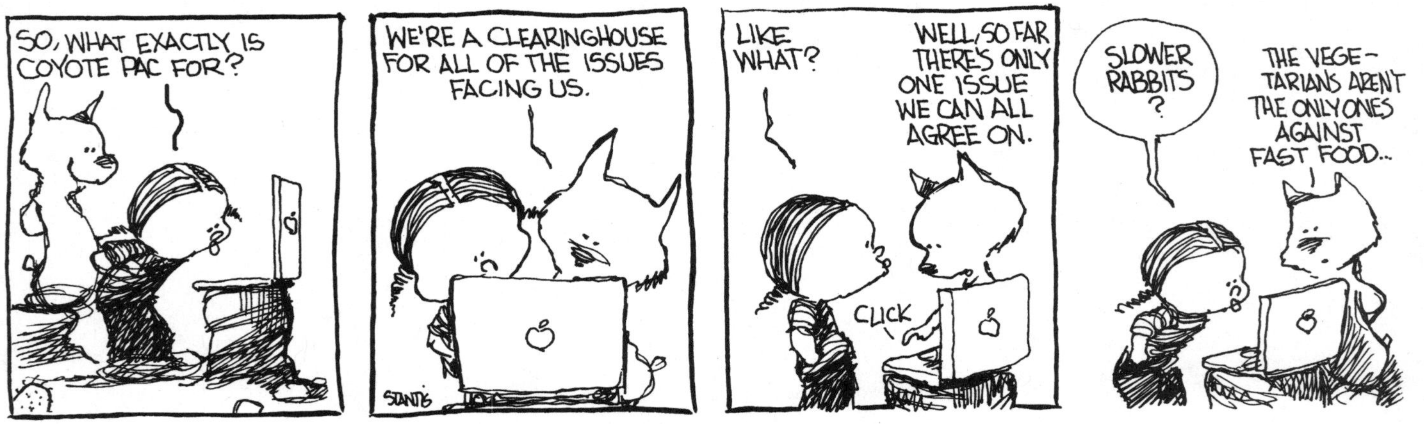
SO, WHAT EXACTLY IS COYOTE PAC FOR?
WE'RE A CLEARINGHOUSE FOR ALL OF THE ISSUES FACING US.
STANTIS
LIKE WHAT?
WELL, SO FAR THERE'S ONLY ONE ISSUE WE CAN ALL AGREE ON.
CLICK
SLOWER RABBITS?
THE VEGE-TARIANS AREN'T THE ONLY ONES AGAINST FAST FOOD...

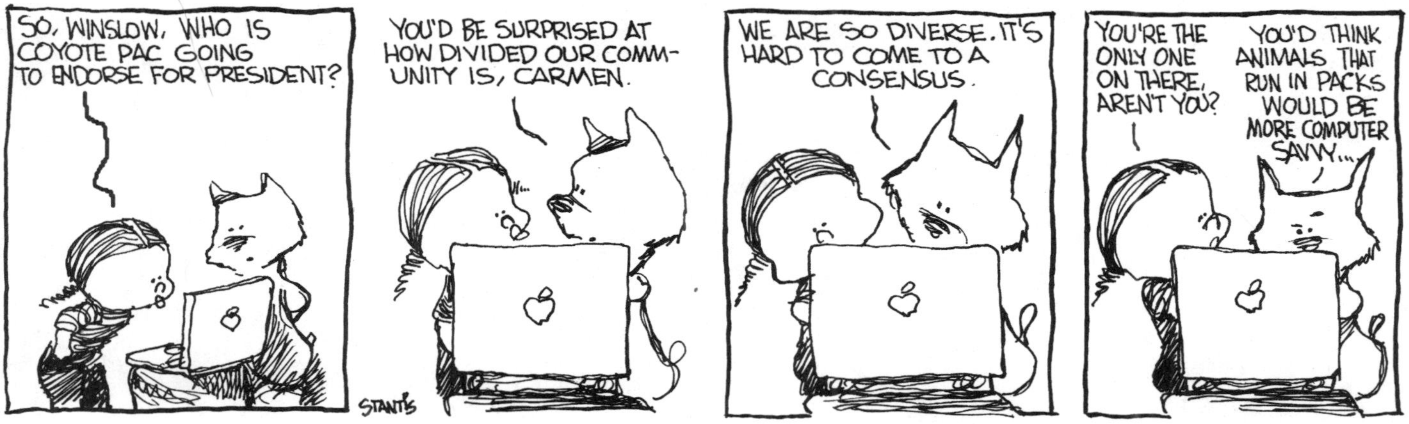
SO, WINSLOW, WHO IS COYOTE PAC GOING TO ENDORSE FOR PRESIDENT?
YOU'D BE SURPRISED AT HOW DIVIDED OUR COMMUNITY IS, CARMEN.
STANTIS
WE ARE SO DIVERSE. IT'S HARD TO COME TO A CONSENSUS.
YOU'RE THE ONLY ONE ON THERE, AREN'T YOU?
YOU'D THINK ANIMALS THAT RUN IN PACKS WOULD BE MORE COMPUTER SAVVY....

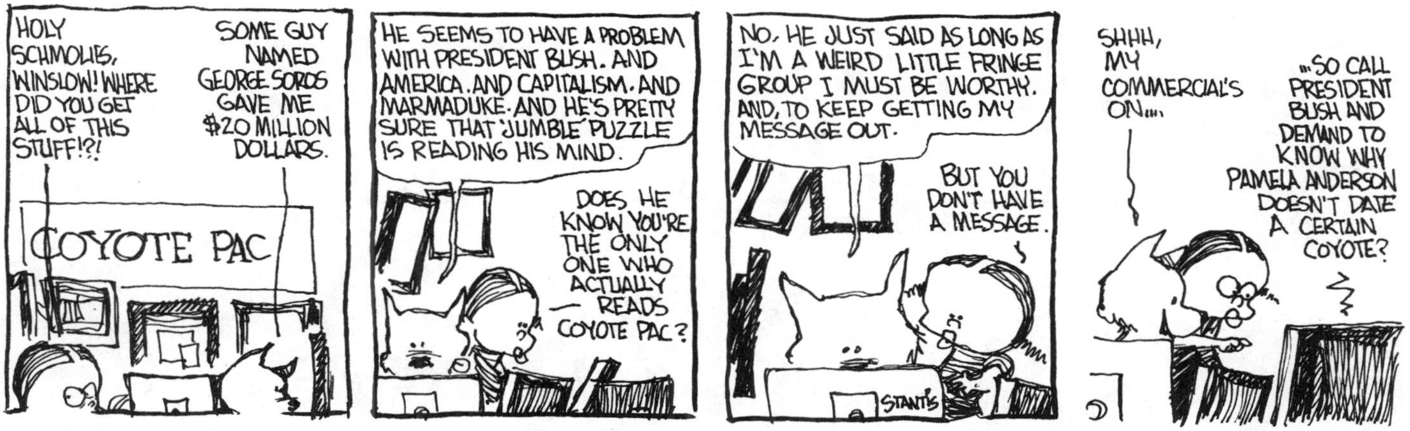
HOLY SCHMOLIES, WINSLOW! WHERE DID YOU GET ALL OF THIS STUFF!?!
SOME GUY NAMED GEORGE SOROS GAVE ME $20 MILLION DOLLARS.
COYOTE PAC
HE SEEMS TO HAVE A PROBLEM WITH PRESIDENT BUSH. AND AMERICA. AND CAPITALISM. AND MARMADUKE. AND HE'S PRETTY SURE THAT 'JUMBLE' PUZZLE IS READING HIS MIND.
DOES HE KNOW YOU'RE THE ONLY ONE WHO ACTUALLY READS COYOTE PAC?
NO, HE JUST SAID AS LONG AS I'M A WEIRD LITTLE FRINGE GROUP I MUST BE WORTHY. AND, TO KEEP GETTING MY MESSAGE OUT.
BUT YOU DON'T HAVE A MESSAGE.
STANTIS
SHHH, MY COMMERCIAL'S ON....
...SO CALL PRESIDENT BUSH AND DEMAND TO KNOW WHY PAMELA ANDERSON DOESN'T DATE A CERTAIN COYOTE?

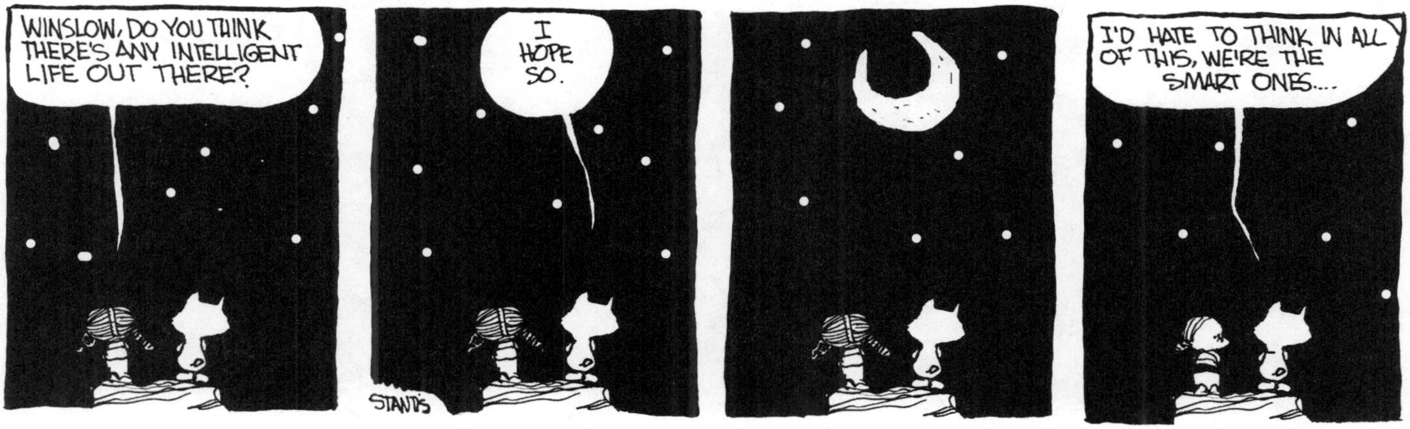
WINSLOW, DO YOU THINK THERE'S ANY INTELLIGENT LIFE OUT THERE?
I HOPE SO.
STANTIS
I'D HATE TO THINK IN ALL OF THIS, WE'RE THE SMART ONES....

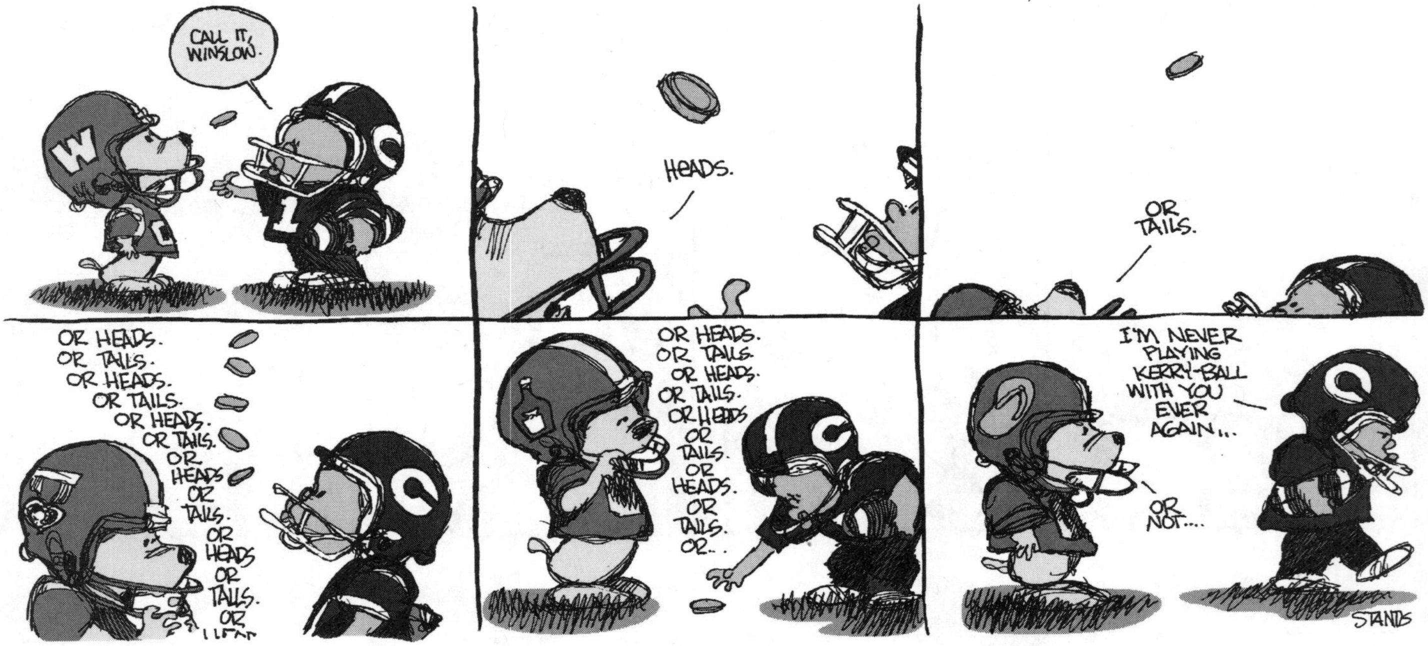
CALL IT, WINSLOW.
HEADS.
OR TAILS.
OR HEADS. OR TAILS. OR HEADS. OR TAILS. OR HEADS. OR TAILS. OR HEADS OR TAILS. OR HEADS OR TAILS. OR
OR HEADS. OR TAILS. OR HEADS. OR TAILS. OR HEADS OR TAILS. OR HEADS. OR TAILS. OR...
I'M NEVER PLAYING KERRY-BALL WITH YOU EVER AGAIN...
OR NOT....
STANTIS

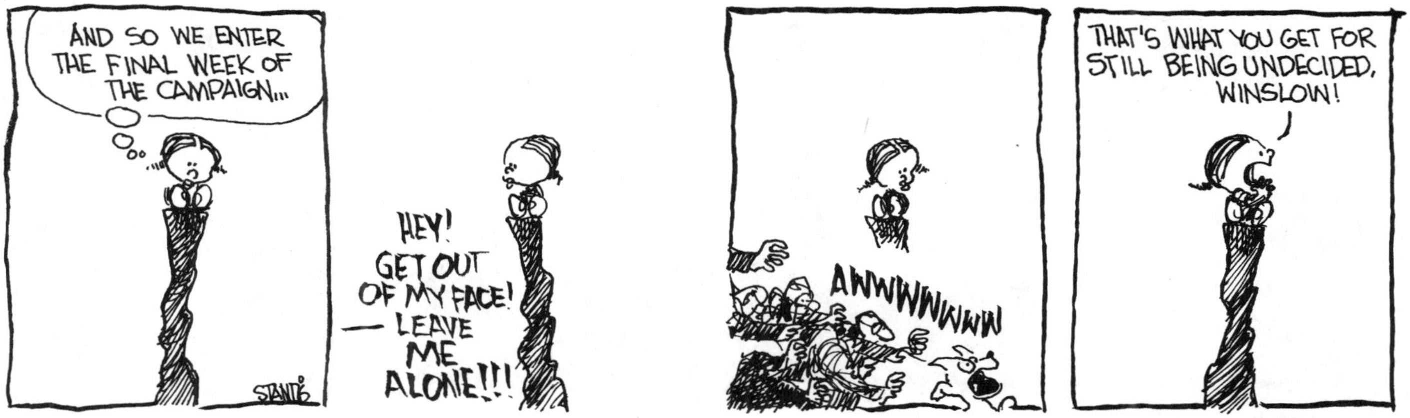
AND SO WE ENTER THE FINAL WEEK OF THE CAMPAIGN...
HEY! GET OUT OF MY FACE! — LEAVE ME ALONE!!!
ANWWWWWWW
THAT'S WHAT YOU GET FOR STILL BEING UNDECIDED, WINSLOW!

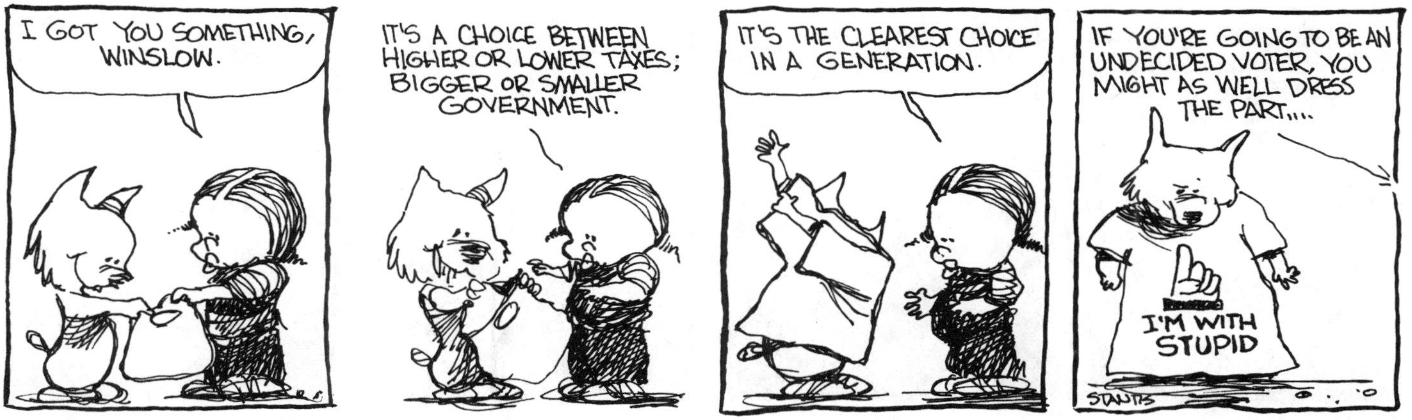
I GOT YOU SOMETHING, WINSLOW.
IT'S A CHOICE BETWEEN HIGHER OR LOWER TAXES; BIGGER OR SMALLER GOVERNMENT.
IT'S THE CLEAREST CHOICE IN A GENERATION.
IF YOU'RE GOING TO BE AN UNDECIDED VOTER, YOU MIGHT AS WELL DRESS THE PART....
I'M WITH STUPID

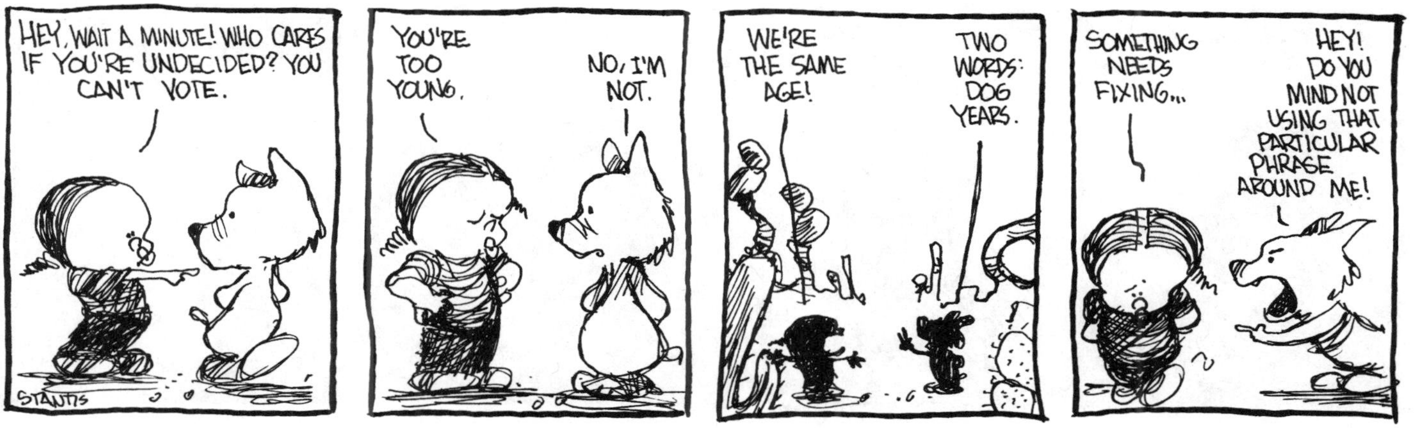
HEY, WAIT A MINUTE! WHO CARES IF YOU'RE UNDECIDED? YOU CAN'T VOTE.
YOU'RE TOO YOUNG.
NO, I'M NOT.
WE'RE THE SAME AGE!
TWO WORDS: DOG YEARS.
SOMETHING NEEDS FIXING...
HEY! DO YOU MIND NOT USING THAT PARTICULAR PHRASE AROUND ME!

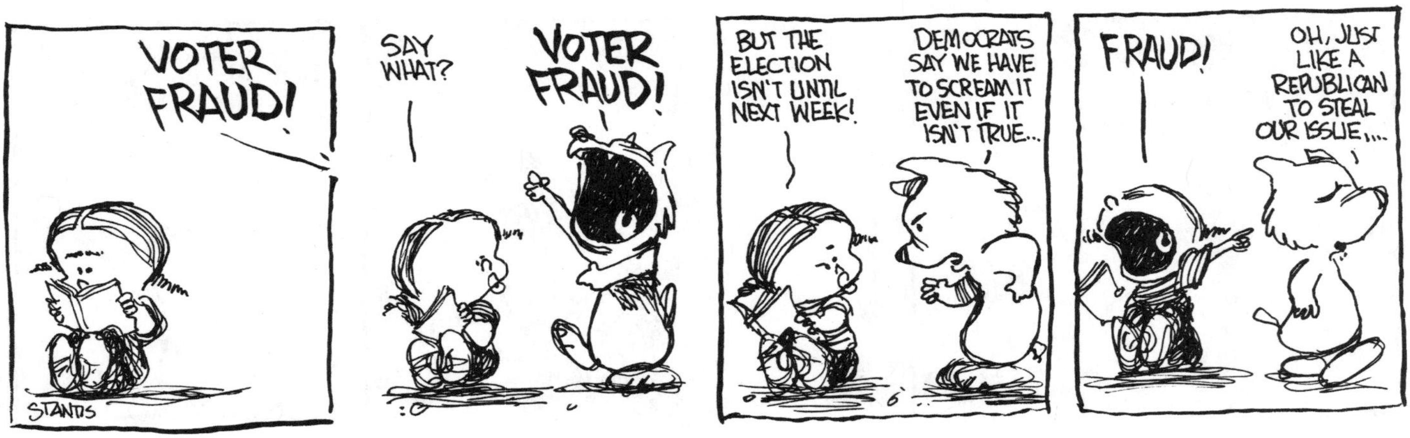
VOTER FRAUD!
SAY WHAT?
VOTER FRAUD!
BUT THE ELECTION ISN'T UNTIL NEXT WEEK!
DEMOCRATS SAY WE HAVE TO SCREAM IT EVEN IF IT ISN'T TRUE...
FRAUD!
OH, JUST LIKE A REPUBLICAN TO STEAL OUR ISSUE,...

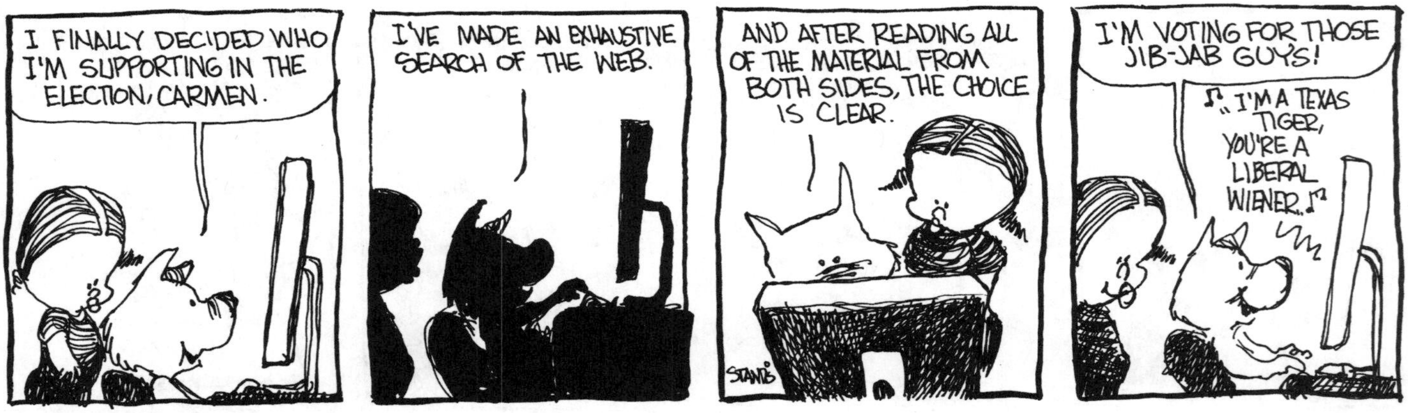
I FINALLY DECIDED WHO I'M SUPPORTING IN THE ELECTION, CARMEN.
I'VE MADE AN EXHAUSTIVE SEARCH OF THE WEB.
AND AFTER READING ALL OF THE MATERIAL FROM BOTH SIDES, THE CHOICE IS CLEAR.
I'M VOTING FOR THOSE JIB-JAB GUYS!
♫.. I'M A TEXAS TIGER, YOU'RE A LIBERAL WIENER..♫

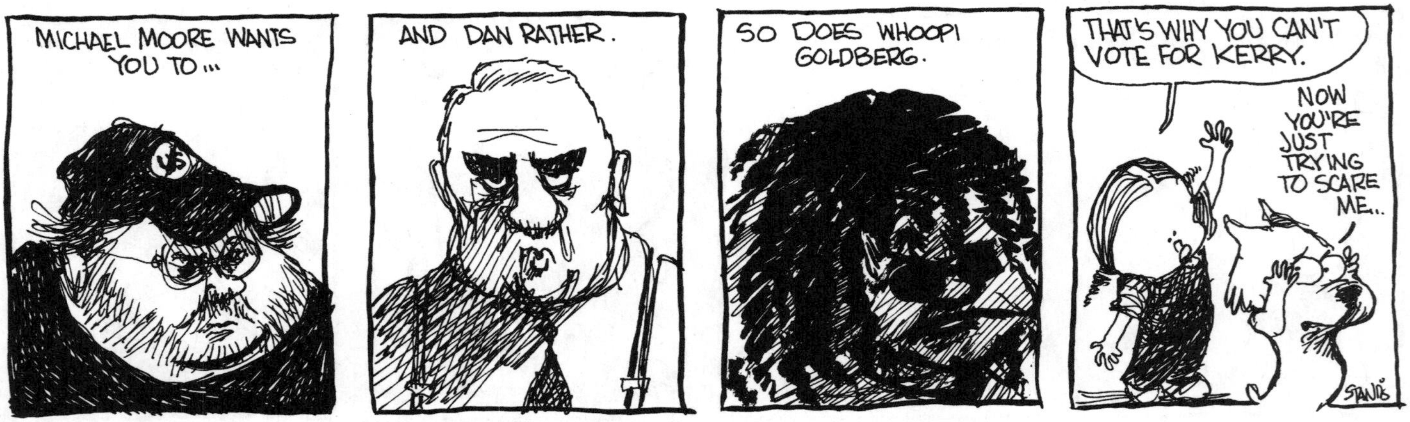
MICHAEL MOORE WANTS YOU TO...
AND DAN RATHER.
SO DOES WHOOPI GOLDBERG.
THAT'S WHY YOU CAN'T VOTE FOR KERRY.
NOW YOU'RE JUST TRYING TO SCARE ME..

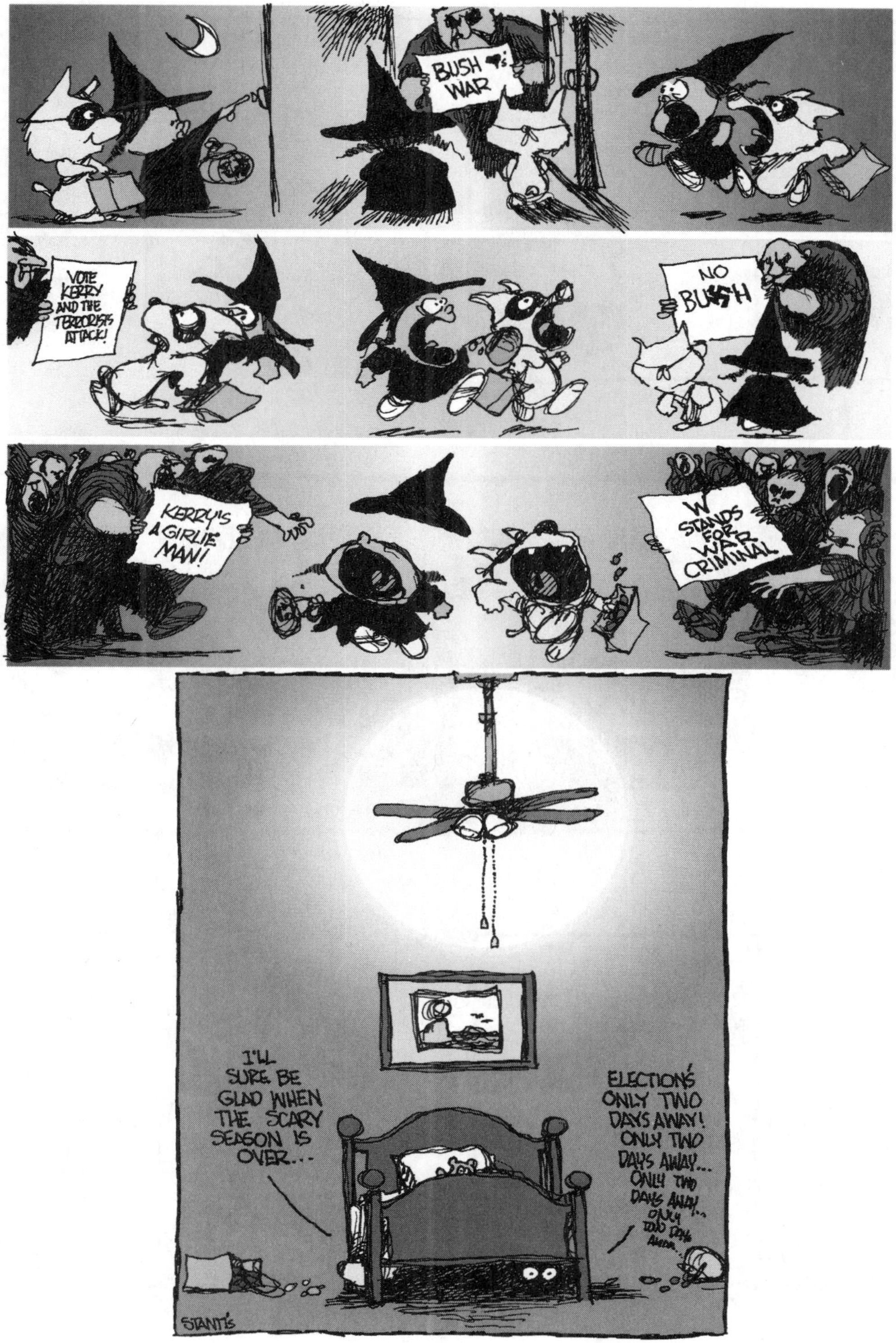
BUSH ♥'s WAR
VOTE KERRY AND THE TERRORISTS ATTACK!
NO BUSH
KERRY'S A GIRLIE MAN!
W STANDS FOR WAR CRIMINAL
I'LL SURE BE GLAD WHEN THE SCARY SEASON IS OVER...
ELECTION'S ONLY TWO DAYS AWAY! ONLY TWO DAYS AWAY... ONLY TWO DAYS AWAY...
STANTIS

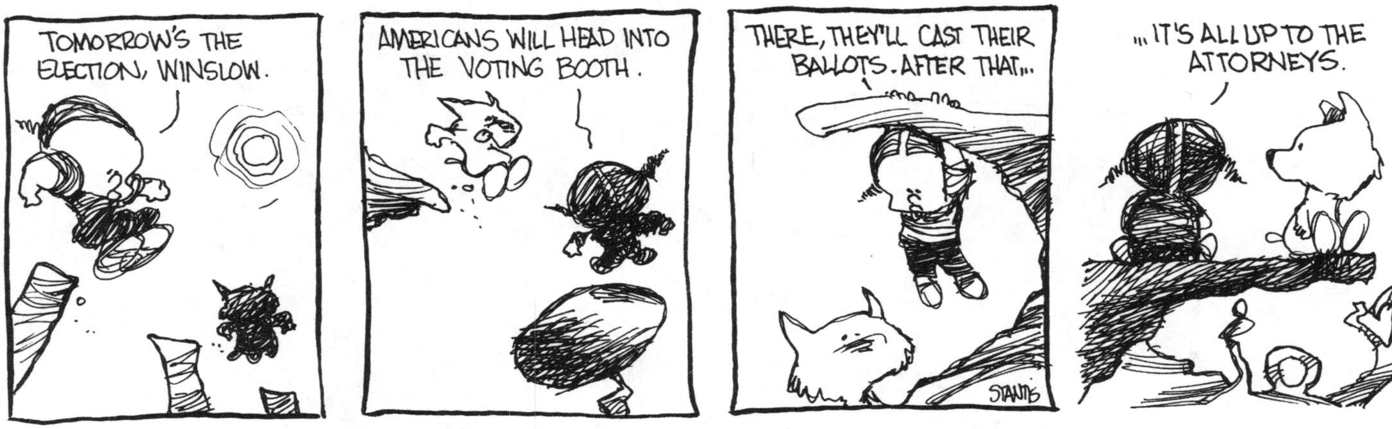
TOMORROW'S THE ELECTION, WINSLOW.
AMERICANS WILL HEAD INTO THE VOTING BOOTH.
THERE, THEY'LL CAST THEIR BALLOTS. AFTER THAT...
...IT'S ALL UP TO THE ATTORNEYS.
STANTIS

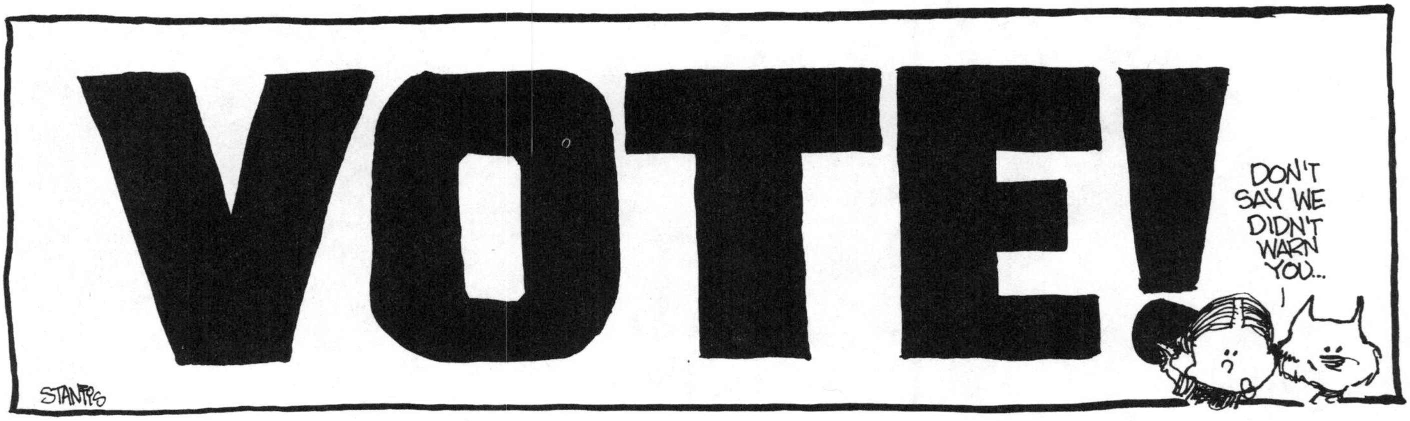
VOTE!
DON'T SAY WE DIDN'T WARN YOU...
STANTIS

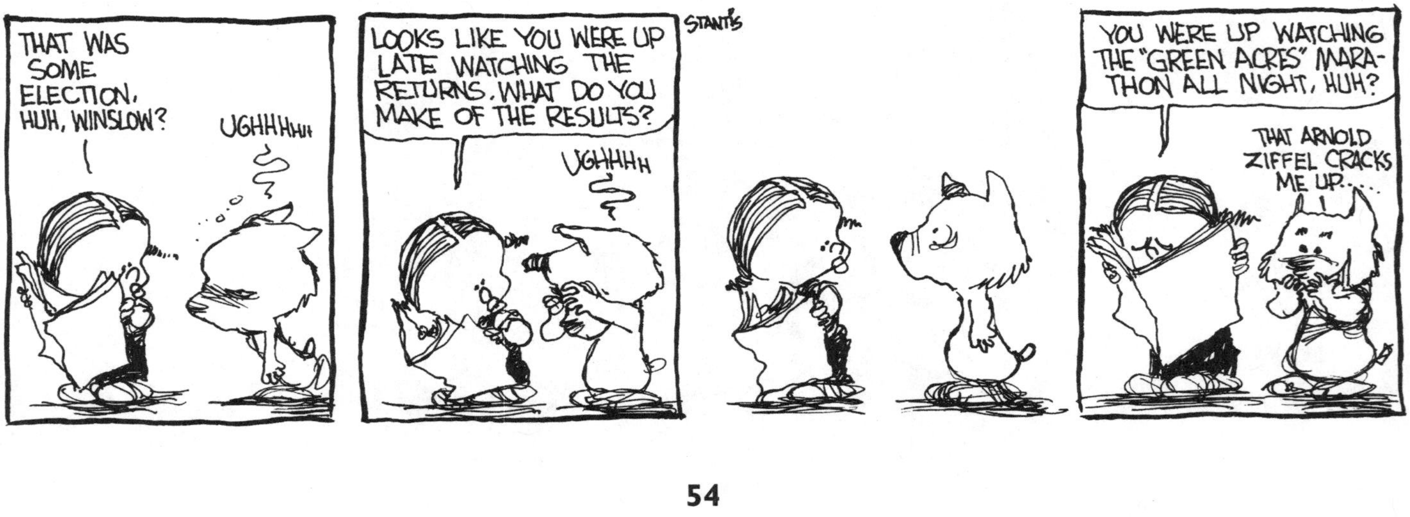
THAT WAS SOME ELECTION, HUH, WINSLOW?
UGHHHHHH
LOOKS LIKE YOU WERE UP LATE WATCHING THE RETURNS. WHAT DO YOU MAKE OF THE RESULTS?
UGHHHH
STANTIS
YOU WERE UP WATCHING THE "GREEN ACRES" MARATHON ALL NIGHT, HUH?
THAT ARNOLD ZIFFEL CRACKS ME UP....

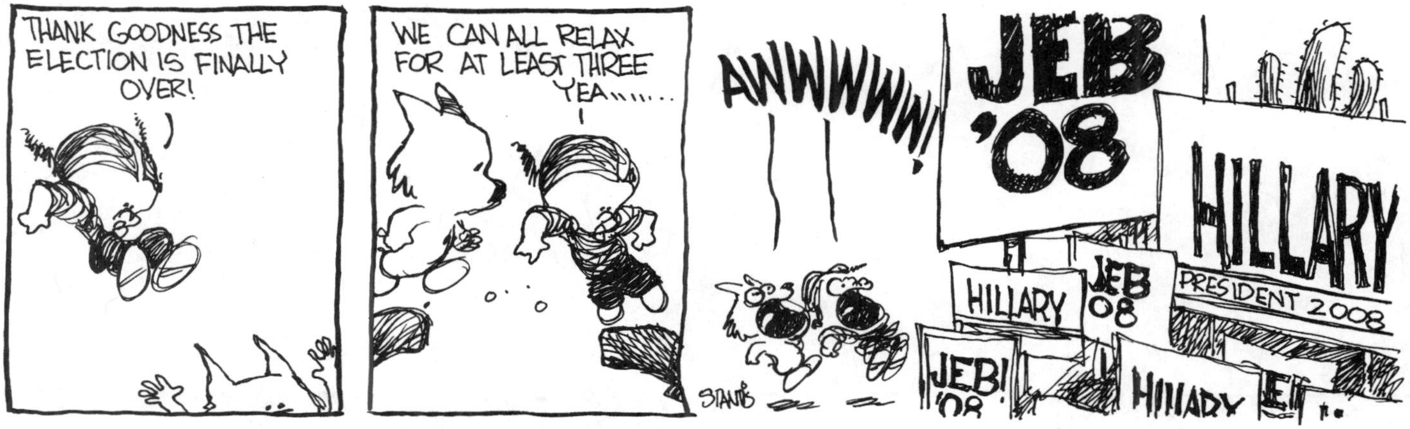
THANK GOODNESS THE ELECTION IS FINALLY OVER!
WE CAN ALL RELAX FOR AT LEAST THREE YEA.......
AWWWWWW!
JEB '08
HILLARY
HILLARY
JEB 08
HILLARY PRESIDENT 2008
JEB! '08
STANTIS

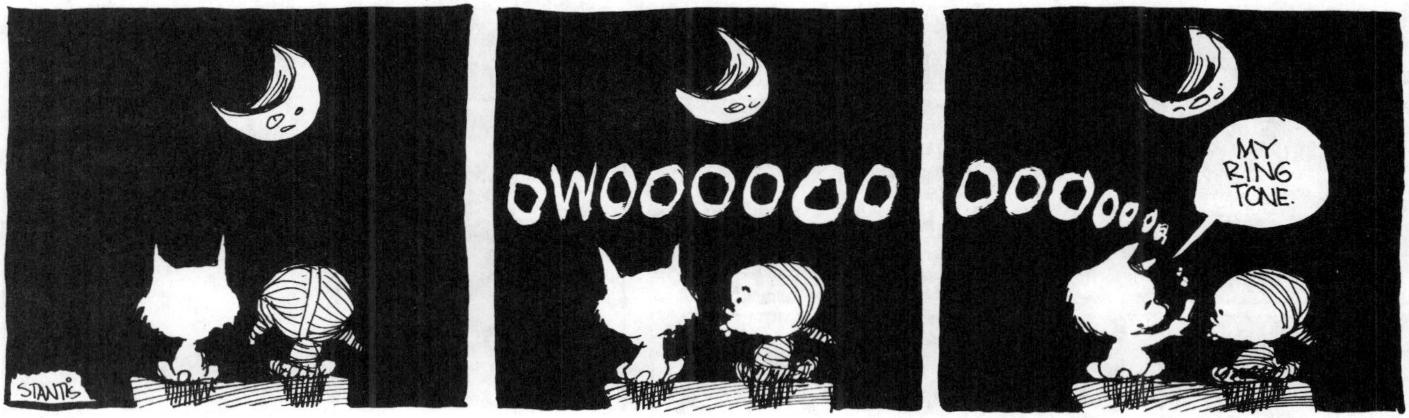
STANTIS
OWOOOOOOO
OOOOooo
MY RING TONE.

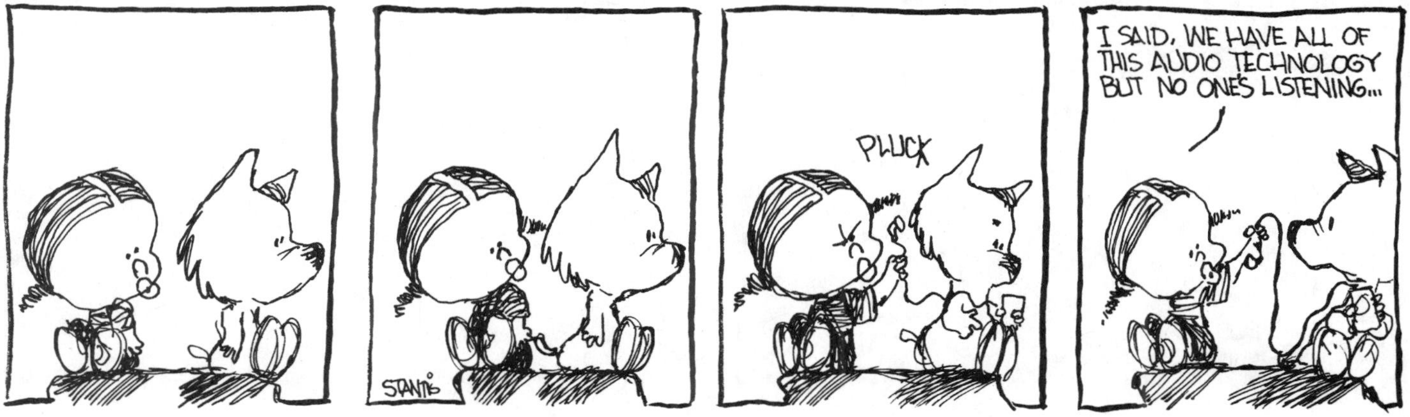
STANTIS
PLUCK
I SAID, WE HAVE ALL OF THIS AUDIO TECHNOLOGY BUT NO ONE'S LISTENING...

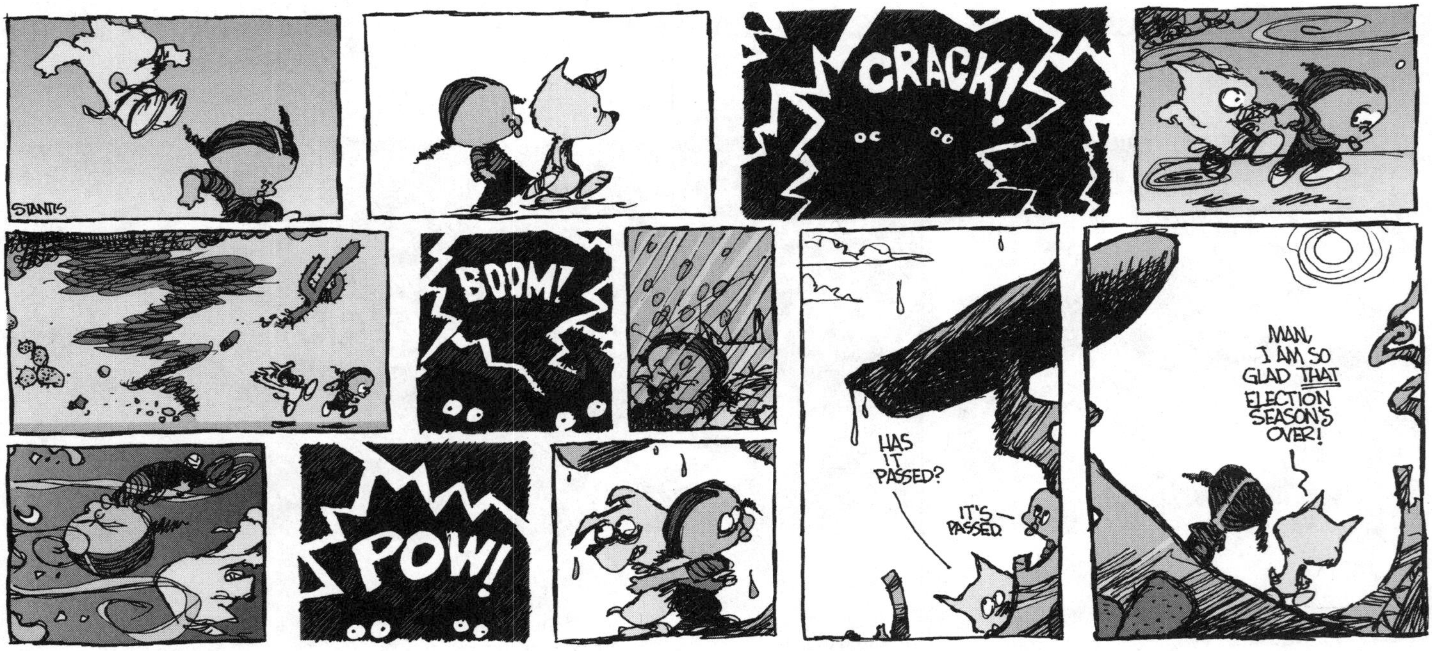
STANTIS
CRACK!
BOOM!
POW!
HAS IT PASSED?
IT'S PASSED.
MAN, I AM SO GLAD THAT ELECTION SEASON'S OVER!

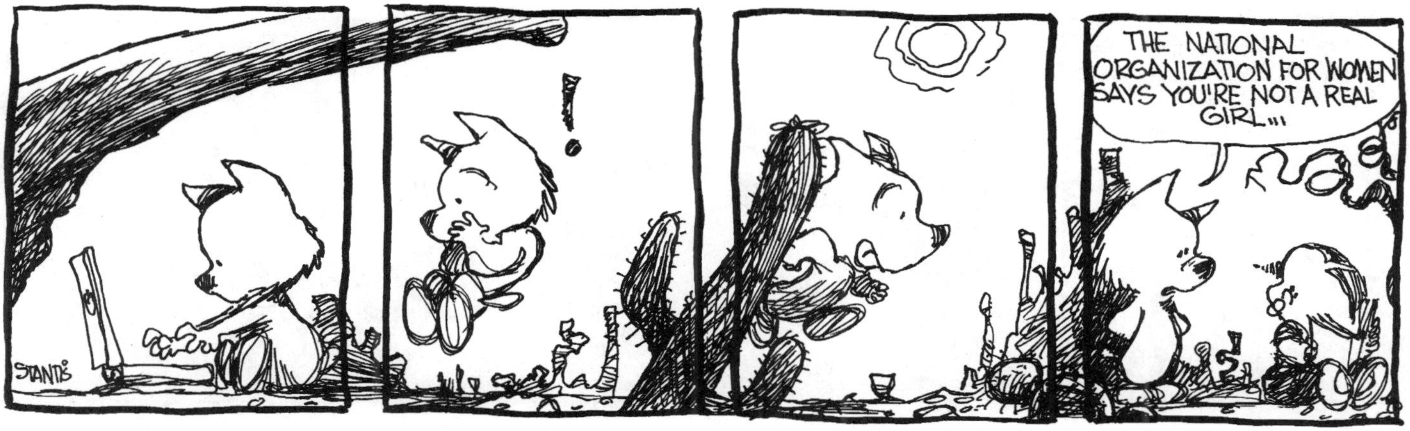
THE NATIONAL ORGANIZATION FOR WOMEN SAYS YOU'RE NOT A REAL GIRL...

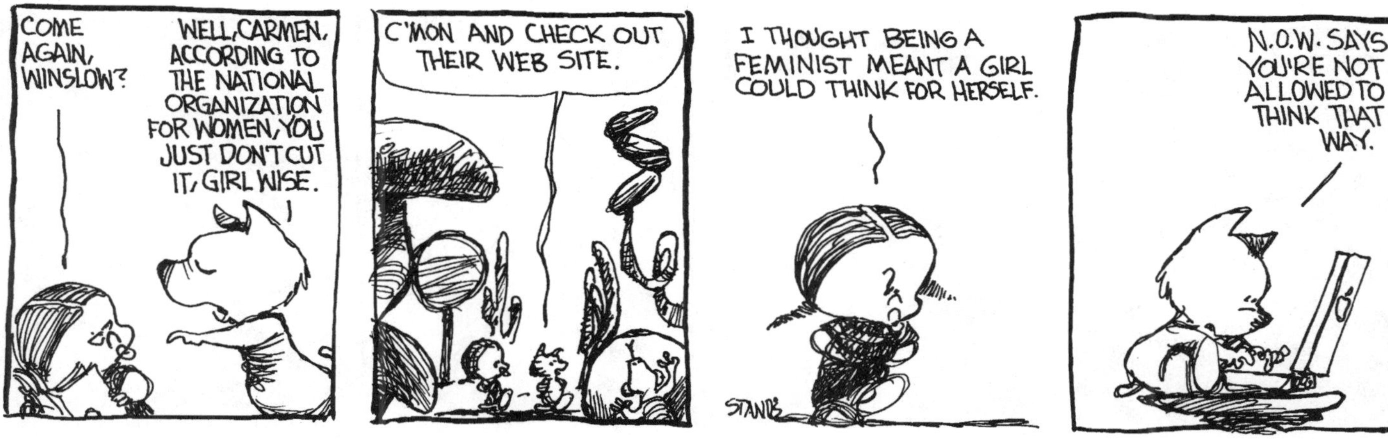
COME AGAIN, WINSLOW?
WELL, CARMEN, ACCORDING TO THE NATIONAL ORGANIZATION FOR WOMEN, YOU JUST DON'T CUT IT, GIRL WISE.
C'MON AND CHECK OUT THEIR WEB SITE.
I THOUGHT BEING A FEMINIST MEANT A GIRL COULD THINK FOR HERSELF.
N.O.W. SAYS YOU'RE NOT ALLOWED TO THINK THAT WAY.

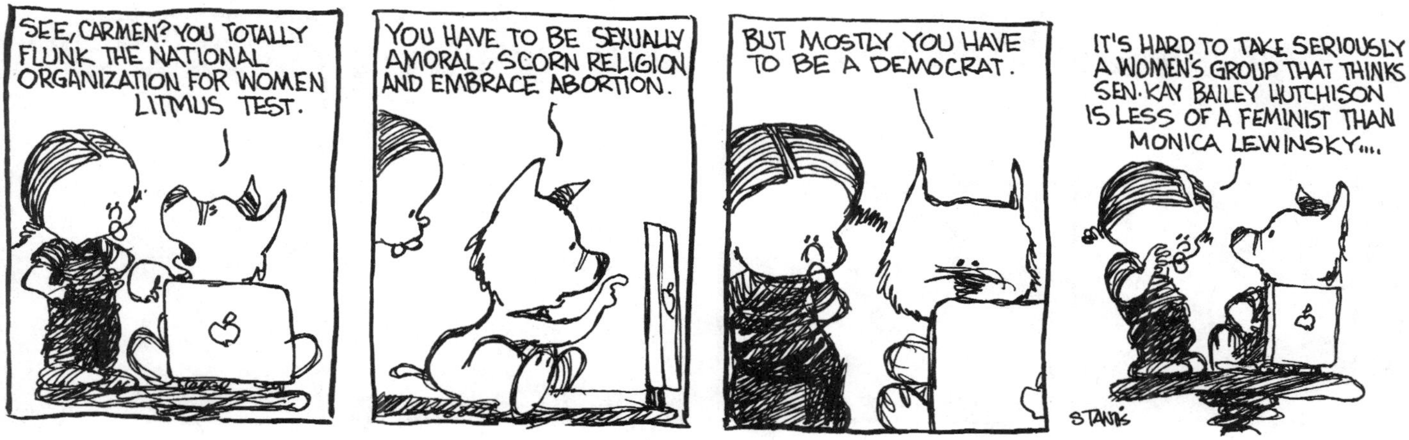
SEE, CARMEN? YOU TOTALLY FLUNK THE NATIONAL ORGANIZATION FOR WOMEN LITMUS TEST.
YOU HAVE TO BE SEXUALLY AMORAL, SCORN RELIGION AND EMBRACE ABORTION.
BUT MOSTLY YOU HAVE TO BE A DEMOCRAT.
IT'S HARD TO TAKE SERIOUSLY A WOMEN'S GROUP THAT THINKS SEN. KAY BAILEY HUTCHISON IS LESS OF A FEMINIST THAN MONICA LEWINSKY....

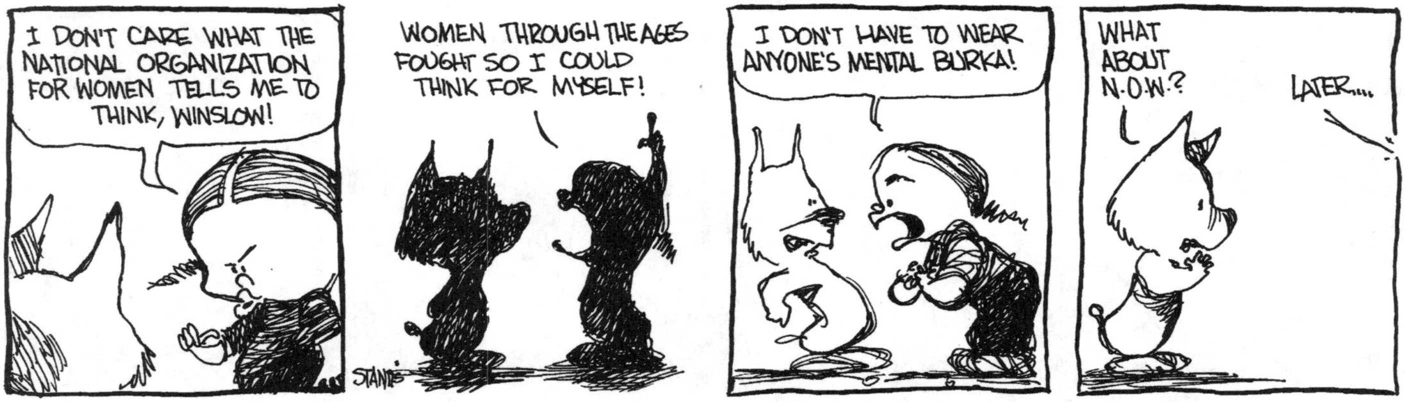
I DON'T CARE WHAT THE NATIONAL ORGANIZATION FOR WOMEN TELLS ME TO THINK, WINSLOW!
WOMEN THROUGH THE AGES FOUGHT SO I COULD THINK FOR MYSELF!
STANIS
I DON'T HAVE TO WEAR ANYONE'S MENTAL BURKA!
WHAT ABOUT N.O.W.?
LATER....

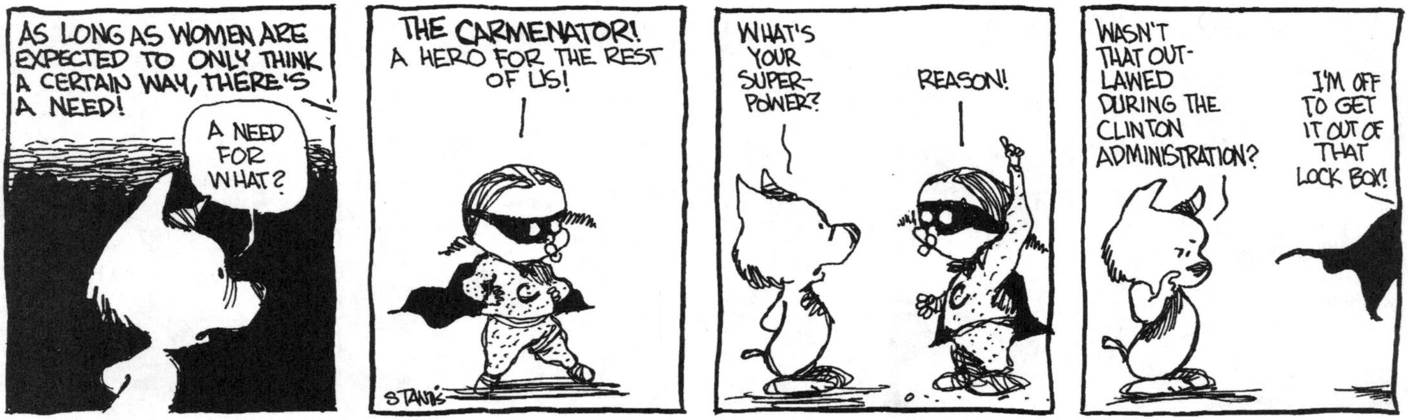
AS LONG AS WOMEN ARE EXPECTED TO ONLY THINK A CERTAIN WAY, THERE'S A NEED!
A NEED FOR WHAT?
THE CARMENATOR! A HERO FOR THE REST OF US!
STANIS
WHAT'S YOUR SUPER-POWER?
REASON!
WASN'T THAT OUT-LAWED DURING THE CLINTON ADMINISTRATION?
I'M OFF TO GET IT OUT OF THAT LOCK BOX!

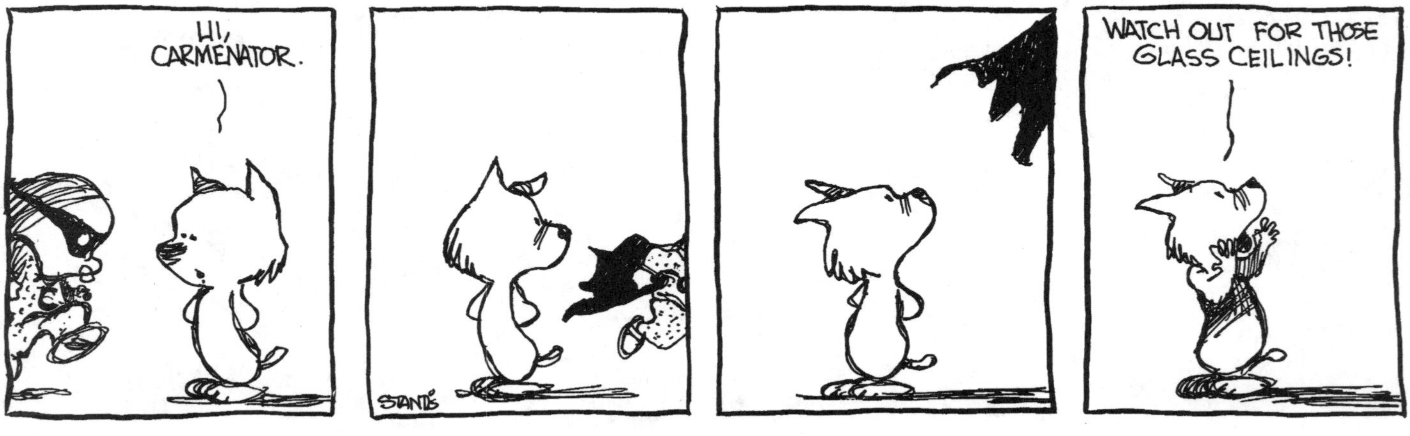
HI, CARMENATOR.
STANIS
WATCH OUT FOR THOSE GLASS CEILINGS!

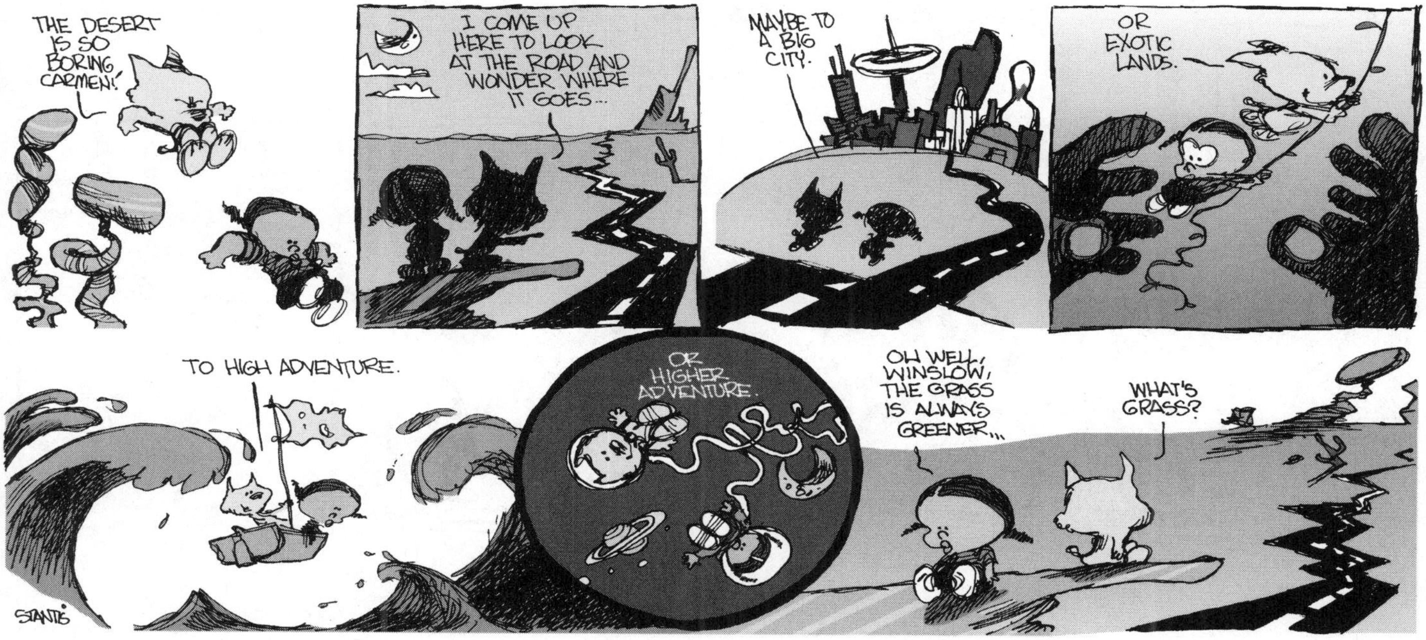
THE DESERT IS SO BORING, CARMEN!
I COME UP HERE TO LOOK AT THE ROAD AND WONDER WHERE IT GOES...
MAYBE TO A BIG CITY.
OR EXOTIC LANDS.
TO HIGH ADVENTURE.
OR HIGHER ADVENTURE.
OH WELL, WINSLOW, THE GRASS IS ALWAYS GREENER...
WHAT'S GRASS?
STANTIS

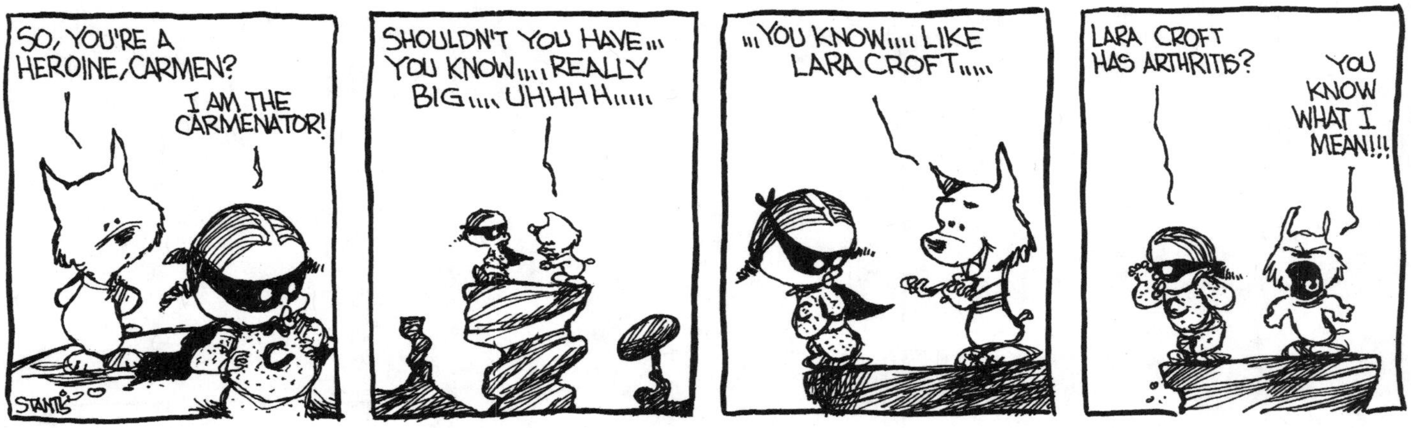
SO, YOU'RE A HEROINE, CARMEN?
I AM THE CARMENATOR!
STANTIS
SHOULDN'T YOU HAVE... YOU KNOW... REALLY BIG... UHHHH...
...YOU KNOW... LIKE LARA CROFT...
LARA CROFT HAS ARTHRITIS?
YOU KNOW WHAT I MEAN!!!

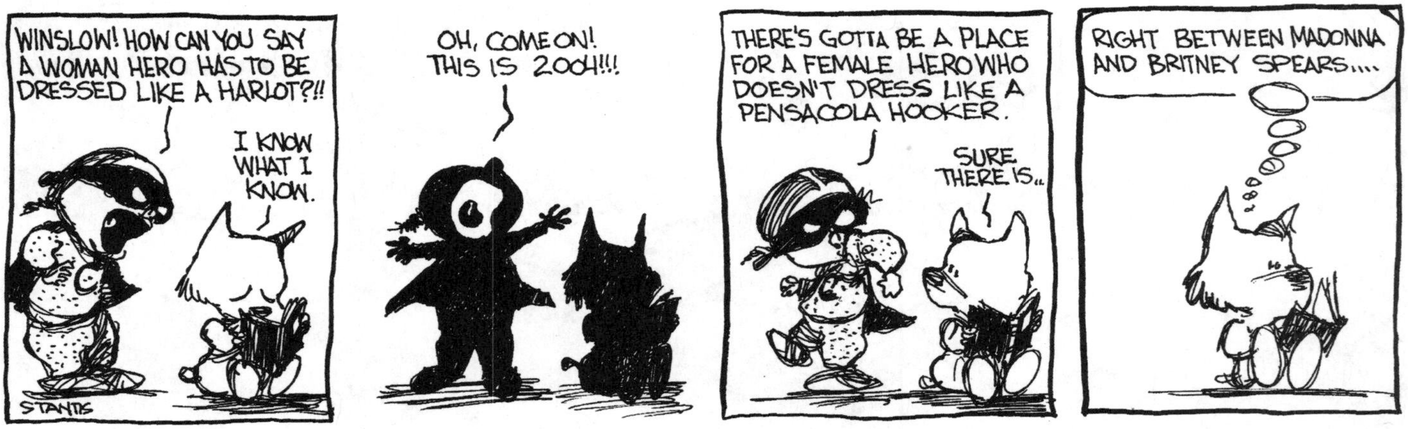
WINSLOW! HOW CAN YOU SAY A WOMAN HERO HAS TO BE DRESSED LIKE A HARLOT?!!
I KNOW WHAT I KNOW.
STANTIS
OH, COME ON! THIS IS 2004!!!
THERE'S GOTTA BE A PLACE FOR A FEMALE HERO WHO DOESN'T DRESS LIKE A PENSACOLA HOOKER.
SURE THERE IS...
RIGHT BETWEEN MADONNA AND BRITNEY SPEARS....

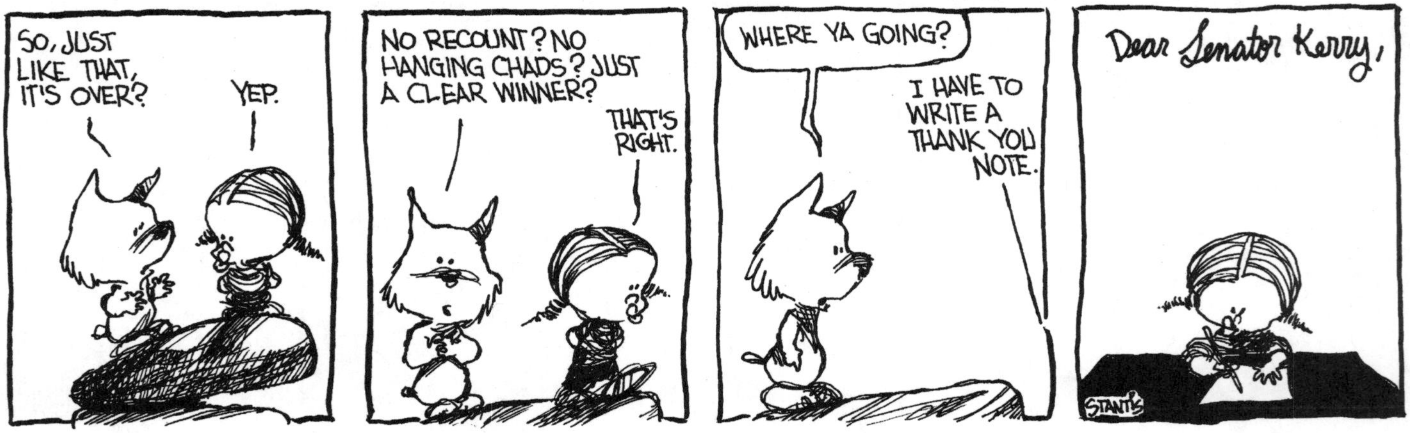
SO, JUST LIKE THAT, IT'S OVER?
YEP.
NO RECOUNT? NO HANGING CHADS? JUST A CLEAR WINNER?
THAT'S RIGHT.
WHERE YA GOING?
I HAVE TO WRITE A THANK YOU NOTE.
Dear Senator Kerry,
STANTIS

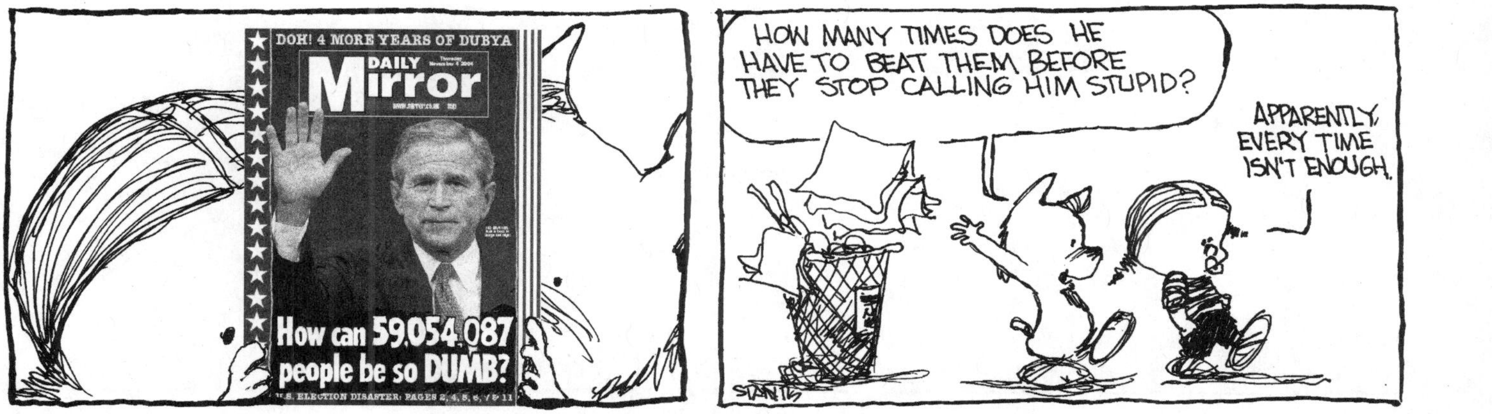
DOH! 4 MORE YEARS OF DUBYA
DAILY Mirror
How can 59,054,087 people be so DUMB?
U.S. ELECTION DISASTER: PAGES 2, 4, 5, 6, 7 & 11
HOW MANY TIMES DOES HE HAVE TO BEAT THEM BEFORE THEY STOP CALLING HIM STUPID?
APPARENTLY, EVERY TIME ISN'T ENOUGH.
STANTIS

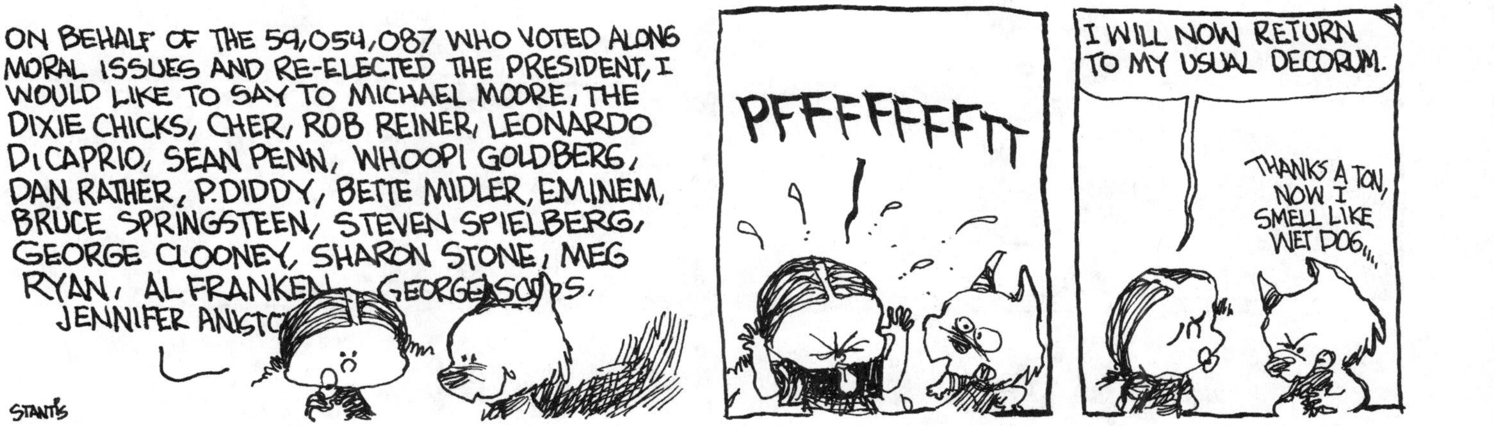
ON BEHALF OF THE 59,054,087 WHO VOTED ALONG MORAL ISSUES AND RE-ELECTED THE PRESIDENT, I WOULD LIKE TO SAY TO MICHAEL MOORE, THE DIXIE CHICKS, CHER, ROB REINER, LEONARDO DiCAPRIO, SEAN PENN, WHOOPI GOLDBERG, DAN RATHER, P.DIDDY, BETTE MIDLER, EMINEM, BRUCE SPRINGSTEEN, STEVEN SPIELBERG, GEORGE CLOONEY, SHARON STONE, MEG RYAN, AL FRANKEN, GEORGE SO S. JENNIFER ANIST
STANTIS
PFFFFFFFFTT
I WILL NOW RETURN TO MY USUAL DECORUM.
THANKS A TON, NOW I SMELL LIKE WET DOG...

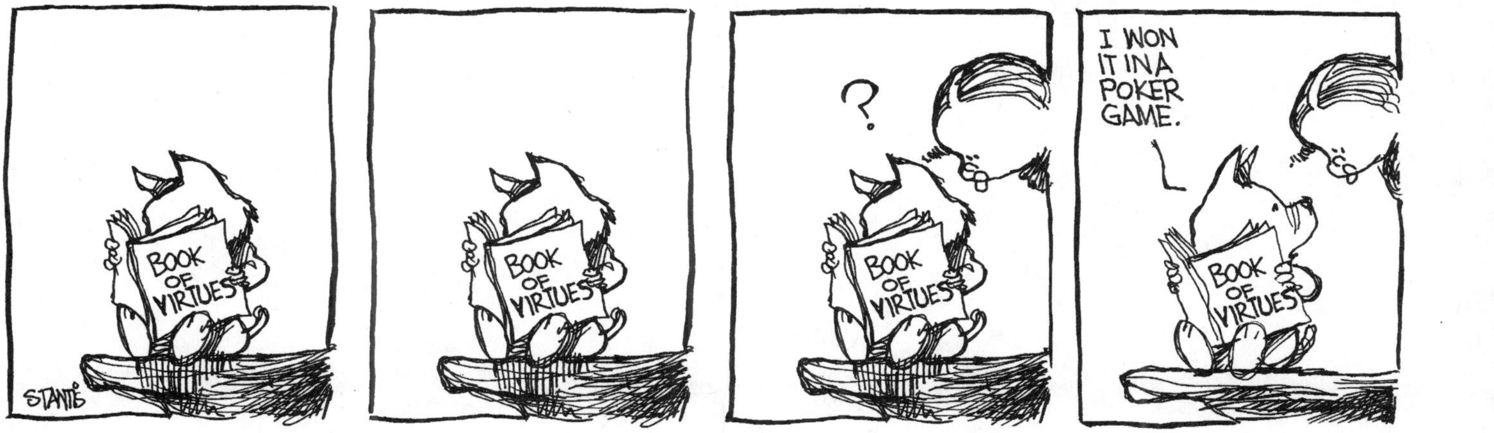
BOOK OF VIRTUES
STANTIS
BOOK OF VIRTUES
?
BOOK OF VIRTUES
I WON IT IN A POKER GAME.
BOOK OF VIRTUES

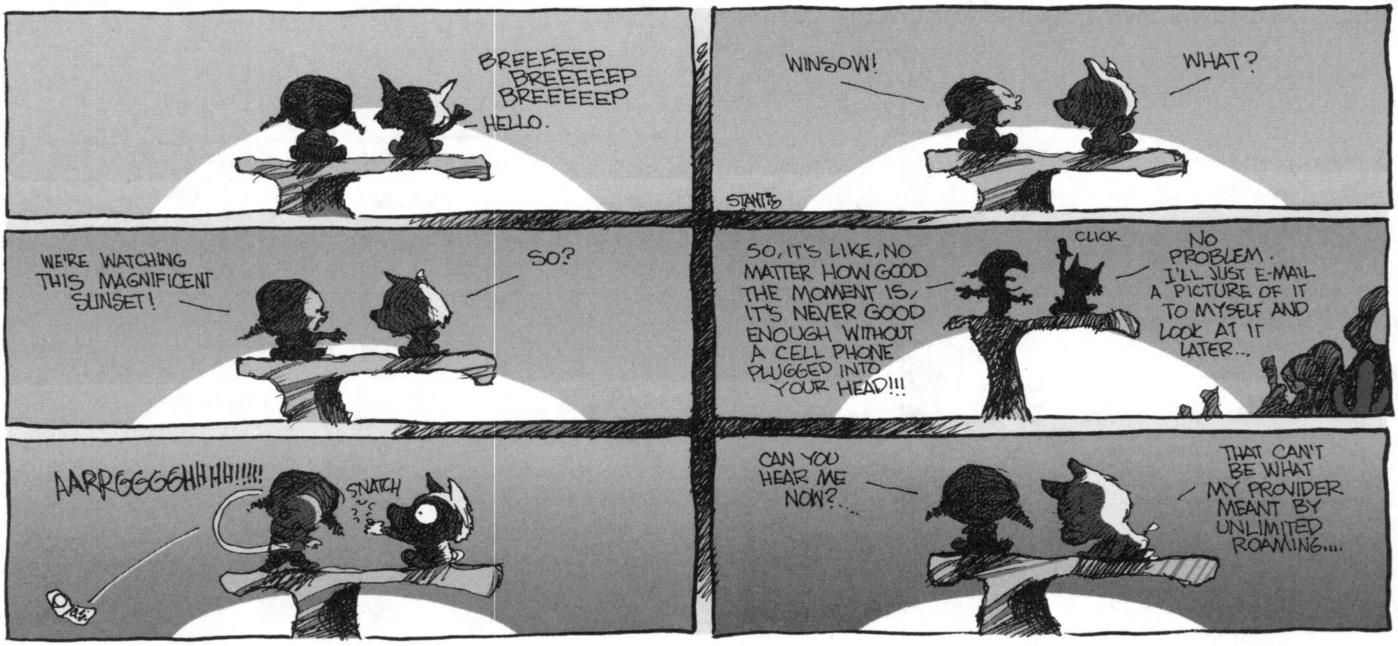

BREEEEEP BREEEEEEP BREEEEEEP
HELLO.
WINSOW!
WHAT?
STANTIS
WE'RE WATCHING THIS MAGNIFICENT SUNSET!
SO?
CLICK
SO, IT'S LIKE, NO MATTER HOW GOOD THE MOMENT IS, IT'S NEVER GOOD ENOUGH WITHOUT A CELL PHONE PLUGGED INTO YOUR HEAD!!!
NO PROBLEM. I'LL JUST E-MAIL A PICTURE OF IT TO MYSELF AND LOOK AT IT LATER...
AARRGGGGHHHHH!!!!!
SNATCH
CAN YOU HEAR ME NOW?...
THAT CAN'T BE WHAT MY PROVIDER MEANT BY UNLIMITED ROAMING....

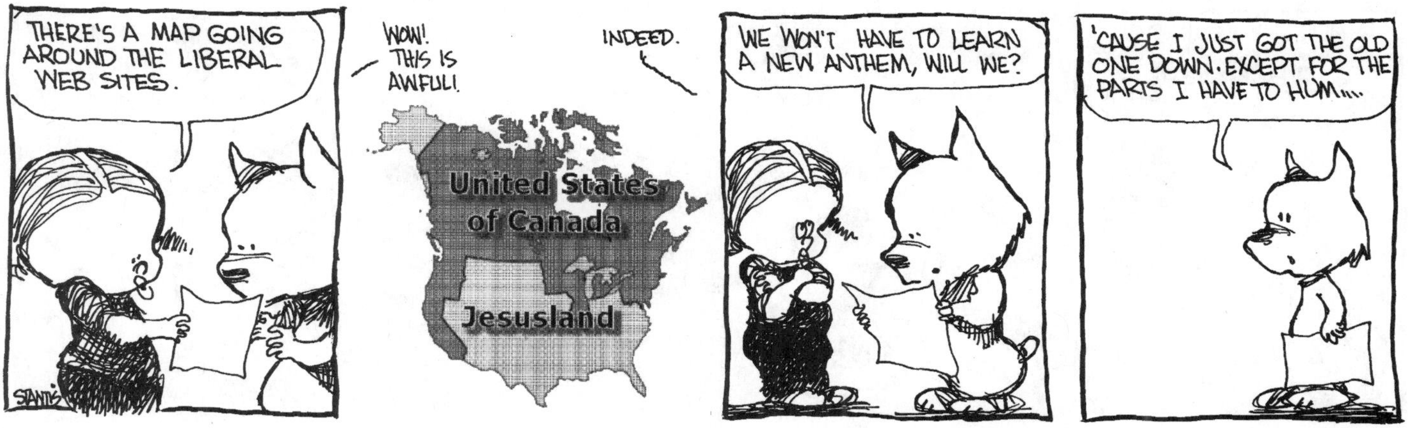
THERE'S A MAP GOING AROUND THE LIBERAL WEB SITES.
WOW! THIS IS AWFUL!
INDEED.
United States of Canada
Jesusland
WE WON'T HAVE TO LEARN A NEW ANTHEM, WILL WE?
'CAUSE I JUST GOT THE OLD ONE DOWN. EXCEPT FOR THE PARTS I HAVE TO HUM...
STANTIS

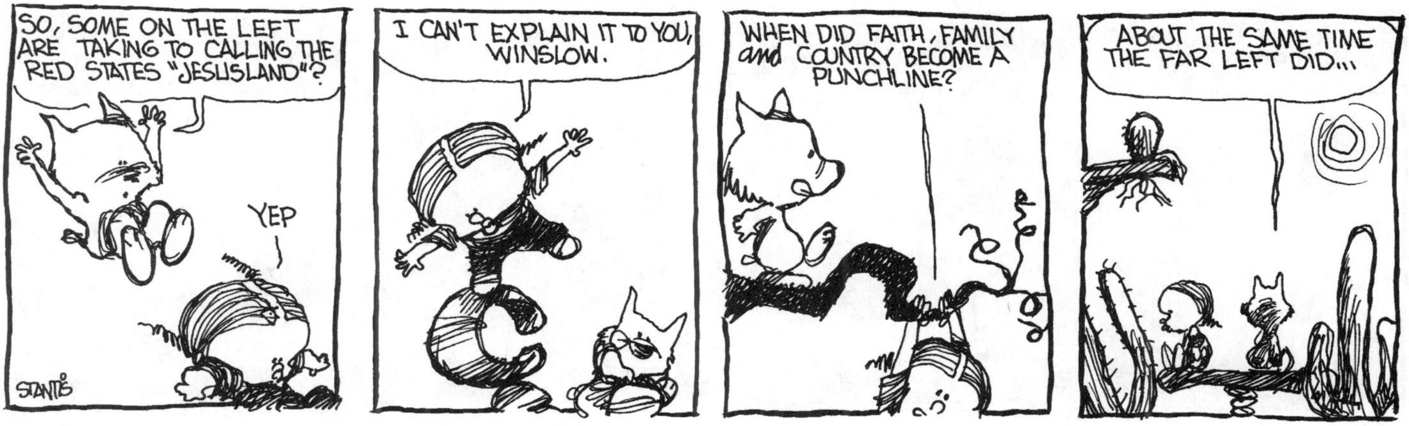
SO, SOME ON THE LEFT ARE TAKING TO CALLING THE RED STATES "JESUSLAND"?
YEP
I CAN'T EXPLAIN IT TO YOU, WINSLOW.
WHEN DID FAITH, FAMILY and COUNTRY BECOME A PUNCHLINE?
ABOUT THE SAME TIME THE FAR LEFT DID...
STANTIS

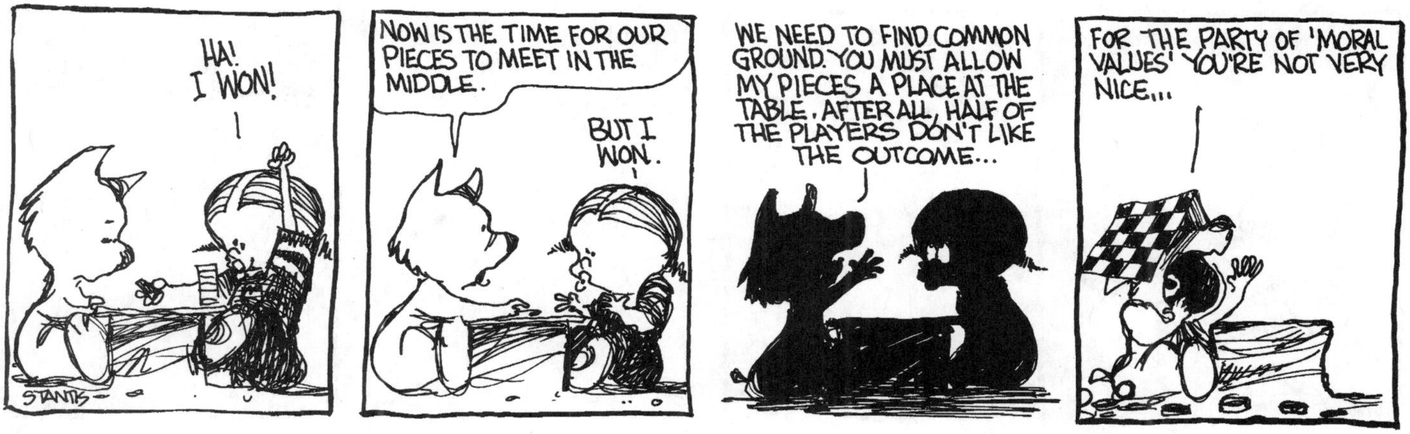
HA! I WON!
NOW IS THE TIME FOR OUR PIECES TO MEET IN THE MIDDLE.
BUT I WON.
WE NEED TO FIND COMMON GROUND. YOU MUST ALLOW MY PIECES A PLACE AT THE TABLE. AFTER ALL, HALF OF THE PLAYERS DON'T LIKE THE OUTCOME...
FOR THE PARTY OF 'MORAL VALUES' YOU'RE NOT VERY NICE...
STANTIS

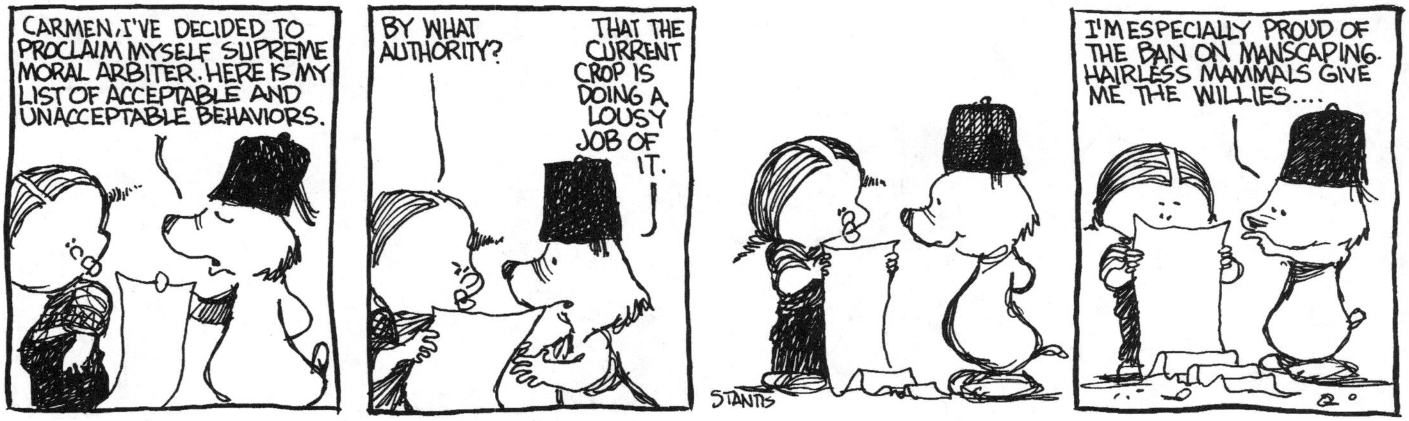
CARMEN, I'VE DECIDED TO PROCLAIM MYSELF SUPREME MORAL ARBITER. HERE IS MY LIST OF ACCEPTABLE AND UNACCEPTABLE BEHAVIORS.
BY WHAT AUTHORITY?
THAT THE CURRENT CROP IS DOING A LOUSY JOB OF IT.
STANTIS
I'M ESPECIALLY PROUD OF THE BAN ON MANSCAPING. HAIRLESS MAMMALS GIVE ME THE WILLIES....

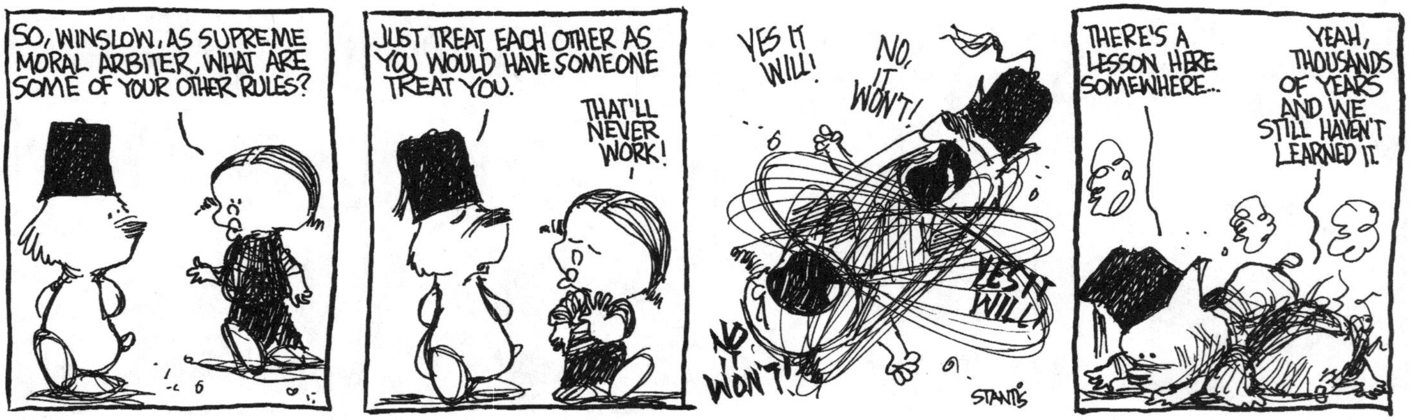
SO, WINSLOW, AS SUPREME MORAL ARBITER, WHAT ARE SOME OF YOUR OTHER RULES?
JUST TREAT EACH OTHER AS YOU WOULD HAVE SOMEONE TREAT YOU.
THAT'LL NEVER WORK!
YES IT WILL!
NO, IT WON'T!
YES IT WILL
NO IT WON'T!
STANTIS
THERE'S A LESSON HERE SOMEWHERE...
YEAH, THOUSANDS OF YEARS AND WE STILL HAVEN'T LEARNED IT.

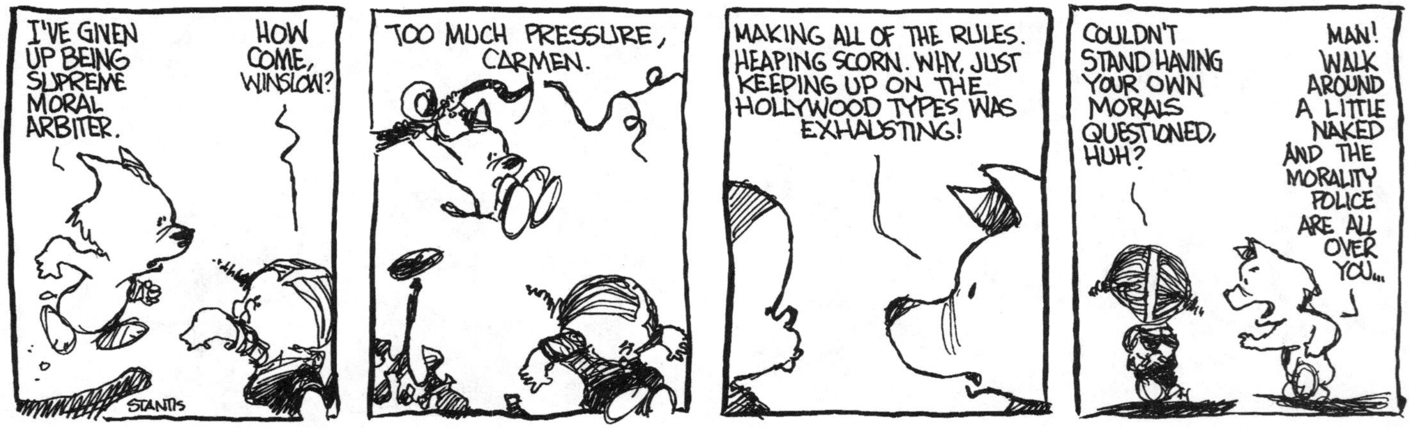
I'VE GIVEN UP BEING SUPREME MORAL ARBITER.
HOW COME, WINSLOW?
STANTIS
TOO MUCH PRESSURE, CARMEN.
MAKING ALL OF THE RULES. HEAPING SCORN. WHY, JUST KEEPING UP ON THE HOLLYWOOD TYPES WAS EXHAUSTING!
COULDN'T STAND HAVING YOUR OWN MORALS QUESTIONED, HUH?
MAN! WALK AROUND A LITTLE NAKED AND THE MORALITY POLICE ARE ALL OVER YOU...

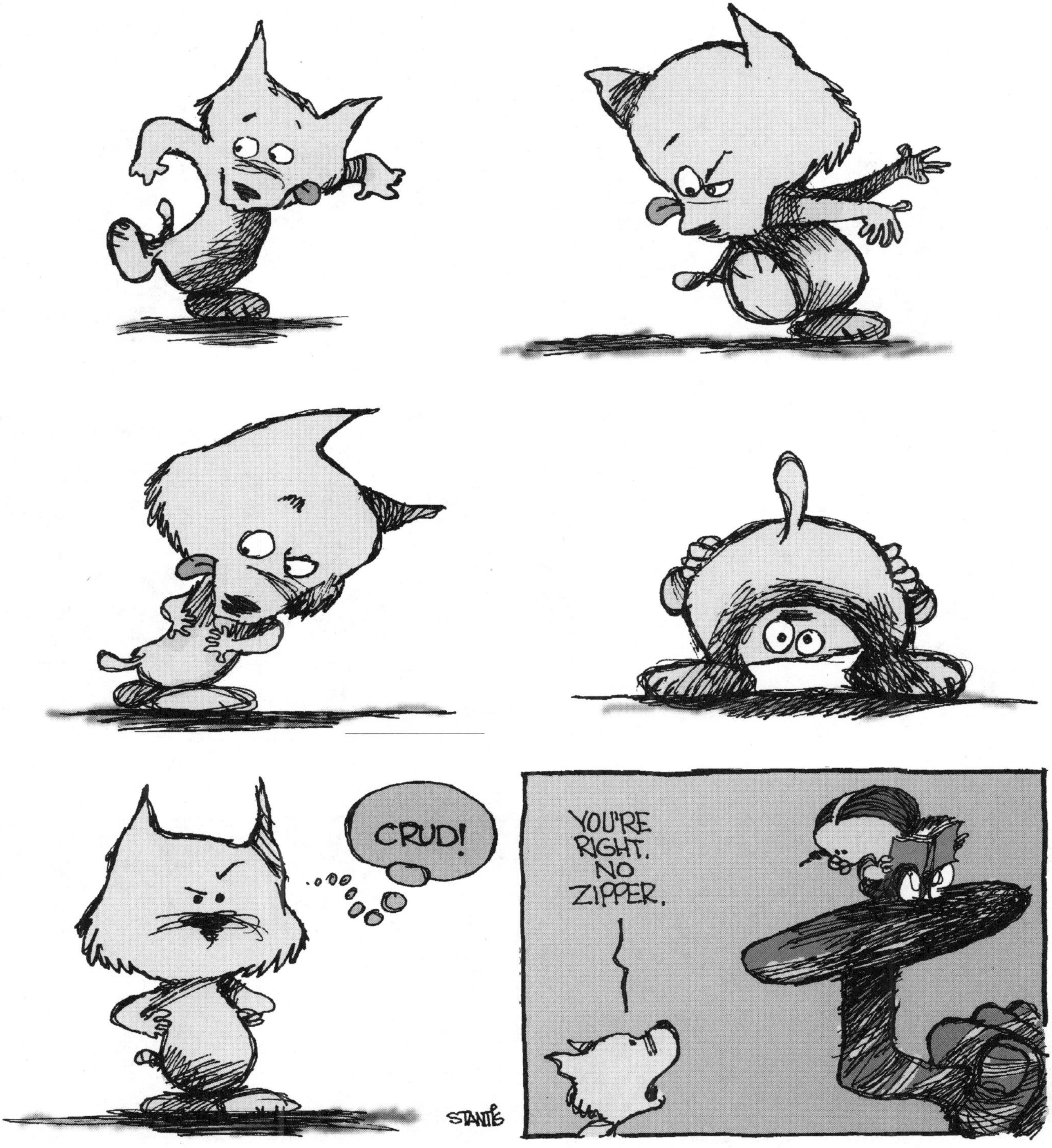
CRUD!
YOU'RE RIGHT. NO ZIPPER.
STANTIS

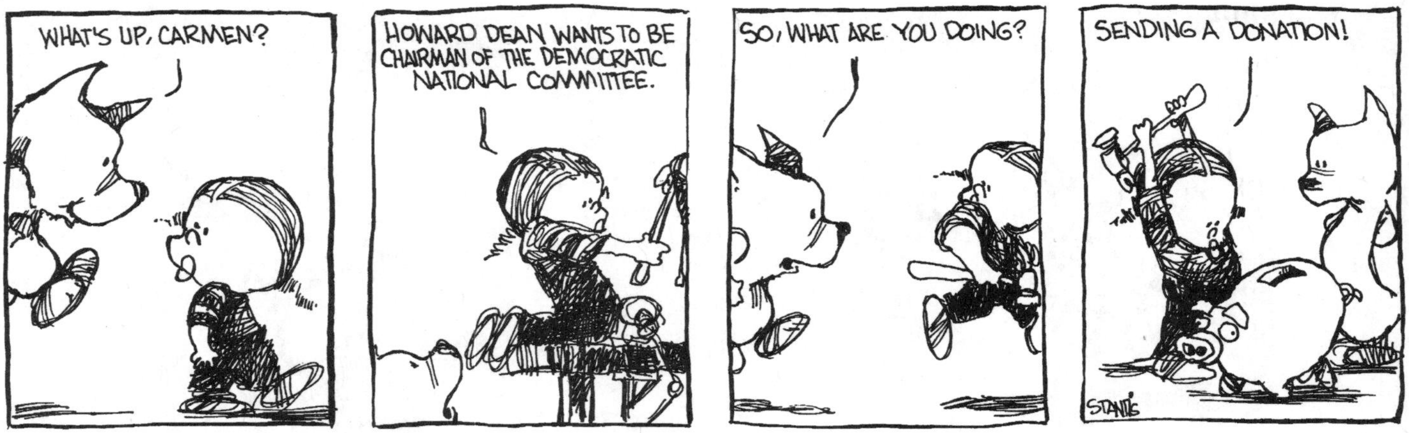
WHAT'S UP, CARMEN?
HOWARD DEAN WANTS TO BE CHAIRMAN OF THE DEMOCRATIC NATIONAL COMMITTEE.
SO, WHAT ARE YOU DOING?
SENDING A DONATION!
STANTIS

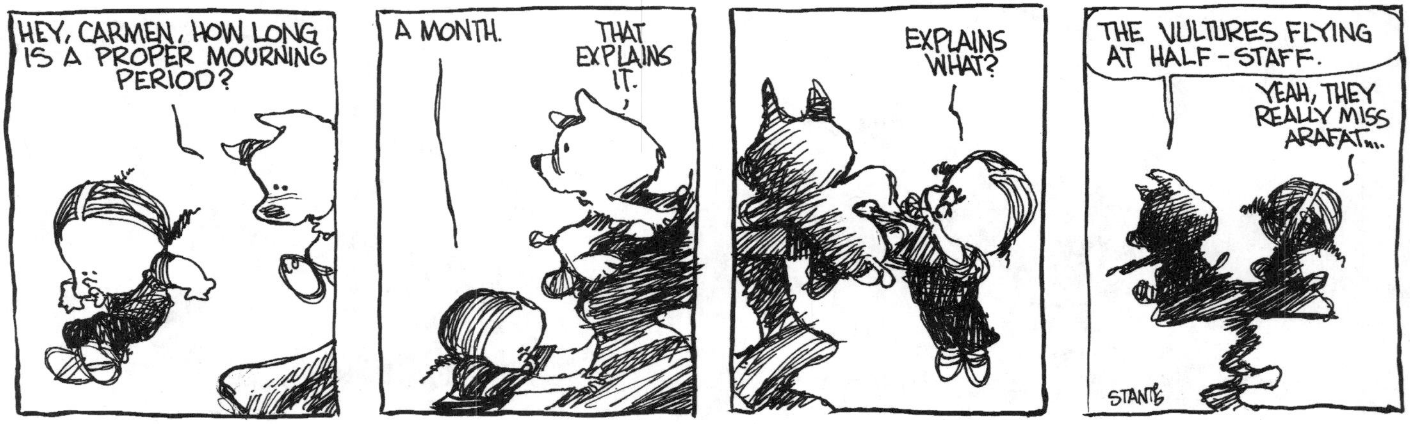
HEY, CARMEN, HOW LONG IS A PROPER MOURNING PERIOD?
A MONTH.
THAT EXPLAINS IT.
EXPLAINS WHAT?
THE VULTURES FLYING AT HALF-STAFF.
YEAH, THEY REALLY MISS ARAFAT...
STANTIS

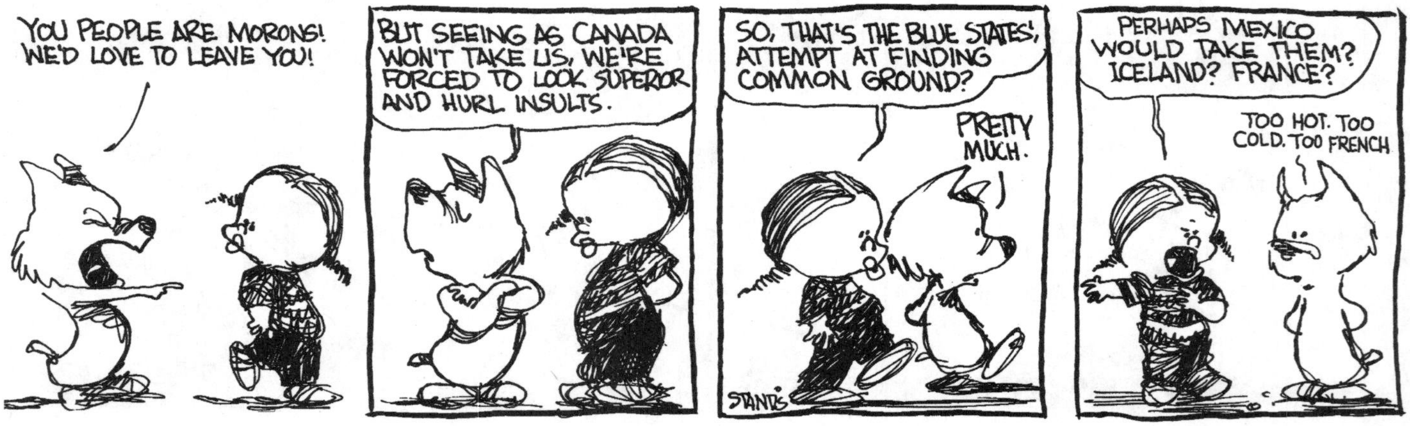
YOU PEOPLE ARE MORONS! WE'D LOVE TO LEAVE YOU!
BUT SEEING AS CANADA WON'T TAKE US, WE'RE FORCED TO LOOK SUPERIOR AND HURL INSULTS.
SO, THAT'S THE BLUE STATES' ATTEMPT AT FINDING COMMON GROUND?
PRETTY MUCH.
STANTIS
PERHAPS MEXICO WOULD TAKE THEM? ICELAND? FRANCE?
TOO HOT. TOO COLD. TOO FRENCH

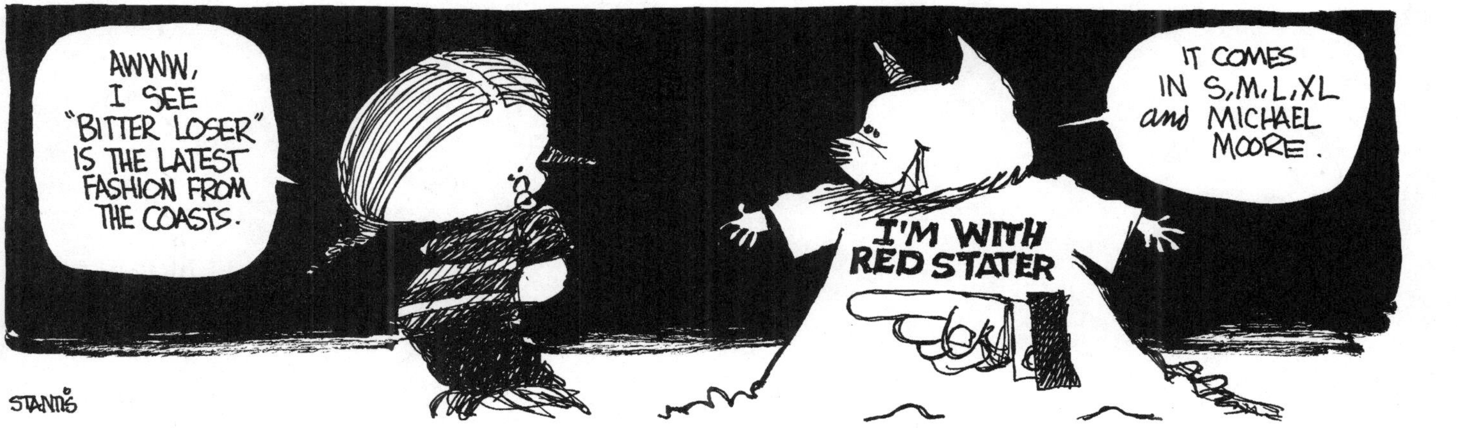

AWWW, I SEE "BITTER LOSER" IS THE LATEST FASHION FROM THE COASTS.
IT COMES IN S,M,L,XL and MICHAEL MOORE.
I'M WITH RED STATER
STANTIS

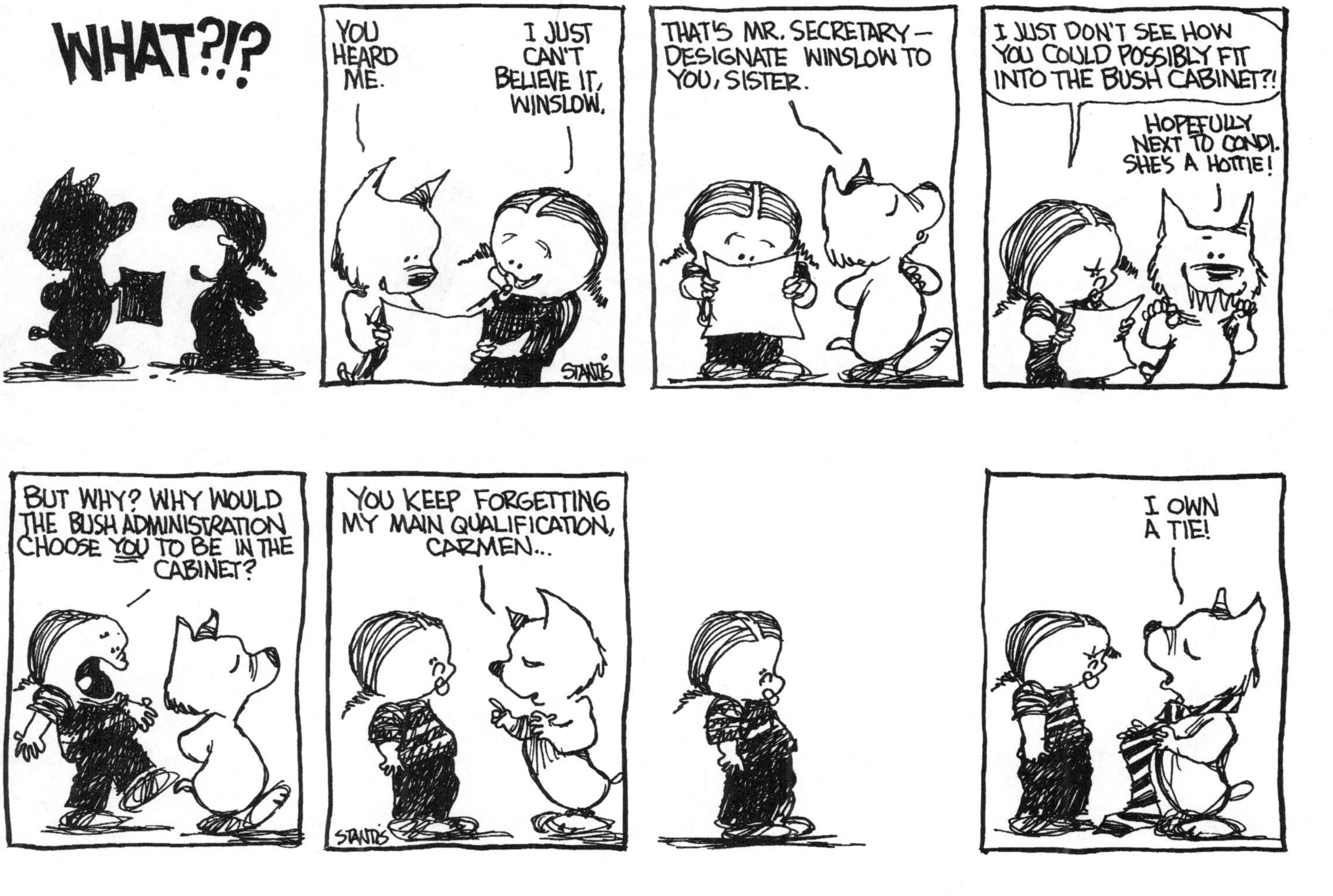

WHAT?!?
YOU HEARD ME.
I JUST CAN'T BELIEVE IT, WINSLOW.
STANTIS
THAT'S MR. SECRETARY-DESIGNATE WINSLOW TO YOU, SISTER.
I JUST DON'T SEE HOW YOU COULD POSSIBLY FIT INTO THE BUSH CABINET?!
HOPEFULLY NEXT TO CONDI. SHE'S A HOTTIE!
BUT WHY? WHY WOULD THE BUSH ADMINISTRATION CHOOSE YOU TO BE IN THE CABINET?
YOU KEEP FORGETTING MY MAIN QUALIFICATION, CARMEN...
STANTIS
I OWN A TIE!

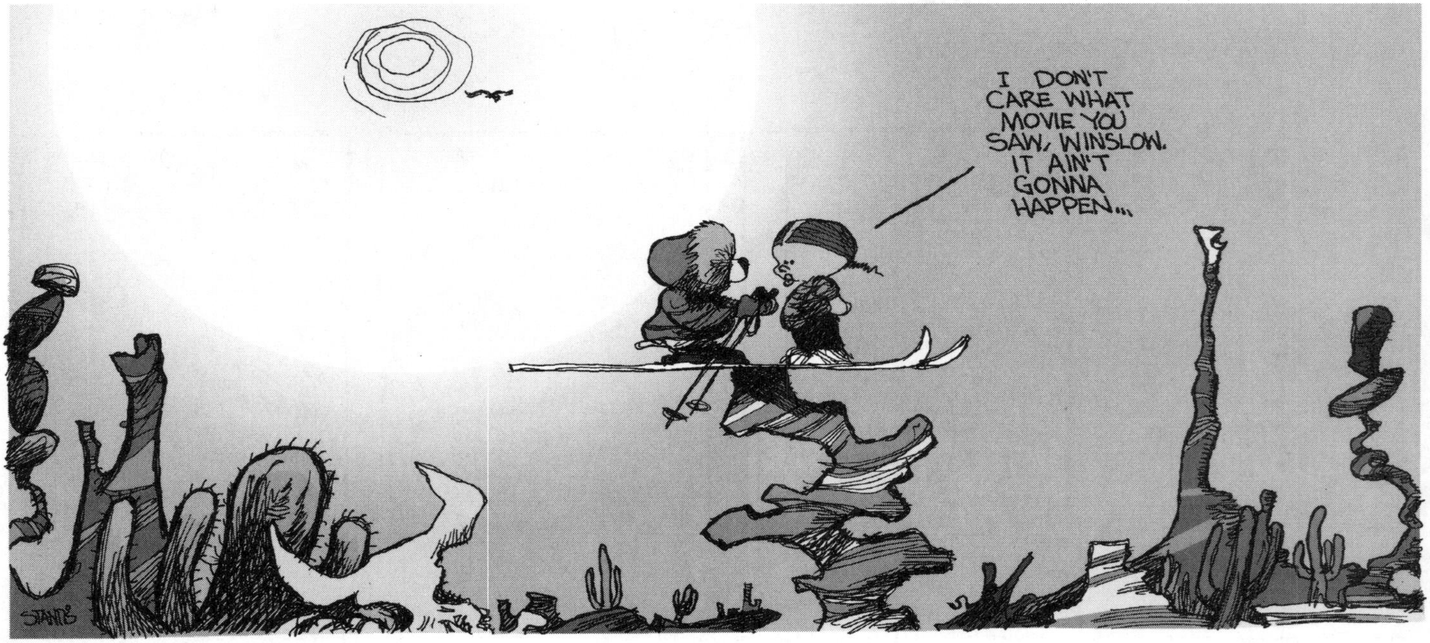
I DON'T CARE WHAT MOVIE YOU SAW, WINSLOW. IT AIN'T GONNA HAPPEN...

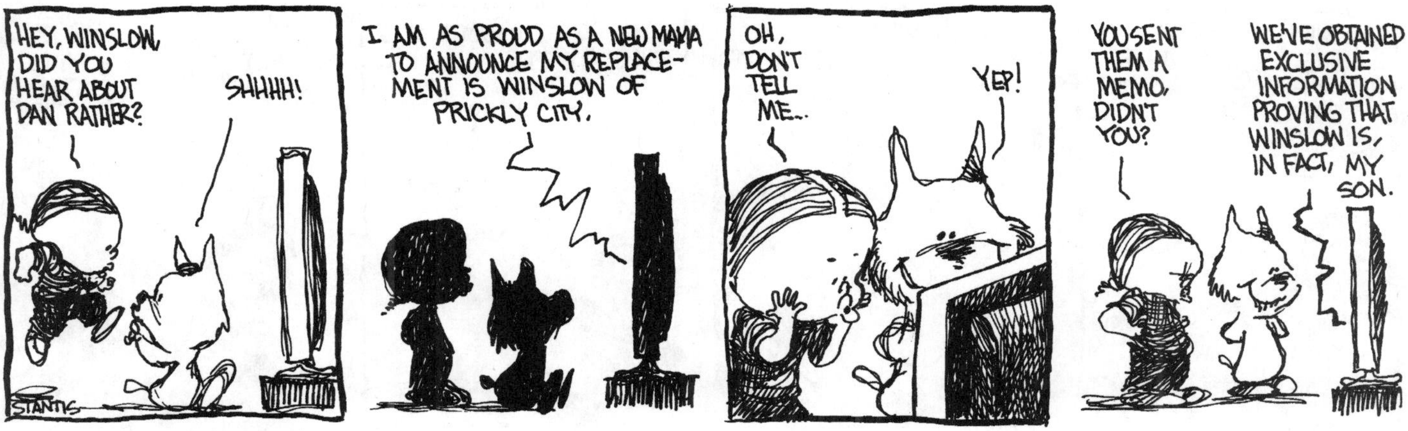
HEY, WINSLOW, DID YOU HEAR ABOUT DAN RATHER?
SHHHH!
I AM AS PROUD AS A NEW MAMA TO ANNOUNCE MY REPLACEMENT IS WINSLOW OF PRICKLY CITY.
OH, DON'T TELL ME...
YEP!
YOU SENT THEM A MEMO, DIDN'T YOU?
WE'VE OBTAINED EXCLUSIVE INFORMATION PROVING THAT WINSLOW IS, IN FACT, MY SON.
STANTIS

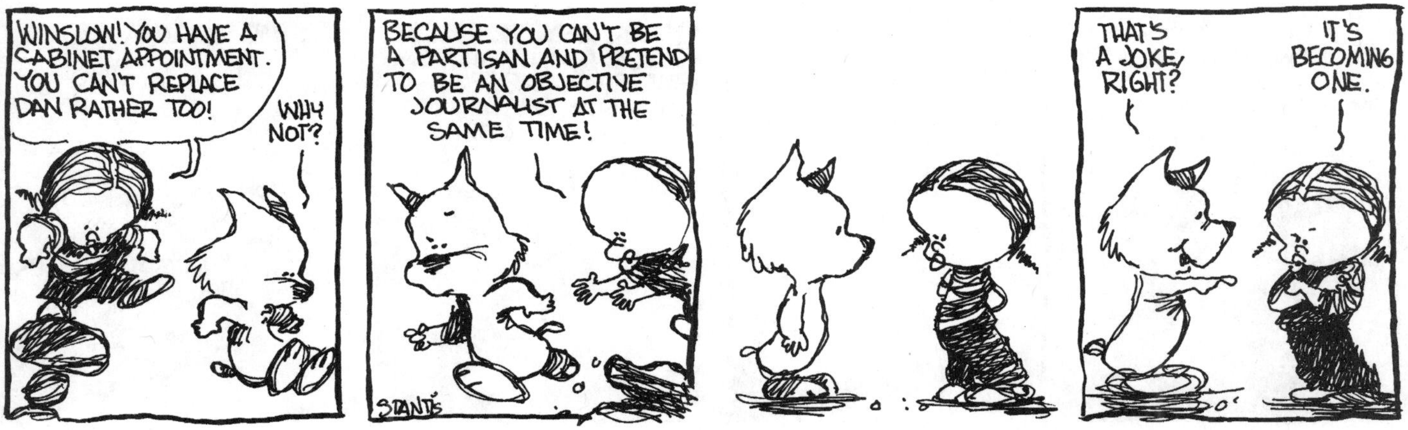
WINSLOW! YOU HAVE A CABINET APPOINTMENT. YOU CAN'T REPLACE DAN RATHER TOO!
WHY NOT?
BECAUSE YOU CAN'T BE A PARTISAN AND PRETEND TO BE AN OBJECTIVE JOURNALIST AT THE SAME TIME!
THAT'S A JOKE, RIGHT?
IT'S BECOMING ONE.
STANTIS

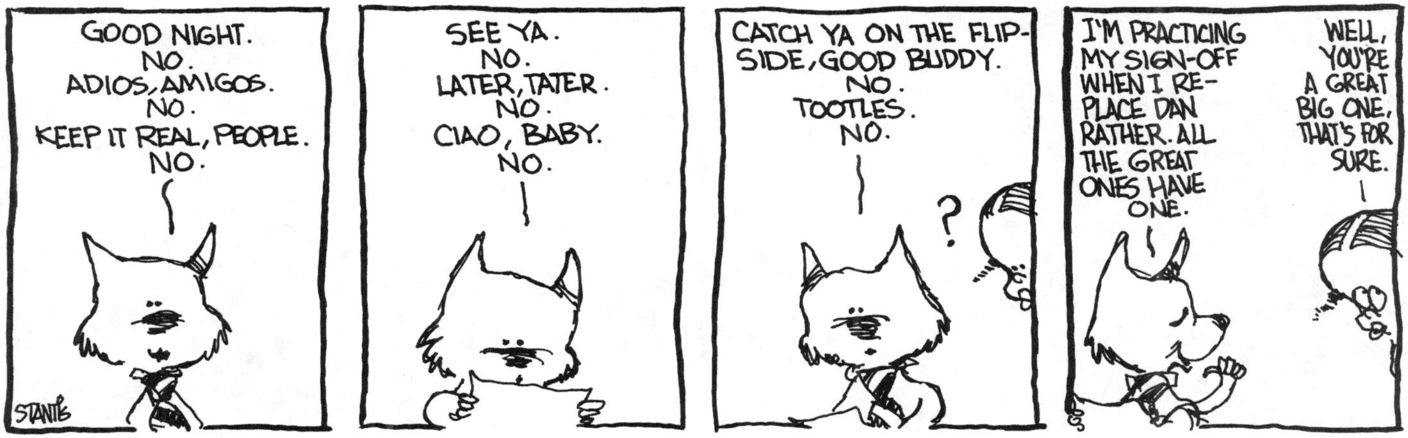
GOOD NIGHT. NO. ADIOS, AMIGOS. NO. KEEP IT REAL, PEOPLE. NO.
SEE YA. NO. LATER, TATER. NO. CIAO, BABY. NO.
CATCH YA ON THE FLIP-SIDE, GOOD BUDDY. NO. TOOTLES. NO.
?
I'M PRACTICING MY SIGN-OFF WHEN I REPLACE DAN RATHER. ALL THE GREAT ONES HAVE ONE.
WELL, YOU'RE A GREAT BIG ONE, THAT'S FOR SURE.
STANTIS

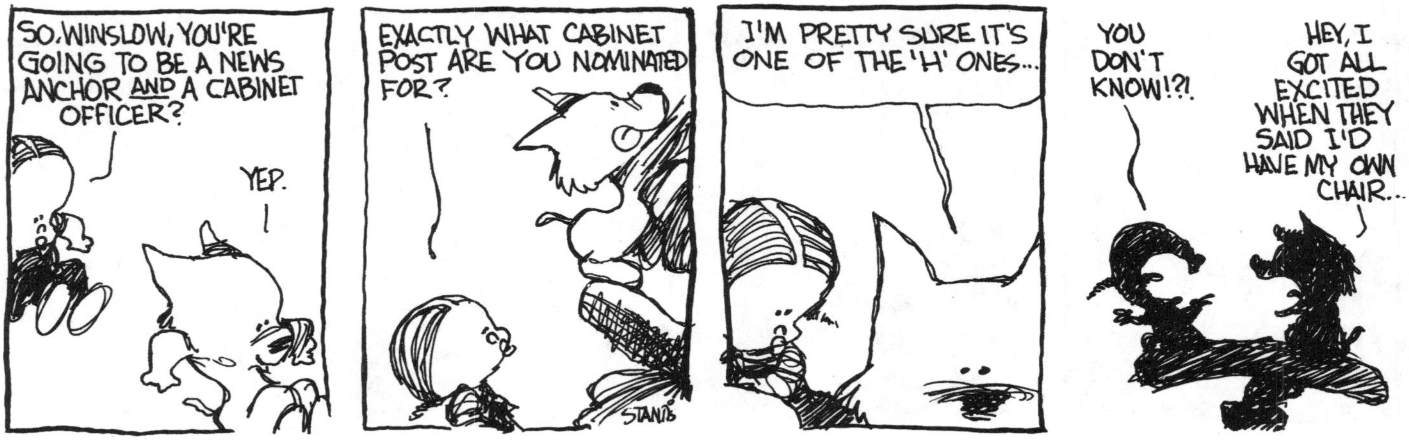
SO, WINSLOW, YOU'RE GOING TO BE A NEWS ANCHOR AND A CABINET OFFICER?
YEP.
EXACTLY WHAT CABINET POST ARE YOU NOMINATED FOR?
I'M PRETTY SURE IT'S ONE OF THE 'H' ONES...
YOU DON'T KNOW!?!
HEY, I GOT ALL EXCITED WHEN THEY SAID I'D HAVE MY OWN CHAIR...
STANTIS

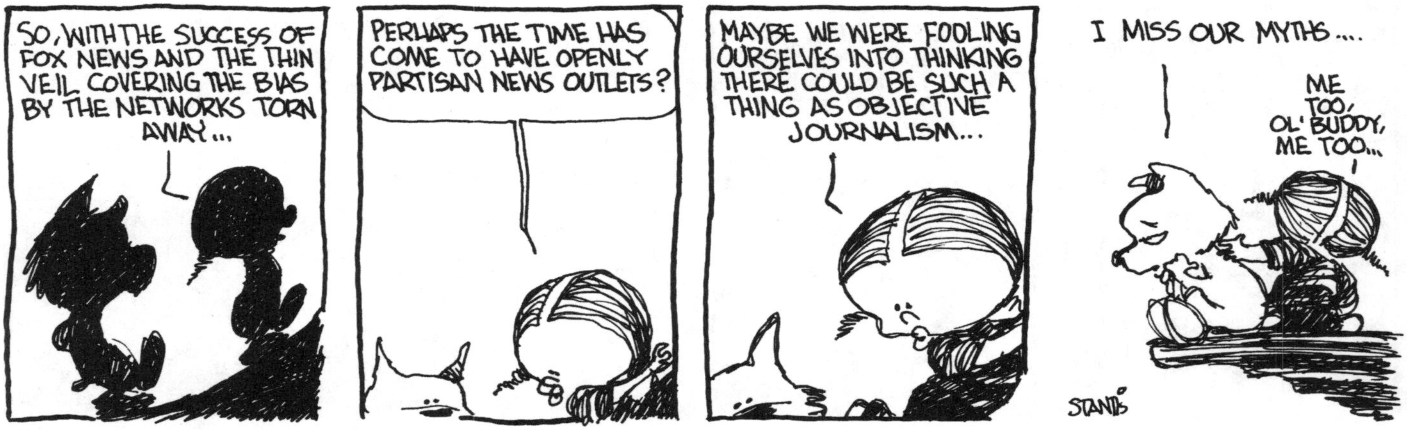
SO, WITH THE SUCCESS OF FOX NEWS AND THE THIN VEIL COVERING THE BIAS BY THE NETWORKS TORN AWAY...
PERHAPS THE TIME HAS COME TO HAVE OPENLY PARTISAN NEWS OUTLETS?
MAYBE WE WERE FOOLING OURSELVES INTO THINKING THERE COULD BE SUCH A THING AS OBJECTIVE JOURNALISM...
I MISS OUR MYTHS....
ME TOO, OL' BUDDY, ME TOO...
STANTIS

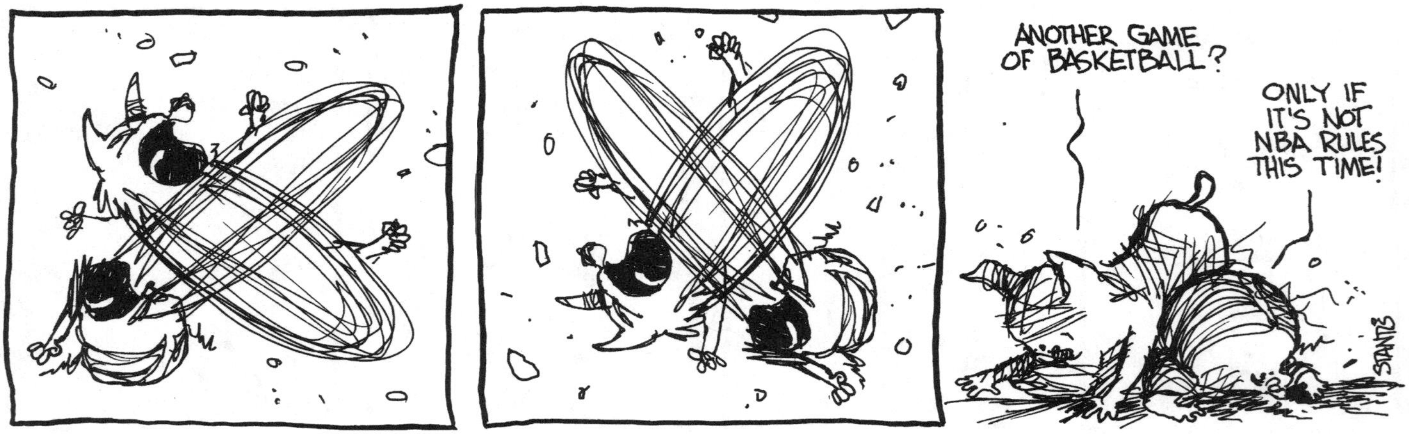
ANOTHER GAME OF BASKETBALL?
ONLY IF IT'S NOT NBA RULES THIS TIME!
STANTIS

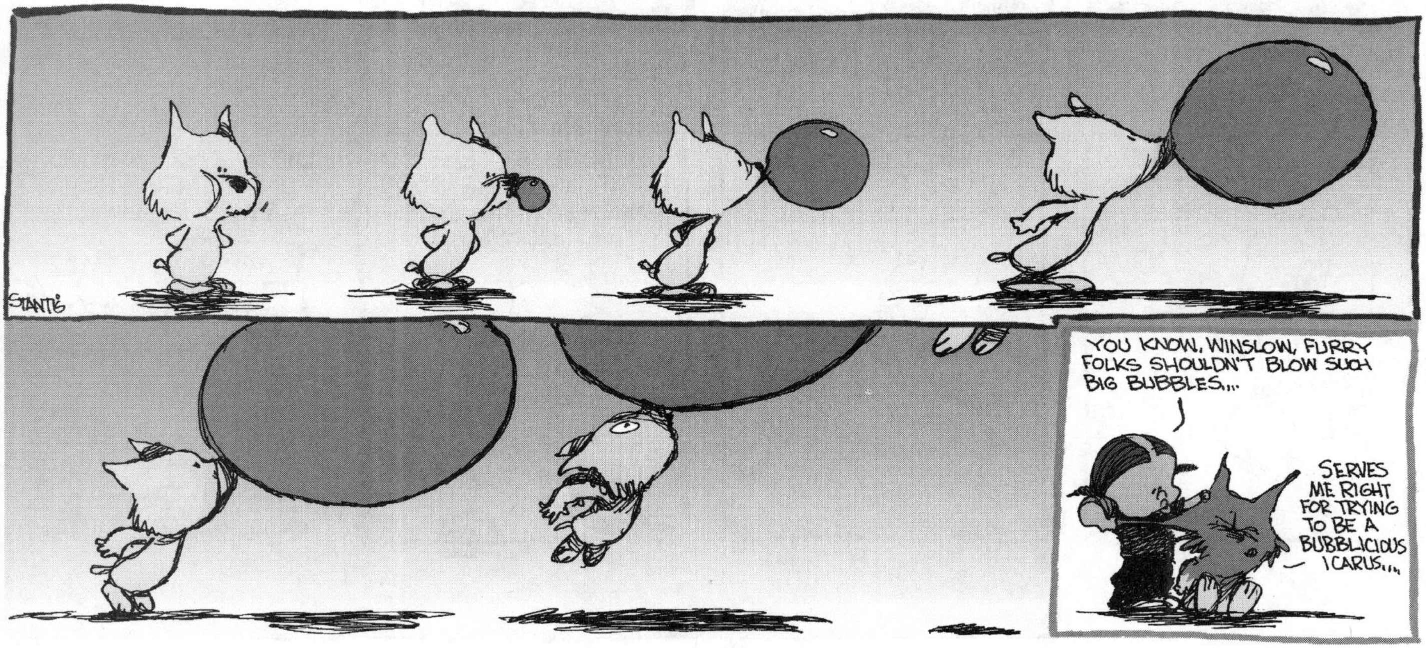
STANTIS
YOU KNOW, WINSLOW, FURRY FOLKS SHOULDN'T BLOW SUCH BIG BUBBLES...
SERVES ME RIGHT FOR TRYING TO BE A BUBBLICIOUS ICARUS...

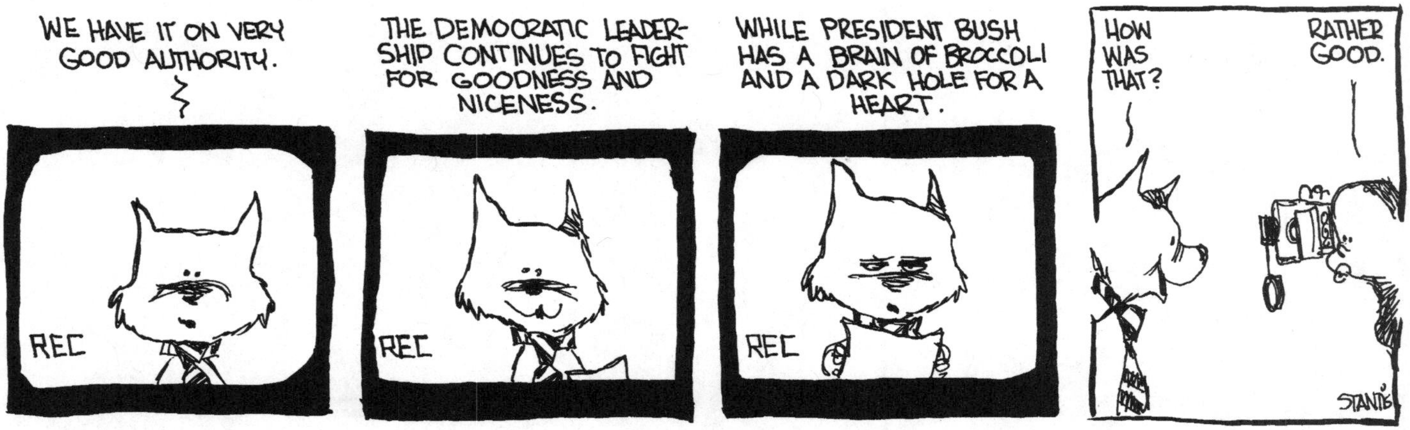
WE HAVE IT ON VERY GOOD AUTHORITY.
REC
THE DEMOCRATIC LEADERSHIP CONTINUES TO FIGHT FOR GOODNESS AND NICENESS.
REC
WHILE PRESIDENT BUSH HAS A BRAIN OF BROCCOLI AND A DARK HOLE FOR A HEART.
REC
HOW WAS THAT?
RATHER GOOD.
STANTIS

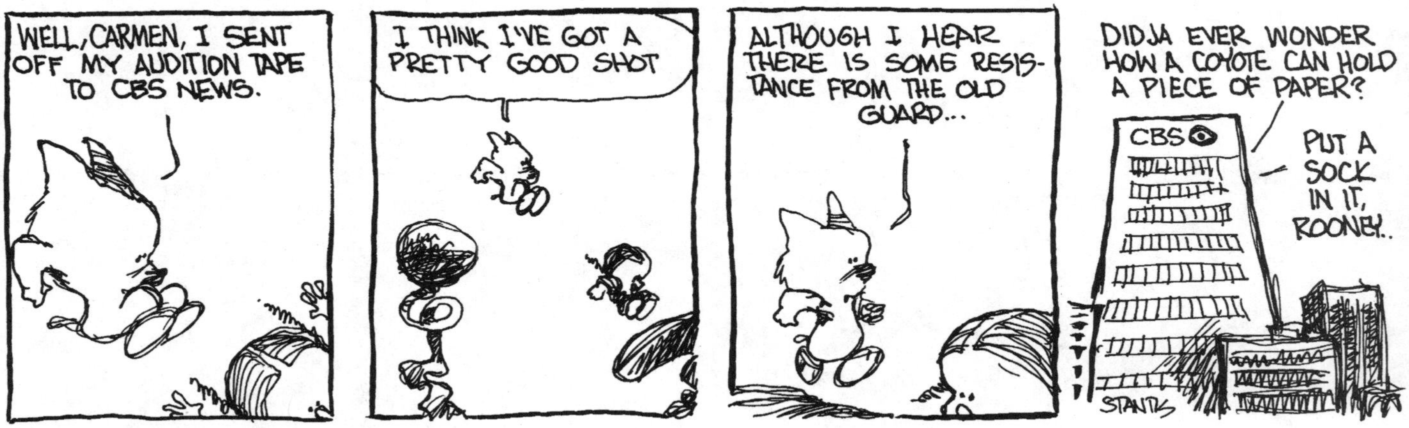
WELL, CARMEN, I SENT OFF MY AUDITION TAPE TO CBS NEWS.
I THINK I'VE GOT A PRETTY GOOD SHOT
ALTHOUGH I HEAR THERE IS SOME RESISTANCE FROM THE OLD GUARD...
DIDJA EVER WONDER HOW A COYOTE CAN HOLD A PIECE OF PAPER?
CBS
PUT A SOCK IN IT, ROONEY..
STANTIS

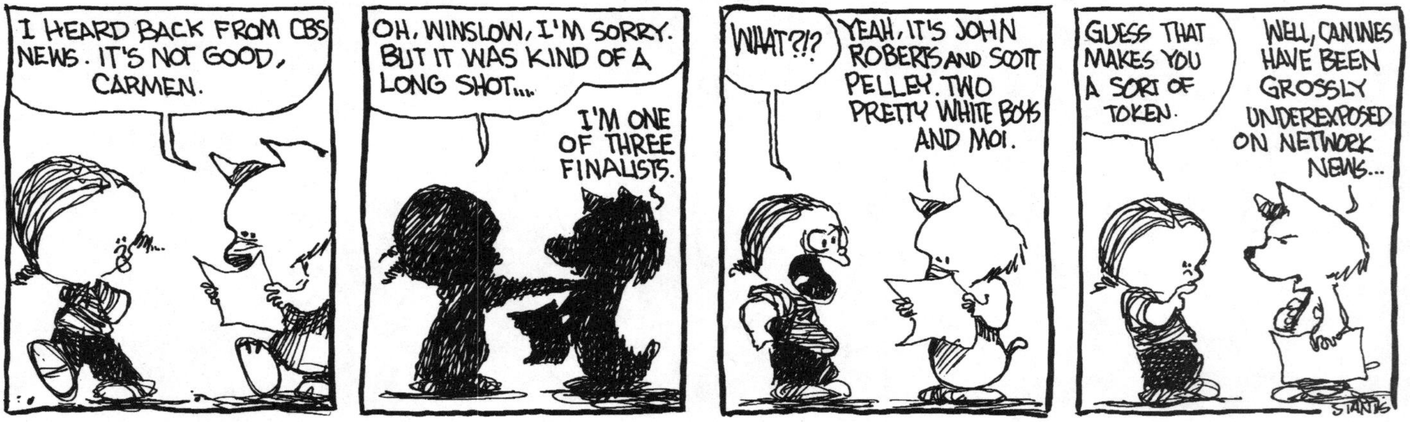
I HEARD BACK FROM CBS NEWS. IT'S NOT GOOD, CARMEN.
OH, WINSLOW, I'M SORRY. BUT IT WAS KIND OF A LONG SHOT...
I'M ONE OF THREE FINALISTS.
WHAT?!?
YEAH, IT'S JOHN ROBERTS AND SCOTT PELLEY. TWO PRETTY WHITE BOYS AND MOI.
GUESS THAT MAKES YOU A SORT OF TOKEN.
WELL, CANINES HAVE BEEN GROSSLY UNDEREXPOSED ON NETWORK NEWS...
STANTIS

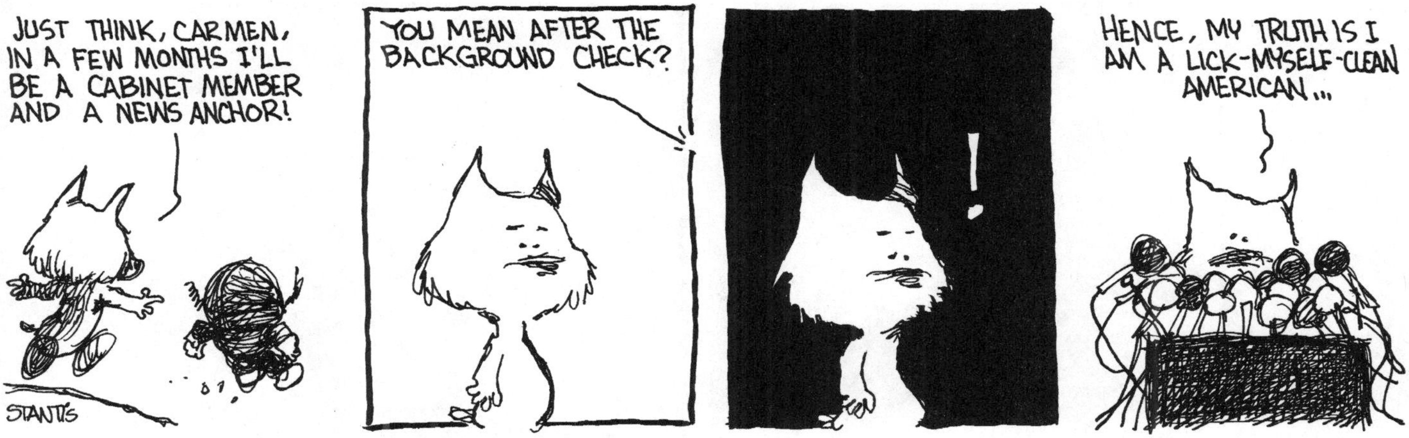
JUST THINK, CARMEN, IN A FEW MONTHS I'LL BE A CABINET MEMBER AND A NEWS ANCHOR!
STANTIS
YOU MEAN AFTER THE BACKGROUND CHECK?
!
HENCE, MY TRUTH IS I AM A LICK-MYSELF-CLEAN AMERICAN...

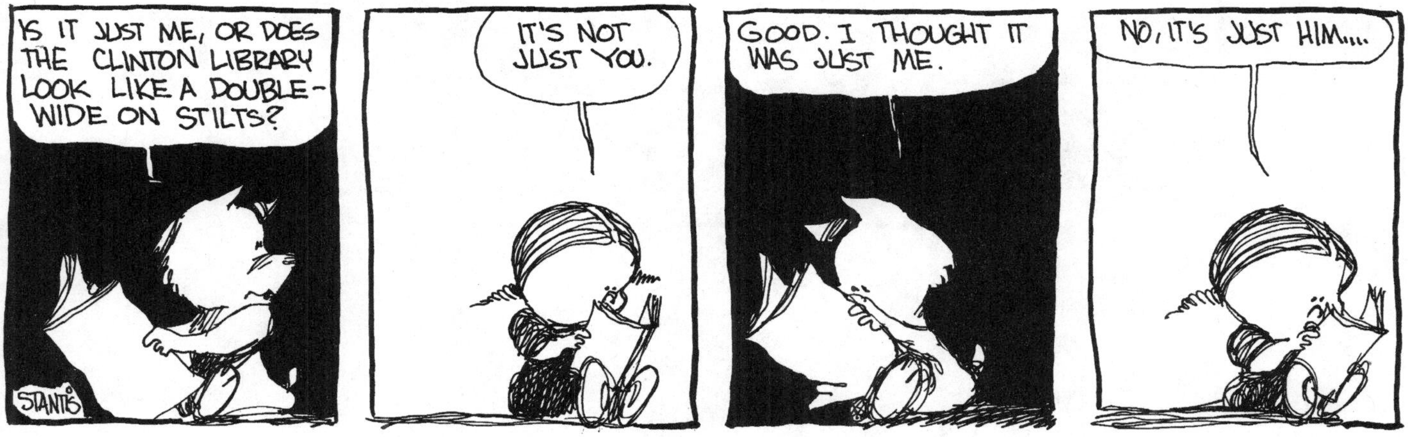
IS IT JUST ME, OR DOES THE CLINTON LIBRARY LOOK LIKE A DOUBLE-WIDE ON STILTS?
STANTIS
IT'S NOT JUST YOU.
GOOD. I THOUGHT IT WAS JUST ME.
NO, IT'S JUST HIM....

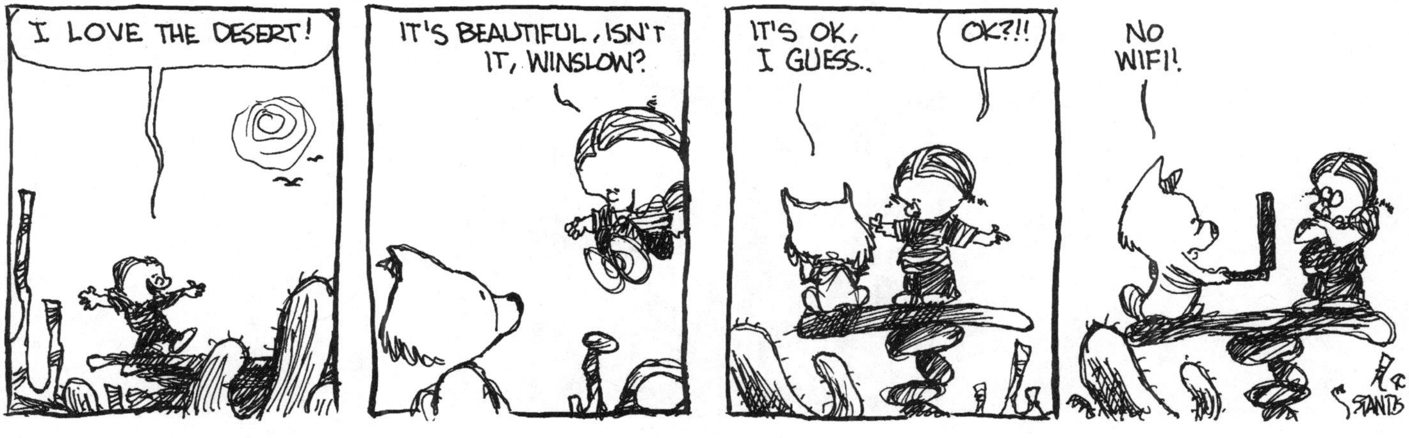
I LOVE THE DESERT!
IT'S BEAUTIFUL, ISN'T IT, WINSLOW?
IT'S OK, I GUESS..
OK?!!
NO WIFI!
STANTIS

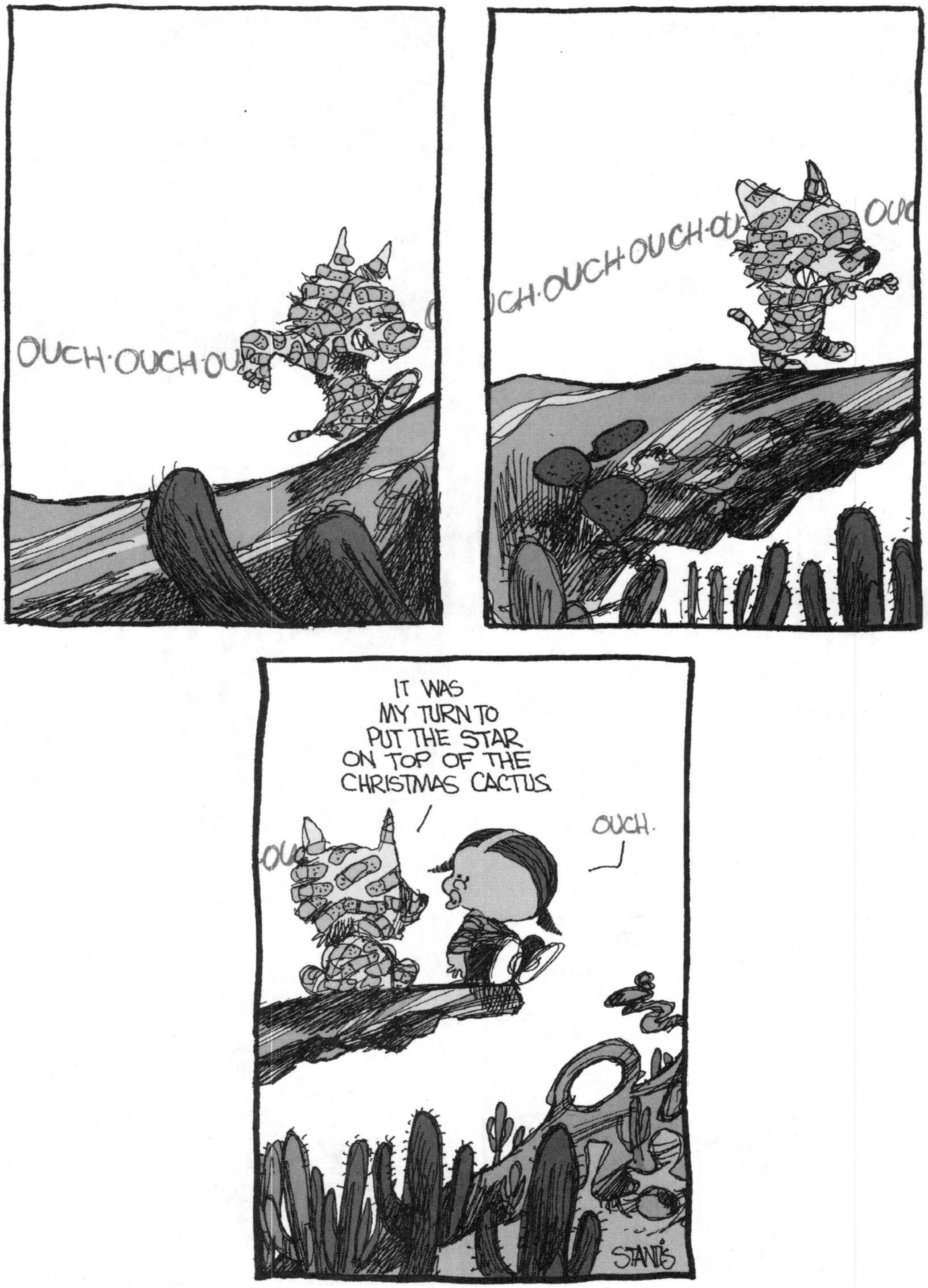
OUCH·OUCH·OU
CH·OUCH·OUCH·OU
OUC
OU
IT WAS MY TURN TO PUT THE STAR ON TOP OF THE CHRISTMAS CACTUS.
OUCH.
STANIS

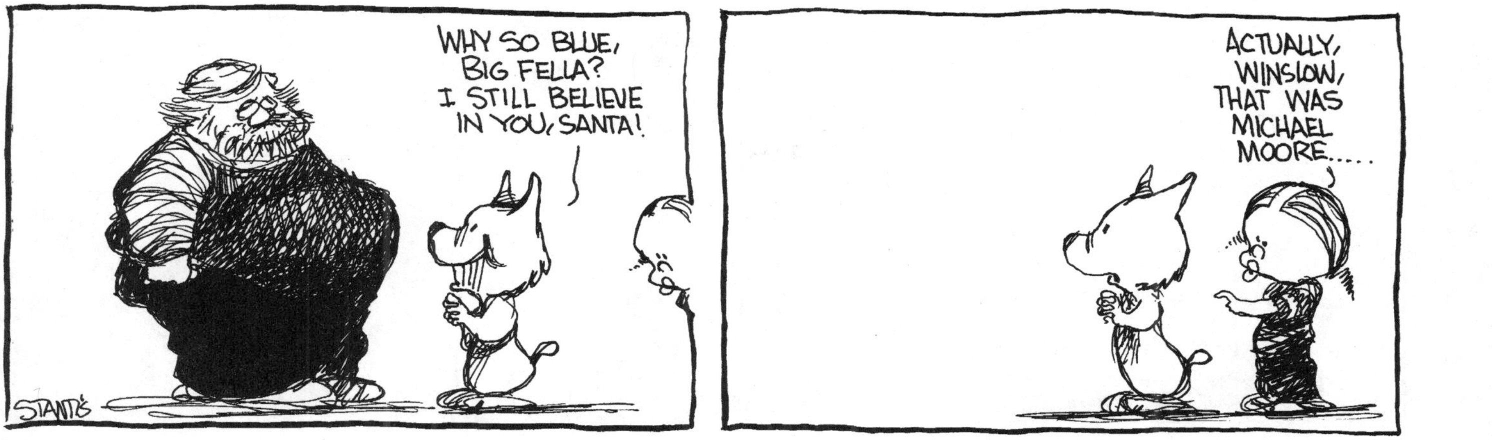
WHY SO BLUE, BIG FELLA? I STILL BELIEVE IN YOU, SANTA!
STANTIS
ACTUALLY, WINSLOW, THAT WAS MICHAEL MOORE.....

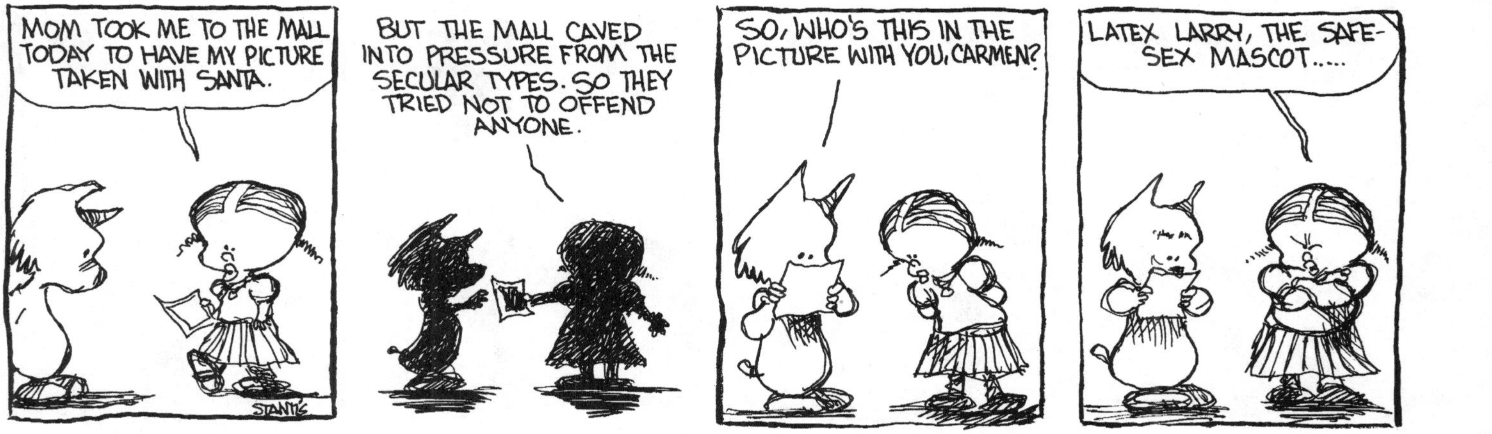
MOM TOOK ME TO THE MALL TODAY TO HAVE MY PICTURE TAKEN WITH SANTA.
STANTIS
BUT THE MALL CAVED INTO PRESSURE FROM THE SECULAR TYPES. SO THEY TRIED NOT TO OFFEND ANYONE.
SO, WHO'S THIS IN THE PICTURE WITH YOU, CARMEN?
LATEX LARRY, THE SAFE-SEX MASCOT.....

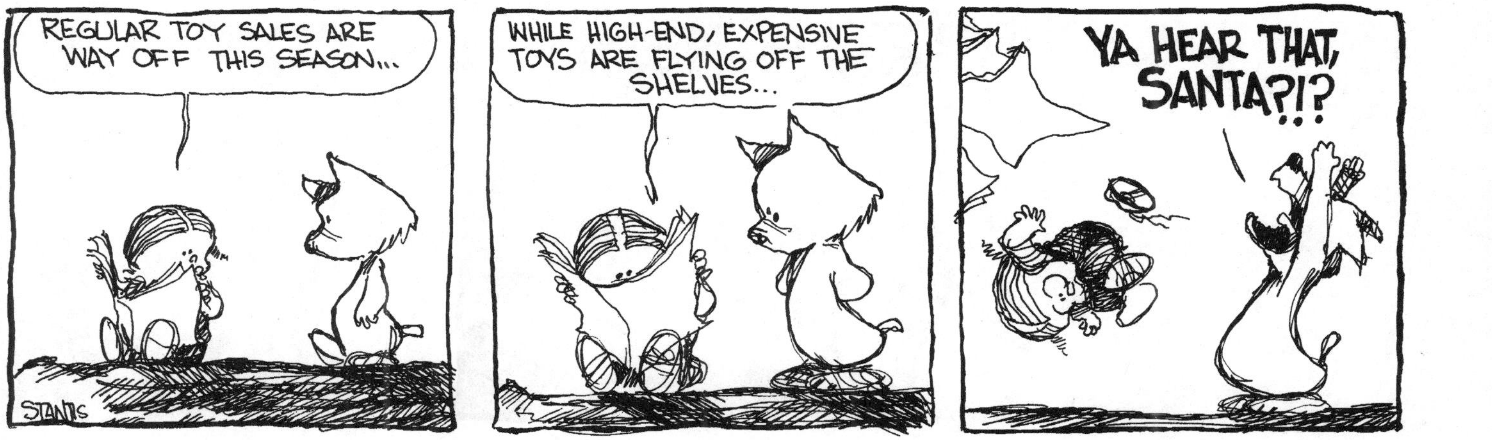
REGULAR TOY SALES ARE WAY OFF THIS SEASON...
STANTIS
WHILE HIGH-END, EXPENSIVE TOYS ARE FLYING OFF THE SHELVES...
YA HEAR THAT, SANTA?!?

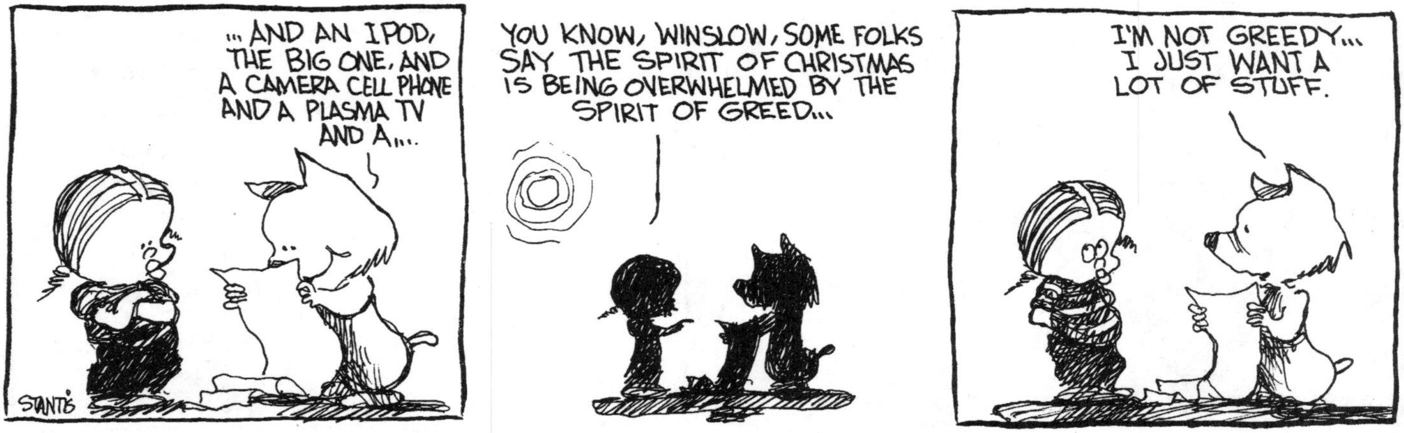
...AND AN IPOD, THE BIG ONE, AND A CAMERA CELL PHONE AND A PLASMA TV AND A....
STANTIS
YOU KNOW, WINSLOW, SOME FOLKS SAY THE SPIRIT OF CHRISTMAS IS BEING OVERWHELMED BY THE SPIRIT OF GREED...
I'M NOT GREEDY... I JUST WANT A LOT OF STUFF.

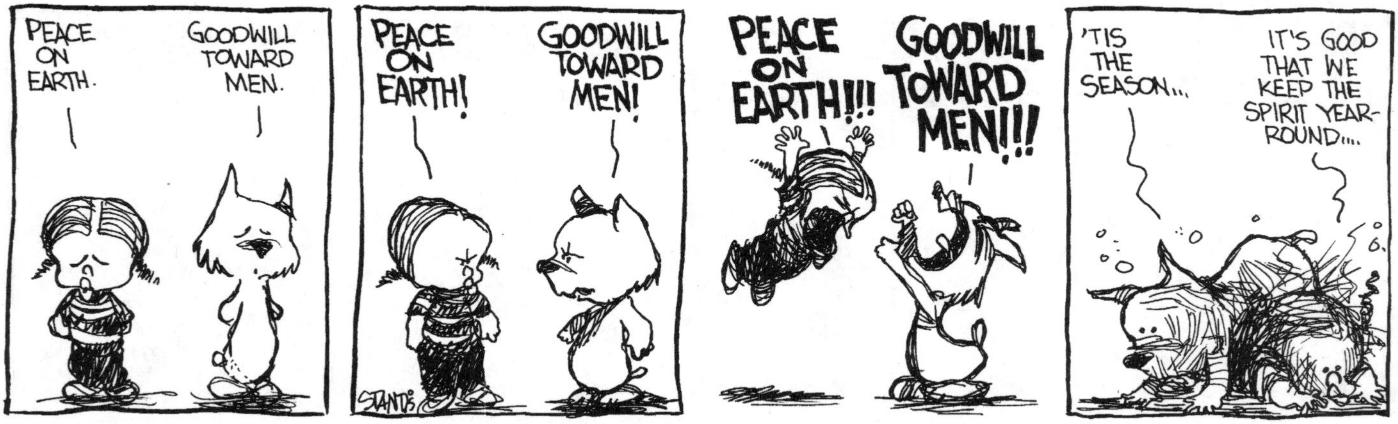
PEACE ON EARTH.
GOODWILL TOWARD MEN.
PEACE ON EARTH!
GOODWILL TOWARD MEN!
STANTIS
PEACE ON EARTH!!!
GOODWILL TOWARD MEN!!!
'TIS THE SEASON...
IT'S GOOD THAT WE KEEP THE SPIRIT YEAR-ROUND....

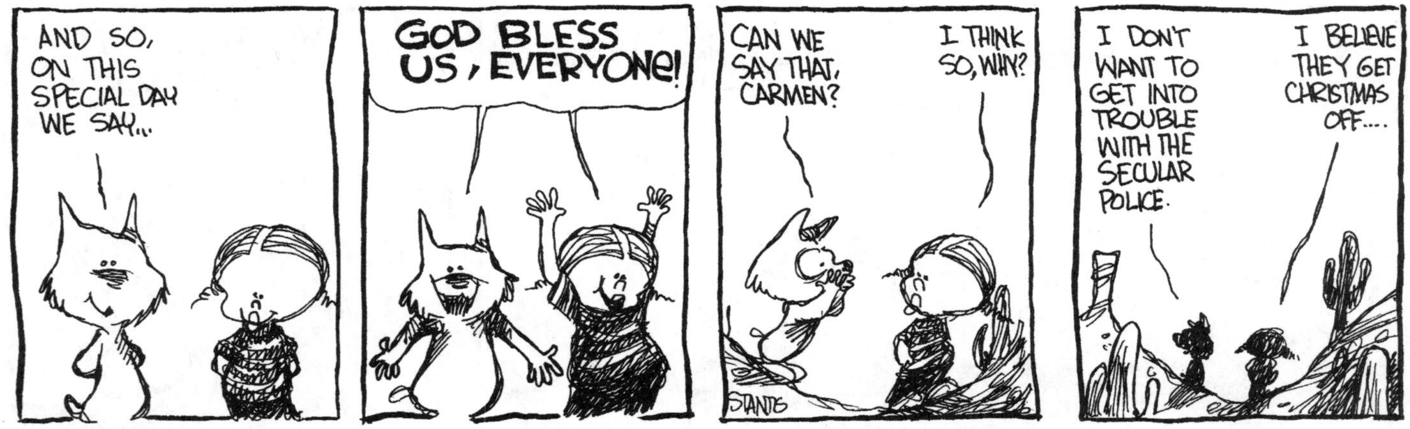
AND SO, ON THIS SPECIAL DAY WE SAY...
GOD BLESS US, EVERYONE!
CAN WE SAY THAT, CARMEN?
I THINK SO, WHY?
STANTIS
I DON'T WANT TO GET INTO TROUBLE WITH THE SECULAR POLICE.
I BELIEVE THEY GET CHRISTMAS OFF....

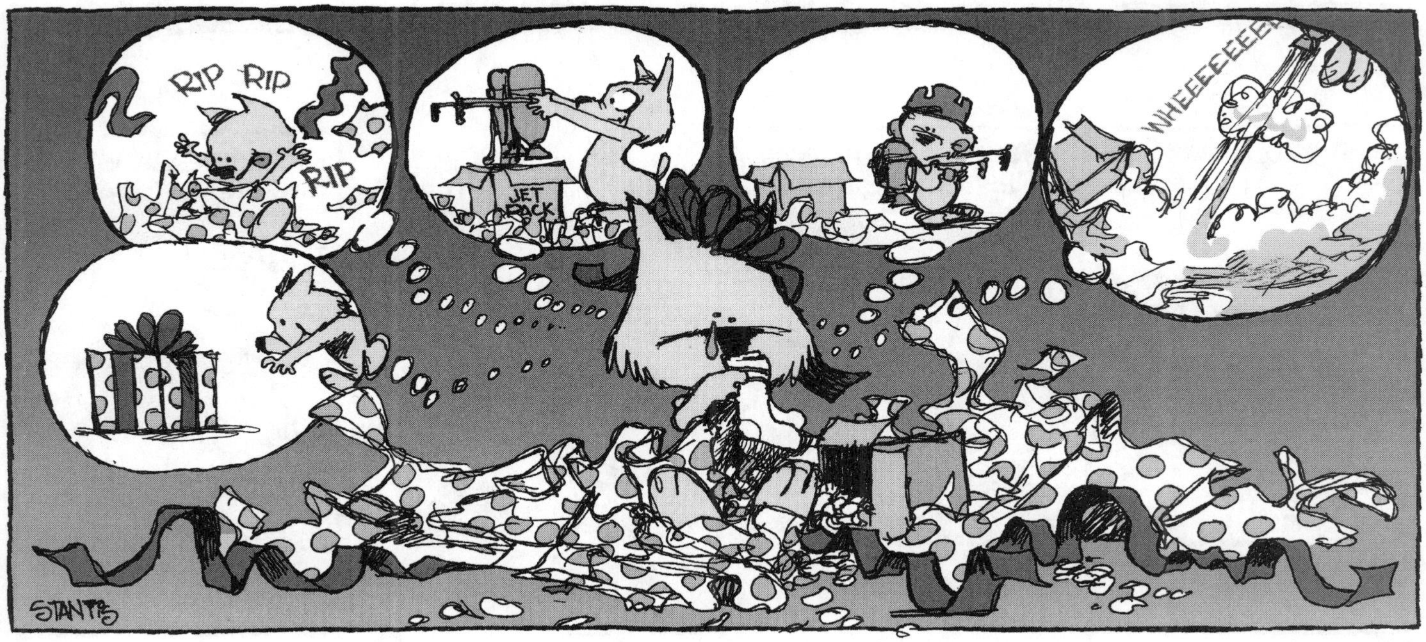
RIP RIP
RIP
JET PACK
WHEEEEEEE
STANT 86

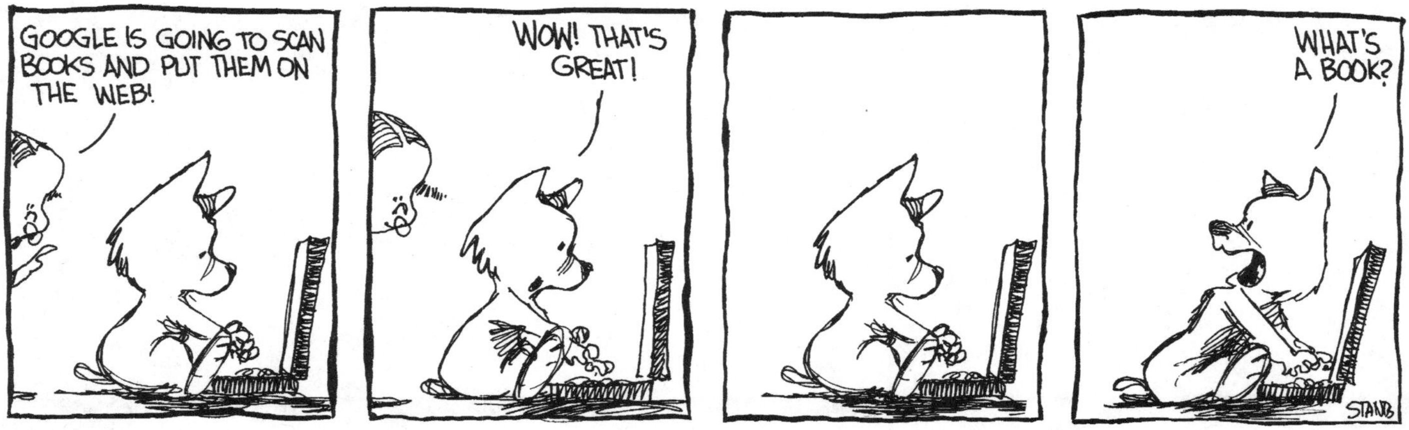
GOOGLE IS GOING TO SCAN BOOKS AND PUT THEM ON THE WEB!
WOW! THAT'S GREAT!
WHAT'S A BOOK?
STANTIS

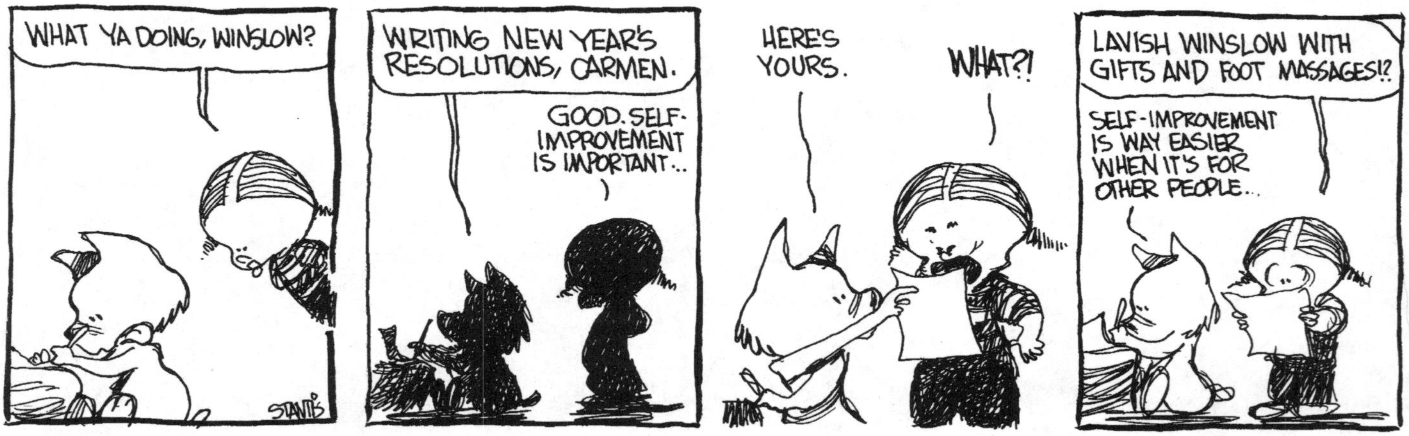
WHAT YA DOING, WINSLOW?
STANTIS
WRITING NEW YEAR'S RESOLUTIONS, CARMEN.
GOOD. SELF-IMPROVEMENT IS IMPORTANT...
HERE'S YOURS.
WHAT?!
LAVISH WINSLOW WITH GIFTS AND FOOT MASSAGES!?
SELF-IMPROVEMENT IS WAY EASIER WHEN IT'S FOR OTHER PEOPLE...

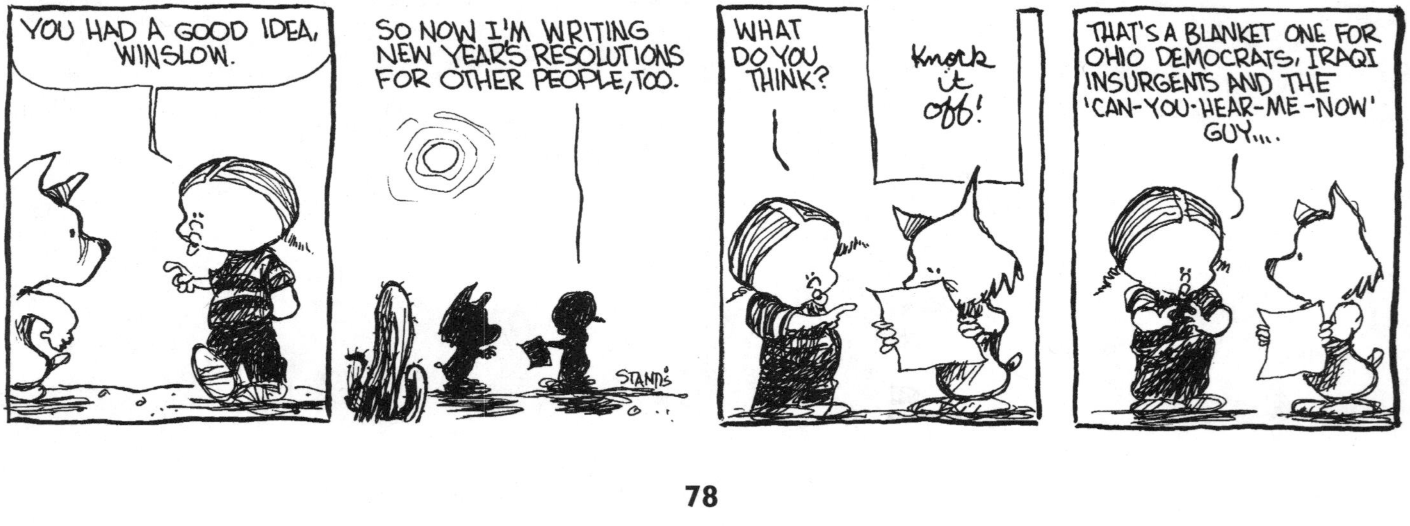
YOU HAD A GOOD IDEA, WINSLOW.
SO NOW I'M WRITING NEW YEAR'S RESOLUTIONS FOR OTHER PEOPLE, TOO.
STANTIS
WHAT DO YOU THINK?
Knock it off!
THAT'S A BLANKET ONE FOR OHIO DEMOCRATS, IRAQI INSURGENTS AND THE 'CAN-YOU-HEAR-ME-NOW' GUY....

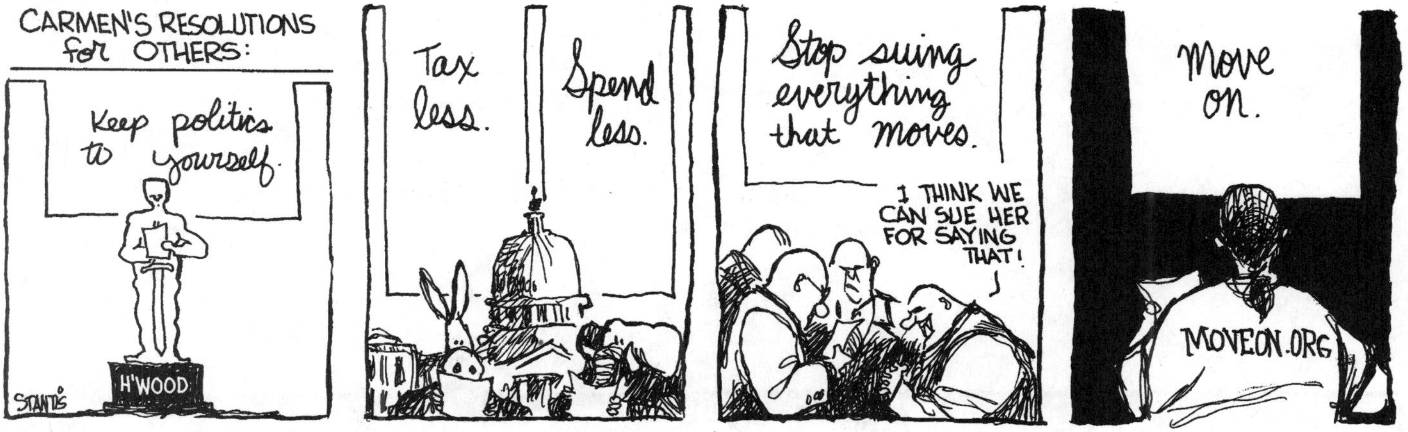
CARMEN'S RESOLUTIONS for OTHERS:
Keep politics to yourself.
H'WOOD
STANTIS
Tax less.
Spend less.
Stop suing everything that moves.
I THINK WE CAN SUE HER FOR SAYING THAT!
Move on.
MOVEON.ORG

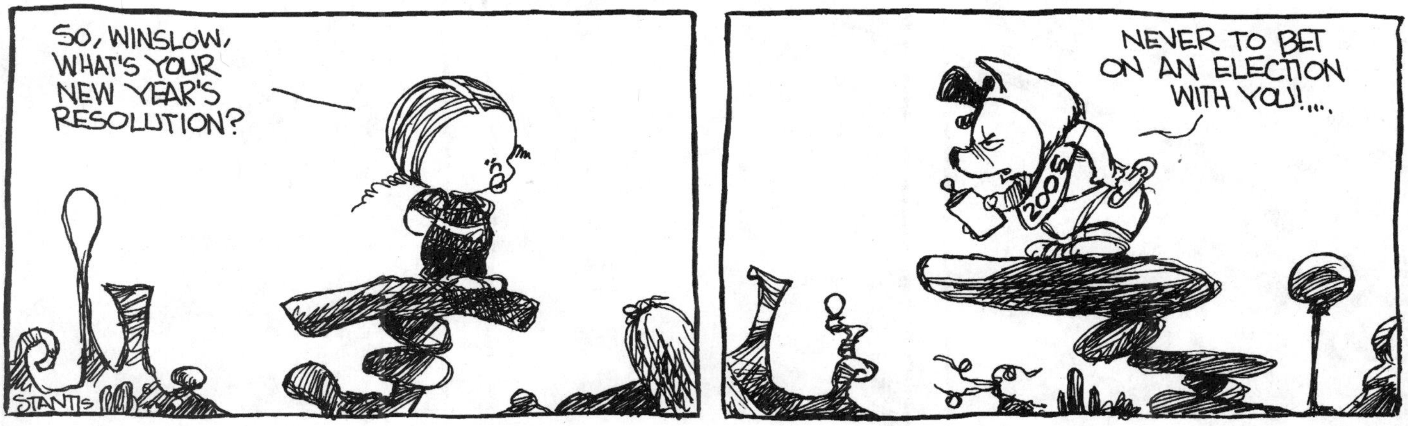
SO, WINSLOW, WHAT'S YOUR NEW YEAR'S RESOLUTION?
STANTIS
NEVER TO BET ON AN ELECTION WITH YOU!....
2005

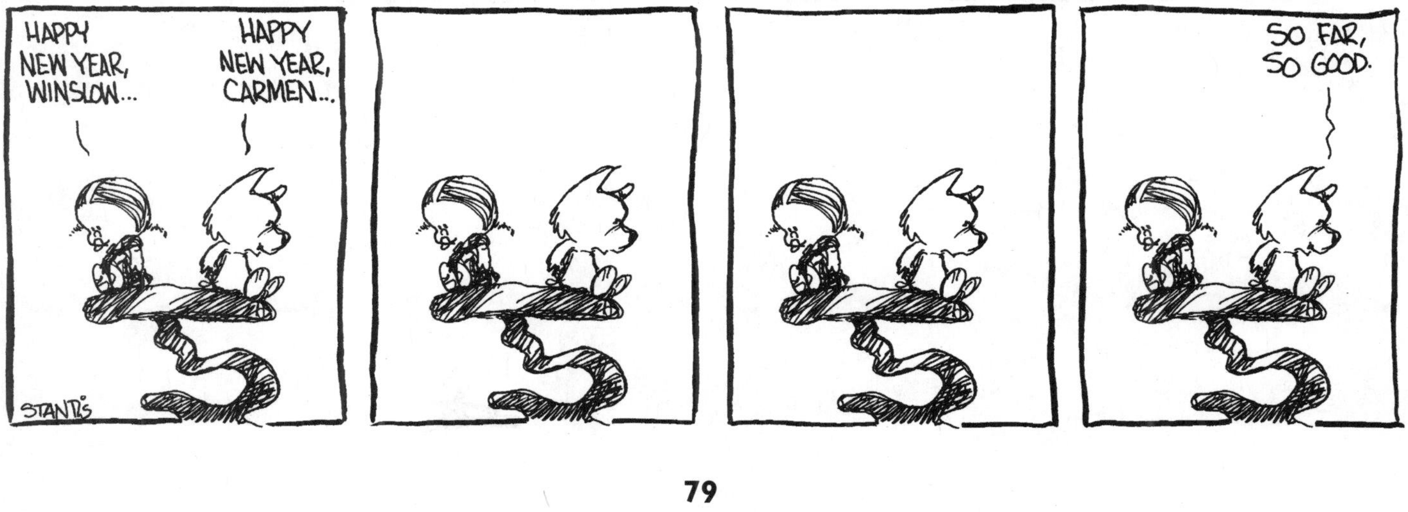
HAPPY NEW YEAR, WINSLOW...
HAPPY NEW YEAR, CARMEN...
STANTIS
SO FAR, SO GOOD.

...3...2... 1
GO!
FLY! –
STANTIS
SO MUCH FOR THAT RESOLUTION.....

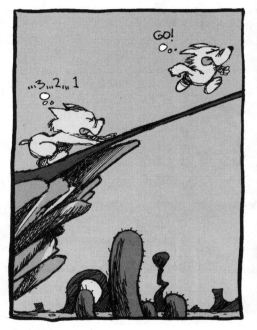

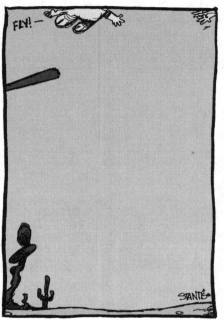

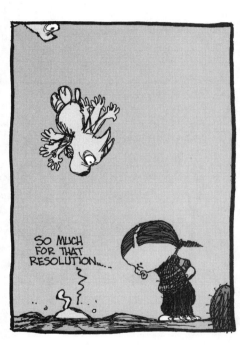

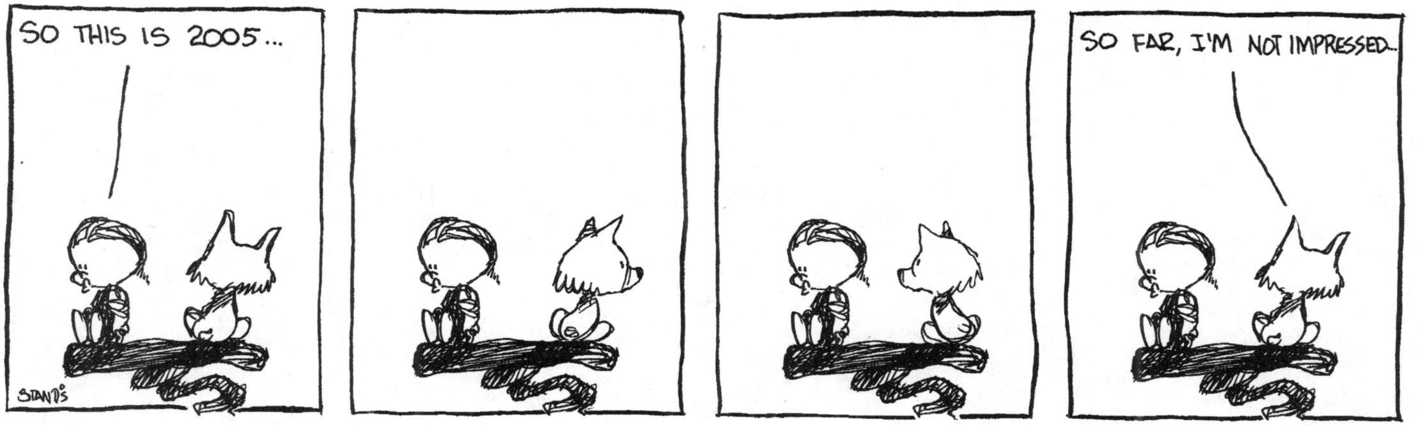
SO THIS IS 2005...
SO FAR, I'M NOT IMPRESSED...

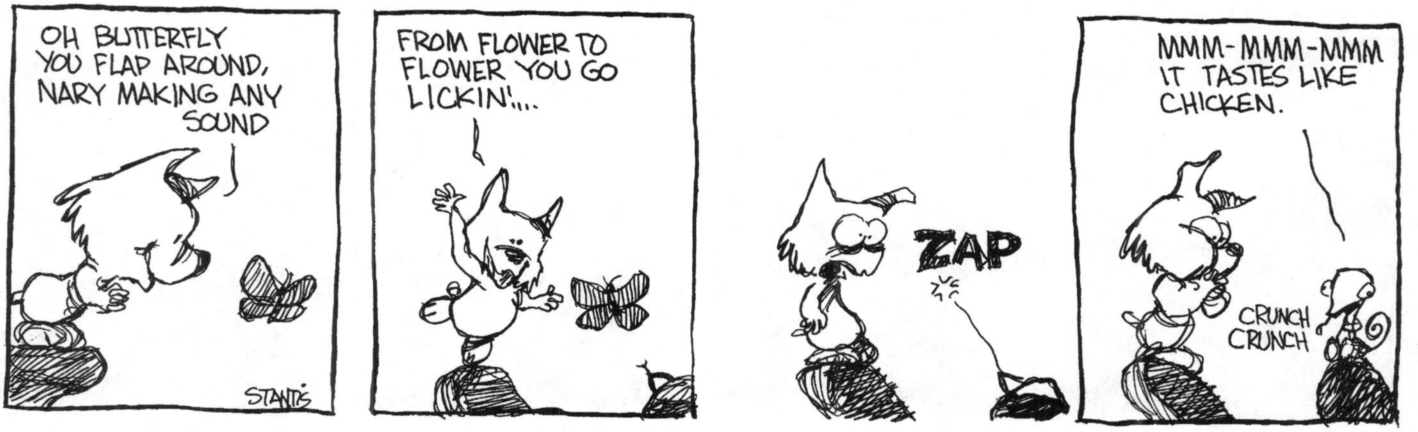
OH BUTTERFLY YOU FLAP AROUND, NARY MAKING ANY SOUND
FROM FLOWER TO FLOWER YOU GO LICKIN'...
ZAP
MMM-MMM-MMM IT TASTES LIKE CHICKEN.
CRUNCH CRUNCH

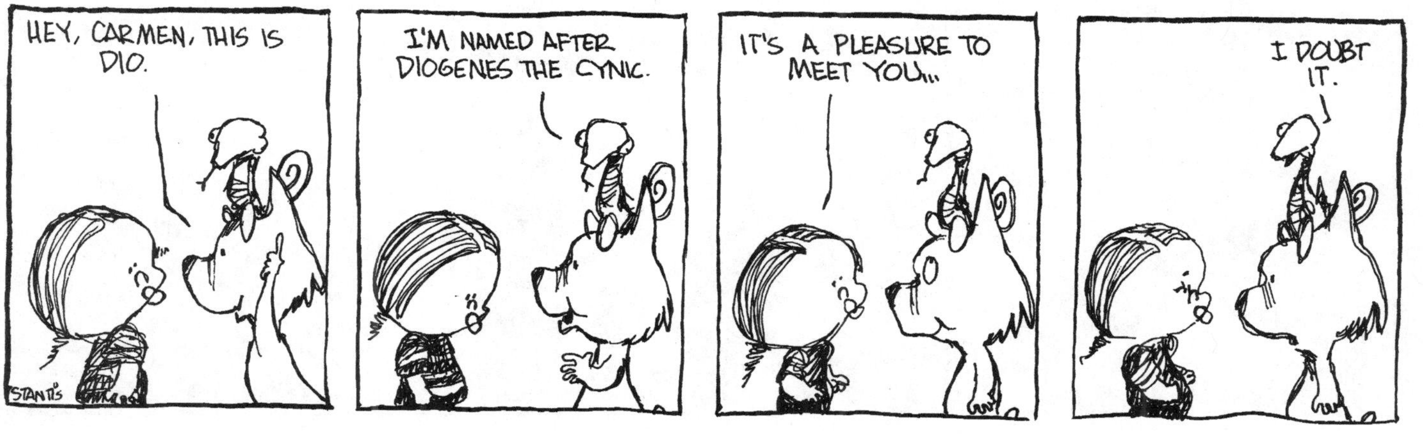
HEY, CARMEN, THIS IS DIO.
I'M NAMED AFTER DIOGENES THE CYNIC.
IT'S A PLEASURE TO MEET YOU...
I DOUBT IT.

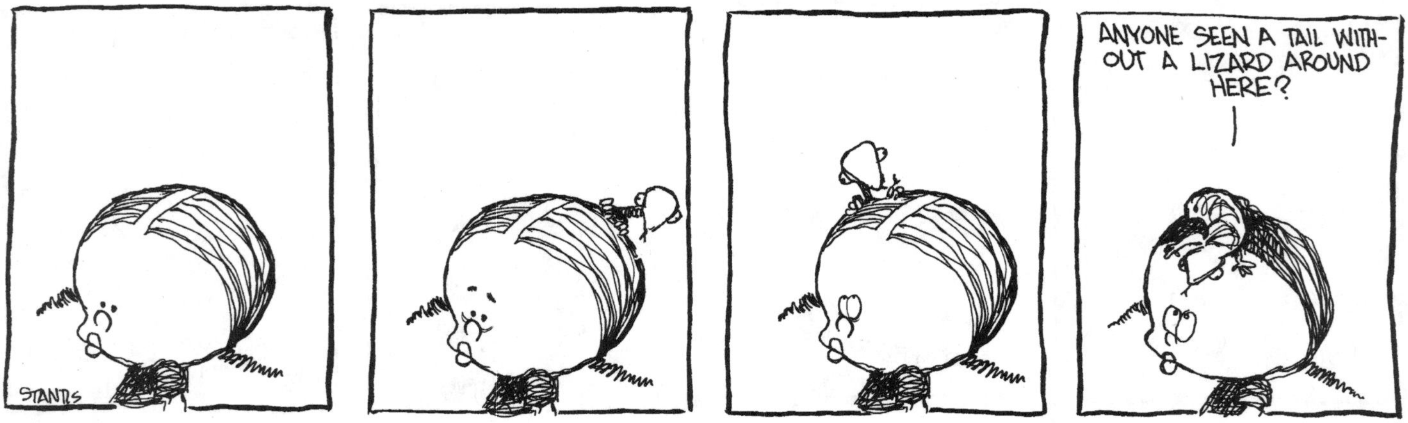
STANTIS
ANYONE SEEN A TAIL WITH-OUT A LIZARD AROUND HERE?

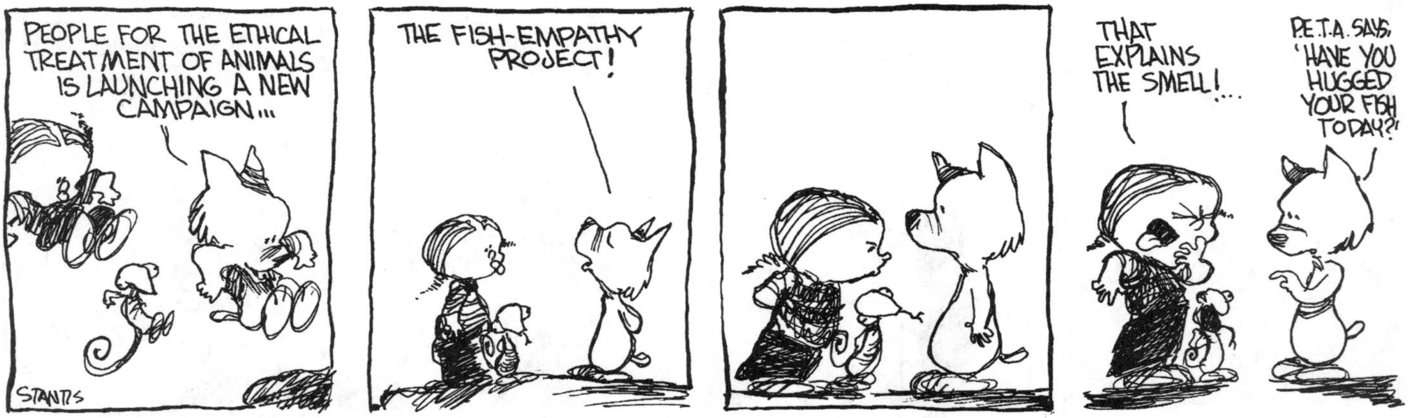
PEOPLE FOR THE ETHICAL TREATMENT OF ANIMALS IS LAUNCHING A NEW CAMPAIGN...
STANTIS
THE FISH-EMPATHY PROJECT!
THAT EXPLAINS THE SMELL!...
P.E.T.A. SAYS, 'HAVE YOU HUGGED YOUR FISH TODAY?'

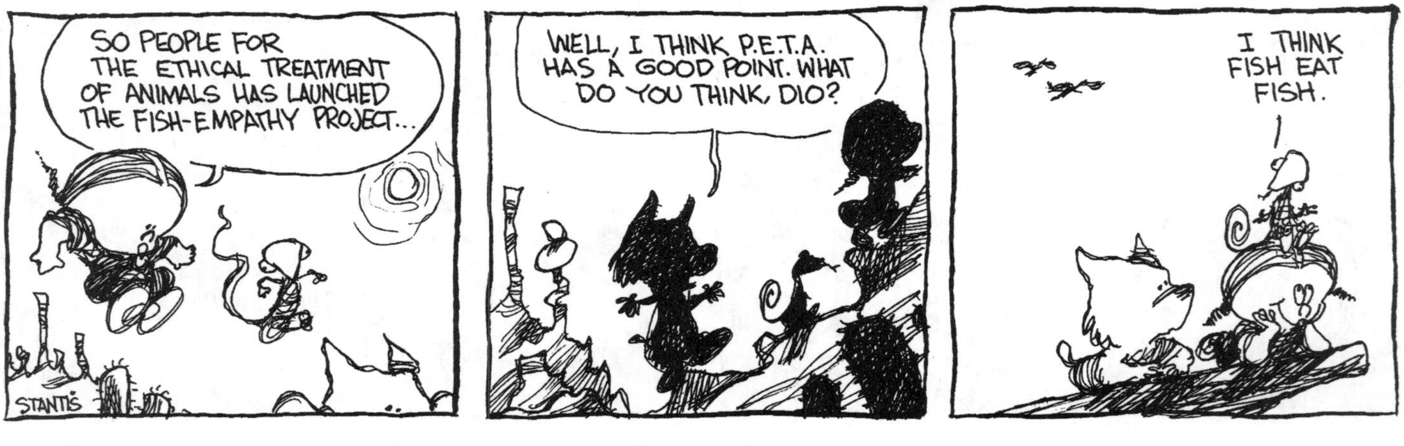
SO PEOPLE FOR THE ETHICAL TREATMENT OF ANIMALS HAS LAUNCHED THE FISH-EMPATHY PROJECT...
STANTIS
WELL, I THINK P.E.T.A. HAS A GOOD POINT. WHAT DO YOU THINK, DIO?
I THINK FISH EAT FISH.

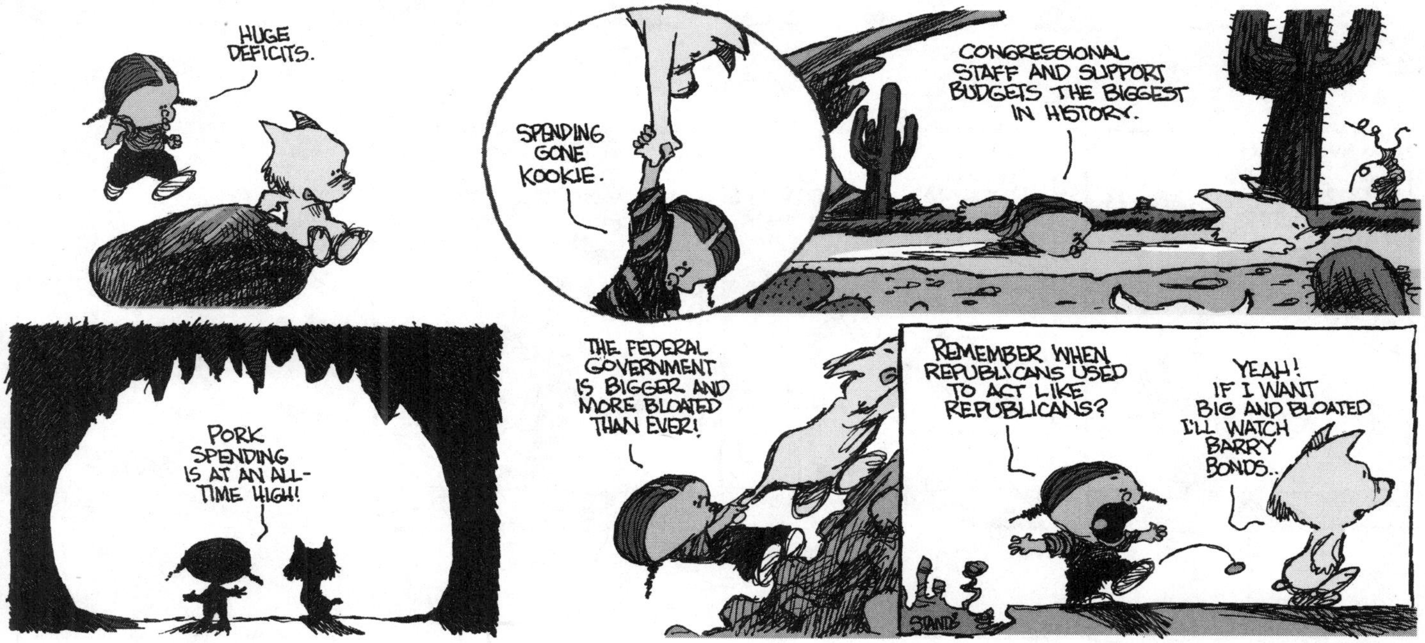
HUGE DEFICITS.
SPENDING GONE KOOKIE.
CONGRESSIONAL STAFF AND SUPPORT BUDGETS THE BIGGEST IN HISTORY.
PORK SPENDING IS AT AN ALL-TIME HIGH!
THE FEDERAL GOVERNMENT IS BIGGER AND MORE BLOATED THAN EVER!
REMEMBER WHEN REPUBLICANS USED TO ACT LIKE REPUBLICANS?
YEAH! IF I WANT BIG AND BLOATED I'LL WATCH BARRY BONDS..

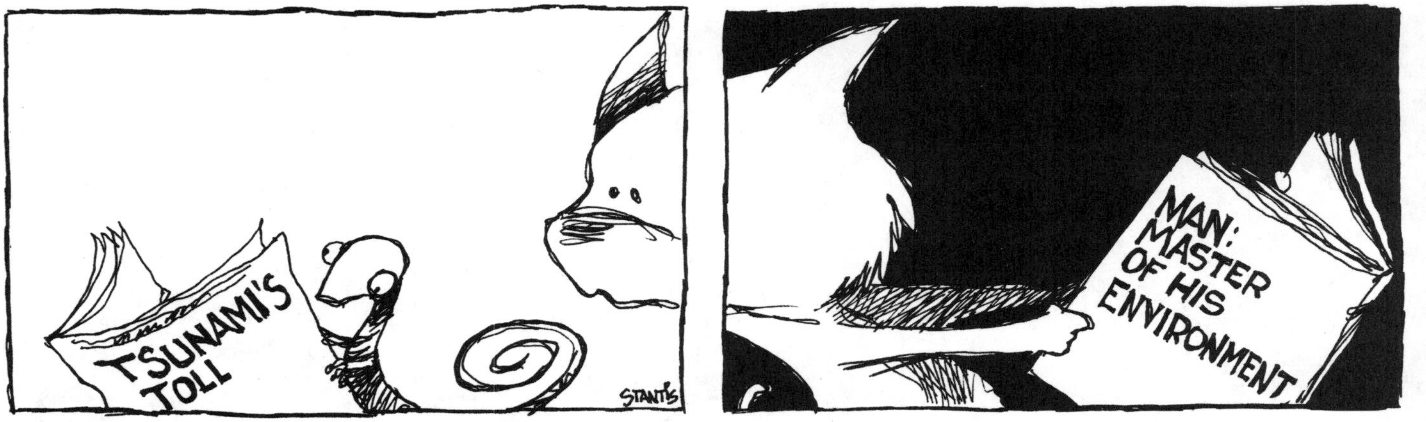
TSUNAMI'S TOLL
STANTIS
MAN: MASTER OF HIS ENVIRONMENT

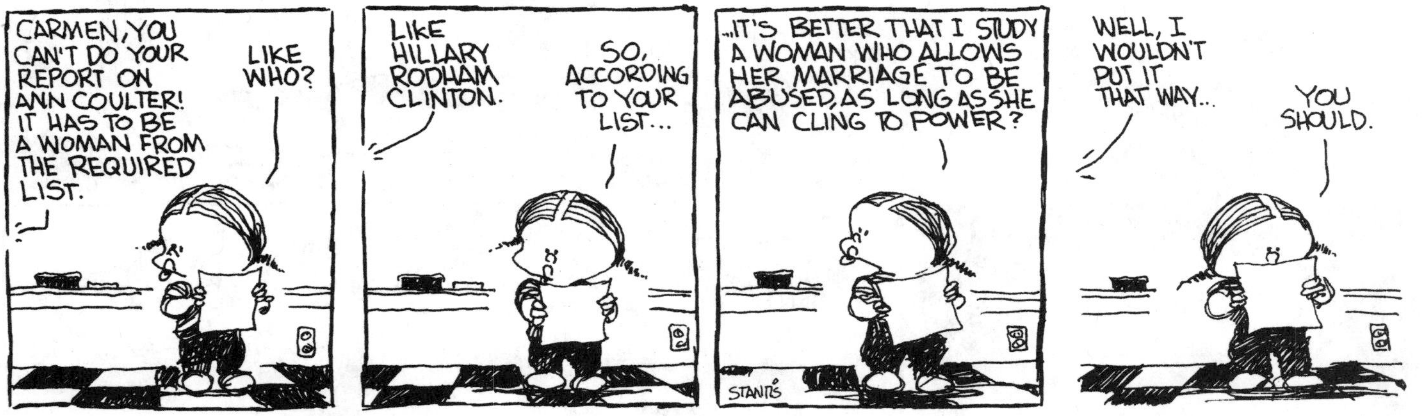
CARMEN, YOU CAN'T DO YOUR REPORT ON ANN COULTER! IT HAS TO BE A WOMAN FROM THE REQUIRED LIST.
LIKE WHO?
LIKE HILLARY RODHAM CLINTON.
SO, ACCORDING TO YOUR LIST...
...IT'S BETTER THAT I STUDY A WOMAN WHO ALLOWS HER MARRIAGE TO BE ABUSED, AS LONG AS SHE CAN CLING TO POWER?
STANTIS
WELL, I WOULDN'T PUT IT THAT WAY...
YOU SHOULD.

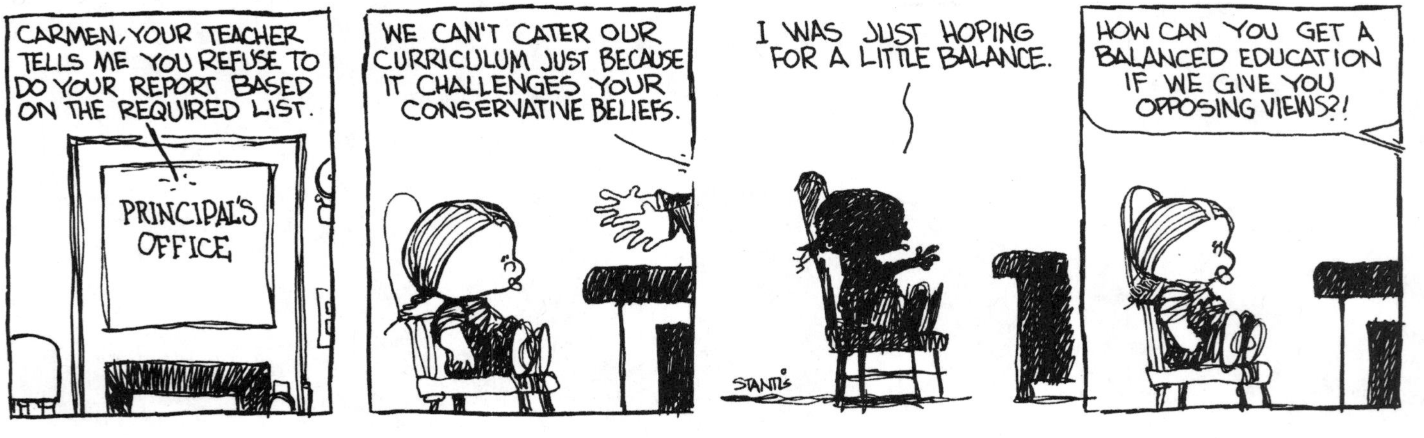
CARMEN, YOUR TEACHER TELLS ME YOU REFUSE TO DO YOUR REPORT BASED ON THE REQUIRED LIST.
PRINCIPAL'S OFFICE
WE CAN'T CATER OUR CURRICULUM JUST BECAUSE IT CHALLENGES YOUR CONSERVATIVE BELIEFS.
I WAS JUST HOPING FOR A LITTLE BALANCE.
STANTIS
HOW CAN YOU GET A BALANCED EDUCATION IF WE GIVE YOU OPPOSING VIEWS?!

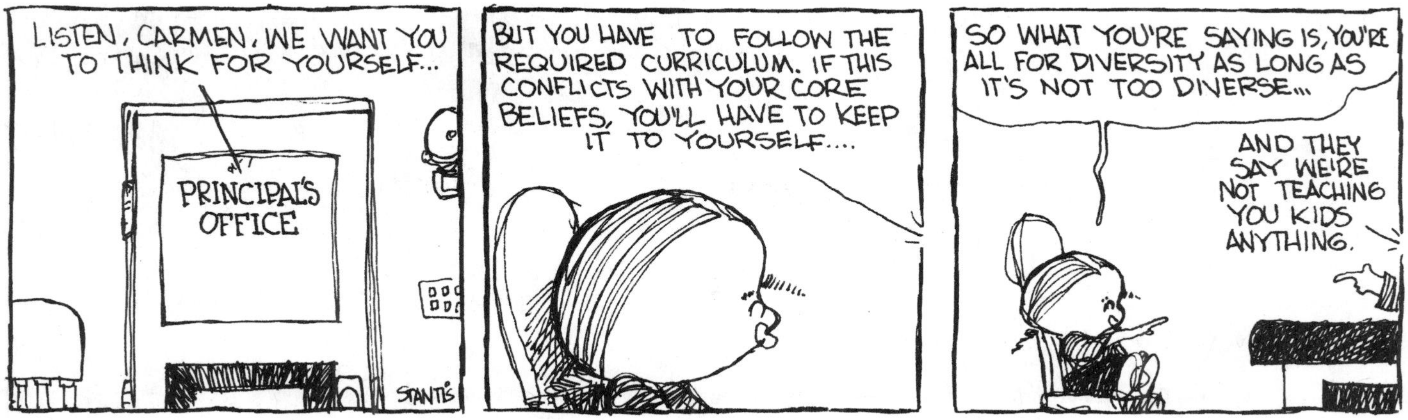
LISTEN, CARMEN, WE WANT YOU TO THINK FOR YOURSELF...
PRINCIPAL'S OFFICE
STANTIS
BUT YOU HAVE TO FOLLOW THE REQUIRED CURRICULUM. IF THIS CONFLICTS WITH YOUR CORE BELIEFS, YOU'LL HAVE TO KEEP IT TO YOURSELF....
SO WHAT YOU'RE SAYING IS, YOU'RE ALL FOR DIVERSITY AS LONG AS IT'S NOT TOO DIVERSE...
AND THEY SAY WE'RE NOT TEACHING YOU KIDS ANYTHING.

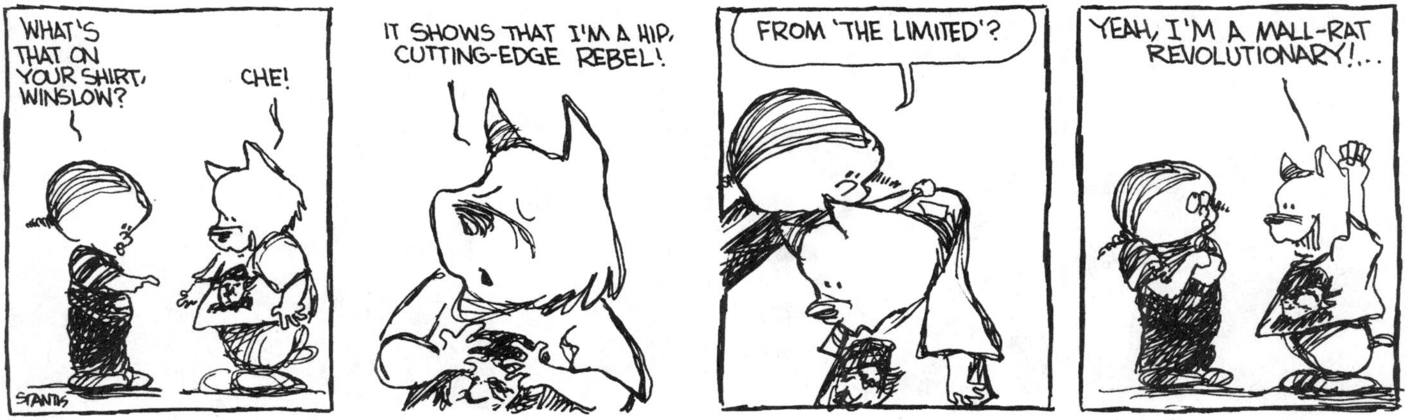
WHAT'S THAT ON YOUR SHIRT, WINSLOW?
CHE!
STANTIS
IT SHOWS THAT I'M A HIP, CUTTING-EDGE REBEL!
FROM 'THE LIMITED'?
YEAH, I'M A MALL-RAT REVOLUTIONARY!...

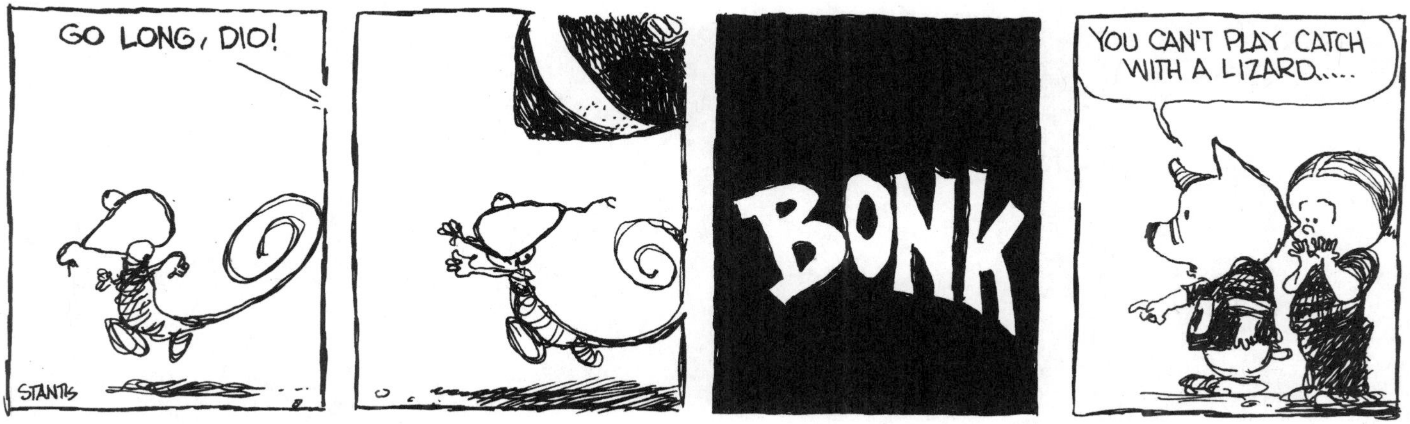
GO LONG, DIO!
STANTIS
BONK
YOU CAN'T PLAY CATCH WITH A LIZARD....

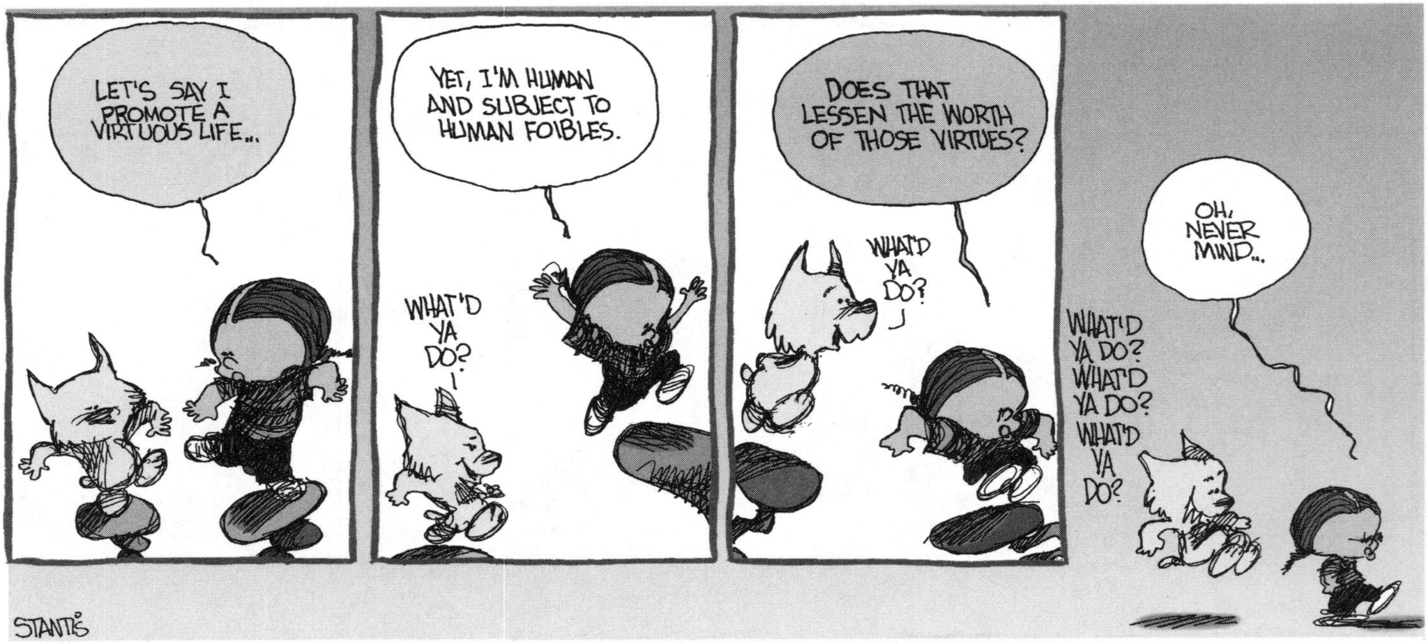
LET'S SAY I PROMOTE A VIRTUOUS LIFE...
YET, I'M HUMAN AND SUBJECT TO HUMAN FOIBLES.
WHAT'D YA DO?
DOES THAT LESSEN THE WORTH OF THOSE VIRTUES?
WHAT'D YA DO?
OH, NEVER MIND...
WHAT'D YA DO? WHAT'D YA DO? WHAT'D YA DO?
STANTIS

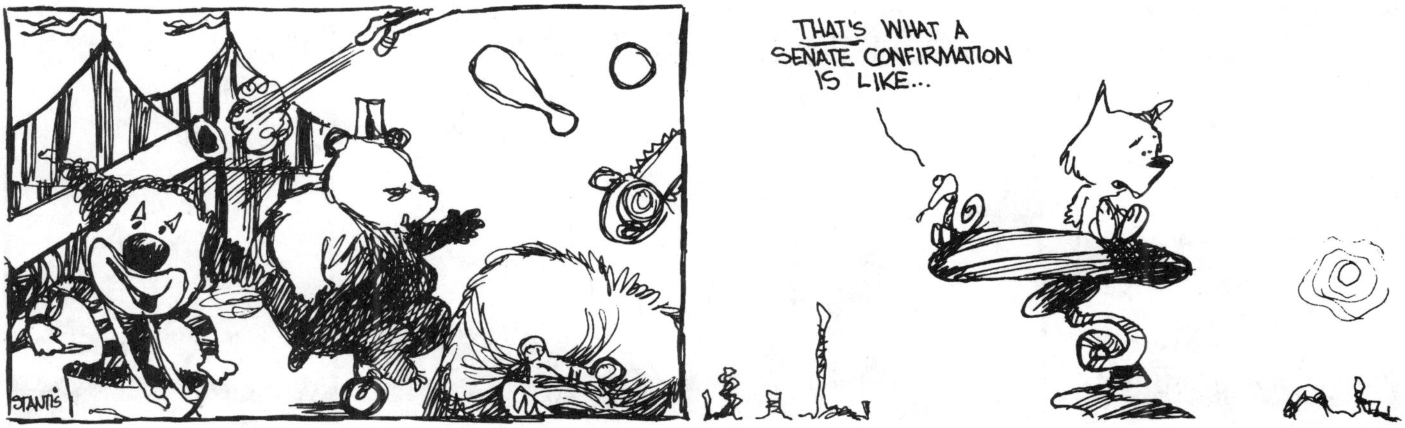
THAT'S WHAT A SENATE CONFIRMATION IS LIKE...

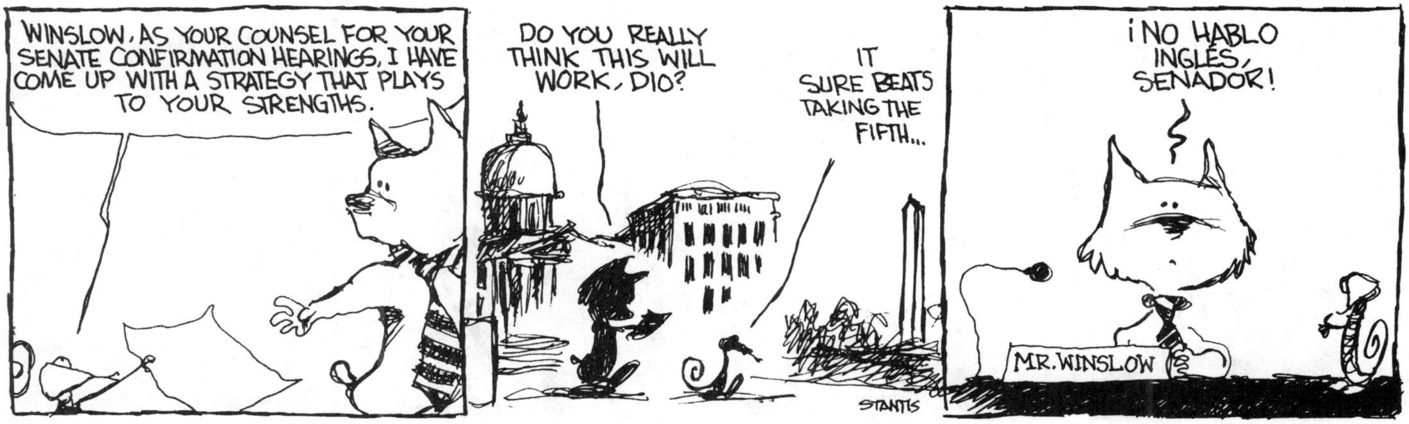
WINSLOW, AS YOUR COUNSEL FOR YOUR SENATE CONFIRMATION HEARINGS, I HAVE COME UP WITH A STRATEGY THAT PLAYS TO YOUR STRENGTHS.
DO YOU REALLY THINK THIS WILL WORK, DIO?
IT SURE BEATS TAKING THE FIFTH...
¡NO HABLO INGLÉS, SENADOR!
MR. WINSLOW

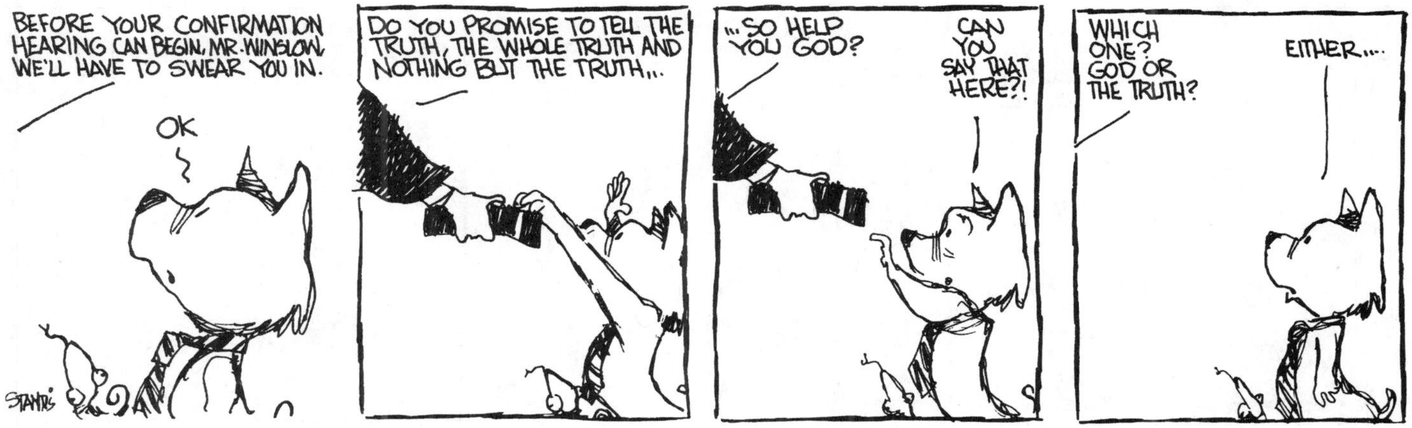
BEFORE YOUR CONFIRMATION HEARING CAN BEGIN, MR. WINSLOW, WE'LL HAVE TO SWEAR YOU IN.
OK
DO YOU PROMISE TO TELL THE TRUTH, THE WHOLE TRUTH AND NOTHING BUT THE TRUTH...
...SO HELP YOU GOD?
CAN YOU SAY THAT HERE?!
WHICH ONE? GOD OR THE TRUTH?
EITHER....

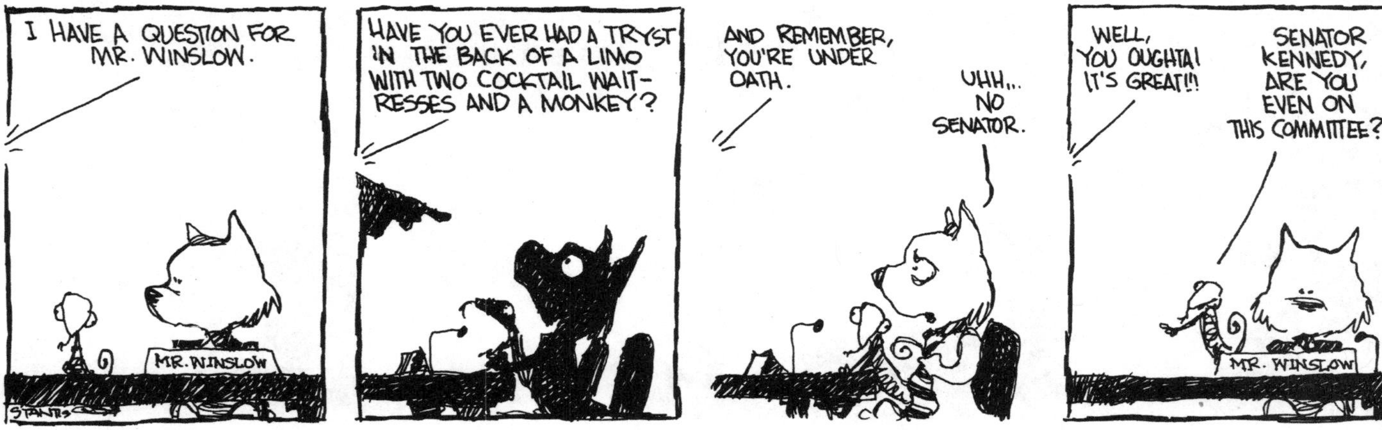
I HAVE A QUESTION FOR MR. WINSLOW.
MR. WINSLOW
STANTIS
HAVE YOU EVER HAD A TRYST IN THE BACK OF A LIMO WITH TWO COCKTAIL WAITRESSES AND A MONKEY?
AND REMEMBER, YOU'RE UNDER OATH.
UHH... NO SENATOR.
WELL, YOU OUGHTA! IT'S GREAT!!
SENATOR KENNEDY, ARE YOU EVEN ON THIS COMMITTEE?
MR. WINSLOW

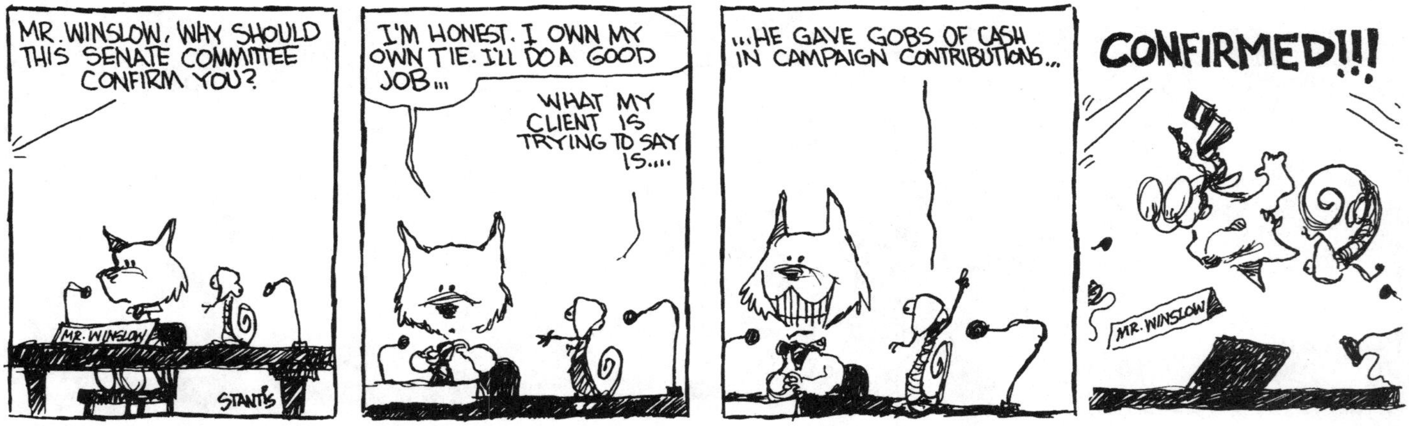
MR. WINSLOW, WHY SHOULD THIS SENATE COMMITTEE CONFIRM YOU?
MR. WINSLOW
STANTIS
I'M HONEST. I OWN MY OWN TIE. I'LL DO A GOOD JOB...
WHAT MY CLIENT IS TRYING TO SAY IS....
...HE GAVE GOBS OF CASH IN CAMPAIGN CONTRIBUTIONS...
CONFIRMED!!!
MR. WINSLOW

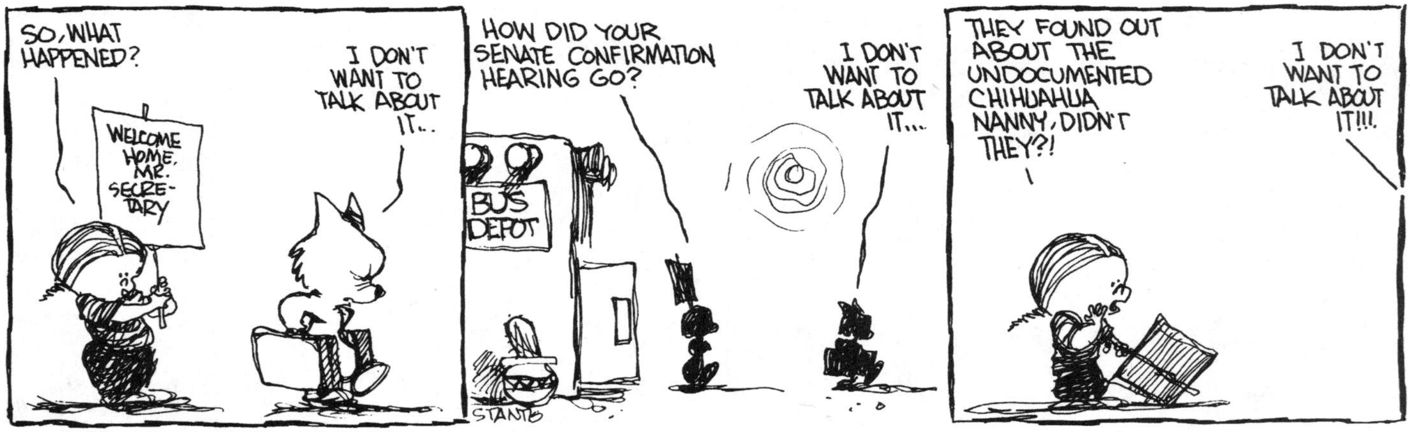
SO, WHAT HAPPENED?
WELCOME HOME, MR. SECRETARY
I DON'T WANT TO TALK ABOUT IT...
HOW DID YOUR SENATE CONFIRMATION HEARING GO?
BUS DEPOT
I DON'T WANT TO TALK ABOUT IT...
STANTIS
THEY FOUND OUT ABOUT THE UNDOCUMENTED CHIHUAHUA NANNY, DIDN'T THEY?!
I DON'T WANT TO TALK ABOUT IT!!!

KNOW WHAT I WISH, CARMEN?
WHAT, WINSLOW?
!
STANTIS
Z
NOOOOO...
NEVER MIND...

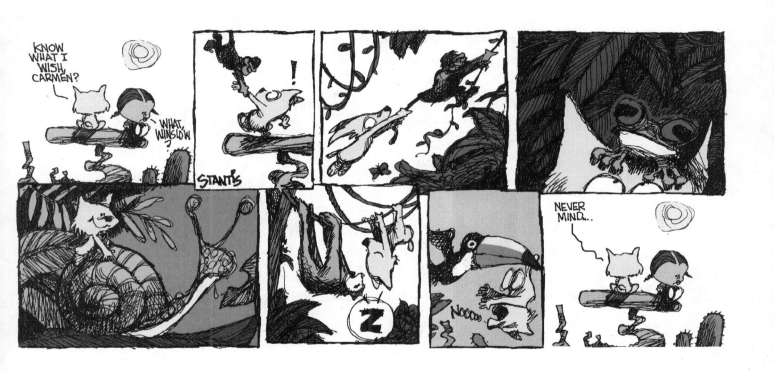

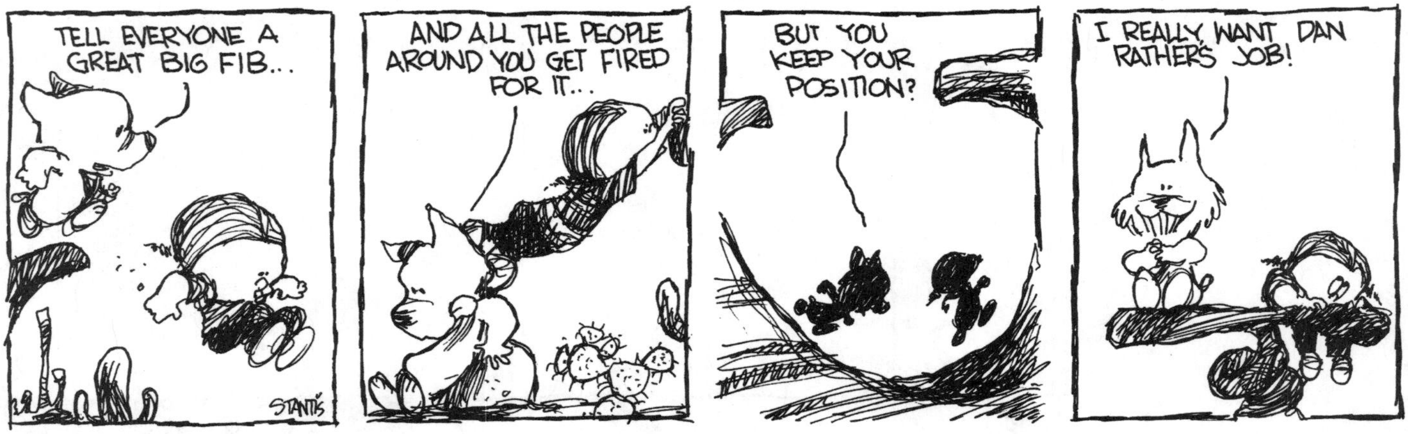
TELL EVERYONE A GREAT BIG FIB...
STANTIS
AND ALL THE PEOPLE AROUND YOU GET FIRED FOR IT...
BUT YOU KEEP YOUR POSITION?
I REALLY WANT DAN RATHER'S JOB!

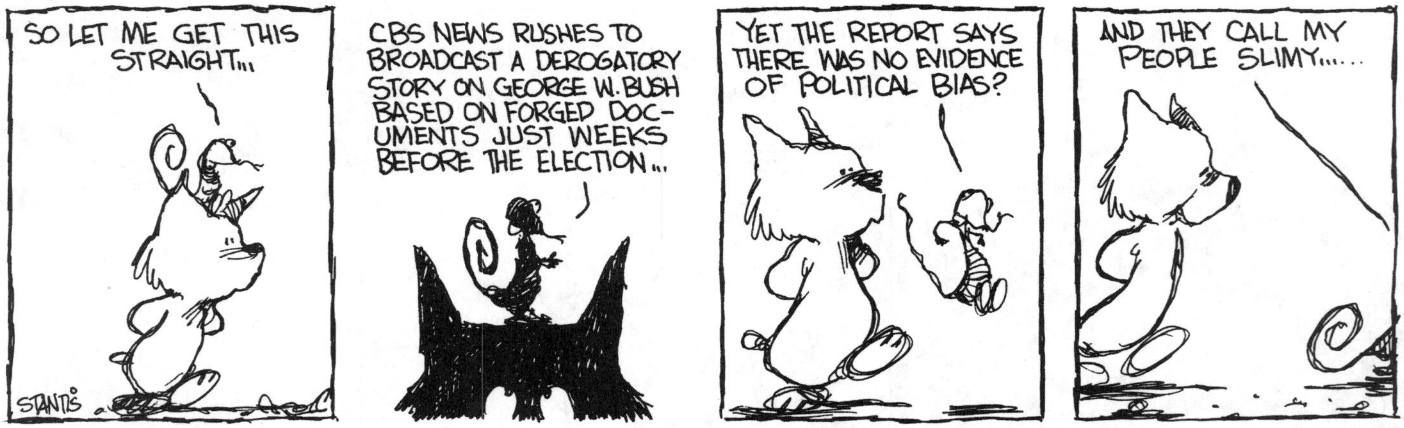
SO LET ME GET THIS STRAIGHT...
STANTIS
CBS NEWS RUSHES TO BROADCAST A DEROGATORY STORY ON GEORGE W. BUSH BASED ON FORGED DOC-UMENTS JUST WEEKS BEFORE THE ELECTION...
YET THE REPORT SAYS THERE WAS NO EVIDENCE OF POLITICAL BIAS?
AND THEY CALL MY PEOPLE SLIMY......

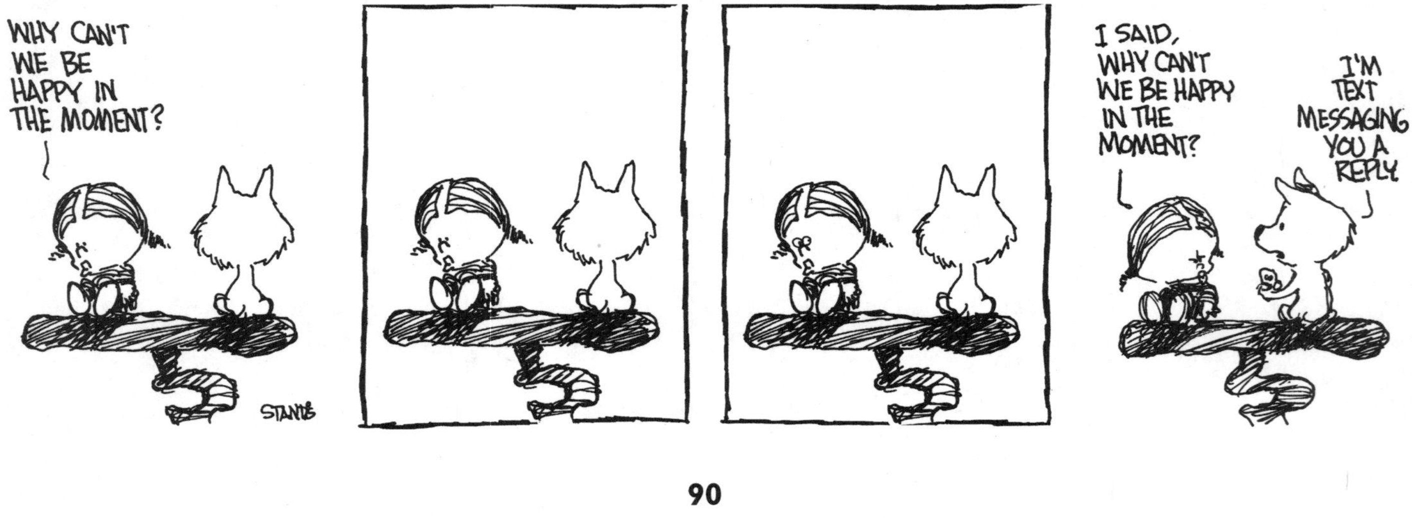
WHY CAN'T WE BE HAPPY IN THE MOMENT?
STANTIS
I SAID, WHY CAN'T WE BE HAPPY IN THE MOMENT?
I'M TEXT MESSAGING YOU A REPLY.

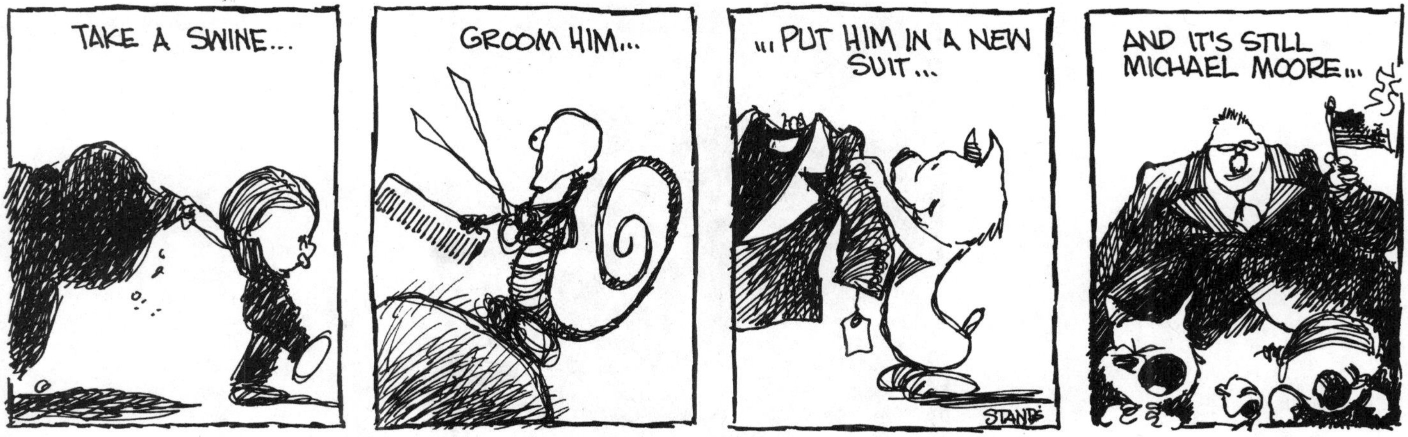
TAKE A SWINE...
GROOM HIM...
...PUT HIM IN A NEW SUIT...
AND IT'S STILL MICHAEL MOORE...
STANTIS

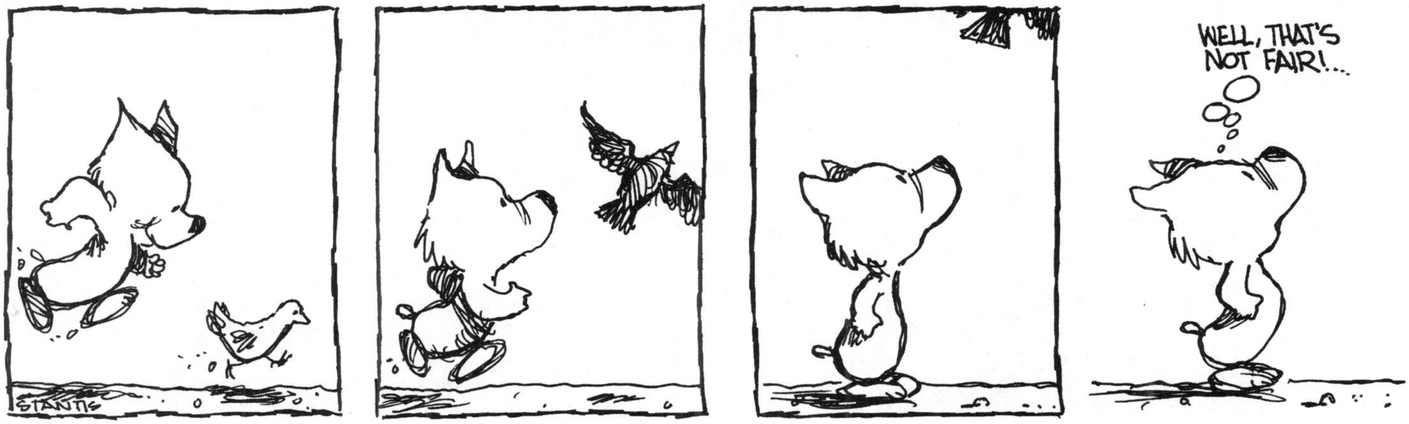
STANTIS
WELL, THAT'S NOT FAIR!...

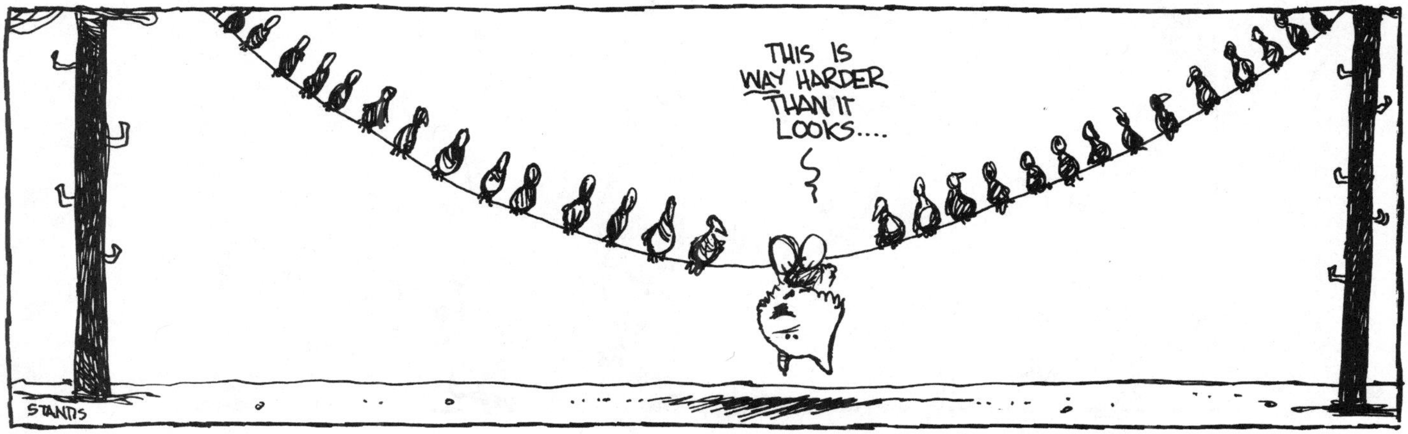
THIS IS WAY HARDER THAN IT LOOKS....
STANTIS

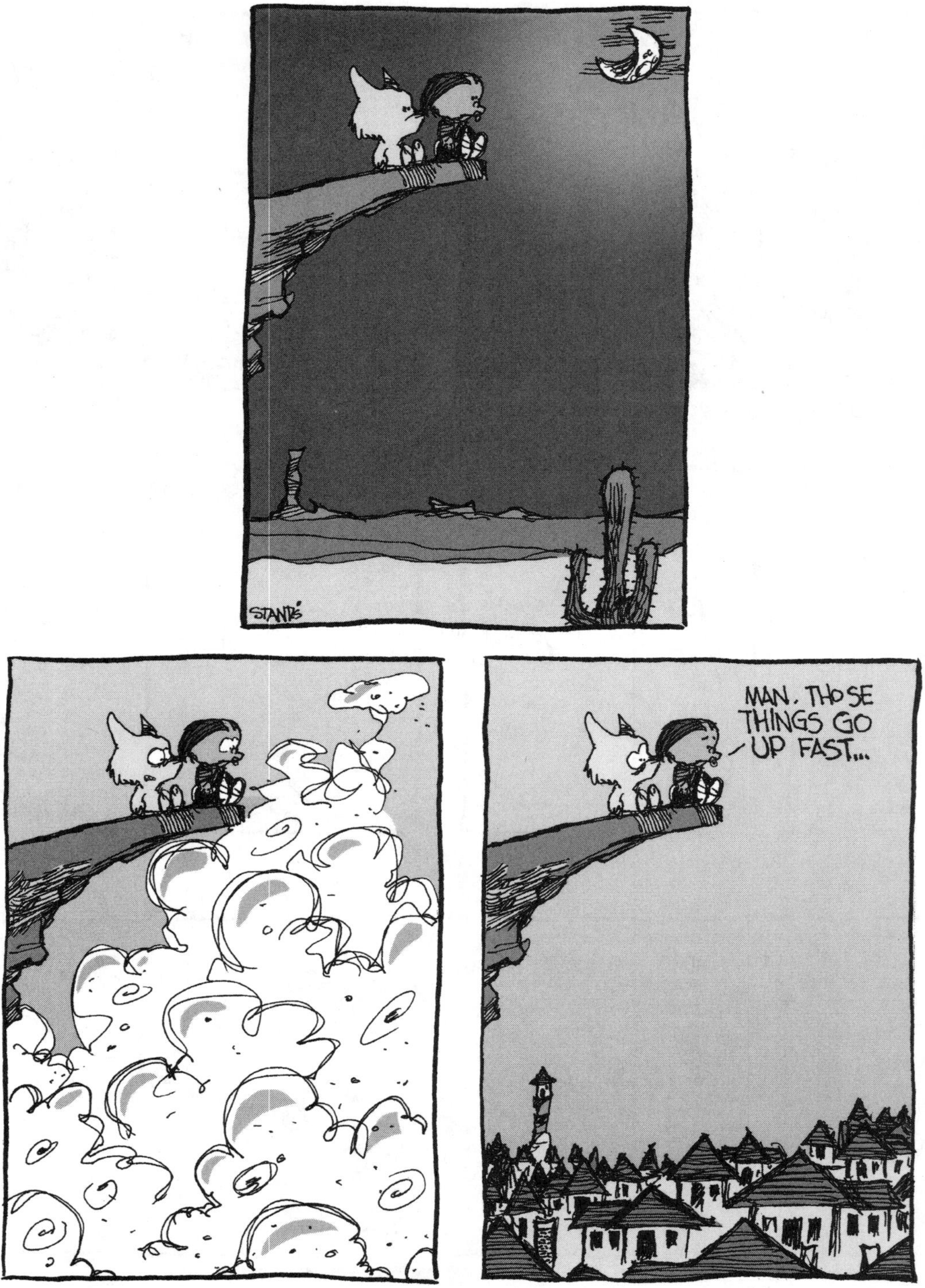
MAN. THOSE THINGS GO UP FAST...

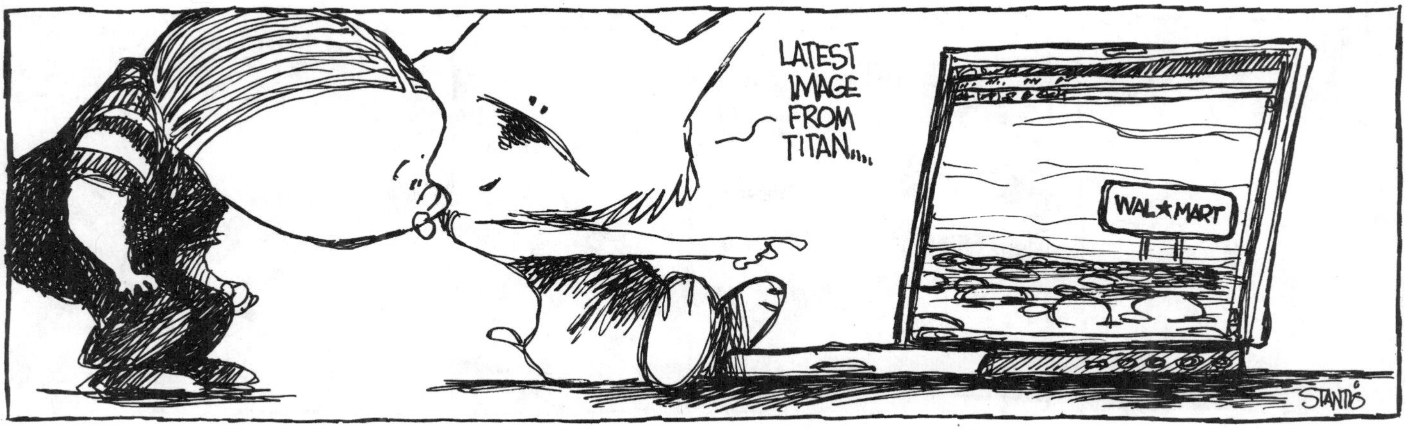
LATEST IMAGE FROM TITAN....
WAL★MART

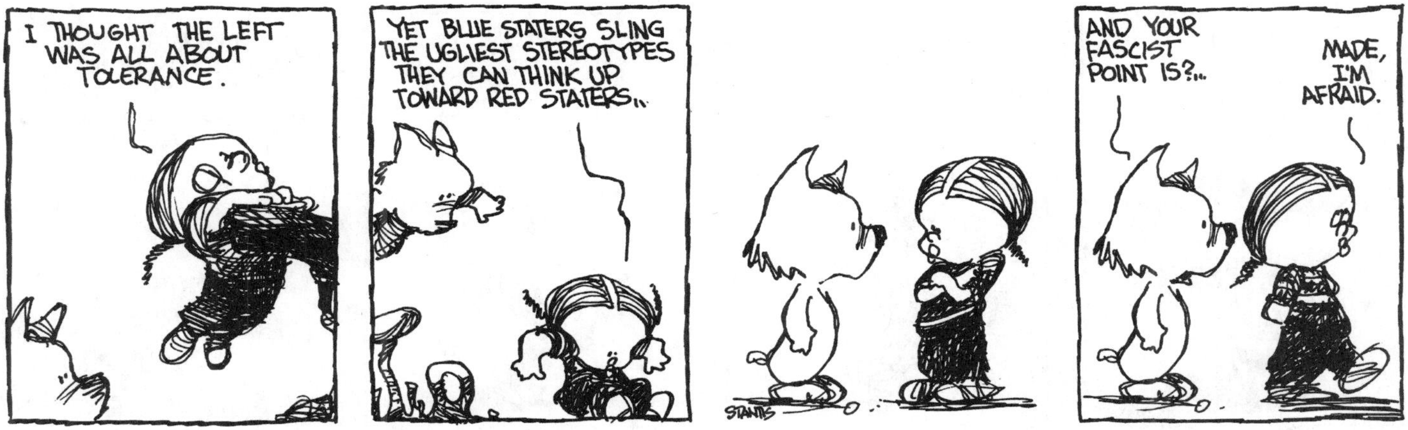
I THOUGHT THE LEFT WAS ALL ABOUT TOLERANCE.
YET BLUE STATERS SLING THE UGLIEST STEREOTYPES THEY CAN THINK UP TOWARD RED STATERS..
AND YOUR FASCIST POINT IS?..
MADE, I'M AFRAID.

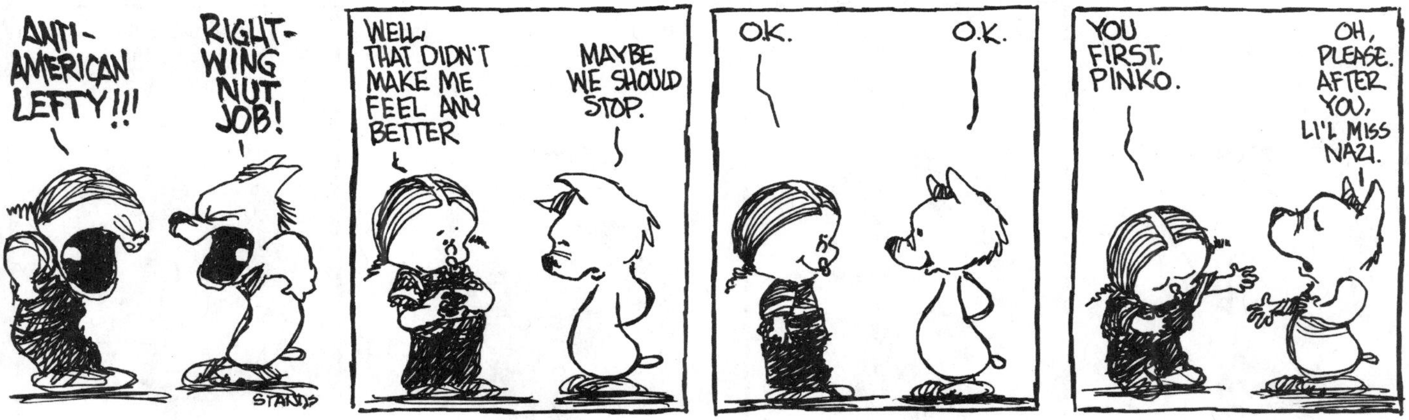
ANTI-AMERICAN LEFTY!!!
RIGHT-WING NUT JOB!
WELL, THAT DIDN'T MAKE ME FEEL ANY BETTER
MAYBE WE SHOULD STOP.
O.K.
O.K.
YOU FIRST, PINKO.
OH, PLEASE. AFTER YOU, LI'L MISS NAZI.

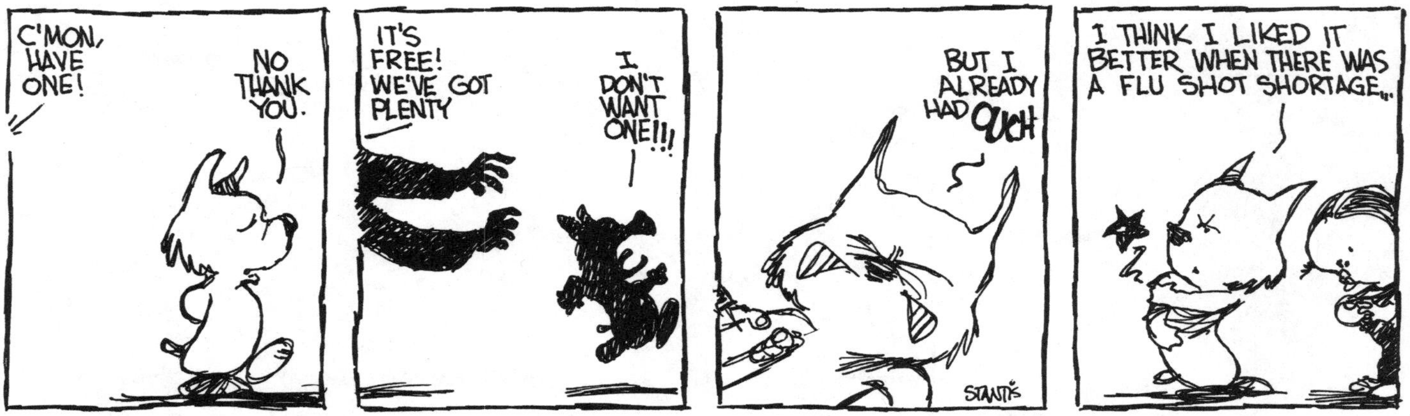
C'MON, HAVE ONE!
NO THANK YOU.
IT'S FREE! WE'VE GOT PLENTY
I DON'T WANT ONE!!!
BUT I ALREADY HAD OUCH
I THINK I LIKED IT BETTER WHEN THERE WAS A FLU SHOT SHORTAGE...

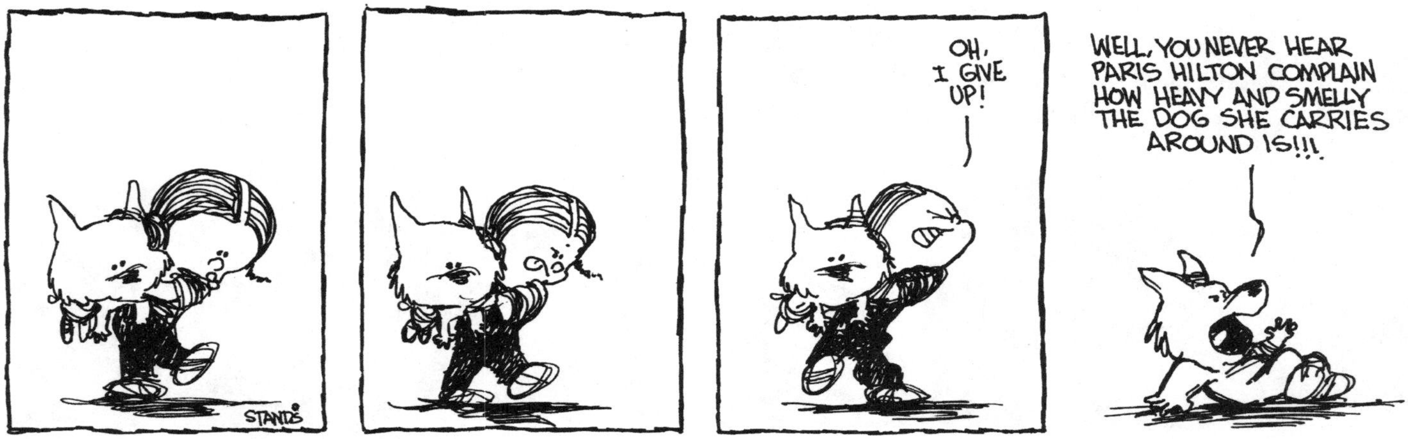
OH, I GIVE UP!
WELL, YOU NEVER HEAR PARIS HILTON COMPLAIN HOW HEAVY AND SMELLY THE DOG SHE CARRIES AROUND IS!!!

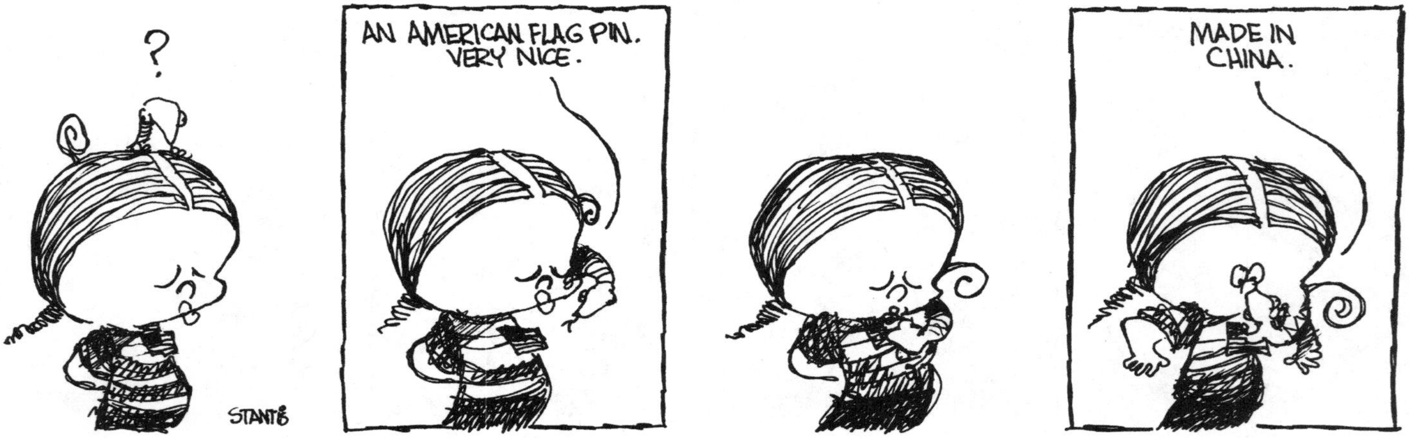
?
AN AMERICAN FLAG PIN. VERY NICE.
MADE IN CHINA.

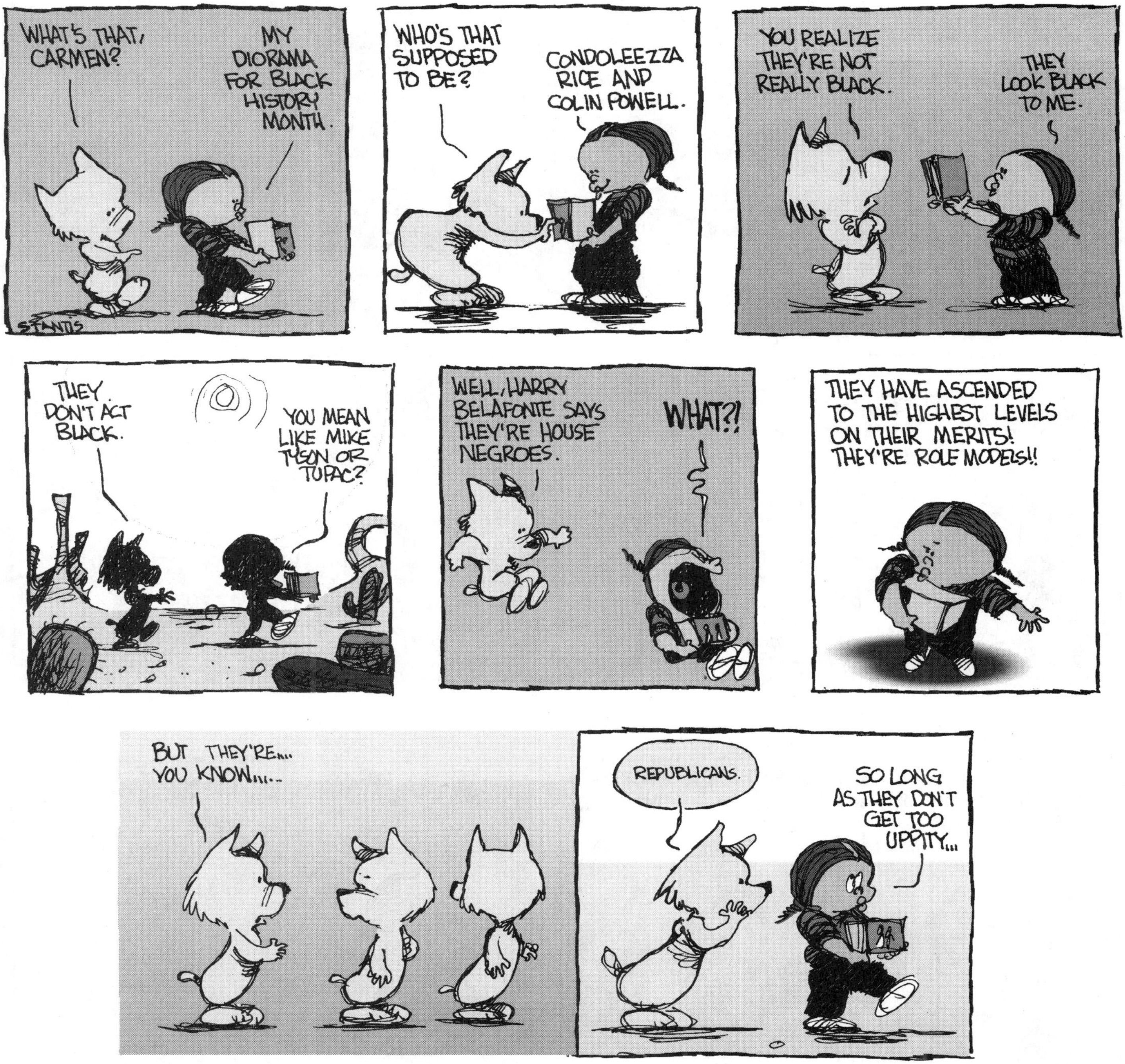
WHAT'S THAT, CARMEN?
MY DIORAMA FOR BLACK HISTORY MONTH.
STANTIS
WHO'S THAT SUPPOSED TO BE?
CONDOLEEZZA RICE AND COLIN POWELL.
YOU REALIZE THEY'RE NOT REALLY BLACK.
THEY LOOK BLACK TO ME.
THEY DON'T ACT BLACK.
YOU MEAN LIKE MIKE TYSON OR TUPAC?
WELL, HARRY BELAFONTE SAYS THEY'RE HOUSE NEGROES.
WHAT?!
THEY HAVE ASCENDED TO THE HIGHEST LEVELS ON THEIR MERITS! THEY'RE ROLE MODELS!!
BUT THEY'RE.... YOU KNOW......
REPUBLICANS.
SO LONG AS THEY DON'T GET TOO UPPITY...

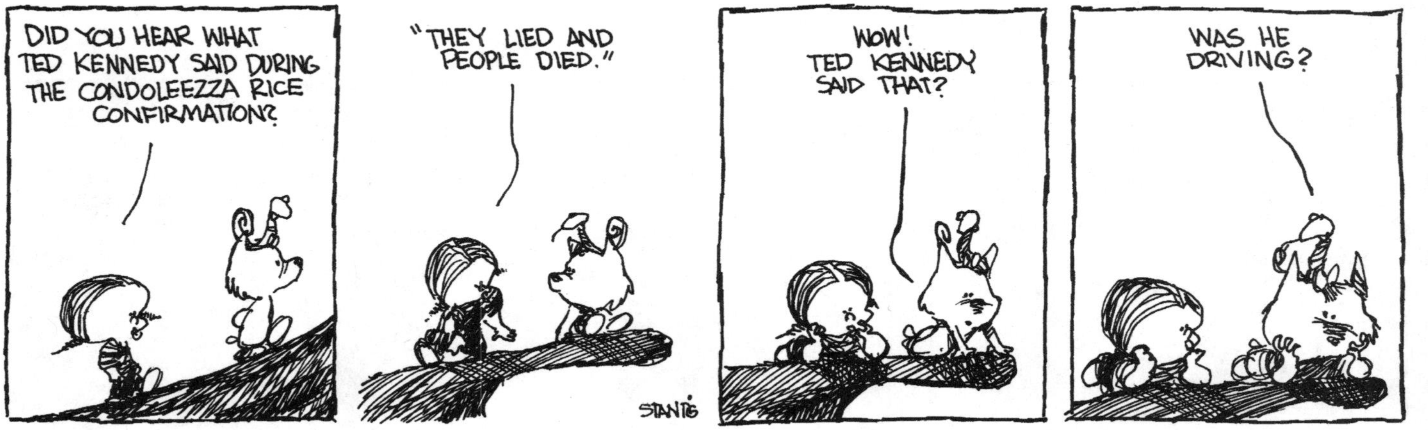
DID YOU HEAR WHAT TED KENNEDY SAID DURING THE CONDOLEEZZA RICE CONFIRMATION?
"THEY LIED AND PEOPLE DIED."
WOW! TED KENNEDY SAID THAT?
WAS HE DRIVING?

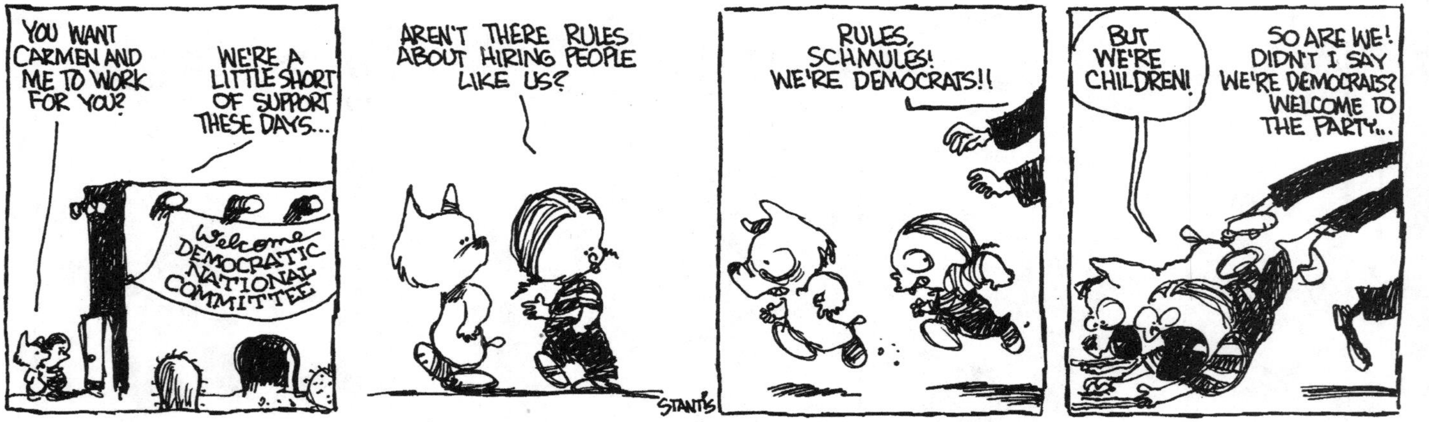
YOU WANT CARMEN AND ME TO WORK FOR YOU?
WE'RE A LITTLE SHORT OF SUPPORT THESE DAYS...
Welcome DEMOCRATIC NATIONAL COMMITTEE
AREN'T THERE RULES ABOUT HIRING PEOPLE LIKE US?
RULES, SCHMULES! WE'RE DEMOCRATS!!
BUT WE'RE CHILDREN!
SO ARE WE! DIDN'T I SAY WE'RE DEMOCRATS? WELCOME TO THE PARTY...

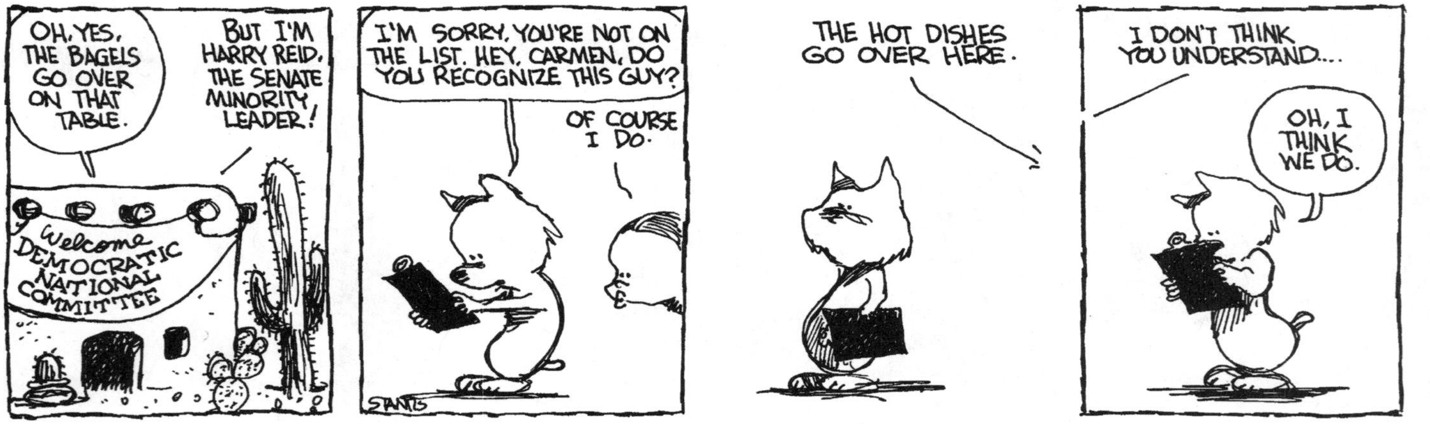
OH, YES, THE BAGELS GO OVER ON THAT TABLE.
BUT I'M HARRY REID, THE SENATE MINORITY LEADER!
Welcome DEMOCRATIC NATIONAL COMMITTEE
I'M SORRY, YOU'RE NOT ON THE LIST. HEY, CARMEN, DO YOU RECOGNIZE THIS GUY?
OF COURSE I DO.
THE HOT DISHES GO OVER HERE.
I DON'T THINK YOU UNDERSTAND....
OH, I THINK WE DO.

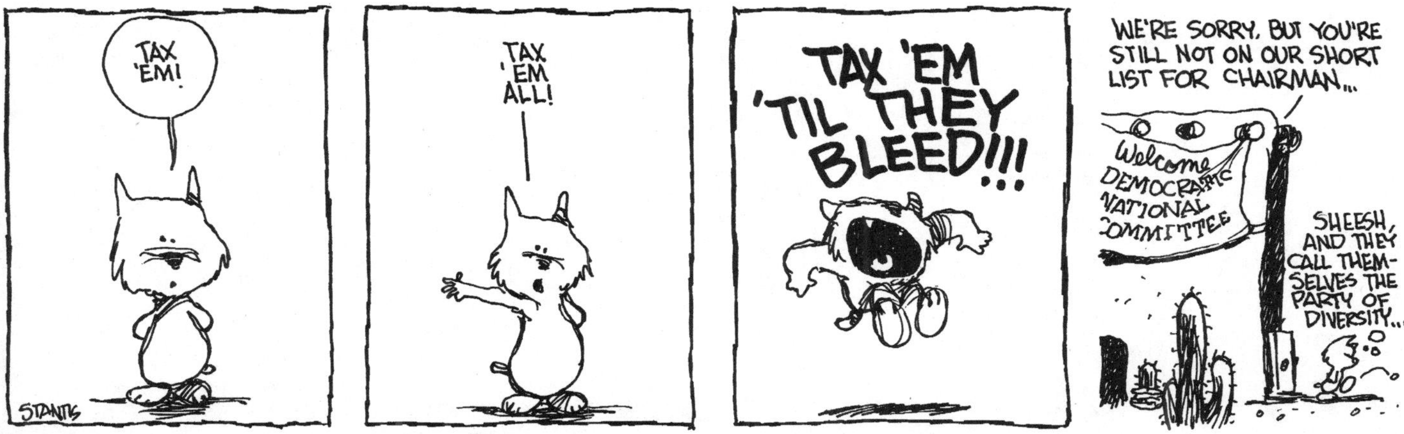
TAX 'EM!
TAX 'EM ALL!
TAX 'EM 'TIL THEY BLEED!!!
WE'RE SORRY, BUT YOU'RE STILL NOT ON OUR SHORT LIST FOR CHAIRMAN...
Welcome DEMOCRATIC NATIONAL COMMITTEE
SHEESH, AND THEY CALL THEM-SELVES THE PARTY OF DIVERSITY...
STANTIS

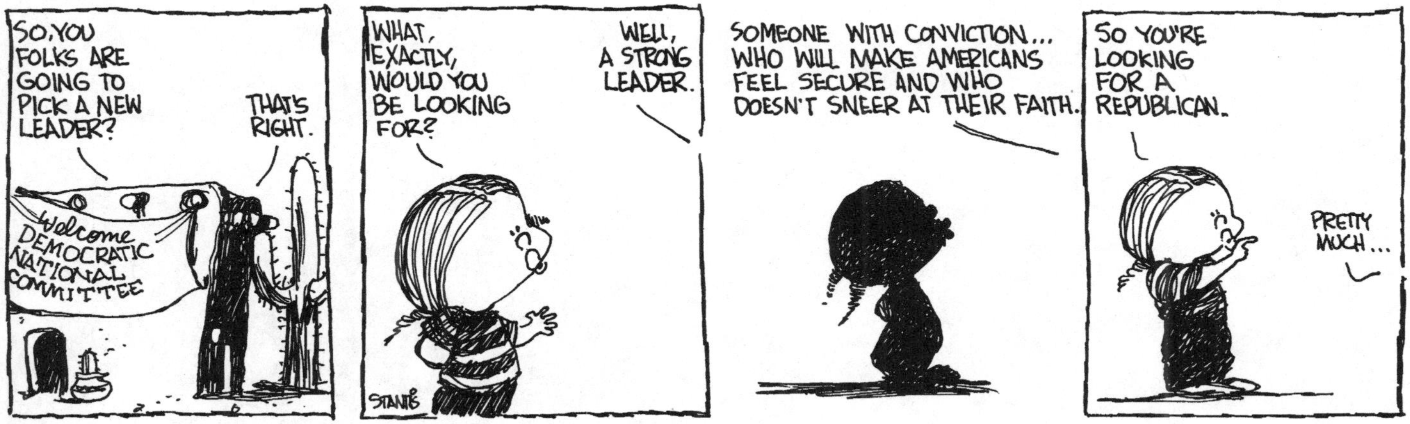
SO, YOU FOLKS ARE GOING TO PICK A NEW LEADER?
THAT'S RIGHT.
Welcome DEMOCRATIC NATIONAL COMMITTEE
WHAT, EXACTLY, WOULD YOU BE LOOKING FOR?
WELL, A STRONG LEADER.
SOMEONE WITH CONVICTION... WHO WILL MAKE AMERICANS FEEL SECURE AND WHO DOESN'T SNEER AT THEIR FAITH.
SO YOU'RE LOOKING FOR A REPUBLICAN.
PRETTY MUCH...
STANTIS

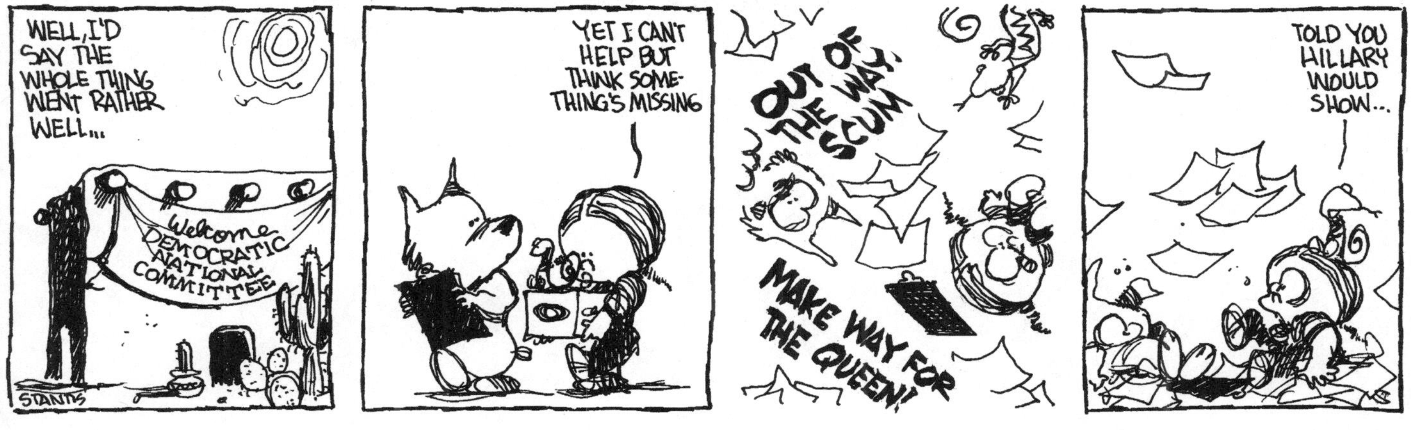
WELL, I'D SAY THE WHOLE THING WENT RATHER WELL...
Welcome DEMOCRATIC NATIONAL COMMITTEE
YET I CAN'T HELP BUT THINK SOME-THING'S MISSING
OUT OF THE WAY, SCUM
MAKE WAY FOR THE QUEEN!
TOLD YOU HILLARY WOULD SHOW...
STANTIS

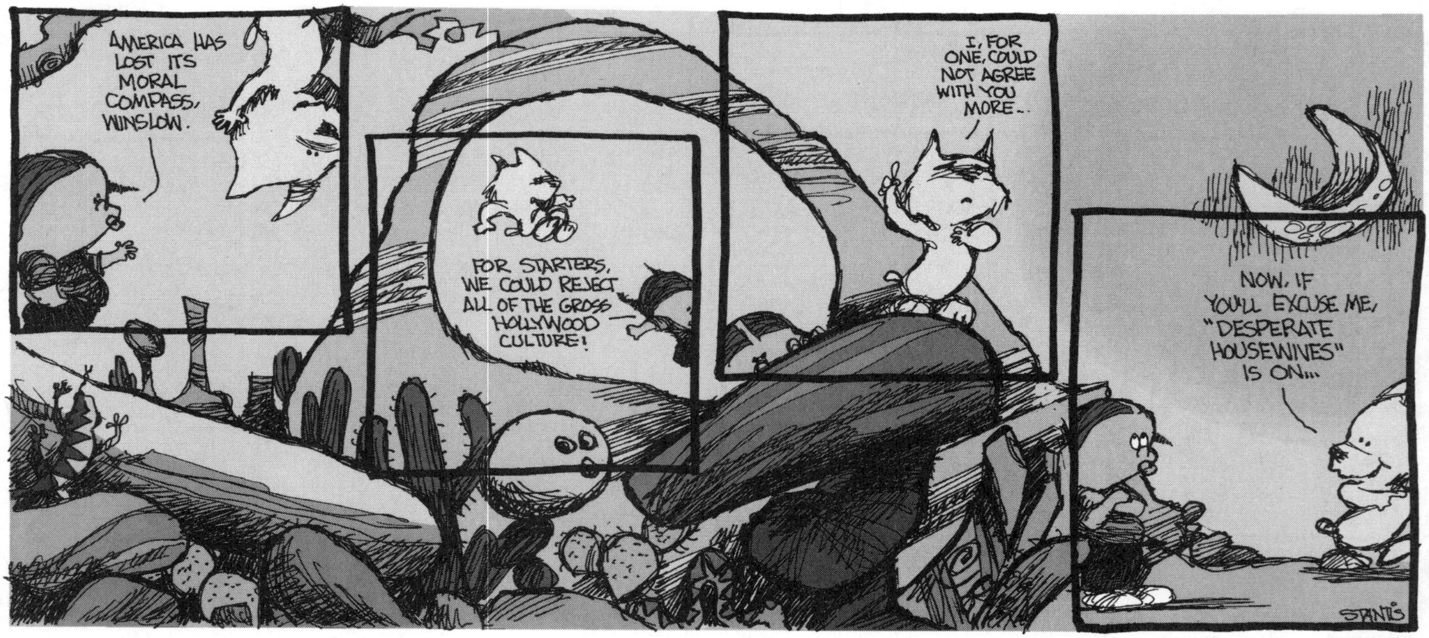
AMERICA HAS LOST ITS MORAL COMPASS, WINSLOW.
FOR STARTERS, WE COULD REJECT ALL OF THE GROSS HOLLYWOOD CULTURE!
I, FOR ONE, COULD NOT AGREE WITH YOU MORE...
NOW, IF YOU'LL EXCUSE ME, "DESPERATE HOUSEWIVES" IS ON...

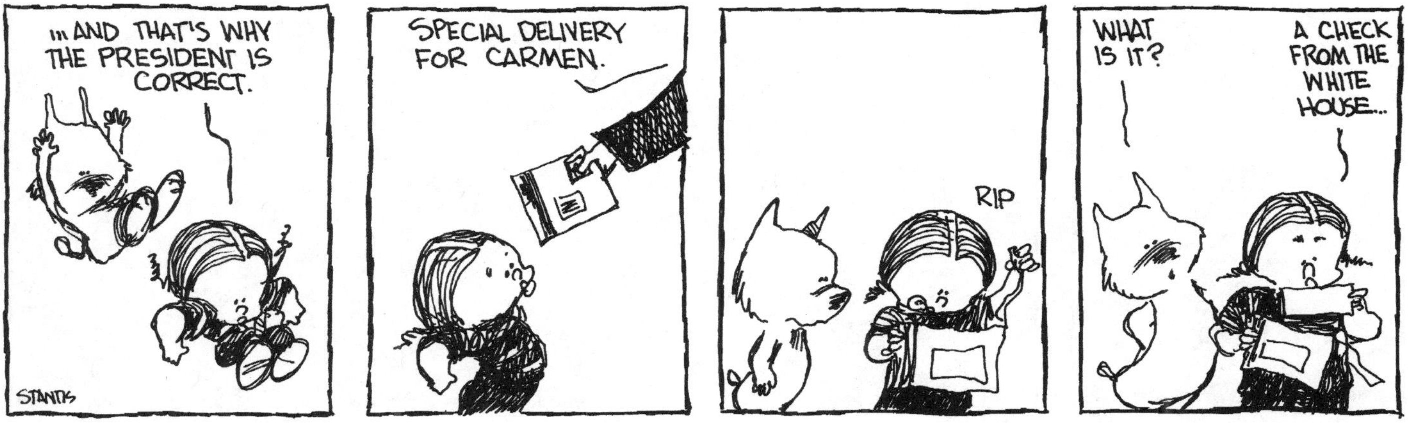
...AND THAT'S WHY THE PRESIDENT IS CORRECT.
STANTIS
SPECIAL DELIVERY FOR CARMEN.
RIP
WHAT IS IT?
A CHECK FROM THE WHITE HOUSE...

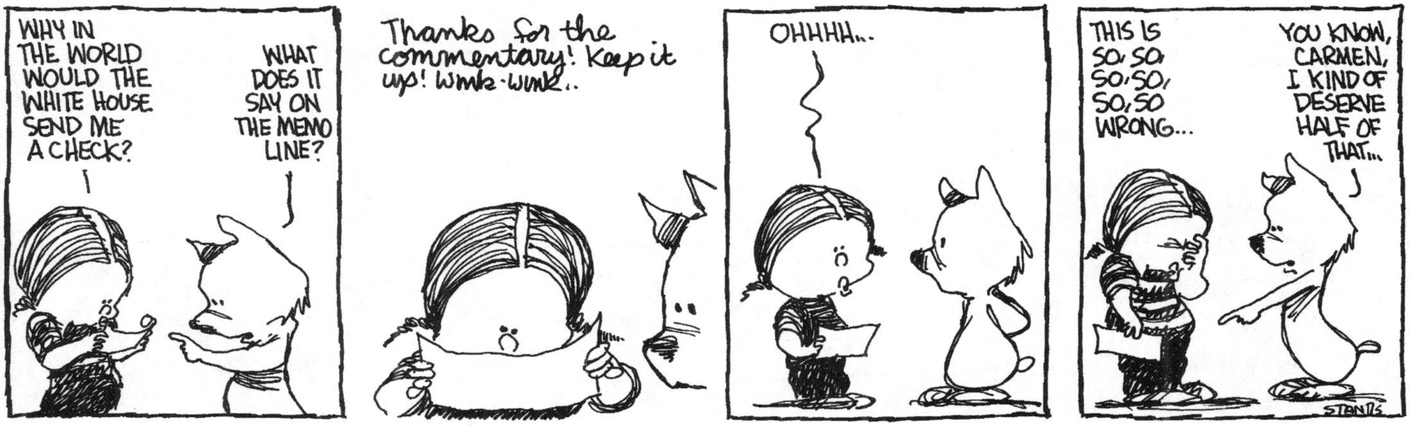
WHY IN THE WORLD WOULD THE WHITE HOUSE SEND ME A CHECK?
WHAT DOES IT SAY ON THE MEMO LINE?
Thanks for the commentary! Keep it up! Wink-wink..
OHHHH...
THIS IS SO, SO, SO, SO, SO, SO WRONG...
YOU KNOW, CARMEN, I KIND OF DESERVE HALF OF THAT...
STANTIS

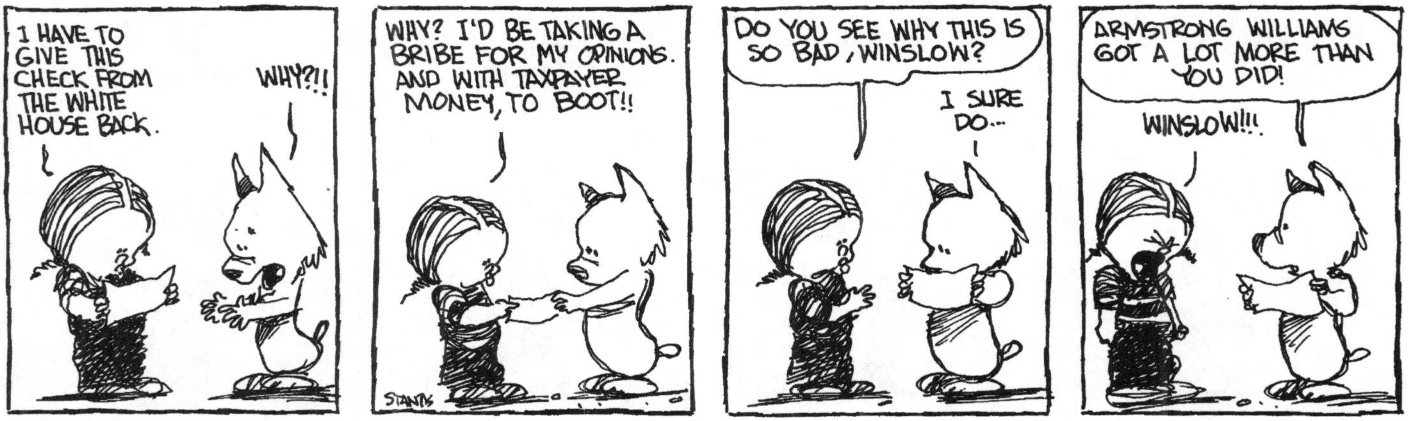
I HAVE TO GIVE THIS CHECK FROM THE WHITE HOUSE BACK.
WHY?!!
WHY? I'D BE TAKING A BRIBE FOR MY OPINIONS. AND WITH TAXPAYER MONEY, TO BOOT!!
STANTIS
DO YOU SEE WHY THIS IS SO BAD, WINSLOW?
I SURE DO...
ARMSTRONG WILLIAMS GOT A LOT MORE THAN YOU DID!
WINSLOW!!!

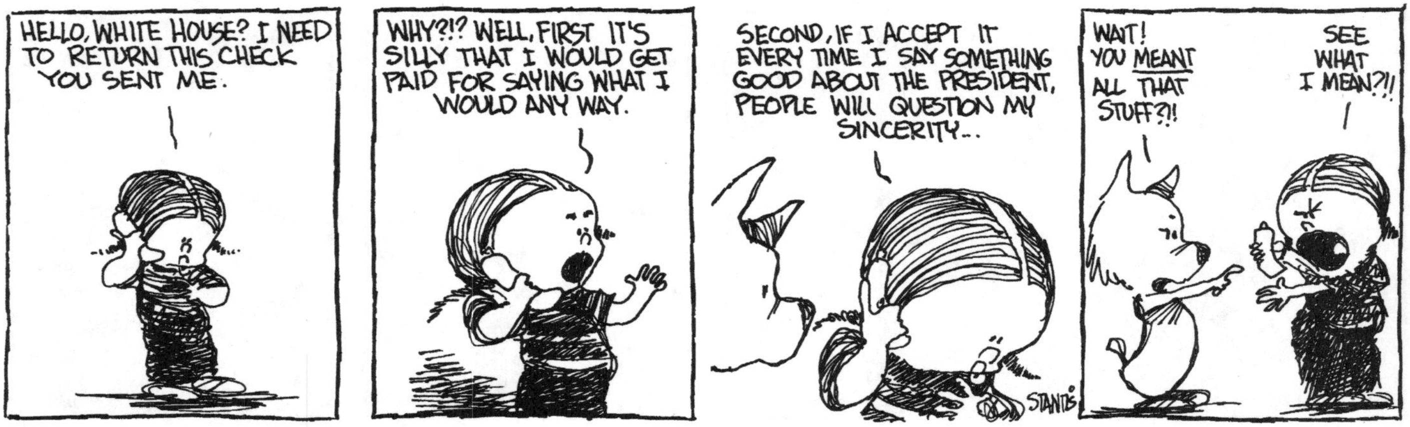
HELLO, WHITE HOUSE? I NEED TO RETURN THIS CHECK YOU SENT ME.
WHY?!? WELL, FIRST IT'S SILLY THAT I WOULD GET PAID FOR SAYING WHAT I WOULD ANY WAY.
SECOND, IF I ACCEPT IT EVERY TIME I SAY SOMETHING GOOD ABOUT THE PRESIDENT, PEOPLE WILL QUESTION MY SINCERITY...
WAIT! YOU MEANT ALL THAT STUFF?!!
SEE WHAT I MEAN?!!
STANTIS

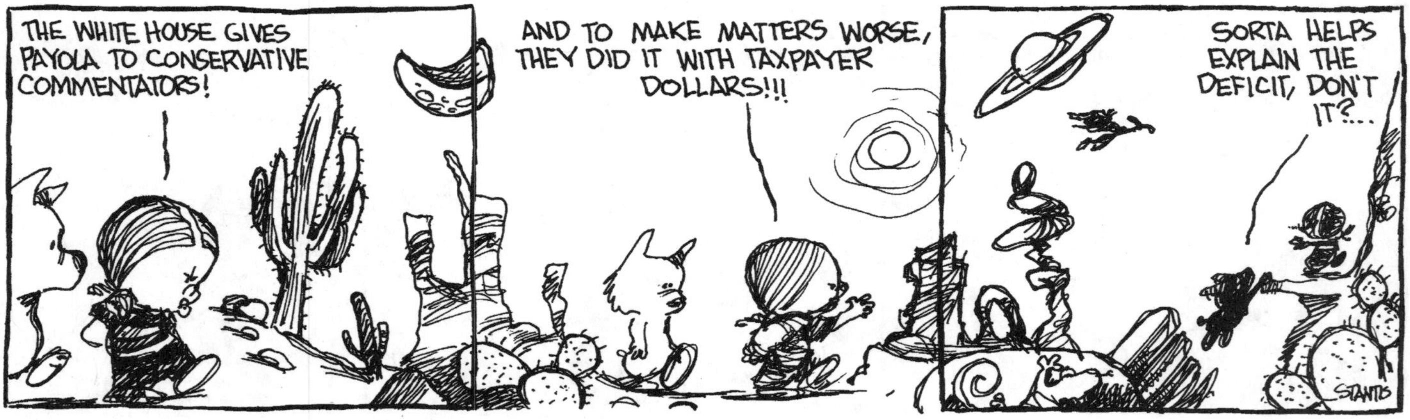
THE WHITE HOUSE GIVES PAYOLA TO CONSERVATIVE COMMENTATORS!
AND TO MAKE MATTERS WORSE, THEY DID IT WITH TAXPAYER DOLLARS!!!
SORTA HELPS EXPLAIN THE DEFICIT, DON'T IT?...
STANTIS

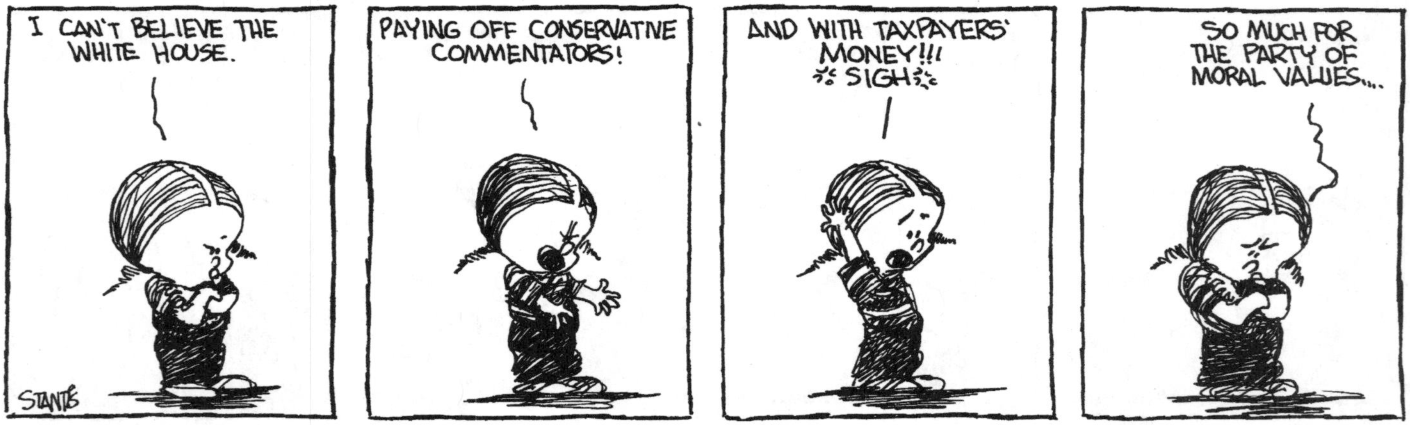
I CAN'T BELIEVE THE WHITE HOUSE.
PAYING OFF CONSERVATIVE COMMENTATORS!
AND WITH TAXPAYERS' MONEY!!! *SIGH*
SO MUCH FOR THE PARTY OF MORAL VALUES...
STANTIS

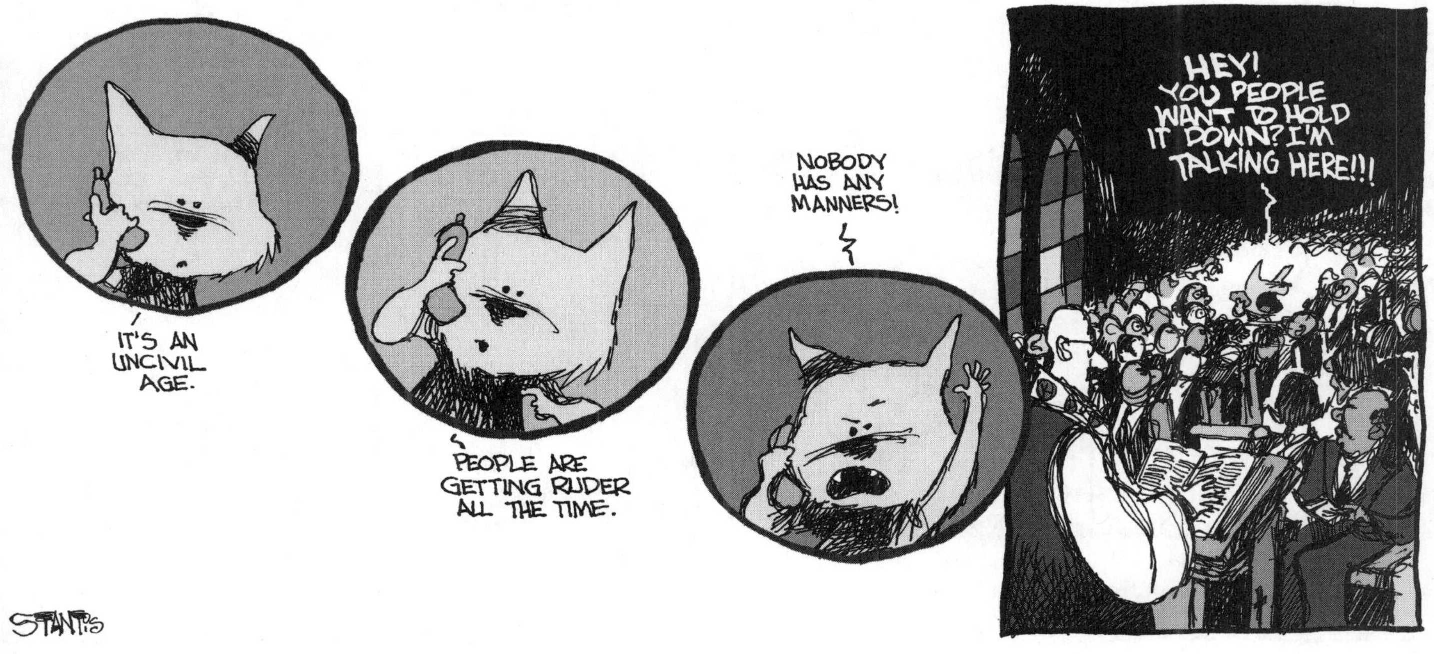
IT'S AN UNCIVIL AGE.
PEOPLE ARE GETTING RUDER ALL THE TIME.
NOBODY HAS ANY MANNERS!
HEY! YOU PEOPLE WANT TO HOLD IT DOWN? I'M TALKING HERE!!!
STANTIS

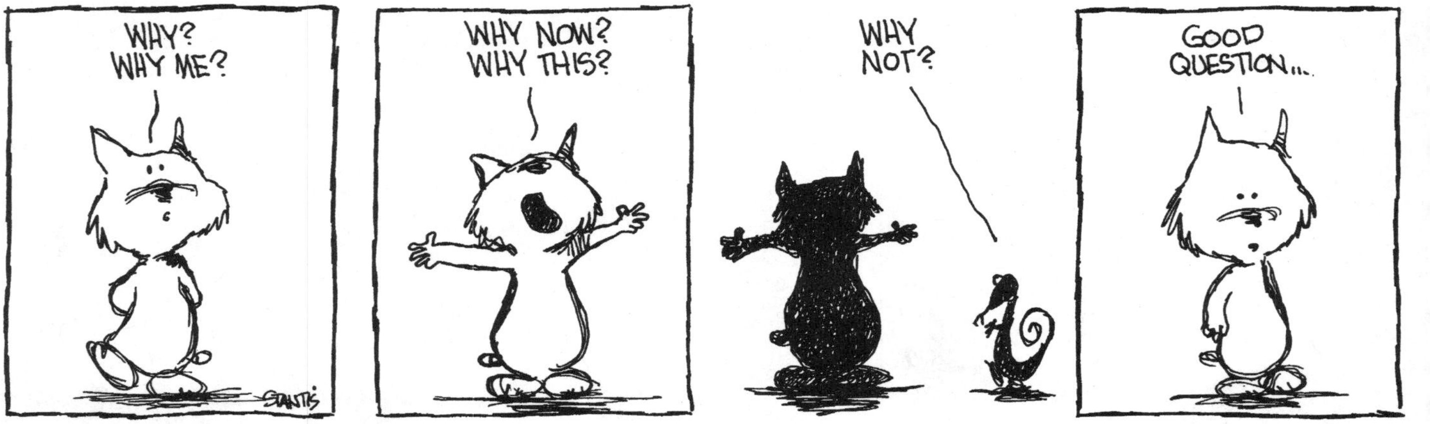
WHY? WHY ME?
STANTIS
WHY NOW? WHY THIS?
WHY NOT?
GOOD QUESTION...

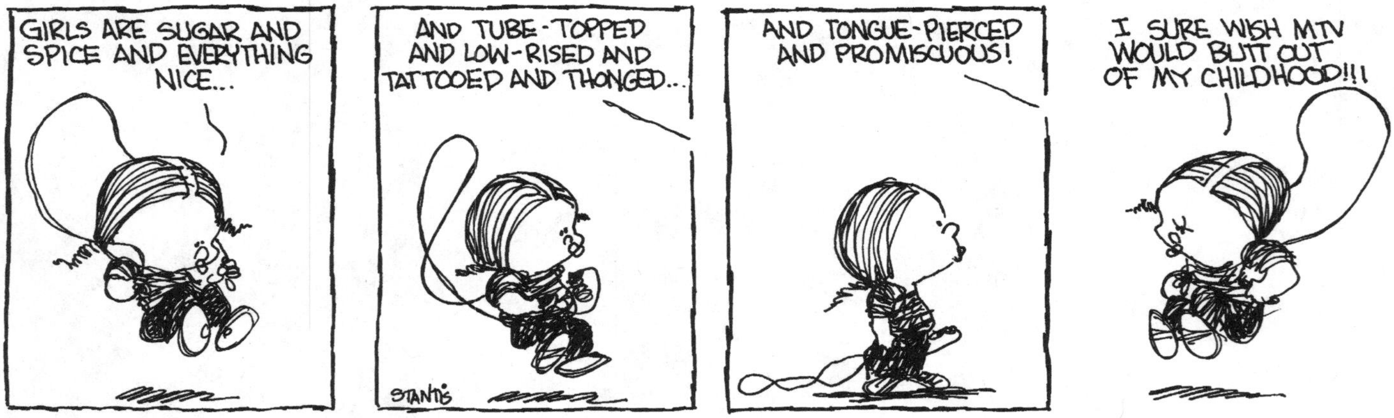
GIRLS ARE SUGAR AND SPICE AND EVERYTHING NICE...
AND TUBE-TOPPED AND LOW-RISED AND TATTOOED AND THONGED...
STANTIS
AND TONGUE-PIERCED AND PROMISCUOUS!
I SURE WISH MTV WOULD BUTT OUT OF MY CHILDHOOD!!!

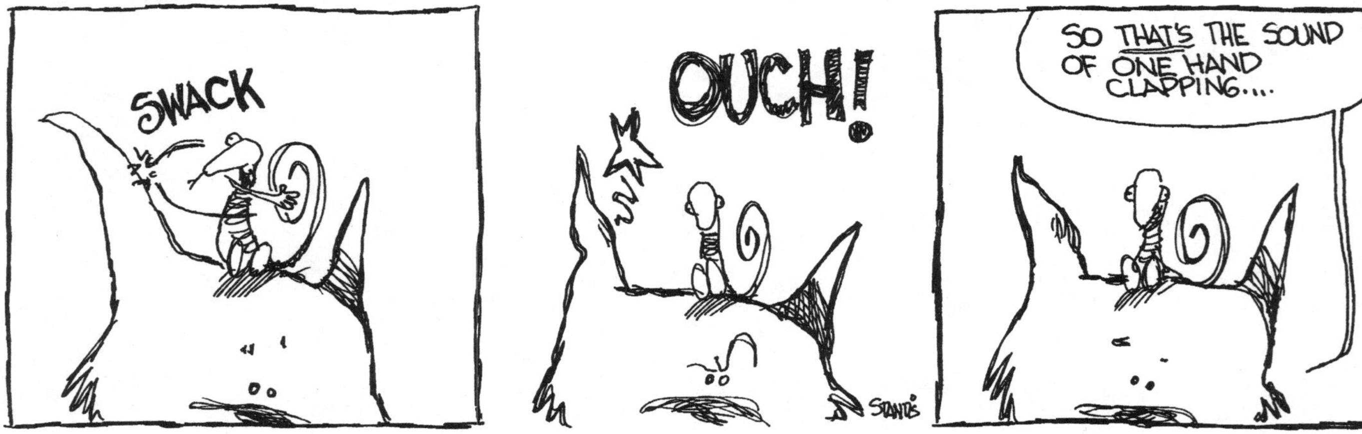
SWACK
OUCH!
STANTIS
SO THAT'S THE SOUND OF ONE HAND CLAPPING....

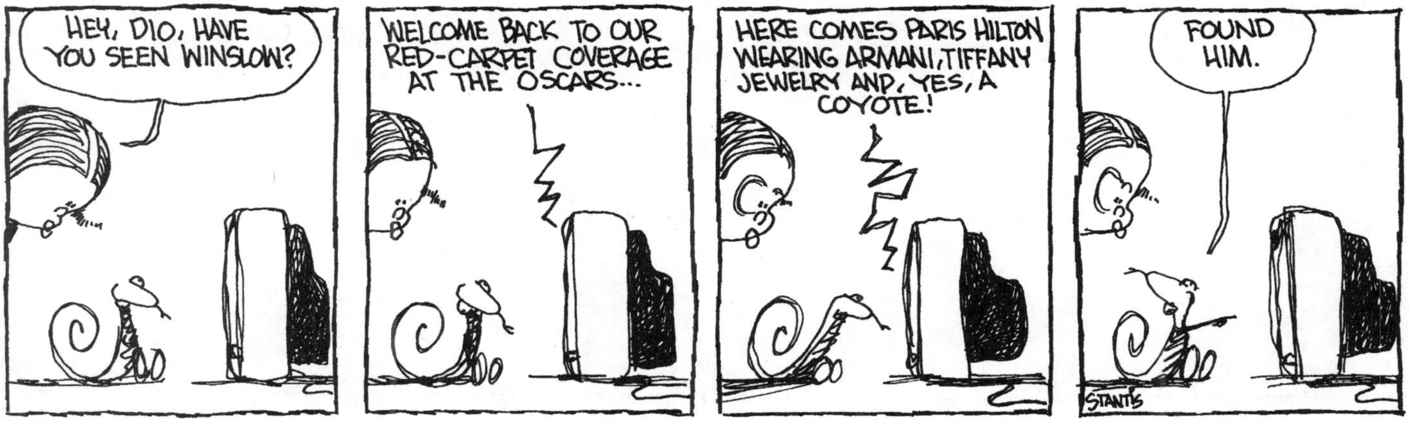
HEY, DIO, HAVE YOU SEEN WINSLOW?
WELCOME BACK TO OUR RED-CARPET COVERAGE AT THE OSCARS...
HERE COMES PARIS HILTON WEARING ARMANI, TIFFANY JEWELRY AND, YES, A COYOTE!
FOUND HIM.
STANTIS

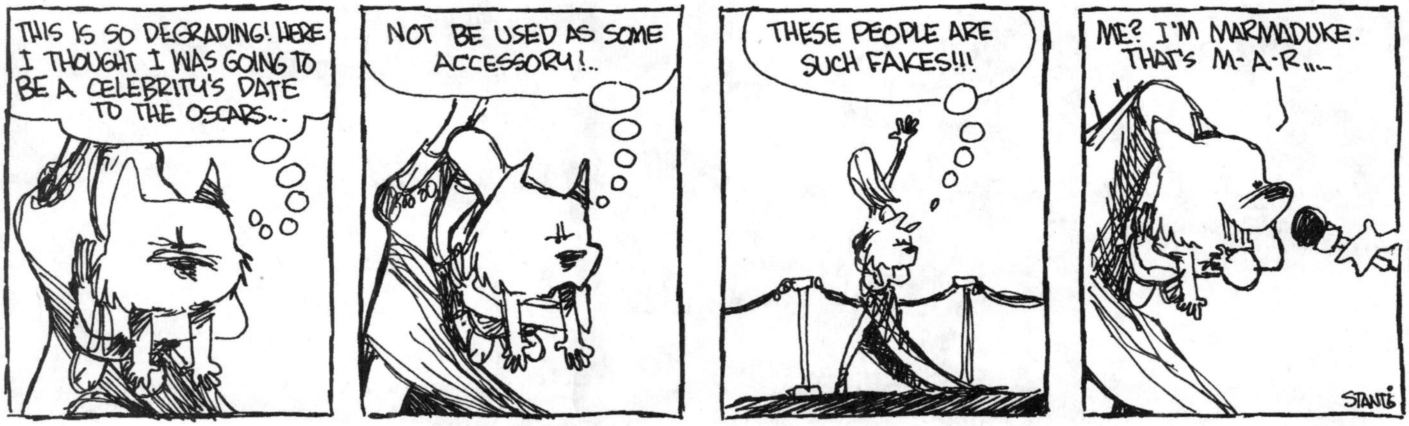
THIS IS SO DEGRADING! HERE I THOUGHT I WAS GOING TO BE A CELEBRITY'S DATE TO THE OSCARS...
NOT BE USED AS SOME ACCESSORY!..
THESE PEOPLE ARE SUCH FAKES!!!
ME? I'M MARMADUKE. THAT'S M-A-R...
STANTIS

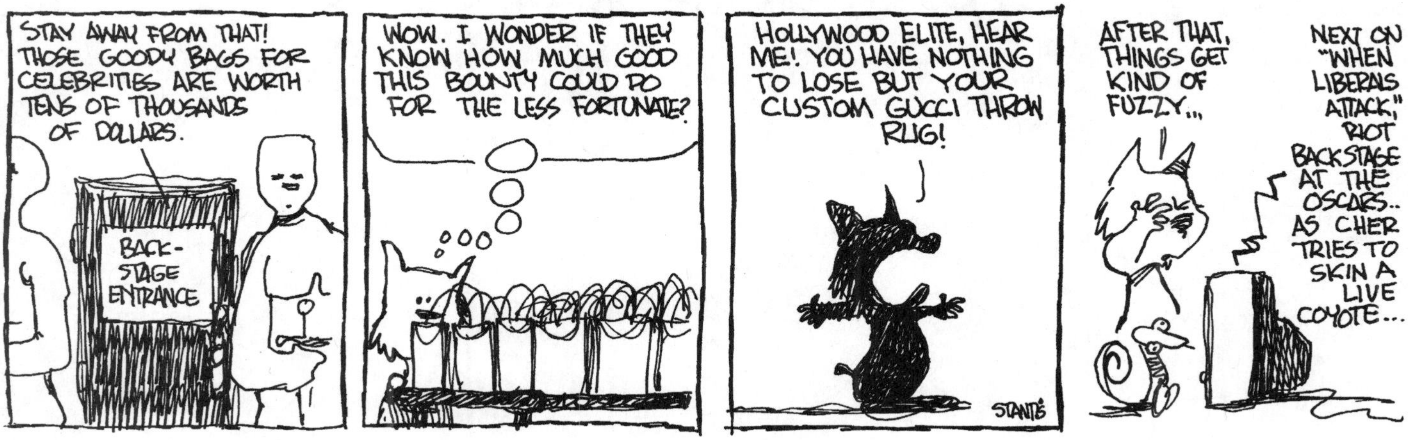
STAY AWAY FROM THAT! THOSE GOODY BAGS FOR CELEBRITIES ARE WORTH TENS OF THOUSANDS OF DOLLARS.
BACK-STAGE ENTRANCE
WOW. I WONDER IF THEY KNOW HOW MUCH GOOD THIS BOUNTY COULD DO FOR THE LESS FORTUNATE?
HOLLYWOOD ELITE, HEAR ME! YOU HAVE NOTHING TO LOSE BUT YOUR CUSTOM GUCCI THROW RUG!
STANTIS
AFTER THAT, THINGS GET KIND OF FUZZY...
NEXT ON "WHEN LIBERALS ATTACK," RIOT BACKSTAGE AT THE OSCARS... AS CHER TRIES TO SKIN A LIVE COYOTE...

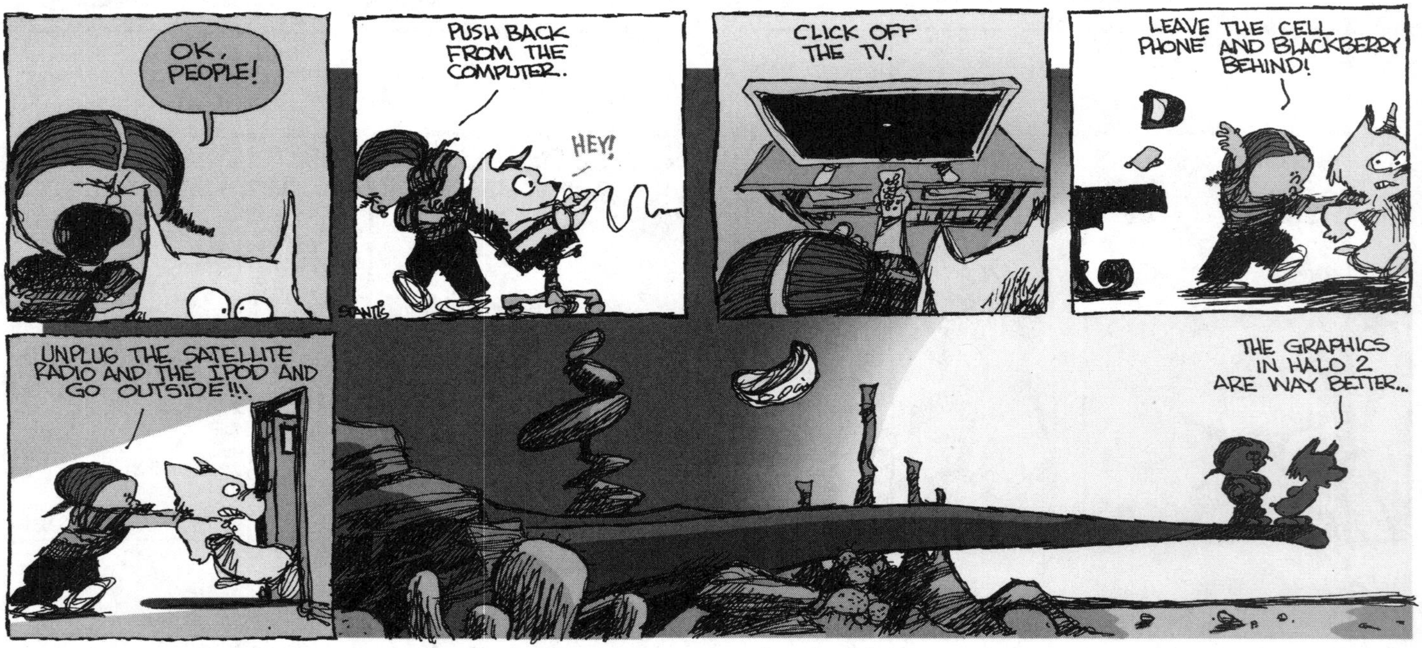
OK, PEOPLE!
PUSH BACK FROM THE COMPUTER.
HEY!
CLICK OFF THE TV.
LEAVE THE CELL PHONE AND BLACKBERRY BEHIND!
UNPLUG THE SATELLITE RADIO AND THE IPOD AND GO OUTSIDE!!!
THE GRAPHICS IN HALO 2 ARE WAY BETTER..

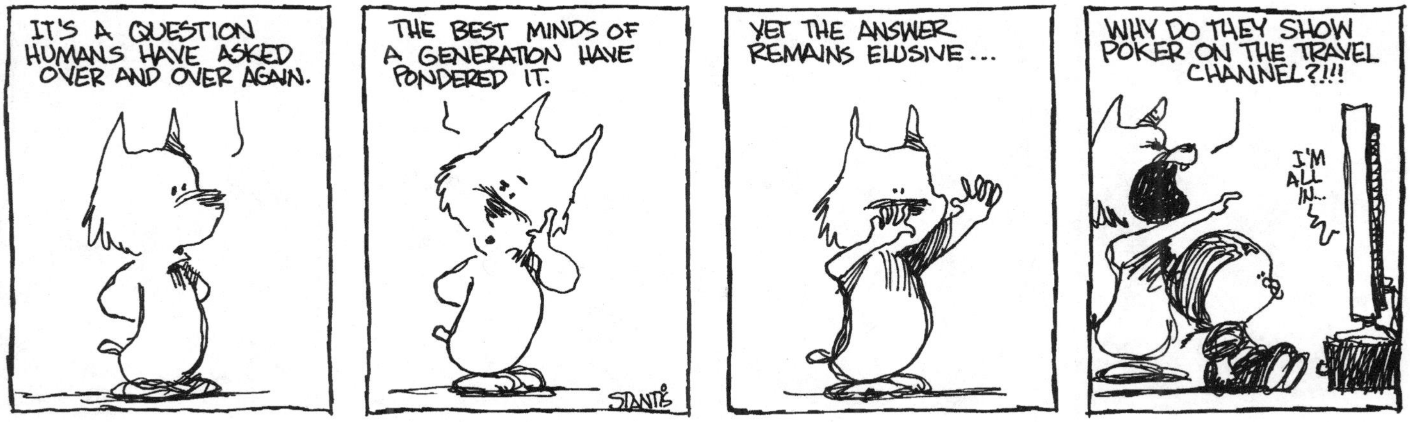
IT'S A QUESTION HUMANS HAVE ASKED OVER AND OVER AGAIN.
THE BEST MINDS OF A GENERATION HAVE PONDERED IT.
YET THE ANSWER REMAINS ELUSIVE...
WHY DO THEY SHOW POKER ON THE TRAVEL CHANNEL?!!!
I'M ALL IN...

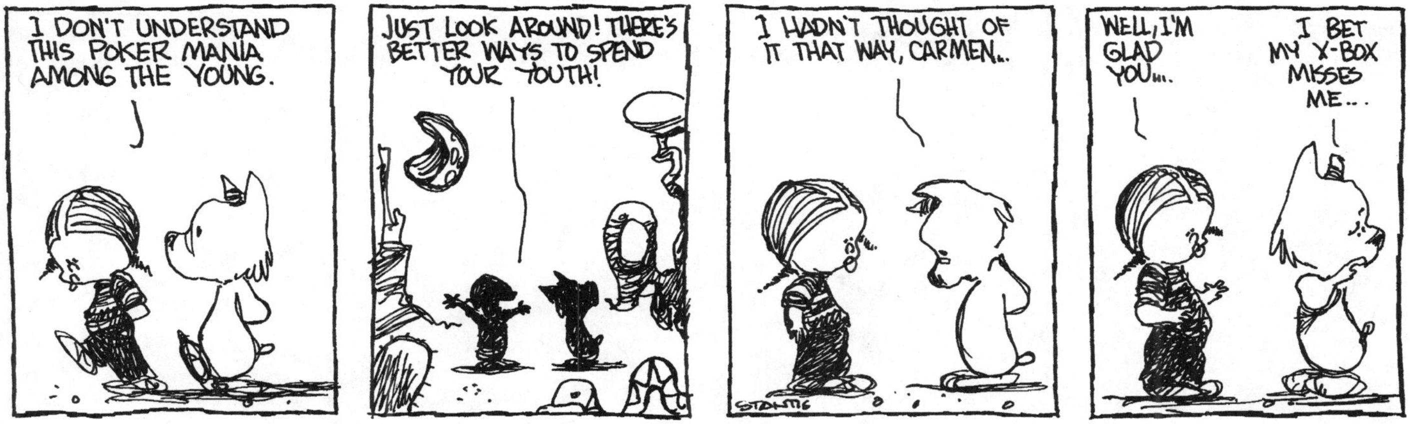
I DON'T UNDERSTAND THIS POKER MANIA AMONG THE YOUNG.
JUST LOOK AROUND! THERE'S BETTER WAYS TO SPEND YOUR YOUTH!
I HADN'T THOUGHT OF IT THAT WAY, CARMEN...
WELL, I'M GLAD YOU...
I BET MY X-BOX MISSES ME...

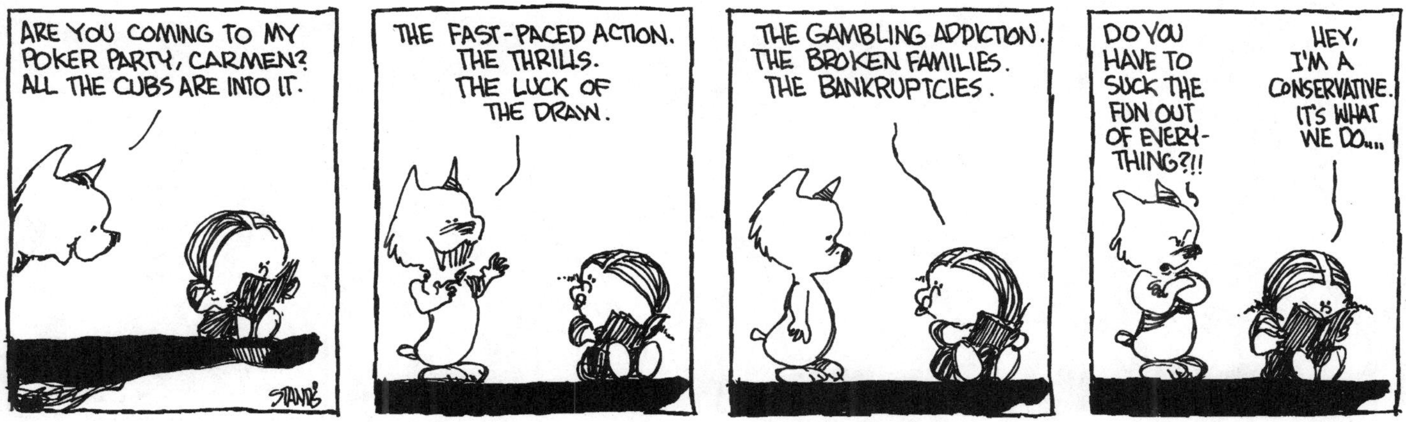
ARE YOU COMING TO MY POKER PARTY, CARMEN? ALL THE CUBS ARE INTO IT.
THE FAST-PACED ACTION. THE THRILLS. THE LUCK OF THE DRAW.
THE GAMBLING ADDICTION. THE BROKEN FAMILIES. THE BANKRUPTCIES.
DO YOU HAVE TO SUCK THE FUN OUT OF EVERY-THING?!!
HEY, I'M A CONSERVATIVE. IT'S WHAT WE DO...

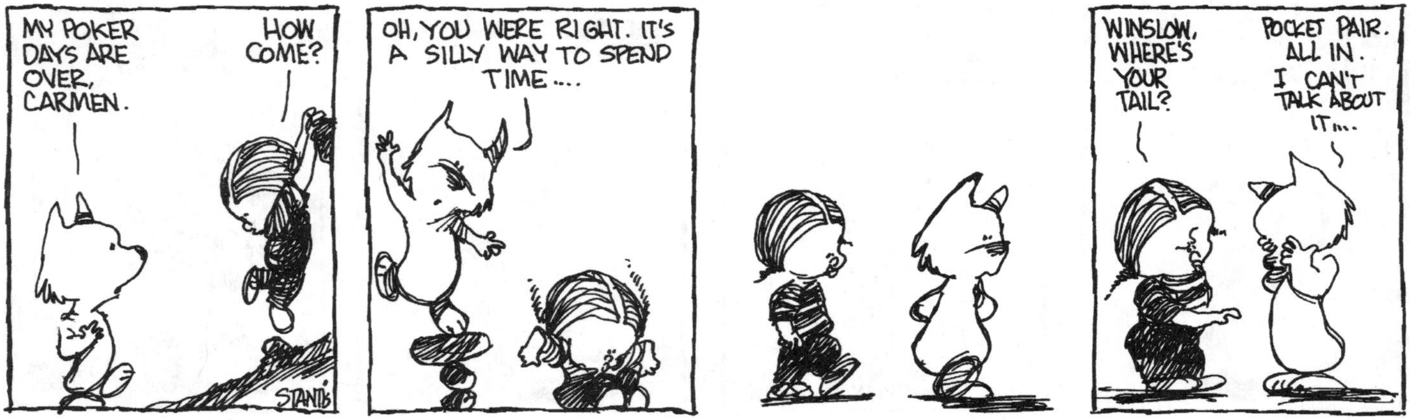
MY POKER DAYS ARE OVER, CARMEN.
HOW COME?
OH, YOU WERE RIGHT. IT'S A SILLY WAY TO SPEND TIME....
WINSLOW, WHERE'S YOUR TAIL?
POCKET PAIR. ALL IN.
I CAN'T TALK ABOUT IT....
STANTIS

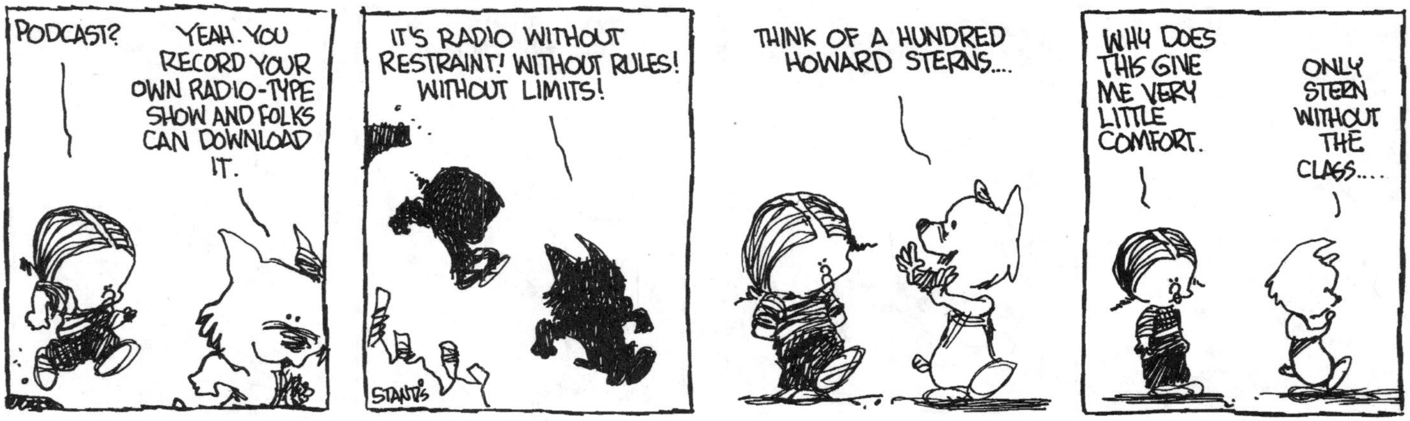
PODCAST?
YEAH. YOU RECORD YOUR OWN RADIO-TYPE SHOW AND FOLKS CAN DOWNLOAD IT.
IT'S RADIO WITHOUT RESTRAINT! WITHOUT RULES! WITHOUT LIMITS!
STANTIS
THINK OF A HUNDRED HOWARD STERNS....
WHY DOES THIS GIVE ME VERY LITTLE COMFORT.
ONLY STERN WITHOUT THE CLASS....

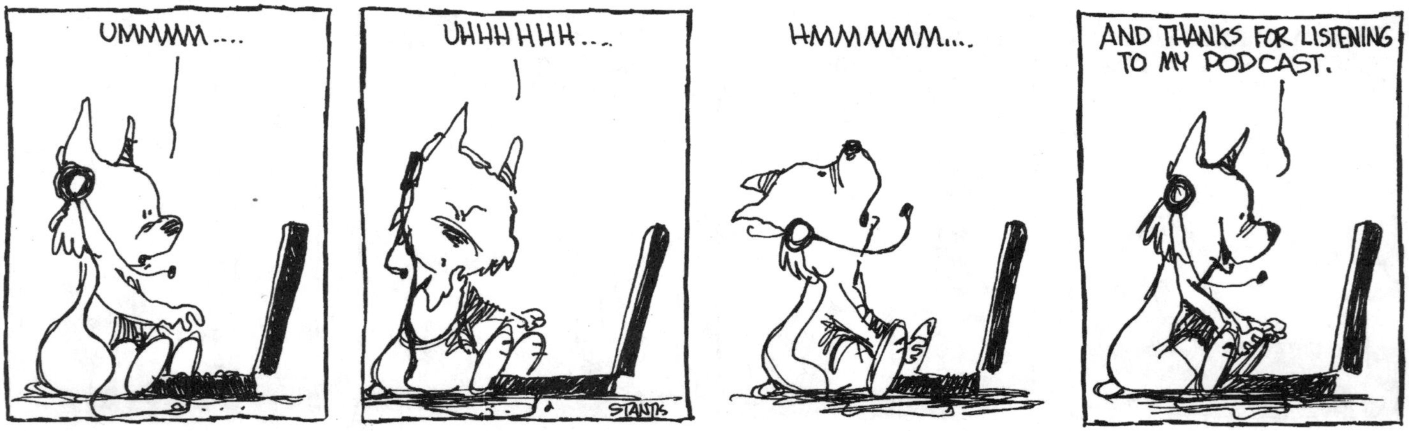
UMMMM....
UHHHHHH....
STANTIS
HMMMMM....
AND THANKS FOR LISTENING TO MY PODCAST.

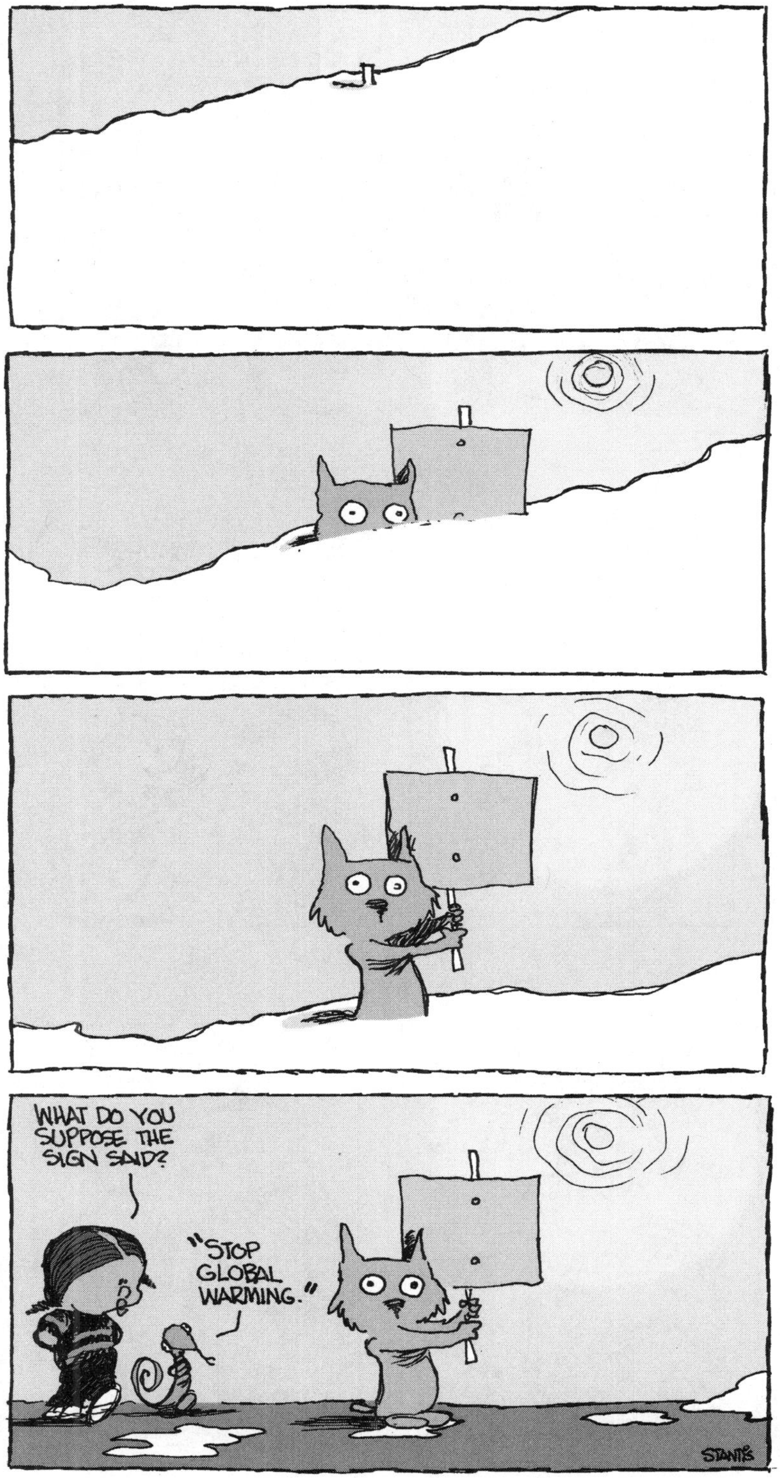
WHAT DO YOU SUPPOSE THE SIGN SAID?
"STOP GLOBAL WARMING."
STANTIS

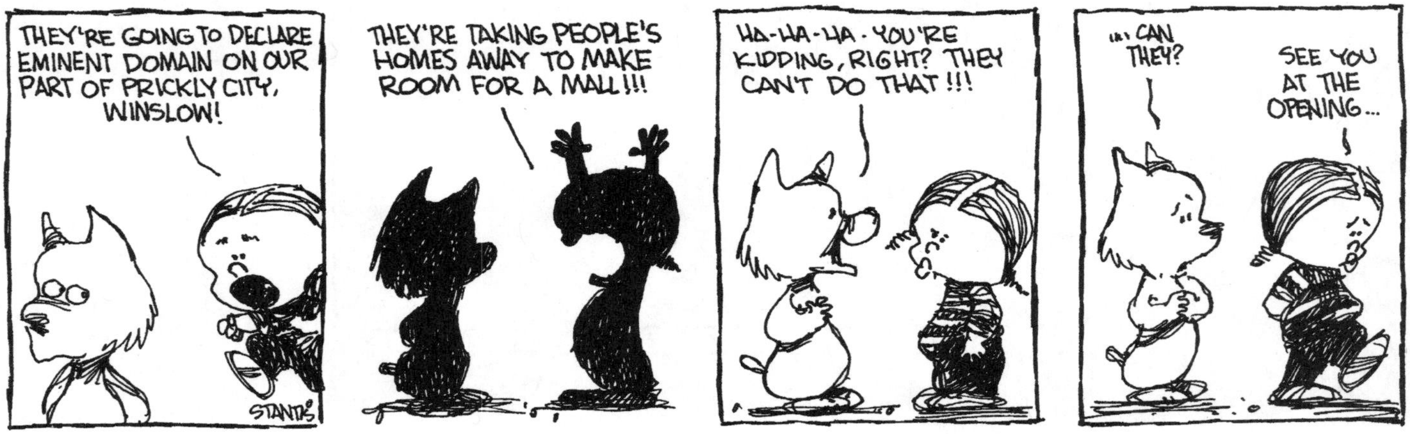
THEY'RE GOING TO DECLARE EMINENT DOMAIN ON OUR PART OF PRICKLY CITY, WINSLOW!
THEY'RE TAKING PEOPLE'S HOMES AWAY TO MAKE ROOM FOR A MALL!!!
HA-HA-HA - YOU'RE KIDDING, RIGHT? THEY CAN'T DO THAT!!!
... CAN THEY?
SEE YOU AT THE OPENING...
STANTIS

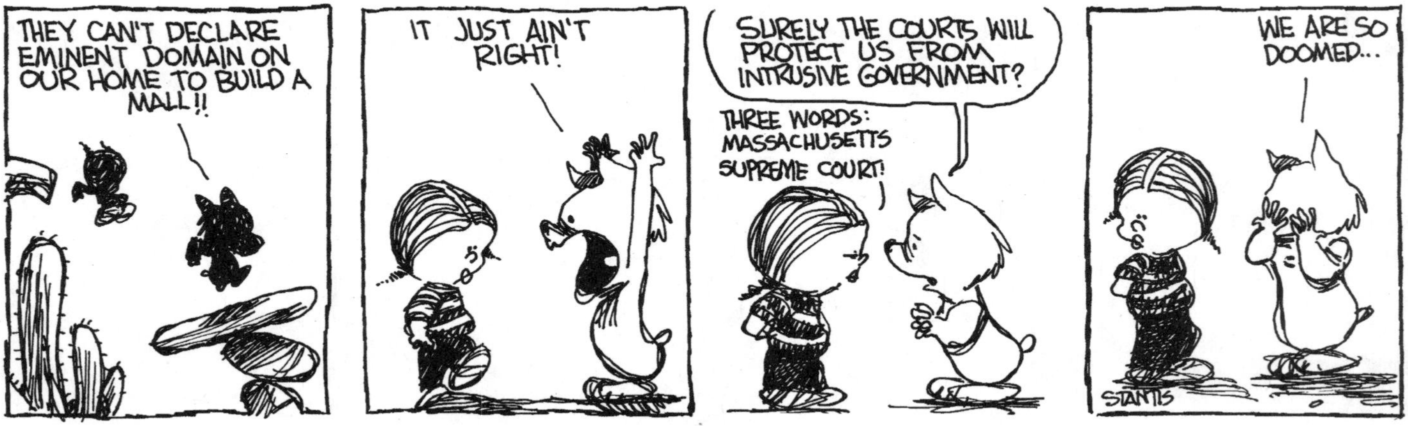
THEY CAN'T DECLARE EMINENT DOMAIN ON OUR HOME TO BUILD A MALL!!
IT JUST AIN'T RIGHT!
SURELY THE COURTS WILL PROTECT US FROM INTRUSIVE GOVERNMENT?
THREE WORDS: MASSACHUSETTS SUPREME COURT!
WE ARE SO DOOMED...
STANTIS

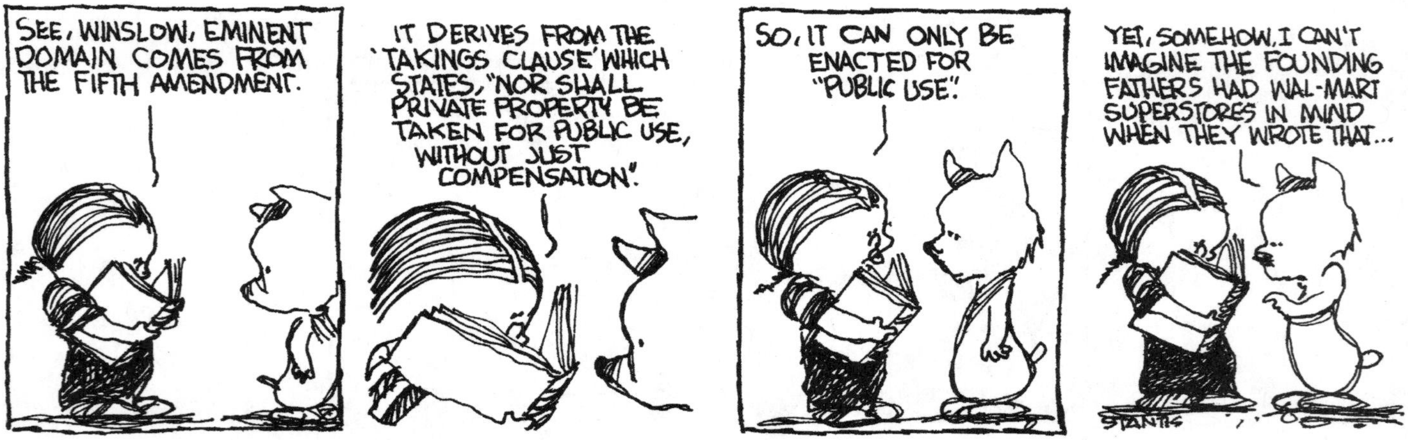
SEE, WINSLOW, EMINENT DOMAIN COMES FROM THE FIFTH AMENDMENT.
IT DERIVES FROM THE 'TAKINGS CLAUSE' WHICH STATES, "NOR SHALL PRIVATE PROPERTY BE TAKEN FOR PUBLIC USE, WITHOUT JUST COMPENSATION".
SO, IT CAN ONLY BE ENACTED FOR "PUBLIC USE".
YET, SOMEHOW, I CAN'T IMAGINE THE FOUNDING FATHERS HAD WAL-MART SUPERSTORES IN MIND WHEN THEY WROTE THAT...
STANTIS

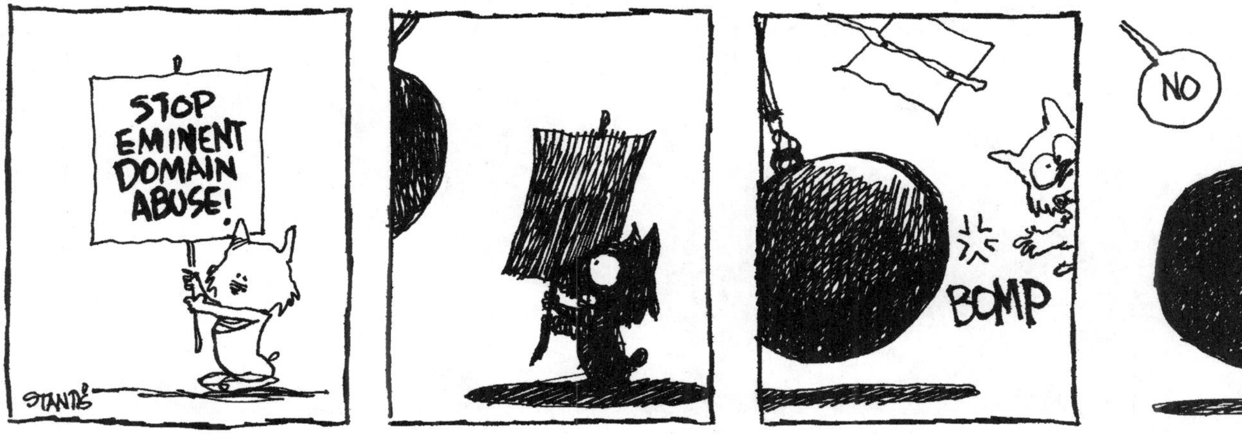
STOP EMINENT DOMAIN ABUSE!
STANTIS
BOMP
NO

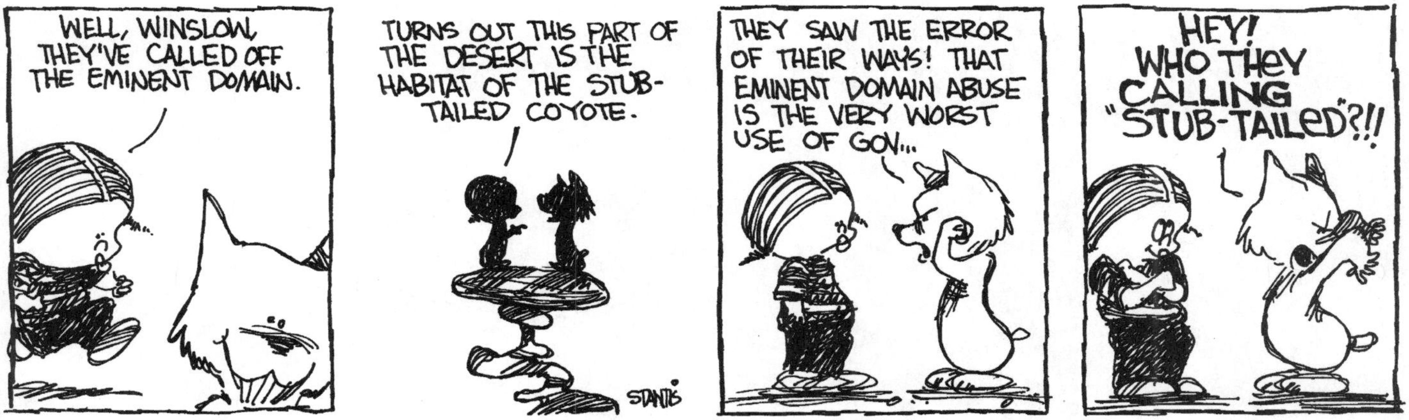
WELL, WINSLOW, THEY'VE CALLED OFF THE EMINENT DOMAIN.
TURNS OUT THIS PART OF THE DESERT IS THE HABITAT OF THE STUB-TAILED COYOTE.
STANTIS
THEY SAW THE ERROR OF THEIR WAYS! THAT EMINENT DOMAIN ABUSE IS THE VERY WORST USE OF GOV...
HEY! WHO THEY CALLING "STUB-TAILED"?!!

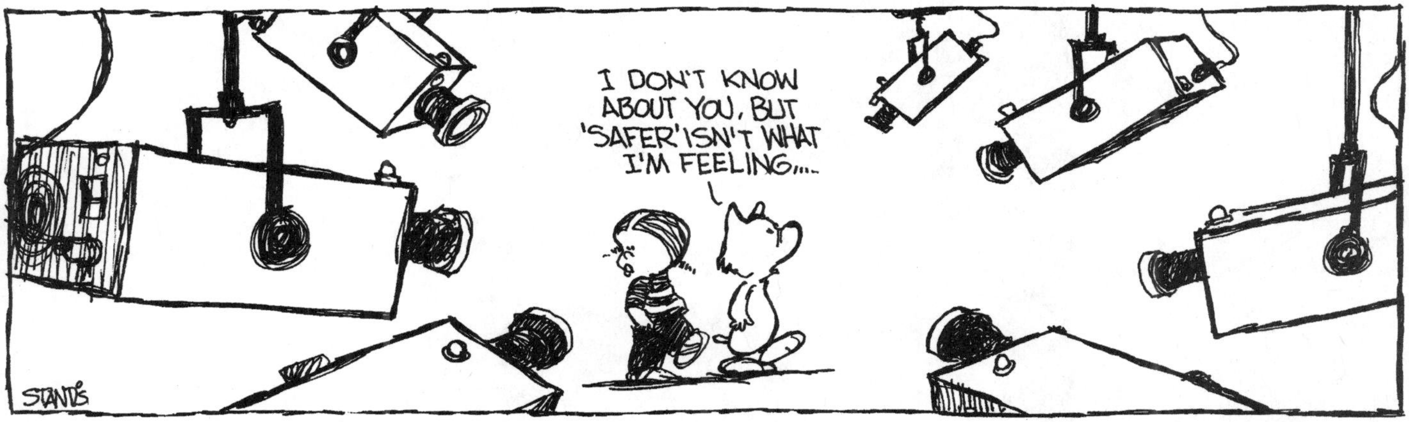
I DON'T KNOW ABOUT YOU, BUT 'SAFER' ISN'T WHAT I'M FEELING....
STANTIS

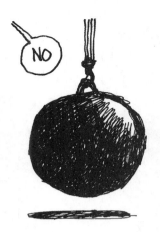

HOPE SPRINGS ETERNAL.
STANT95

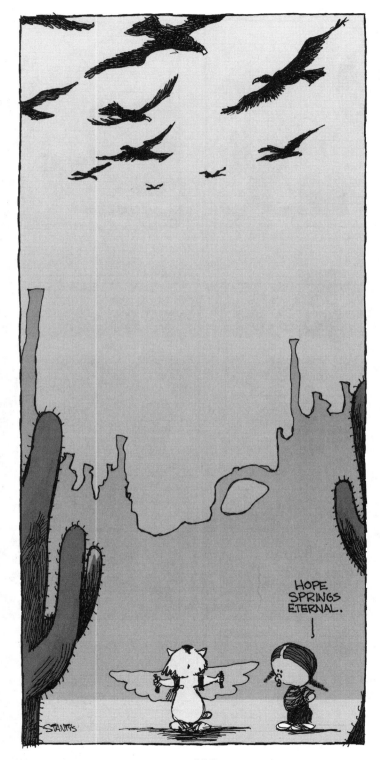

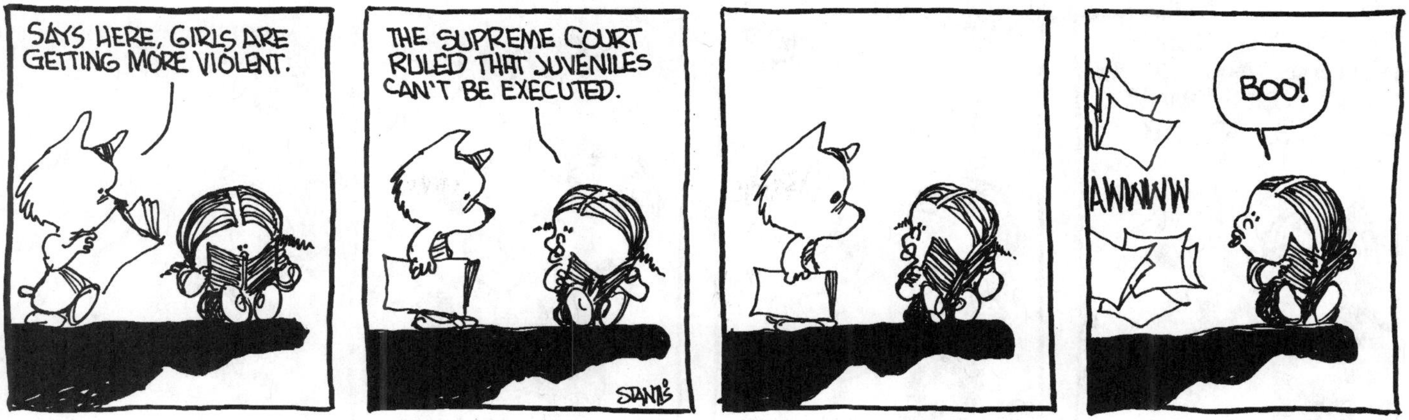
SAYS HERE, GIRLS ARE GETTING MORE VIOLENT.
THE SUPREME COURT RULED THAT JUVENILES CAN'T BE EXECUTED.
AWWWW
BOO!
STANTIS

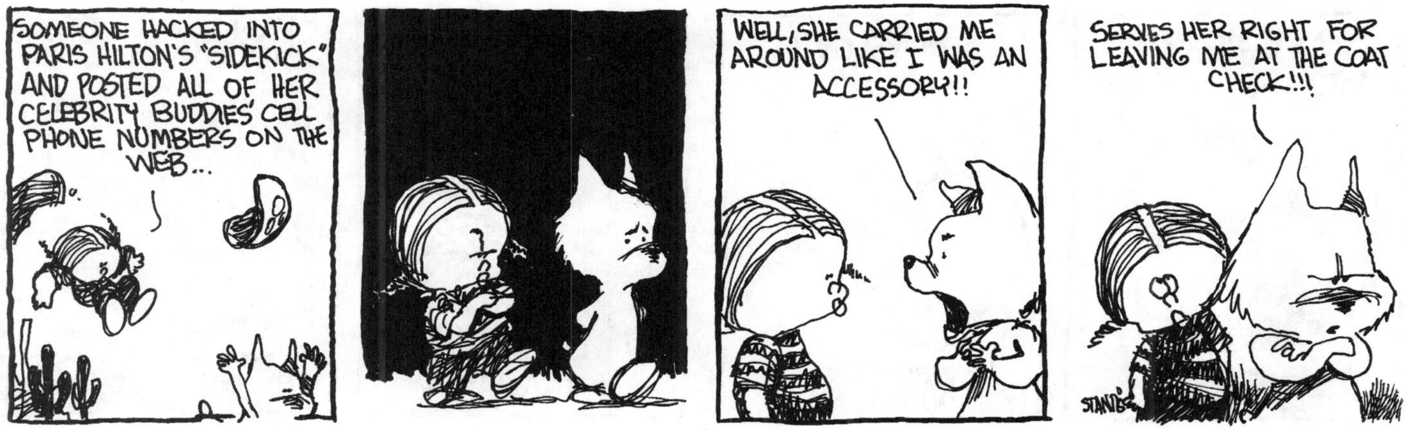
SOMEONE HACKED INTO PARIS HILTON'S "SIDEKICK" AND POSTED ALL OF HER CELEBRITY BUDDIES' CELL PHONE NUMBERS ON THE WEB...
WELL, SHE CARRIED ME AROUND LIKE I WAS AN ACCESSORY!!
SERVES HER RIGHT FOR LEAVING ME AT THE COAT CHECK!!!
STANTIS

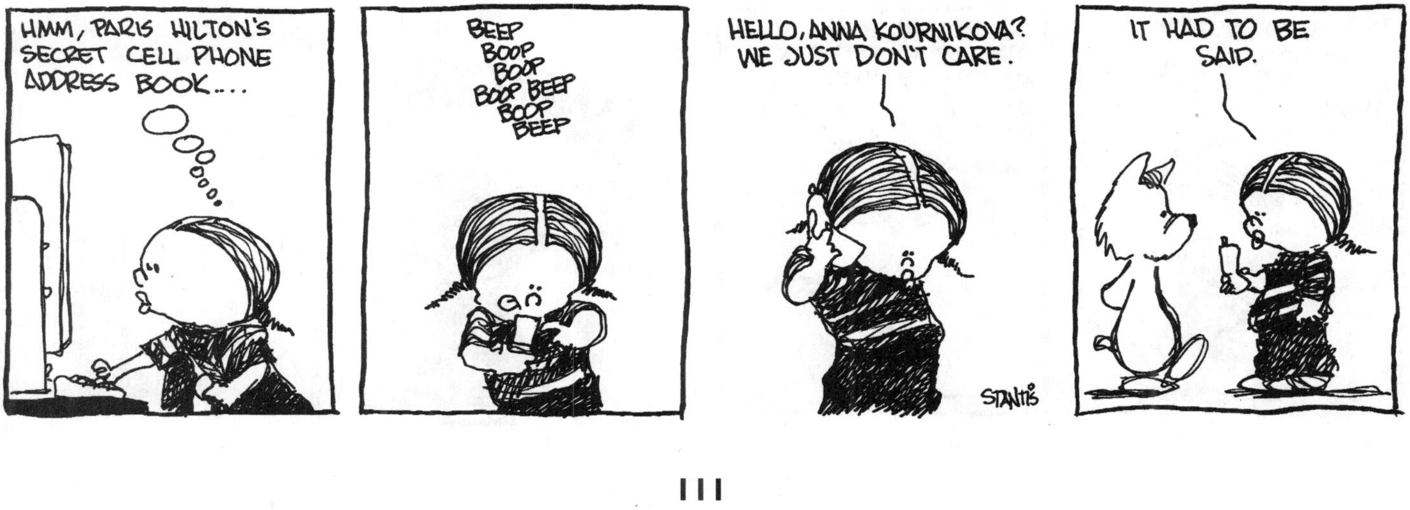
HMM, PARIS HILTON'S SECRET CELL PHONE ADDRESS BOOK....
BEEP
BOOP
BOOP
BOOP BEEP
BOOP
BEEP
HELLO, ANNA KOURNIKOVA? WE JUST DON'T CARE.
STANTIS
IT HAD TO BE SAID.

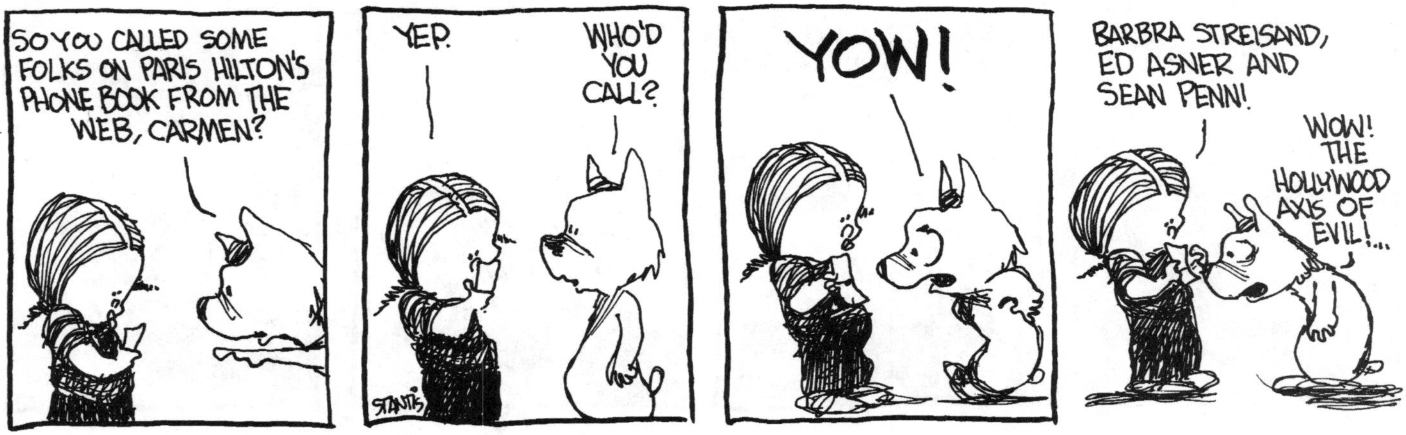
SO YOU CALLED SOME FOLKS ON PARIS HILTON'S PHONE BOOK FROM THE WEB, CARMEN?
YEP.
WHO'D YOU CALL?
STANTIS
YOW!
BARBRA STREISAND, ED ASNER AND SEAN PENN!
WOW! THE HOLLYWOOD AXIS OF EVIL!...

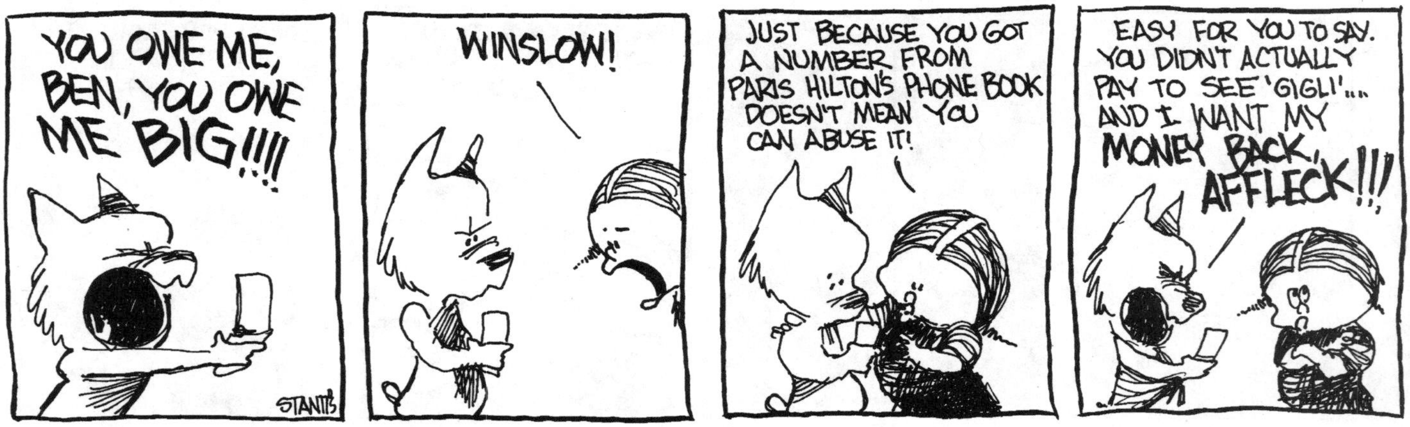
YOU OWE ME, BEN, YOU OWE ME BIG!!!!
STANTIS
WINSLOW!
JUST BECAUSE YOU GOT A NUMBER FROM PARIS HILTON'S PHONE BOOK DOESN'T MEAN YOU CAN ABUSE IT!
EASY FOR YOU TO SAY. YOU DIDN'T ACTUALLY PAY TO SEE 'GIGLI'... AND I WANT MY MONEY BACK, AFFLECK!!!

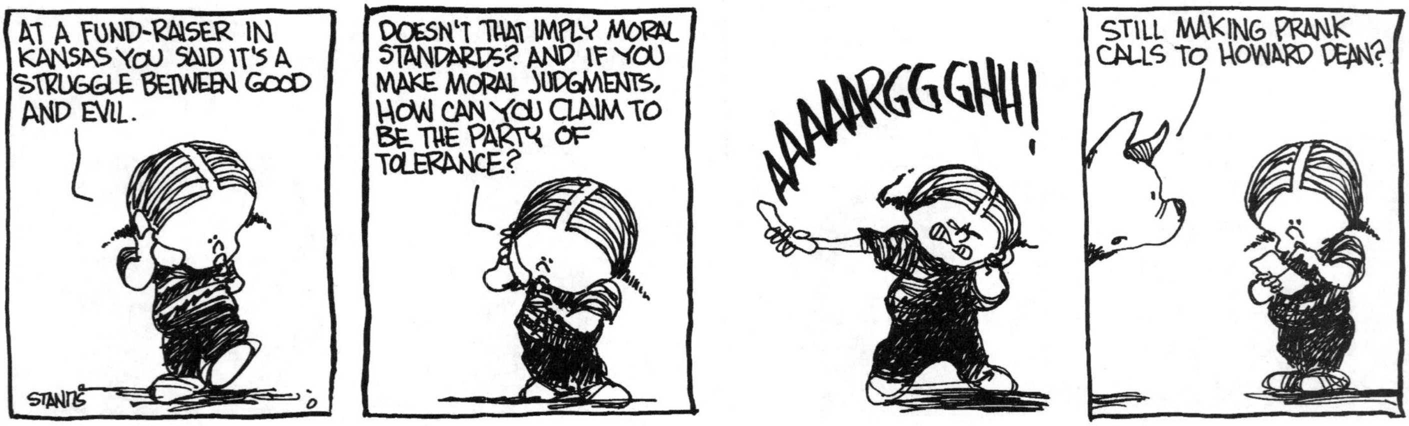
AT A FUND-RAISER IN KANSAS YOU SAID IT'S A STRUGGLE BETWEEN GOOD AND EVIL.
STANTIS
DOESN'T THAT IMPLY MORAL STANDARDS? AND IF YOU MAKE MORAL JUDGMENTS, HOW CAN YOU CLAIM TO BE THE PARTY OF TOLERANCE?
AAAAARGGGHH!
STILL MAKING PRANK CALLS TO HOWARD DEAN?

STANTIS
MANSCAPING?
MANSCAPING.
WHAT IS MANSCAPING?
IT'S THE MANAGEMENT OF MALE BODY HAIR.
SO, YOU MANSCAPE?
OF COURSE! ALL US METROSEXUALS DO....
MANSCAPING.
GONE HORRIBLY AWRY....

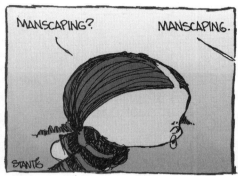

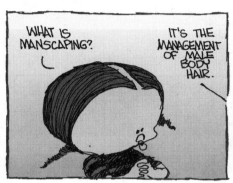

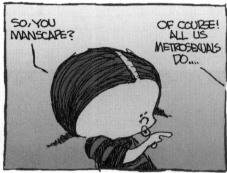

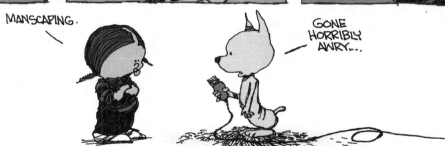

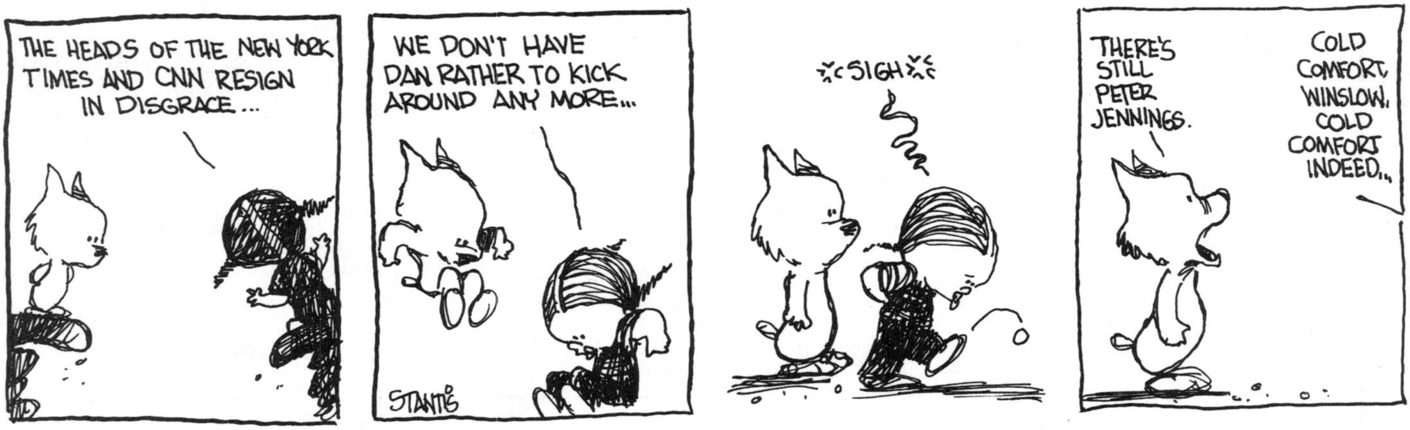
THE HEADS OF THE NEW YORK TIMES AND CNN RESIGN IN DISGRACE...
WE DON'T HAVE DAN RATHER TO KICK AROUND ANY MORE...
STANTIS
SIGH
THERE'S STILL PETER JENNINGS.
COLD COMFORT, WINSLOW, COLD COMFORT INDEED...

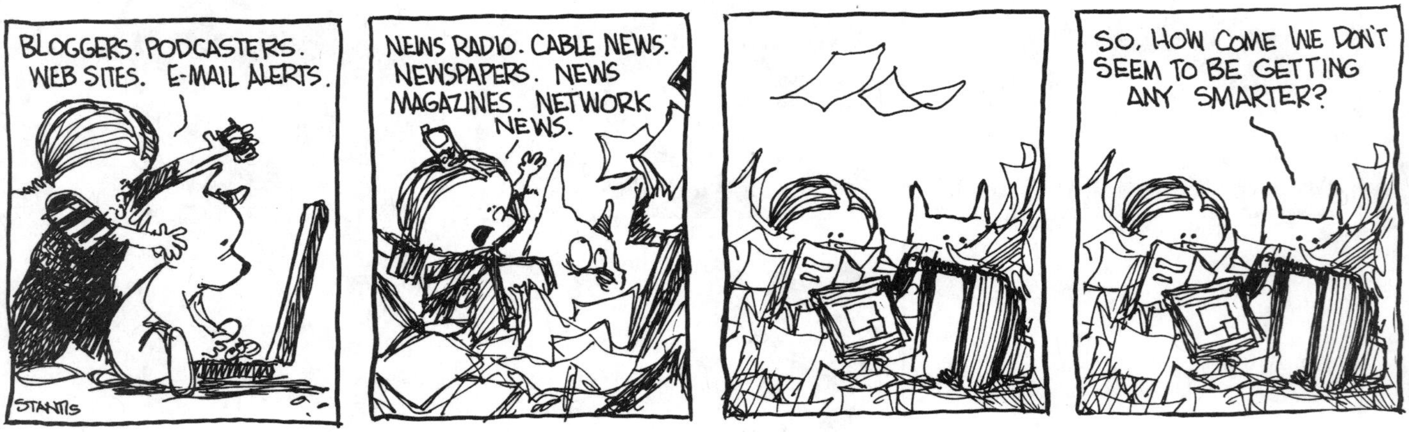
BLOGGERS. PODCASTERS. WEB SITES. E-MAIL ALERTS.
STANTIS
NEWS RADIO. CABLE NEWS. NEWSPAPERS. NEWS MAGAZINES. NETWORK NEWS.
SO, HOW COME WE DON'T SEEM TO BE GETTING ANY SMARTER?

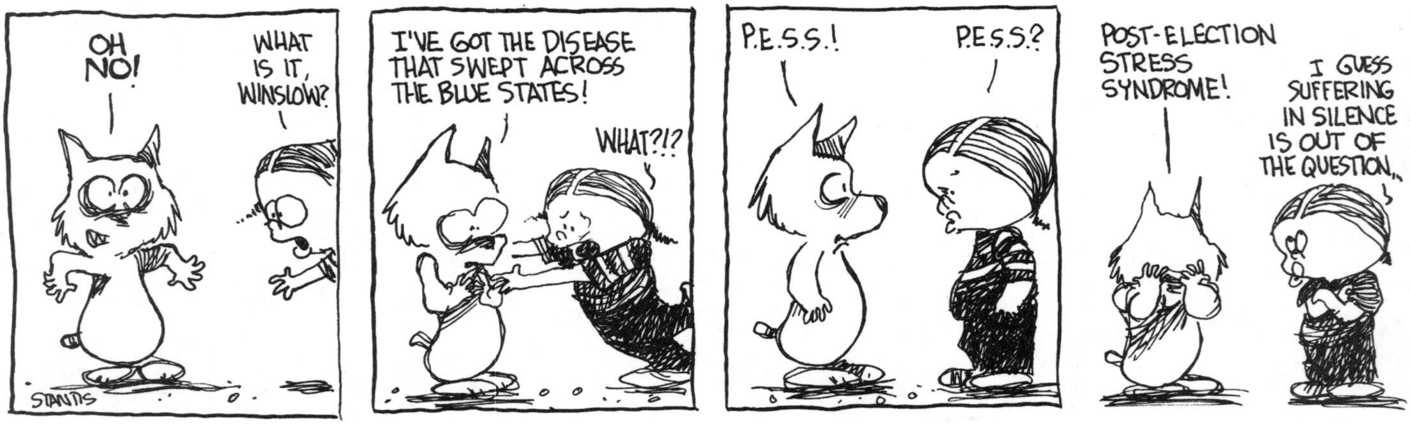
OH NO!
WHAT IS IT, WINSLOW?
STANTIS
I'VE GOT THE DISEASE THAT SWEPT ACROSS THE BLUE STATES!
WHAT?!?
P.E.S.S.!
P.E.S.S.?
POST-ELECTION STRESS SYNDROME!
I GUESS SUFFERING IN SILENCE IS OUT OF THE QUESTION...

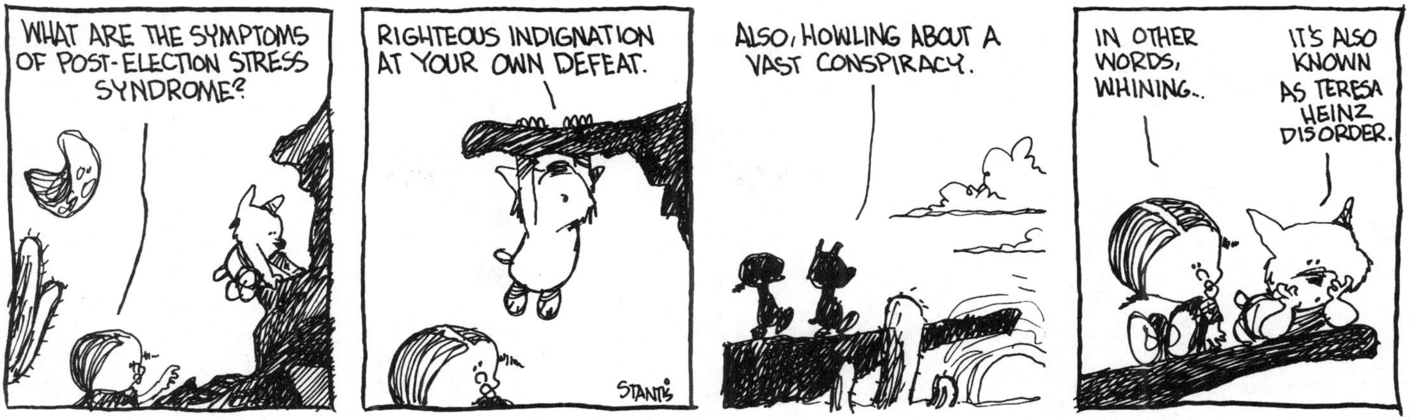
WHAT ARE THE SYMPTOMS OF POST-ELECTION STRESS SYNDROME?
RIGHTEOUS INDIGNATION AT YOUR OWN DEFEAT.
STANTIS
ALSO, HOWLING ABOUT A VAST CONSPIRACY.
IN OTHER WORDS, WHINING..
IT'S ALSO KNOWN AS TERESA HEINZ DISORDER.

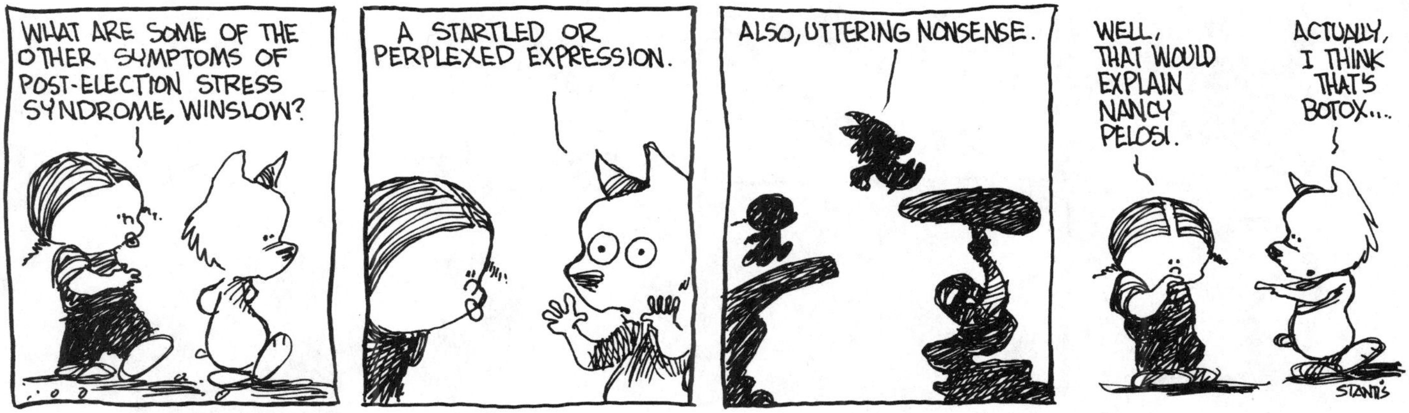
WHAT ARE SOME OF THE OTHER SYMPTOMS OF POST-ELECTION STRESS SYNDROME, WINSLOW?
A STARTLED OR PERPLEXED EXPRESSION.
ALSO, UTTERING NONSENSE.
WELL, THAT WOULD EXPLAIN NANCY PELOSI.
ACTUALLY, I THINK THAT'S BOTOX....
STANTIS

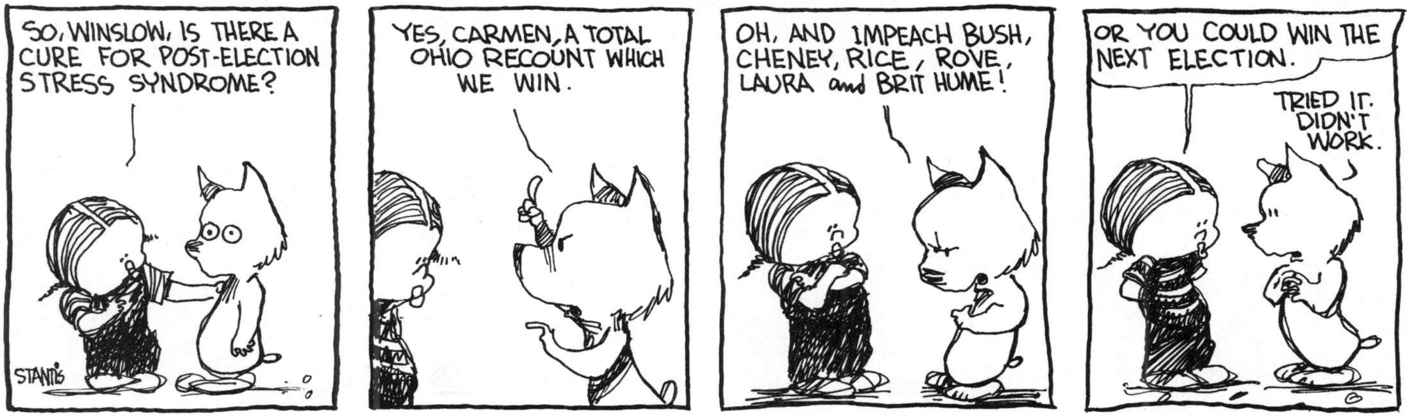
SO, WINSLOW, IS THERE A CURE FOR POST-ELECTION STRESS SYNDROME?
STANTIS
YES, CARMEN, A TOTAL OHIO RECOUNT WHICH WE WIN.
OH, AND IMPEACH BUSH, CHENEY, RICE, ROVE, LAURA and BRIT HUME!
OR YOU COULD WIN THE NEXT ELECTION.
TRIED IT. DIDN'T WORK.

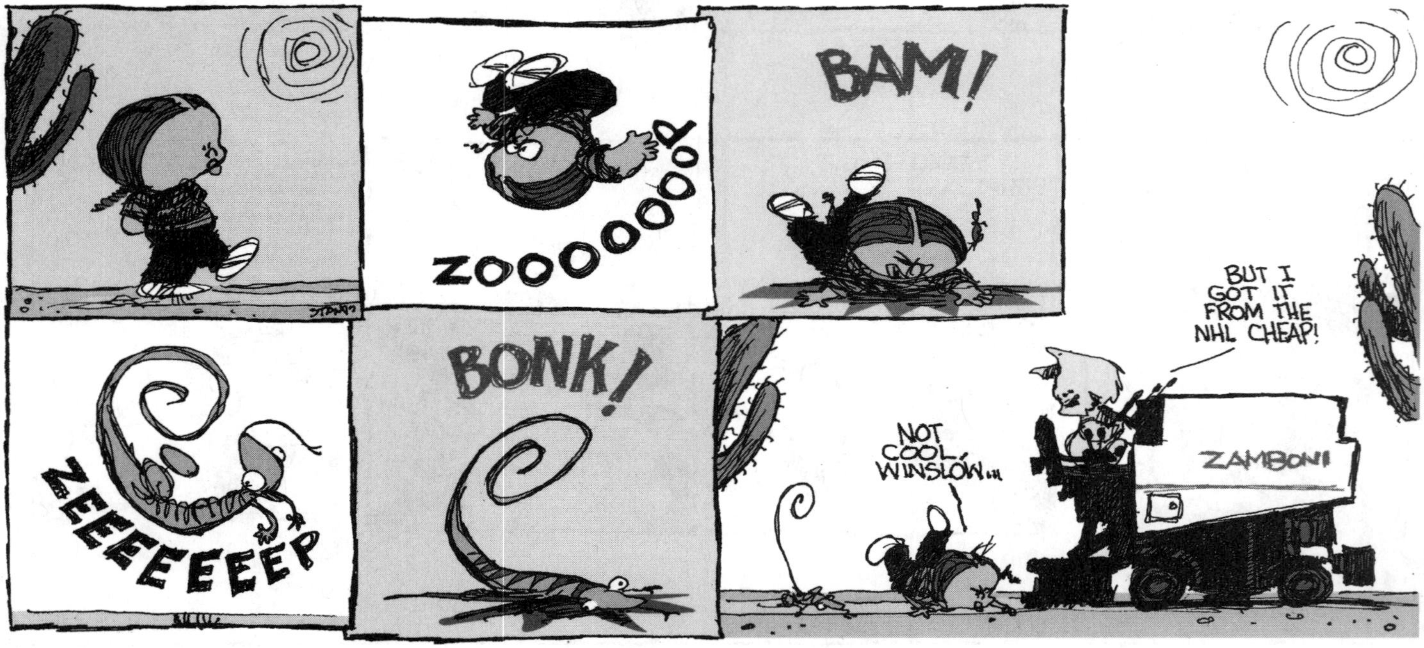
ZOOOOOOOOOP
BAM!
ZEEEEEEEEP
BONK!
NOT COOL, WINSLOW...
BUT I GOT IT FROM THE NHL CHEAP!
ZAMBONI

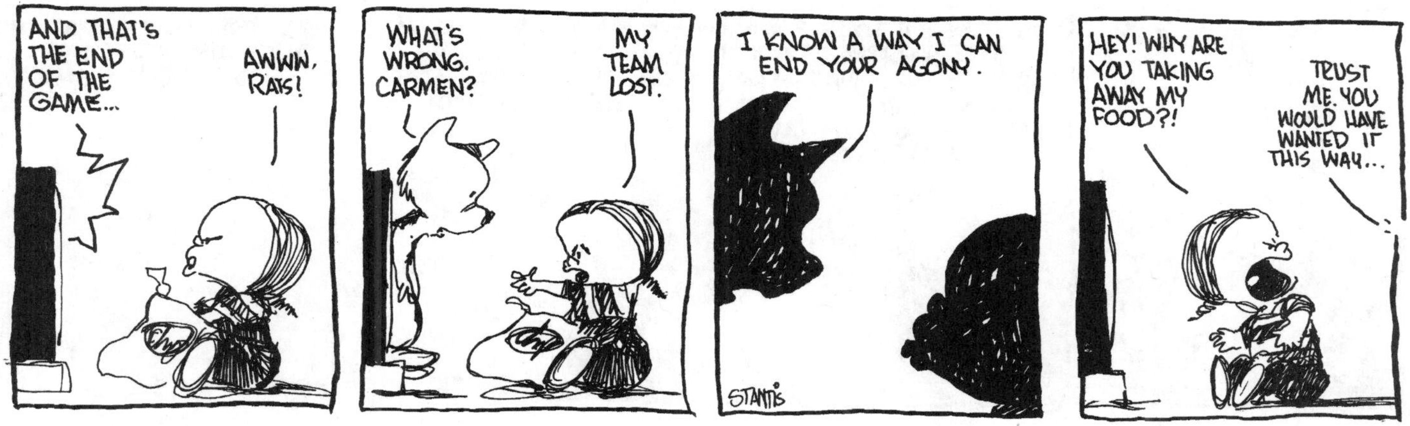
AND THAT'S THE END OF THE GAME...
AWWW, RATS!
WHAT'S WRONG, CARMEN?
MY TEAM LOST.
I KNOW A WAY I CAN END YOUR AGONY.
STANTIS
HEY! WHY ARE YOU TAKING AWAY MY FOOD?!
TRUST ME. YOU WOULD HAVE WANTED IT THIS WAY...

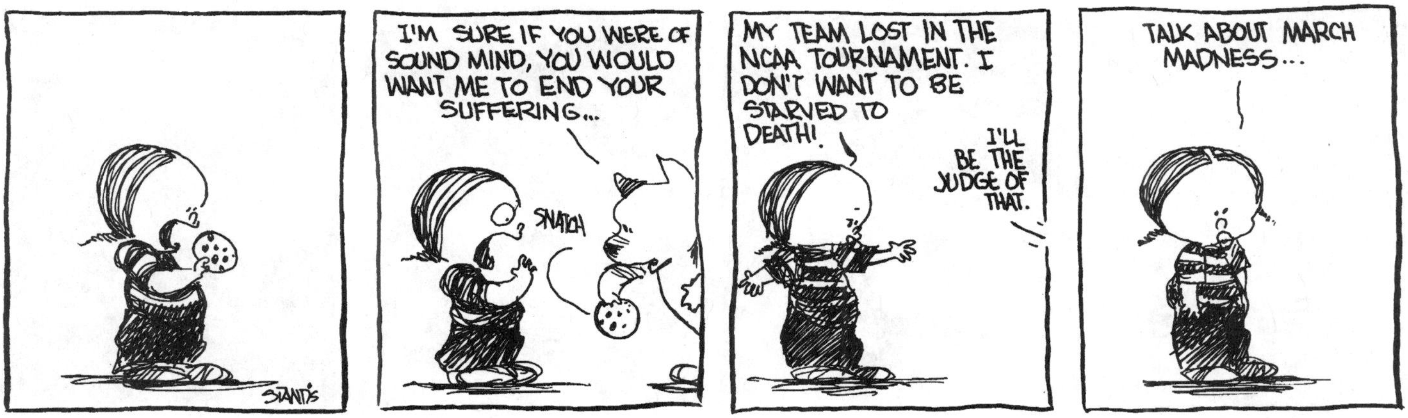
STANTIS
I'M SURE IF YOU WERE OF SOUND MIND, YOU WOULD WANT ME TO END YOUR SUFFERING...
SNATCH
MY TEAM LOST IN THE NCAA TOURNAMENT. I DON'T WANT TO BE STARVED TO DEATH!
I'LL BE THE JUDGE OF THAT.
TALK ABOUT MARCH MADNESS...

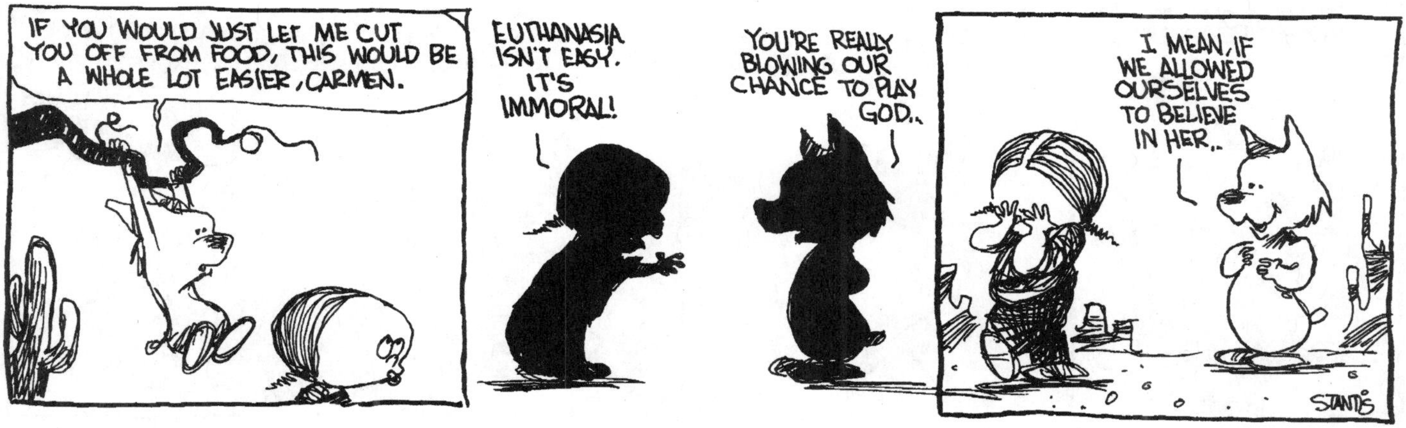
IF YOU WOULD JUST LET ME CUT YOU OFF FROM FOOD, THIS WOULD BE A WHOLE LOT EASIER, CARMEN.
EUTHANASIA ISN'T EASY. IT'S IMMORAL!
YOU'RE REALLY BLOWING OUR CHANCE TO PLAY GOD..
I MEAN, IF WE ALLOWED OURSELVES TO BELIEVE IN HER..
STANTIS

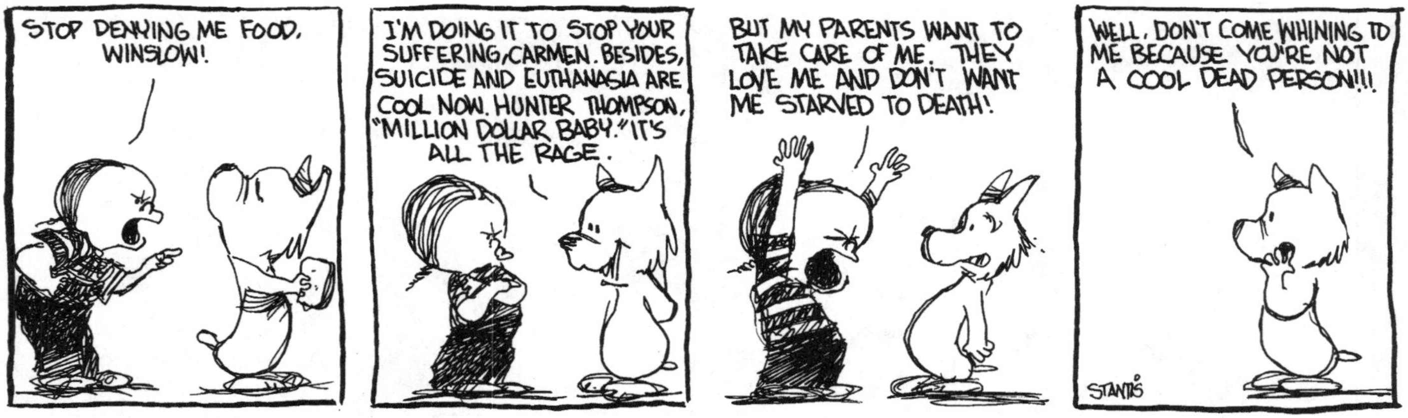
STOP DENYING ME FOOD, WINSLOW!
I'M DOING IT TO STOP YOUR SUFFERING, CARMEN. BESIDES, SUICIDE AND EUTHANASIA ARE COOL NOW. HUNTER THOMPSON, "MILLION DOLLAR BABY." IT'S ALL THE RAGE.
BUT MY PARENTS WANT TO TAKE CARE OF ME. THEY LOVE ME AND DON'T WANT ME STARVED TO DEATH!
WELL, DON'T COME WHINING TO ME BECAUSE YOU'RE NOT A COOL DEAD PERSON!!!
STANTIS

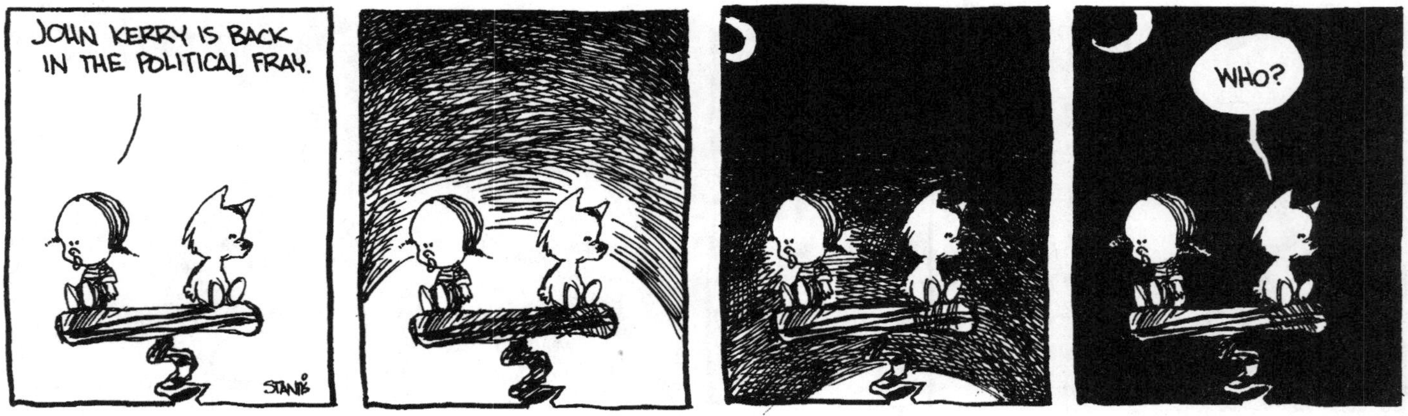
JOHN KERRY IS BACK IN THE POLITICAL FRAY.
STANTIS
WHO?

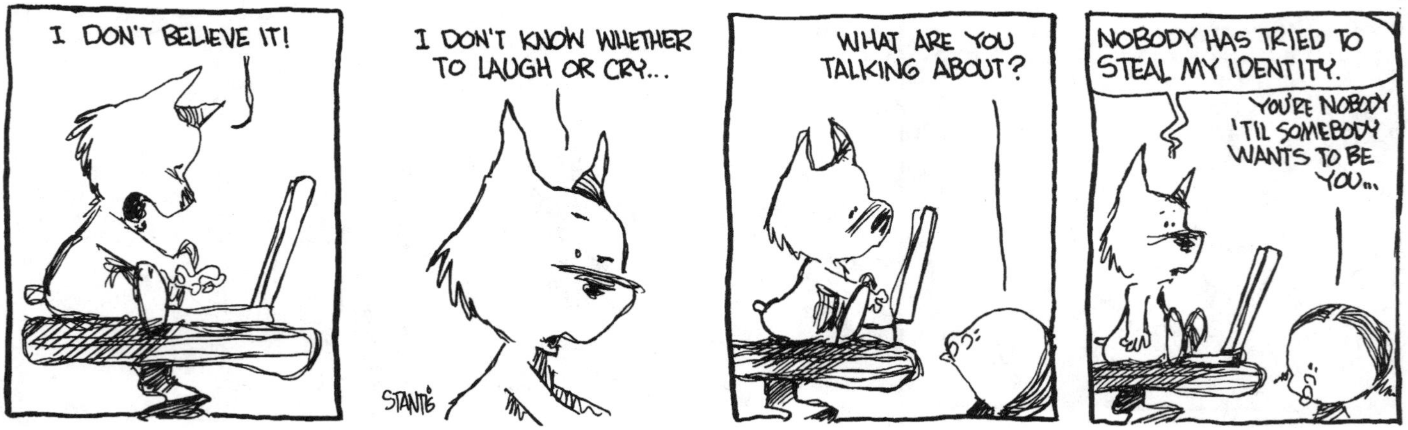
I DON'T BELIEVE IT!
I DON'T KNOW WHETHER TO LAUGH OR CRY...
STANTIS
WHAT ARE YOU TALKING ABOUT?
NOBODY HAS TRIED TO STEAL MY IDENTITY.
YOU'RE NOBODY 'TIL SOMEBODY WANTS TO BE YOU...

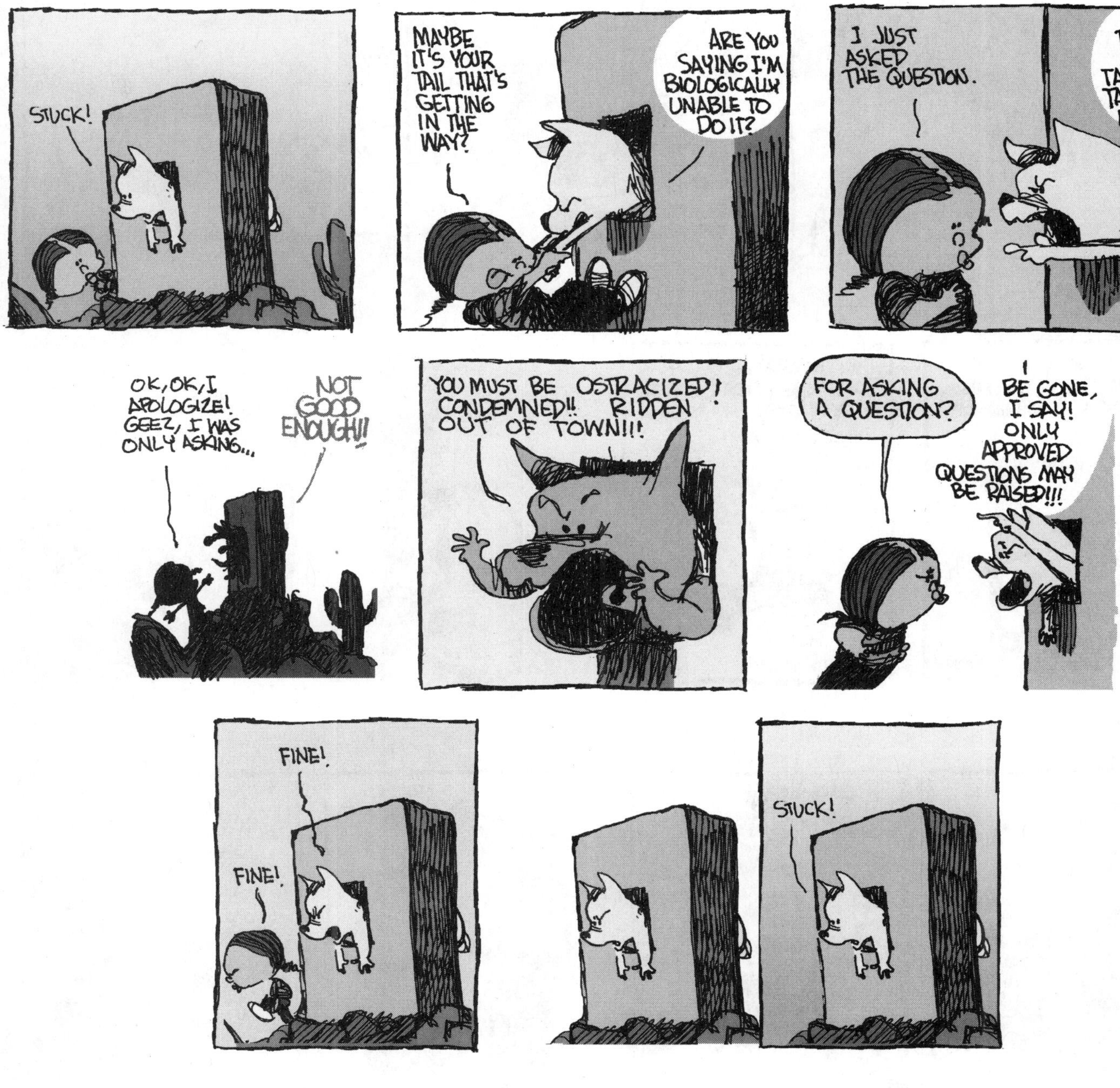

STUCK!
MAYBE IT'S YOUR TAIL THAT'S GETTING IN THE WAY?
ARE YOU SAYING I'M BIOLOGICALLY UNABLE TO DO IT?
I JUST ASKED THE QUESTION.
THAT'S ANTI-TAILISM! TAKE IT BACK!
OK, OK, I APOLOGIZE! GEEZ, I WAS ONLY ASKING...
NOT GOOD ENOUGH!!
YOU MUST BE OSTRACIZED! CONDEMNED!! RIDDEN OUT OF TOWN!!!
FOR ASKING A QUESTION?
BE GONE, I SAY! ONLY APPROVED QUESTIONS MAY BE RAISED!!!
FINE!
FINE!
STUCK!

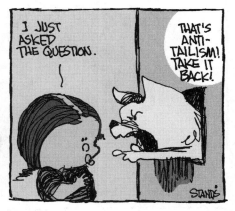

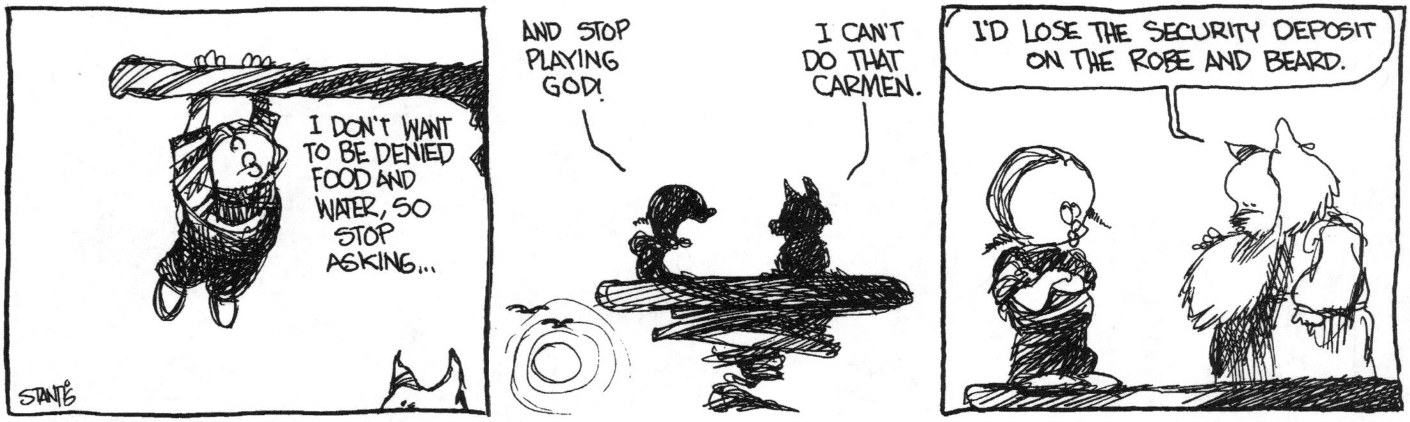
I DON'T WANT TO BE DENIED FOOD AND WATER, SO STOP ASKING...
STANTIS
AND STOP PLAYING GOD!
I CAN'T DO THAT CARMEN.
I'D LOSE THE SECURITY DEPOSIT ON THE ROBE AND BEARD.

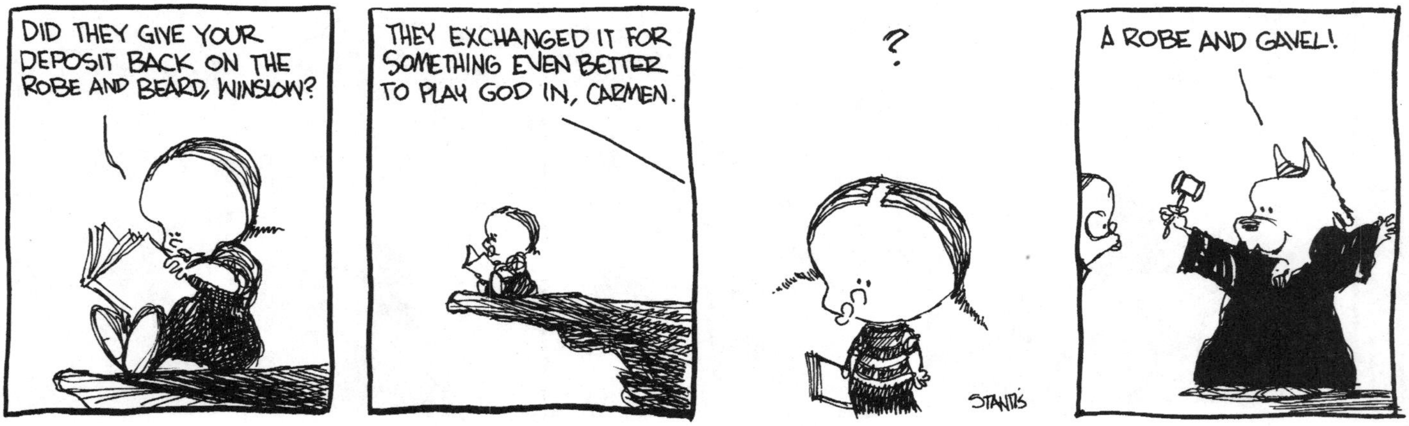
DID THEY GIVE YOUR DEPOSIT BACK ON THE ROBE AND BEARD, WINSLOW?
THEY EXCHANGED IT FOR SOMETHING EVEN BETTER TO PLAY GOD IN, CARMEN.
?
STANTIS
A ROBE AND GAVEL!

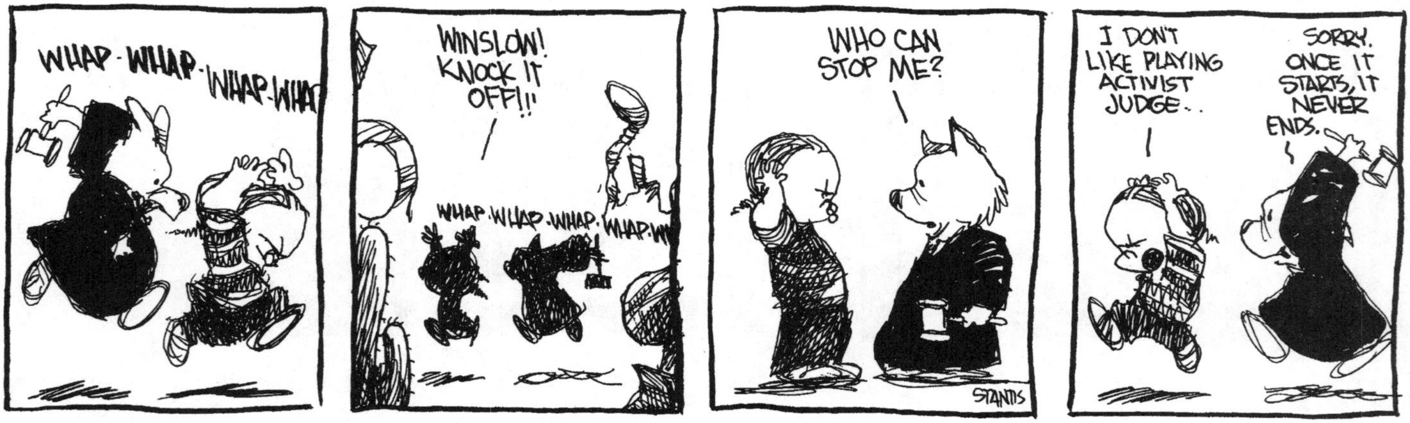
WHAP-WHAP-WHAP-WHA
WINSLOW! KNOCK IT OFF!!
WHAP-WHAP-WHAP-WHAP-WH
WHO CAN STOP ME?
STANTIS
I DON'T LIKE PLAYING ACTIVIST JUDGE...
SORRY. ONCE IT STARTS, IT NEVER ENDS.

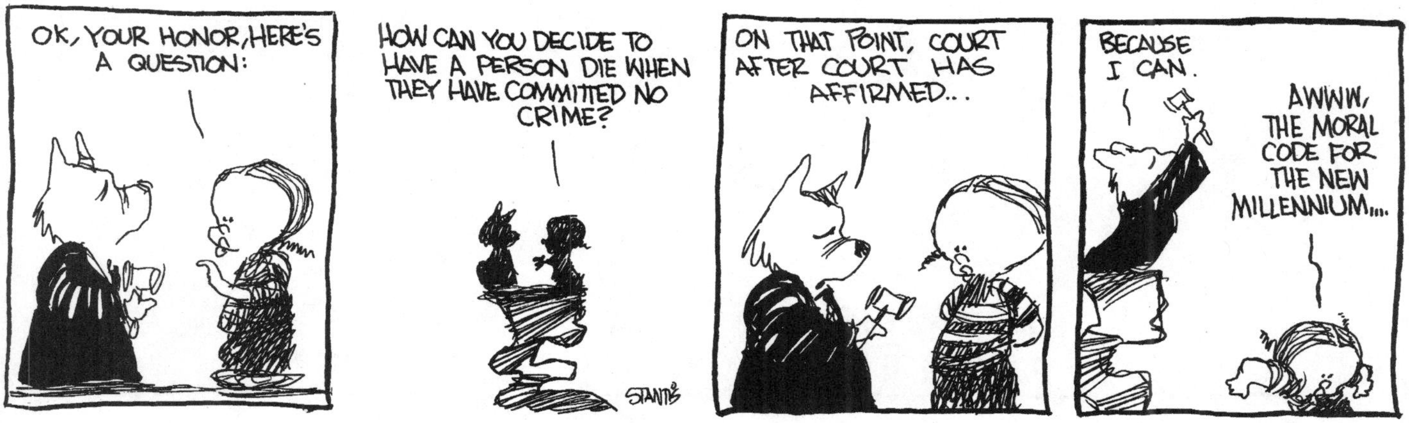
OK, YOUR HONOR, HERE'S A QUESTION:
HOW CAN YOU DECIDE TO HAVE A PERSON DIE WHEN THEY HAVE COMMITTED NO CRIME?
STANTIS
ON THAT POINT, COURT AFTER COURT HAS AFFIRMED...
BECAUSE I CAN.
AWWW, THE MORAL CODE FOR THE NEW MILLENNIUM....

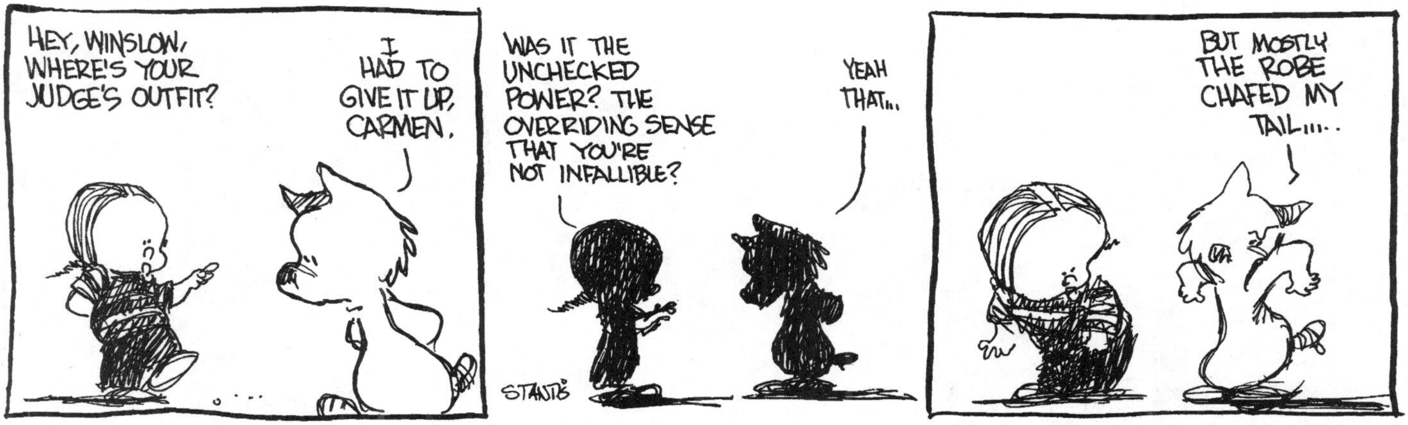
HEY, WINSLOW, WHERE'S YOUR JUDGE'S OUTFIT?
I HAD TO GIVE IT UP, CARMEN.
WAS IT THE UNCHECKED POWER? THE OVERRIDING SENSE THAT YOU'RE NOT INFALLIBLE?
YEAH THAT...
STANTIS
BUT MOSTLY THE ROBE CHAFED MY TAIL.....

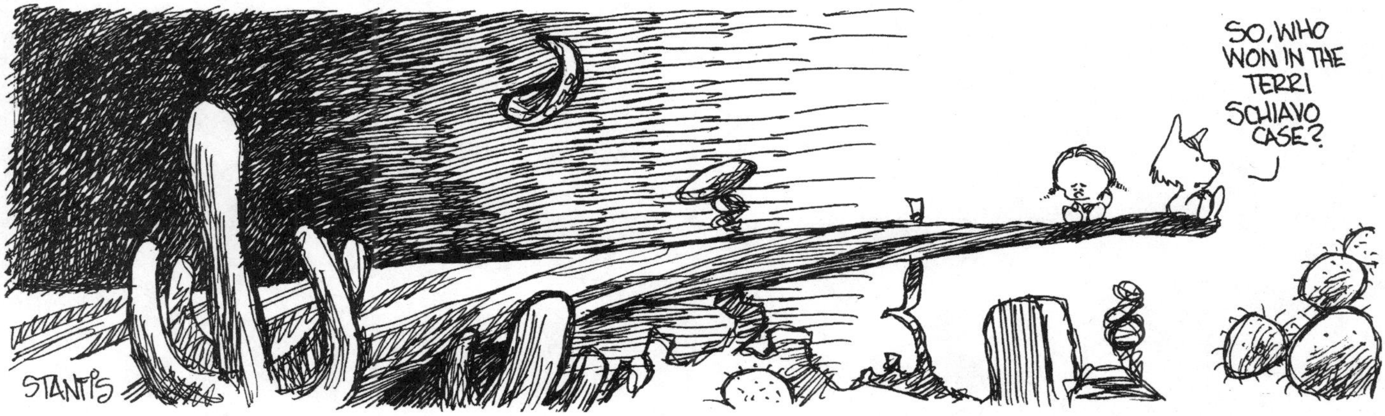
SO, WHO WON IN THE TERRI SCHIAVO CASE?
STANTIS

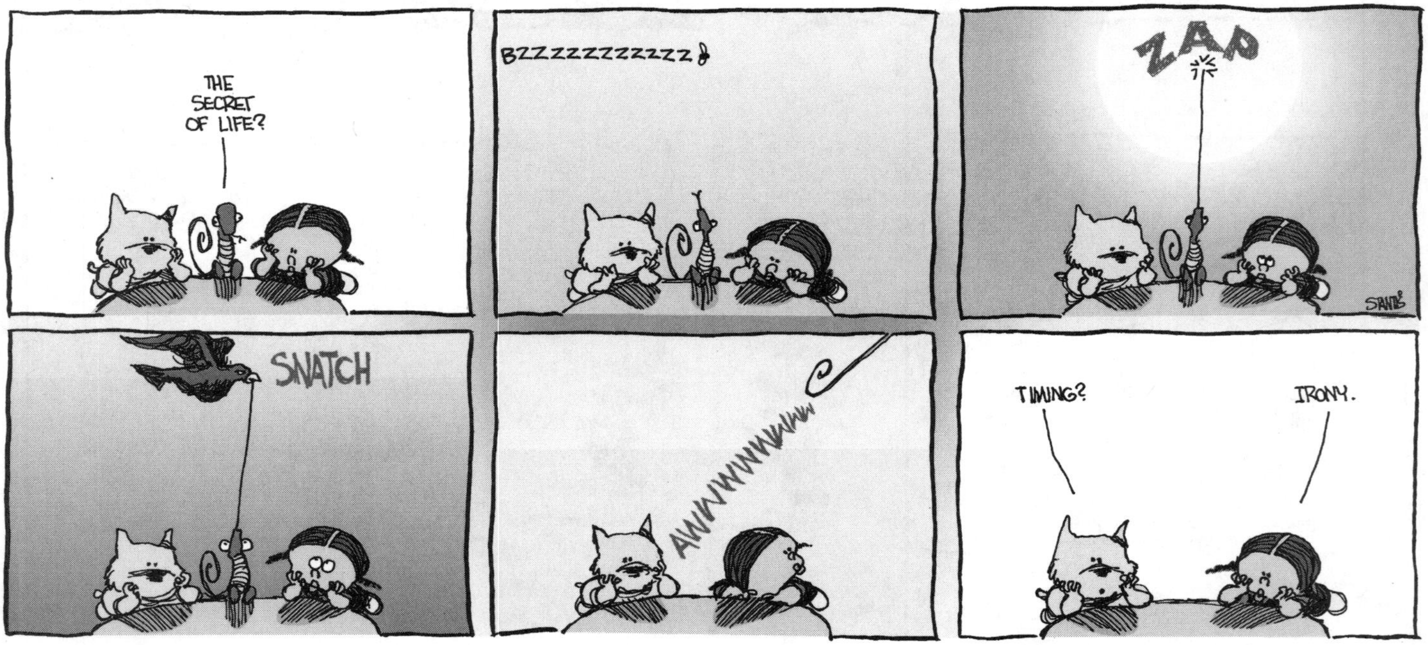
THE SECRET OF LIFE?
BZZZZZZZZZZZ
ZAP
SNATCH
AWWWWWWW
TIMING?
IRONY.

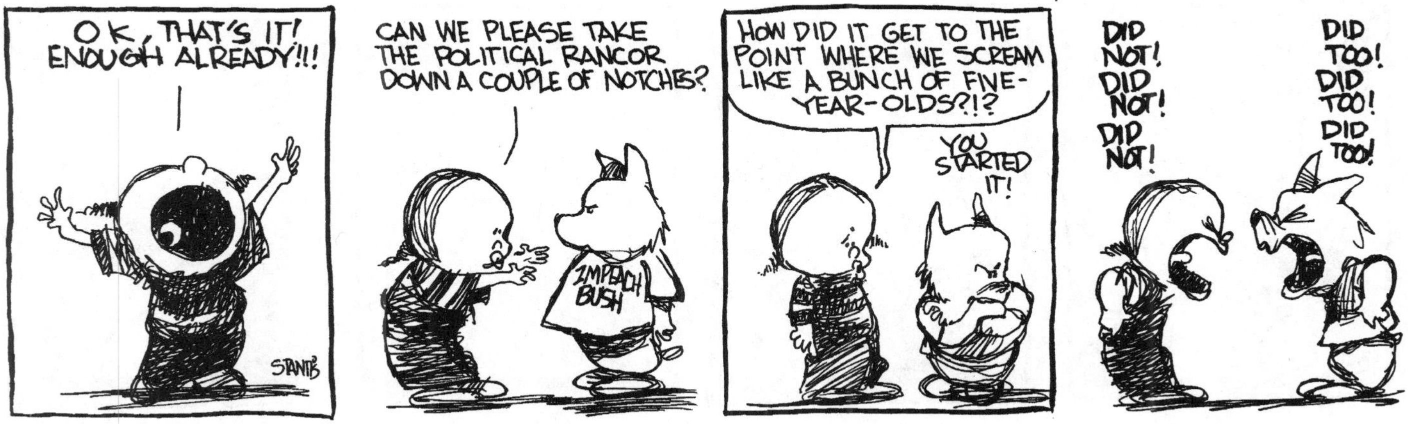
OK, THAT'S IT! ENOUGH ALREADY!!!
STANTIS
CAN WE PLEASE TAKE THE POLITICAL RANCOR DOWN A COUPLE OF NOTCHES?
IMPEACH BUSH
HOW DID IT GET TO THE POINT WHERE WE SCREAM LIKE A BUNCH OF FIVE-YEAR-OLDS?!?
YOU STARTED IT!
DID NOT! DID NOT! DID NOT!
DID TOO! DID TOO! DID TOO!

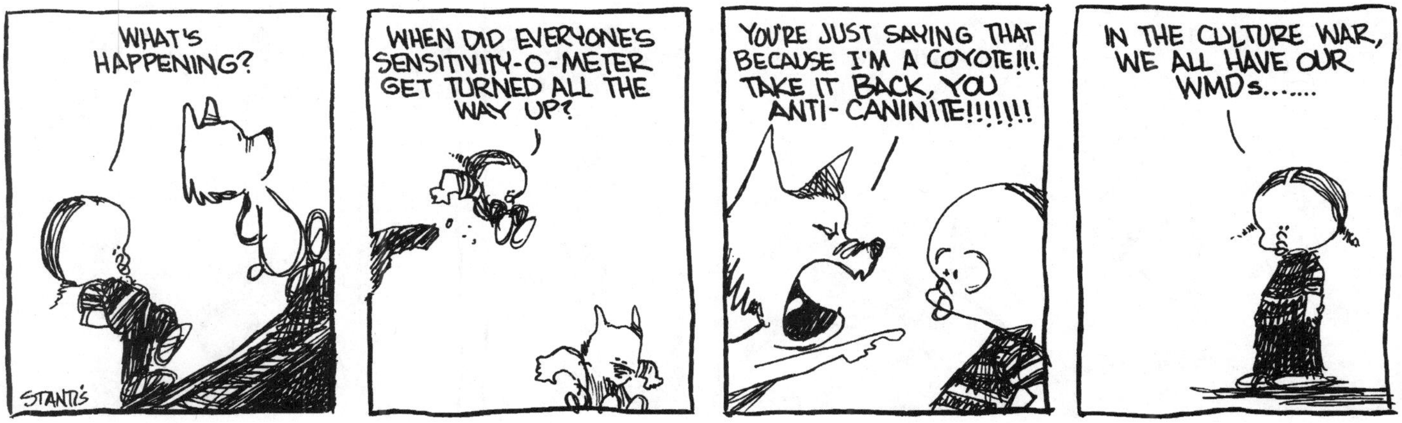
WHAT'S HAPPENING?
STANTIS
WHEN DID EVERYONE'S SENSITIVITY-O-METER GET TURNED ALL THE WAY UP?
YOU'RE JUST SAYING THAT BECAUSE I'M A COYOTE!!! TAKE IT BACK, YOU ANTI-CANINITE!!!!!!!
IN THE CULTURE WAR, WE ALL HAVE OUR WMDs.......

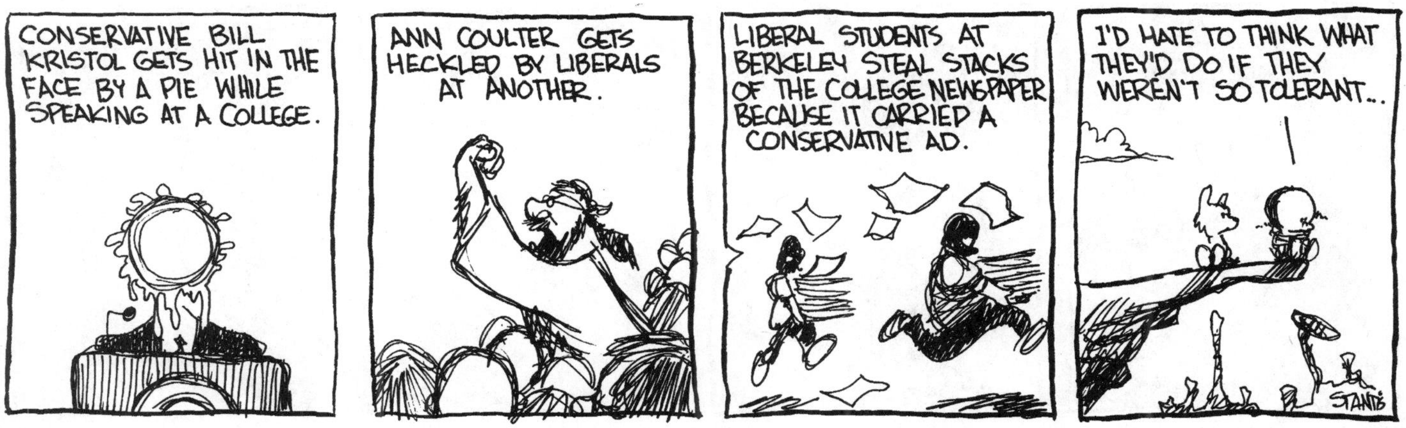
CONSERVATIVE BILL KRISTOL GETS HIT IN THE FACE BY A PIE WHILE SPEAKING AT A COLLEGE.
ANN COULTER GETS HECKLED BY LIBERALS AT ANOTHER.
LIBERAL STUDENTS AT BERKELEY STEAL STACKS OF THE COLLEGE NEWSPAPER BECAUSE IT CARRIED A CONSERVATIVE AD.
I'D HATE TO THINK WHAT THEY'D DO IF THEY WEREN'T SO TOLERANT...
STANTIS

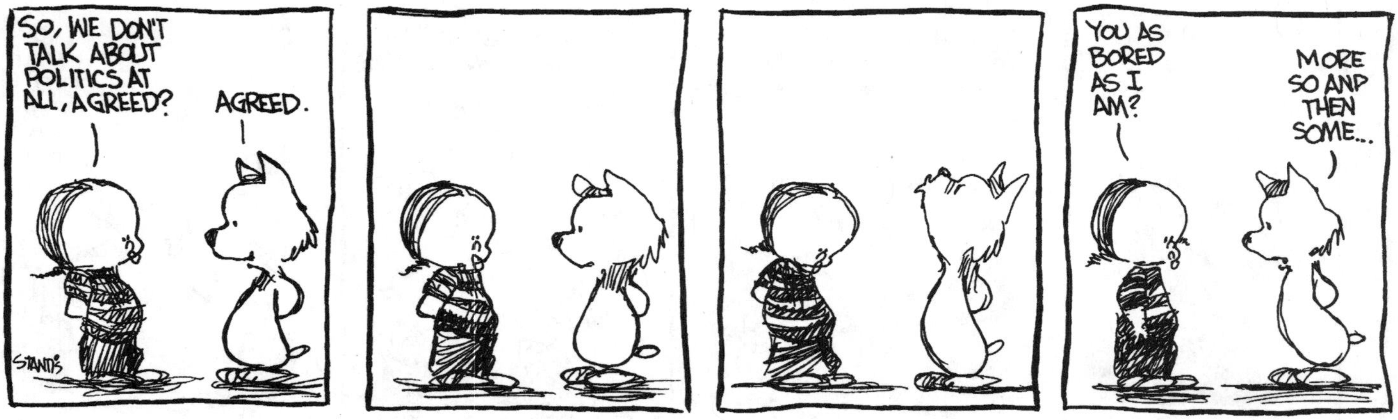
SO, WE DON'T TALK ABOUT POLITICS AT ALL, AGREED?
AGREED.
YOU AS BORED AS I AM?
MORE SO AND THEN SOME...
STANTIS

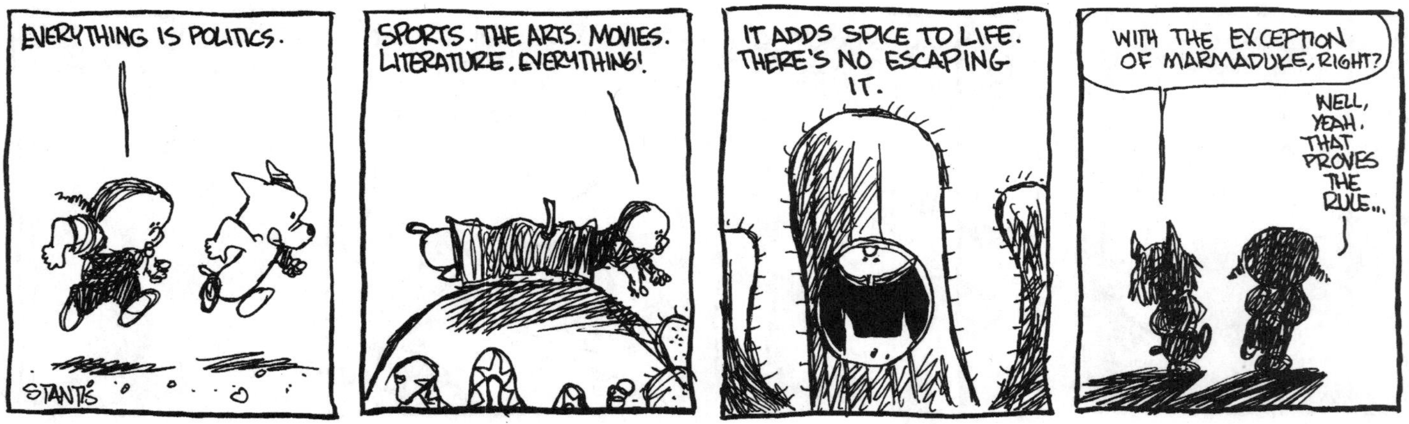
EVERYTHING IS POLITICS.
SPORTS. THE ARTS. MOVIES. LITERATURE. EVERYTHING!
IT ADDS SPICE TO LIFE. THERE'S NO ESCAPING IT.
WITH THE EXCEPTION OF MARMADUKE, RIGHT?
WELL, YEAH. THAT PROVES THE RULE...
STANTIS

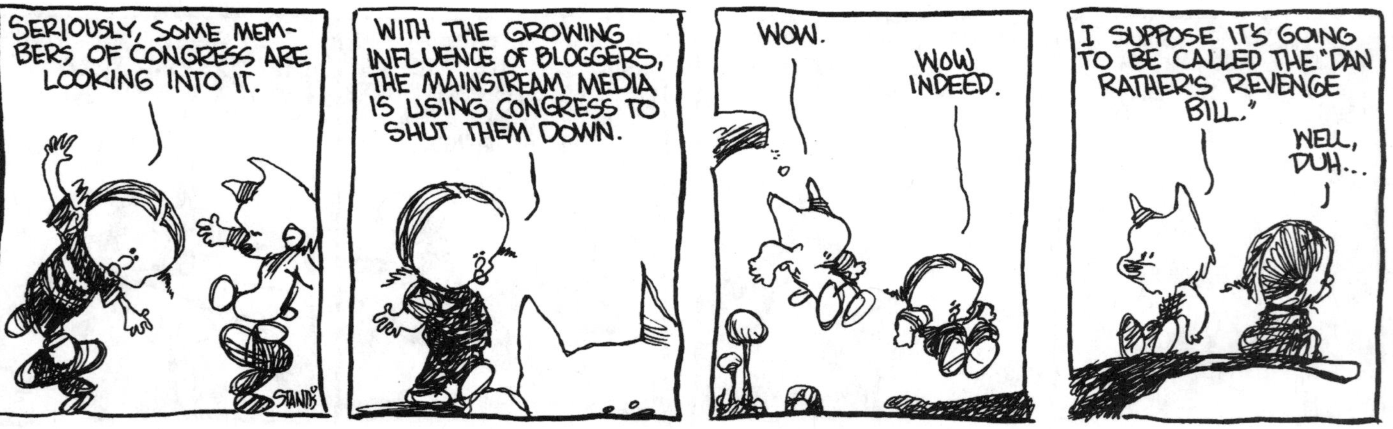
SERIOUSLY, SOME MEMBERS OF CONGRESS ARE LOOKING INTO IT.
WITH THE GROWING INFLUENCE OF BLOGGERS, THE MAINSTREAM MEDIA IS USING CONGRESS TO SHUT THEM DOWN.
WOW.
WOW INDEED.
I SUPPOSE IT'S GOING TO BE CALLED THE "DAN RATHER'S REVENGE BILL."
WELL, DUH...
STANTIS

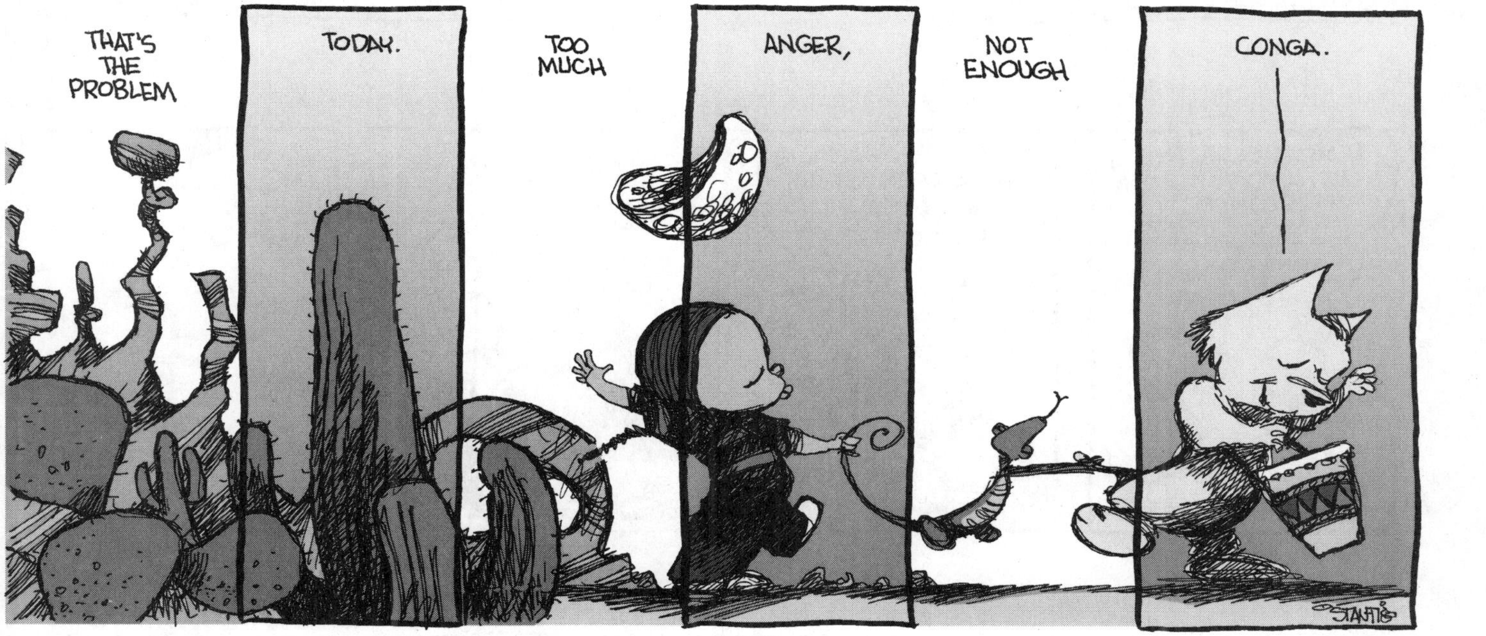
THAT'S THE PROBLEM
TODAY.
TOO MUCH
ANGER,
NOT ENOUGH
CONGA.
STANTIS

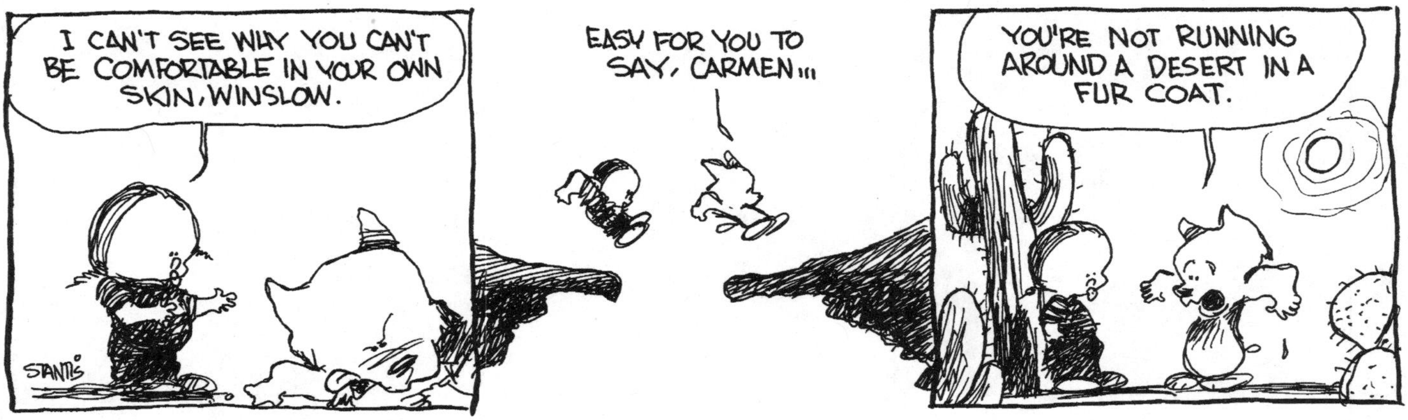
I CAN'T SEE WHY YOU CAN'T BE COMFORTABLE IN YOUR OWN SKIN, WINSLOW.
STANTIS
EASY FOR YOU TO SAY, CARMEN...
YOU'RE NOT RUNNING AROUND A DESERT IN A FUR COAT.

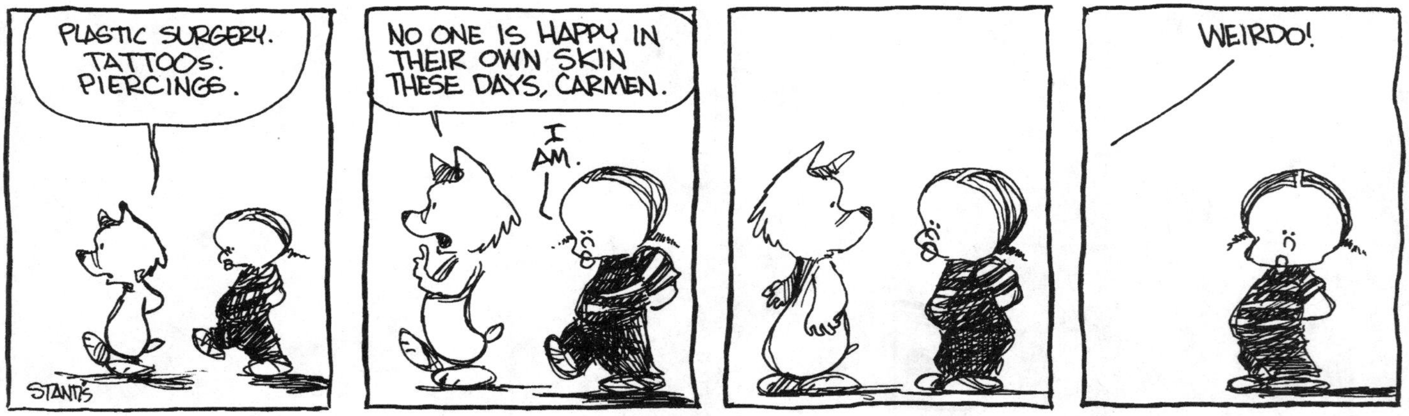
PLASTIC SURGERY. TATTOOS. PIERCINGS.
STANTIS
NO ONE IS HAPPY IN THEIR OWN SKIN THESE DAYS, CARMEN.
I AM.
WEIRDO!

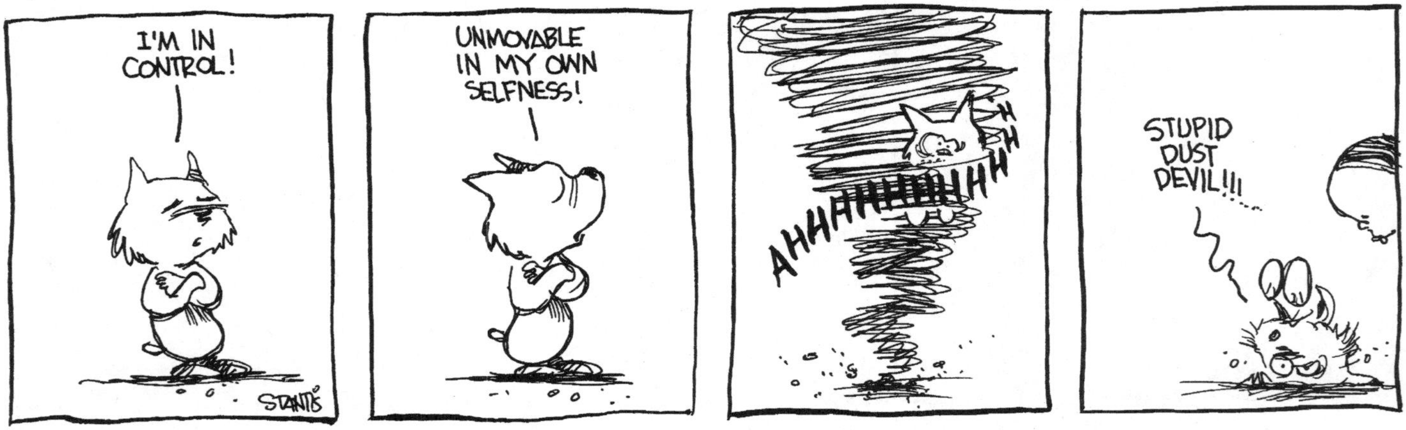
I'M IN CONTROL!
STANTIS
UNMOVABLE IN MY OWN SELFNESS!
AHHHHHHHHHHHH
STUPID DUST DEVIL!!!

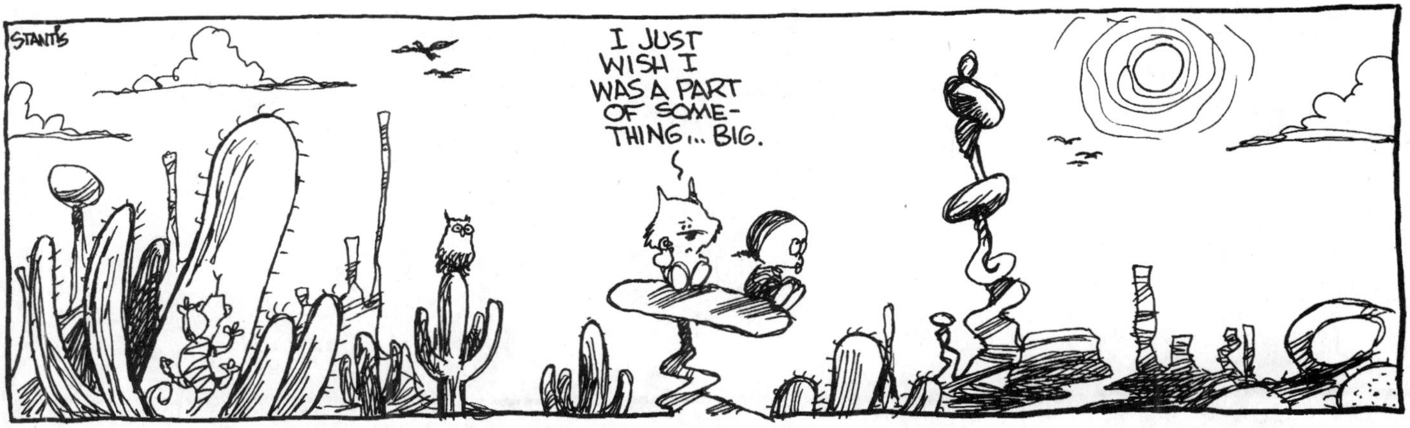
STANTIS
I JUST WISH I WAS A PART OF SOME-THING... BIG.

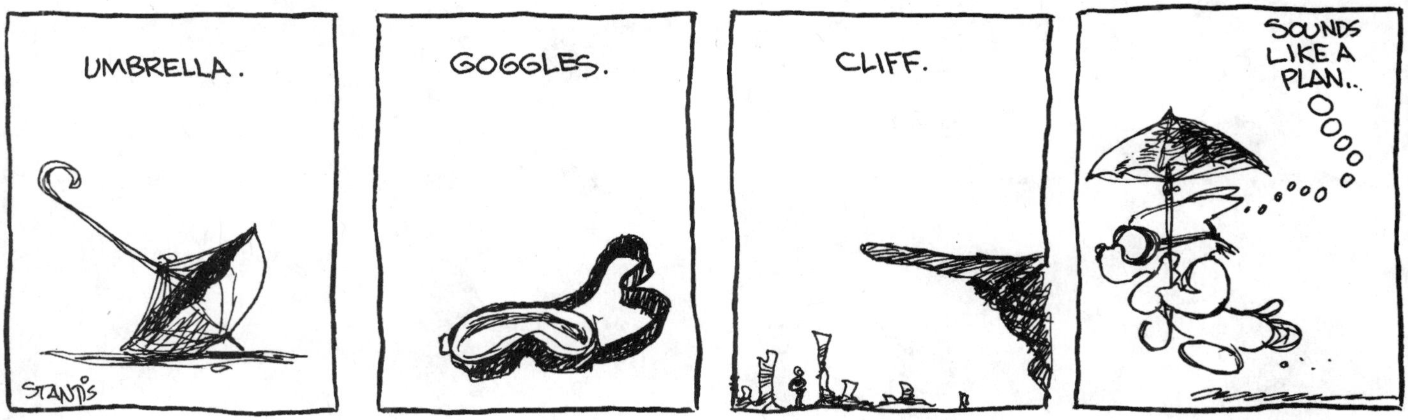
UMBRELLA.
STANTIS
GOGGLES.
CLIFF.
SOUNDS LIKE A PLAN..

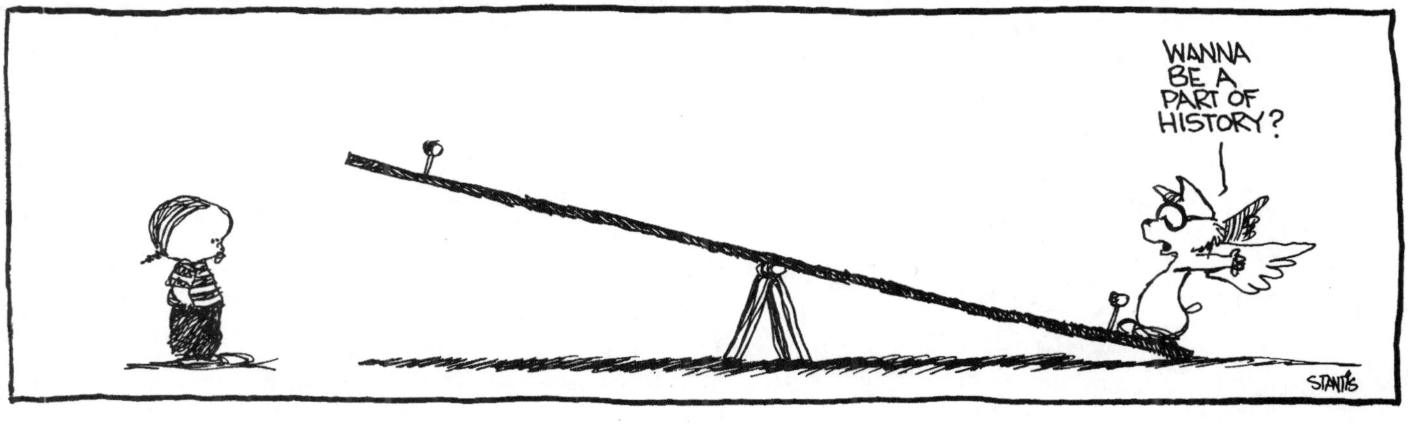
WANNA BE A PART OF HISTORY?
STANTIS

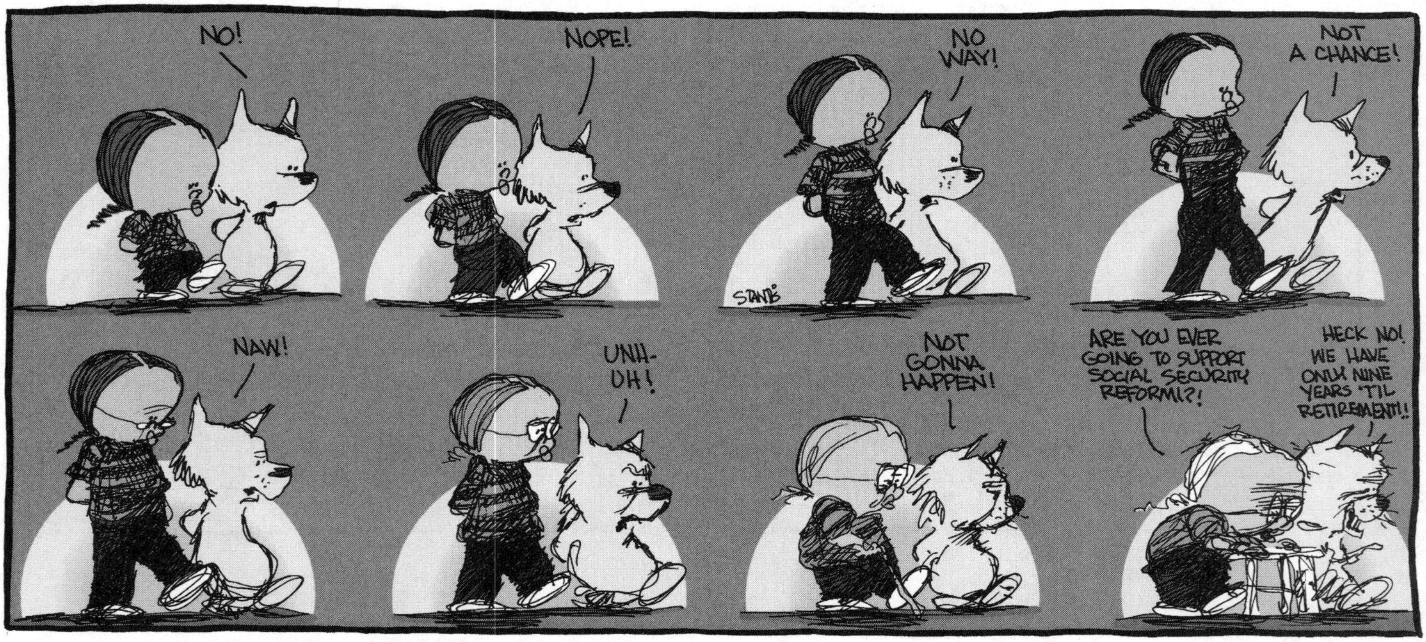
NO!
NOPE!
NO WAY!
NOT A CHANCE!
STANTIS
NAW!
UNH-UH!
NOT GONNA HAPPEN!
ARE YOU EVER GOING TO SUPPORT SOCIAL SECURITY REFORM!?!
HECK NO! WE HAVE ONLY NINE YEARS 'TIL RETIREMENT!!